To Dorothy and Jim

With fondest memories of
Christian Friendship to both
Mike and I.

Barbara.

BUXTON: A PEOPLE'S HISTORY

Buxton
A People's History

MIKE LANGHAM

Carnegie Publishing Ltd

Published by Carnegie Publishing Ltd
Carnegie House, Chatsworth Road
Lancaster LA1 4SL
+44 (0) 1524 840111
publishing website: www.carnegiepub.co.uk
book production website: www.wooof.net

British Library Cataloguing-in-Publication data
A catalogue record for this book is available from the British Library

ISBN 1-85936-086-6

Typeset in Adobe Garamond by Carnegie Publishing
Printed and bound in the UK by
The Cromwell Press, Trowbridge, Wilts

Contents

Acknowledgements

This research has involved a fascinating journey to places, archives, collections and libraries in search of new data and supporting evidence and I have been helped on my way by a number of people to whom I owe a debt of gratitude. I thank the Trustees of the Chatsworth Settlement for permission to study a huge range of Buxton material and am particularly grateful to Mr Peter Day, keeper of the Devonshire Collections and Mr Tom Askey, the archivist, for excellent and friendly research facilities. I have invariably found the staff at libraries and archive collections to be most helpful and wish to thank: Dr Margaret O'Sullivan and her staff at the Derbyshire Record Office, Matlock; University of Sheffield Library; Lincoln Theological Institute Library, Sheffield; Matlock Local Studies; Harrogate Local Studies; Scarborough library; Manchester Central; Manchester University Kantorowich Library; Stockport Local Studies. In London the Wellcome Foundation, Euston Road; Institute of Historical Research, at the University of London; RIBA Library Portland Place and the library of the Royal Institute of Chartered Surveyors in Great George Street. In Buxton staff at the Local Studies Library and the Museum & Art Gallery took a particular interest in my work and were always ready to help with queries and requests. I am grateful to a number of local people who have allowed me access to private papers and proffered information about their own property. The Buxton Archaeological and Natural History Society members have given their customary support and encouragement.

I should like to thank a number of people who have offered practical help: David Barton on Matlock; John Bishop on architecture; Revd Phillip Bridgwater on clerical vestments; Martin Brooke-Taylor on legal matters; Mike Bryant, Senior Hydrotherapist, Devonshire Royal Hospital; Professor David Cannadine has taken time to discuss my research and give me some useful pointers; Ian Clements for help with plan drawings; Richard Crook for loaning me his thesis on Henry Currey; Professor Mark Greengrass for guidance on internet citations; John Leach, now curator at Tiverton Museum, for discussion on some of the finer points of Buxton's history; Jane McGrother on rheumatic disease; Dr Bruce Osborne on spas; Robin Price at the Wellcome Institute on hydropathy; Dr Peter Smith on domed buildings and Mr Peter Whitfield for valuable information on the Catholic Apostolic movement and for showing me the wonderful Gordon Square Church which John Betjeman called 'the cathedral of Bloomsbury'. Fellow travellers in the Department of History at Sheffield, Dr John Gratton and Mr Julian Holder have offered encouragement and practical guidance, usually over a pint after a seminar. My thanks also to Cheryl Plant, the postgraduate secretary, who looked after my work and kept me up-to-date with happenings in the department.

Now to those who have been with me right through the research and to whom I want to offer special thanks. My supervisor, Professor Clyde Binfield, has guided me through the process, offering challenges which caused me fruitfully to extend my channels of enquiry and to develop the quality of my work. He has also found ways of gently pointing out to an old(ish) local history writer the differences between writing a book and writing a thesis. I have much enjoyed our regular progress meetings. My two firmest friends in Buxton's history, Oliver Gomersal and Colin Wells, have gladly listened to my enthusiastic reports of the 'eurekas' I have found in this or that archive as well as encouraging me when progress has been slow.

Finally, I could not have set out on a course of research and writing such as this without the full support of my family. I have been a 'continuous learner' throughout my working life and my wife, Barbara, has been hugely supportive, thus setting the tone for our sons, Robert and Thomas, to be the same. Now their own families are supporting me and grandchildren have made regular inquiries as to progress. With such encouragement I could hardly lack motivation.

I am grateful to the following individuals and organisations who have given permission for illustrations to be used. Particular illustrations may be identified in the book by the shortened reference given in square brackets. E.M. & G.J. Barton [E.M. & G.J.B.]; J.M. Bentley [J.M.B.]; The British Spas Federation [B.S.F.]; The Builder Group plc [B.G.PLC]; Buxton Museum and Art Gallery [B.M.A.G.]; Derbyshire County Council: Derbyshire Record Office, by permission of the County and Diocesan Archivist [D.R.O.]; Derbyshire County Council, Local Studies Library, Buxton [D.C.C. Lib.]; Devonshire Collection, Chatsworth, by permission of the Duke of Devonshire and the Chatsworth Settlement Trustees [D.C. Chat.]; Longmans Green & Co. [L.G. & Co.]; Image of Henry Currey by courtesy of the National Portrait Gallery, London. [N.P.G.]; A reproduction from the Ordnance Survey map of Buxton 1878 by kind permission of the Ordnance Survey NC/01/23929 [O.S.]; Three images from Hardwick Hall, The Devonshire Collection (The National Trust). Photographs: Photographic Survey, Courtauld Institute of Art. [N.T./Courtauld Inst.]; The Wellcome Library, London [Wellcome]; A line drawing from the N.A.H.T. Conference Souvenir – 'Buxton' 1934 is by Mr R. McLellan Sim [R.Mc.L.S.]. All other illustrations are from the author's collection. Much care has been taken to obtain permission to use illustrations and the author apologises in advance for the accidental omission of any acknowledgement.

MJL, Autumn 2001

List of Appendices

Introduction

Chapter One

Chapter Two

Chapter Three

Chapter Four

Foreword

by His Grace The Duke of Devonshire KG PC MC

The inland resort of Buxton has been associated with my family for more than four hundred years, since Bess of Hardwick and her husband George Talbot, Sixth Earl of Shrewsbury, built the Hall there. In the eighteenth century the Fifth Duke commissioned the northern architect John Carr to built the magnificent Crescent and Stables and subsequently developed the town as a fashionable spa. But the most significant growth occurred under the patronage of the Sixth and Seventh Dukes, when the reputation of Buxton as an important and influential inland medical resort was forged. Buxton in unique, as an inland resort, in that it was developed as an estate town through the mid-nineteenth century. Much of the land upon which the town was built was owned by my family and the shaping of the town owes much to the agents and architects employed by the Devonshire Buxton Estate. Whilst this influence progressively gave way to control by an emerging local democracy, both the Devonshire Estate and the local authority could take credit for the high reputation reached by the town. In 1905 more than four thousand visitors each week stayed in the many hotels and lodging houses and an impressive range of treatments was on offer at the baths and hydros.

It is fitting that I should write a foreword to this book which covers the nineteenth and early twentieth centuries in detail, a period of very close involvement by my family in the town. In his research, the author has been able to draw extensively from original records kept in the archives at Chatsworth. But most importantly that close interest has been maintained; both my father and myself have been mayors of Buxton and my family is proud of its long and continuing connection with the town.

Introduction

DESCRIPTIONS of Buxton as a healing spa have been recorded by travellers and doctors from the sixteenth century. John Leland, an early modern English antiquary, began his travels in the twenty-fifth year of Henry Vlll (1533/34). He records the

> ... Wye River good for Troutes risith in Darbyshire nere S. Anne of Buckstanes Welle ...[1]

The earliest medical treatise on the spa is that of John Jones writing in 1572 who did much to promote the medical value of the springs.[2] Dr Jones engendered a flow of books and papers on Buxton, many by learned doctors but others, such as the work of Hobbes and Cotton, more descriptive of the topography of Buxton and the surrounding area.[3] Whilst the seventeenth and eighteenth centuries saw a number of seminal works on the medical use of Buxton water, in the nineteenth century such treatises were more prolific (though not all so formative) due not simply to the developing technology of print but to the upsurge of interest of Buxton as a medical health resort.[4] The promotion of Buxton as a health resort, as opposed to the more fashionable leisure attractions of, say Bath or Tunbridge Wells of the mid eighteenth century, is an important distinction to which this research will return. Coterminous with this medical literature were more general descriptive guides, many offering a potted history of the town, quite a number repeating historical inaccuracies presented in earlier volumes.

Given this body of literature it is, perhaps, surprising that no real attempt to chronicle the history of the town was made until Jewitt's work of 1811 and even this was more directory and topography than history.[5] Apart from a useful range of work by Victorian amateur archæologists,[6] much of the detailed work on aspects of the town has taken place in the twentieth century. A number of significant historical periods have been researched and described, in more or less detail, including the Roman urban civilian settlement,[7] the Elizabethan court intrigue and the visits of Mary Queen of Scots,[8] and the Georgian development of the town.[9] Recent work has attempted to document the history of the town from its genesis to the present day and other work has focused on particular aspects, for example the baths, turnpike roads, coal mining and theatre.[10]

Why select the Victorian/Edwardian period for this research? One

John Leland (*c.* 1506–1552) was the earliest of modern English antiquaries. He was authorised by Henry VIII to travel the kingdom to locate and identify all records, writings and secrets of antiquity. His close and careful observations over six years of travel, *Leland's Itinerary* were first published in nine volumes at Oxford in 1710. This title page is from an edition of 1770.

1

Thomas Hobbes (1588–1679), philosopher. He was tutor to William Cavendish, afterwards Second Earl of Devonshire, and became his secretary and companion. From 1640 he spent eleven years in Paris as a member of the first group of Royalist emigrés and was appointed tutor to the Prince of Wales, later Charles II. Hobbes spent much time at Chatsworth and his long association with the Cavendish family allowed him to travel and meet such thinkers as Galileo and Descartes and to work in fine libraries. He published *Leviathan* in 1651 and was a profound thinker and writer who provoked much valuable political and philosophical debate in the seventeenth century. [N.T./Courtauld Inst.]

part of the answer lies in the manner in which this Victorian spa has been underrated by recent historians.[11] Buxton is undoubtedly an early spa and ranks with Bath as one of the only two spas with a natural thermal water. The Romans recognised this naming Buxton *Aquae Arnemetiae* and Bath *Aquae Sulis*. A line of continuous use of the springs may be traced tenuously through the Dark Ages and more firmly from the early medieval period to the sixteenth century which saw growth in accommodation to house, amongst others, Mary Queen of Scots on her visits to take the waters. But it is the investment of the Fifth Duke of Devonshire between 1780 and 1811 leaving the town with a splendid legacy of Georgian buildings in the Crescent, stables, church and town houses which placed Buxton in the setting of a spa. It is not surprising, therefore, that modern writers have classified the town in such terms as

The Church of St John the Baptist, the last gift of the Fifth Duke of Devonshire to the town, was dedicated in 1812. This drawing, from A. Jewitt's *History of Buxton* 1811, shows the church as a new building standing alone in, what was then, the township of Fairfield.

… an early spa of noble patronage …[12]

Phyllis Hembry offers a well researched description of the Elizabethan and Georgian periods in the town but the same cannot be said of the coverage of the Victorian and Edwardian era in a second volume published after her death.[13] Alderson's description is '… an early watering place …', and he does not include it amongst the four resorts he particularly associates with Victorian growth.[14] Yet a large part of Buxton stands today as a reminder of solid Victorian values and innovation. The town's apogee was undoubtedly the period of the second half of the nineteenth century and first decade of the twentieth. At no time, before or since, has the spa offered so many medical water treatments and so many doctors specialising in this branch of medicine. Moreover the town, though situated in a bowl at 1,000 feet in the hills of the High Peak, experienced very significant growth in population and prosperity between 1848 and 1905. Between 1861 and 1901 the population of Buxton grew at a pace far greater than the national average; house building quadrupled as did the number of roads. In 1905 twenty-seven hotels and more than 300 lodging houses provided facilities for a weekly influx of 4,000 visitors.[15] Buxton has fine examples of a wide range of Victorian and Edwardian architecture in both public and private buildings.

Buxton is, in essence, a Victorian and Edwardian health resort.

This view of the entrance to
Poole's Cavern, a show cave, is
redolent of the bucolic setting
of Buxton in 1842.

The fortunes of the town and the way it grew and was shaped during this time presents a potentially rich area for study. No detailed study has been made of this major period of growth, though the life of one significant townsman of the period (the builder/architect Robert Rippon Duke, 1817–1909) has revealed valuable insights and the work of Grundy Heape offers some useful social observations.[16] A detailed investigation would be an important contribution to the history of the town.

A second consideration is the value which such a study can offer to the body of knowledge on Victorian urban development. The importance of detailed local work and its contribution to more generalised writing which develops concepts and classifications cannot be underestimated.[17] Indeed, the historian who wishes to generalise about land ownership and Victorian towns will not easily succeed without access to well researched particular studies.[18] Such studies can add significantly to an understanding of the changing balance between the aristocratic land-owning elite and middle-class leadership in the growth and shape of nineteenth-century towns. Every particular study adds to the evidence needed to paint the broad canvas. So this work identifies the extent to which Buxton conformed to the pattern of landed power giving way to middle-class influence as the century proceeded; it observes the similarities and differences between this town and comparable towns in that respect; and it portrays specific ↄ⃦

aspects of its growth which are unusual or different in the development of a civic mentality.[19]

Finally, the proposed research takes place at a time when there is a resurgence of interest in the heritage of the town. This interest is being demonstrated by the investment of finance from the European Community, the National Lottery, through English Heritage, government agencies and elsewhere, into conservation and refurbishment. Inevitably this raises the level of interest of townspeople in their heritage and in the history of their surroundings. The need for well researched study manifests itself in questions and requests for information from individuals and groups, particularly those involved in the survey and listing of buildings for conservation purposes.

The research concentrates on particular detailed aspects of the growth of Buxton between the years 1848 and 1905. The rationale for the starting date is straightforward, 1848 being the year of the town's renascence after forty years of moribundity. While a fairly superficial examination of Buxton's nineteenth-century history will identify this as an obvious date, what is not so obvious is the reason why this is so. Indeed, so sparse is the existing literature on the first half of the century that it has been necessary for this research to provide a preliminary chapter to identify the key events and influences in the period from 1811. This has the secondary benefit of identifying necessary preconditions for the advancement from 1848. The determination of an end date was not so clear cut. The town enjoyed reputation and wealth as an inland resort right up to the start of the Great War, substantial new houses for the wealthy were still being built in 1910–12. But, as research proceeded, it became increasingly clear that the point at which the town had reached its optimum, in both physical growth and changes in the exercise of power, could be set at 1905. The influence of the Devonshire Estate was diminishing, the last major investment, the Baths, had been acquired by the Urban District Council in 1904 and local councillors were now the prime authority in directing the town. Furthermore, though building continued, the shape of the twentieth-century town, its actual road layout, was determined by 1905 and all public buildings of any note were completed by that time. The Eighth Duke of Devonshire (1833–1908) was to be the last to exert any direct ducal influence on the affairs of the town and, after 1904, his agent, Frank Drewry, found his influence, only indirectly, as a County Councillor. Thus the year 1905 represents the point at which the town had reached its apogee as an inland health resort.

The focus of this research is on the physical growth of the town, its development as a health resort and the changes in the balance of power and influence in the way in which the town developed. The town in this time presents an interesting crucible in which events

DE
Mirabilibus Pecci:
BEING THE
VONDERS
OF THE
PEAK
IN
DARBY-SHIRE,
Commonly called
The Devil's Arse of Peak.

In English and Latine.

The Latine Written by *Thomas Hobbes* of *Malmsbury*.

The English by a Person of Quality.

on, Printed for *Williams Crook* at the Green *Dragon* without *Temple-Bar*, 1678.

Title page of *The Wonders of the Peak* by Thomas Hobbes, 1678.

and actors combined to shape a distinct 'Buxton personality'. For so long the style of administration had been determined by the aristocratic Devonshires whose values in political, economic and social terms had been dominant. Like a baby learning to walk, the movement towards self direction and the social strengthening needed to enhance the town's resources and reputation were not easy. The process was not helped by the physical remoteness of the place, especially in the winter, and the Buxton psyche born out of this insularity. Yet when social and political change came it was rapid, not evolutionary but part of the wider middle-class revolution in which Buxton, like others, became a distinctive self-managing unit of local government. How did this 'personality' evolve? who contributed to its type? The first four chapters describe the *how* in detail moving from aristocratic to local government in politics, commerce, land management and physical growth, each chapter identifying a distinctive thesis. The second four chapters identify the *who*, the principal movers and shapers reflecting the concerns of land sales, the politics of urban growth, the shaping of a health resort, topography and the built environment. The principal drivers have been identified in land agency, water medicine, religion and architecture. Inevitably some other areas of influence do not receive the same depth of treatment and may only be included within the context of a chapter. Areas such as commerce, education, law and order, mutual societies including freemasonry, foresters, oddfellows, and social aspects of visiting and living in a burgeoning resort, which fall outside the boundaries of the present study, may merit future examination.

Land ownership

Because the development of Buxton in the nineteenth century is inextricably bound up with the Devonshire Estate, before proceeding to chapter one it is necessary to clarify the ownership of land on which urban Buxton was built. The Duke of Devonshire was the major landowner in the town through the period of the study and well into the twentieth century. In fact the position did not materially change until 1951 when death duties necessitated the sale of Buxton properties and Chief Rents. Despite very careful financial planning, the Tenth Duke's untimely death left his heir with an unprecedented debt to the Inland Revenue. Buxton assets were in the first instalment of disposals, his agent, Hugo Read, winding up the affairs of an estate office which had been at the heart of the nineteenth-century growth, and closing a long chapter of direct influence on the shape of the town by the Devonshire Cavendish family.[20]

The ownership of land in Buxton by the Cavendish family begins with the marriage of Elizabeth Hardwick (*c.* 1527–1608), a young

Elizabeth, Countess of Shrewsbury, 'Bess of Hardwick' (1518–1608). She acquired much land in Derbyshire through her second marriage to Sir William Cavendish and consolidated her land holdings by her fourth marriage to the Sixth Earl of Shrewsbury. A shrewd business woman, she used her commercial acumen to promote Buxton as a fashionable watering place when members of the Elizabethan court were visiting in the wake of Mary Queen of Scots and when the idea of the secular holiday was just beginning to emerge. [N.T./Courtauld Inst.]

widow, to William Cavendish (1505–57), a Suffolk landowner, in 1547.[21] William Cavendish had made his reputation as a commissioner for the surrender of the monasteries and had acquired both a knighthood and substantial monastic land through the dissolution. He held the office of Treasurer of the Royal Chamber to both Henry VIII and Edward VI.[22] Persuaded by his wife, William sold and exchanged land in the south of England for estates in North Derbyshire; these included the land upon which Bess of Hardwick was, subsequently, to build her great houses at Chatsworth and Hardwick. It also included lands, rents and tithes in Buxton, the origins of the Buxton holdings. Sir William died in 1557 and Bess of Hardwick married twice more, her fourth husband being George Talbot, the Sixth Earl of Shrewsbury, gaoler to Mary Queen of Scots. This marriage united the Cavendish Derbyshire holdings with those of Shrewsbury and provided for the

GEORGIVS TALBOTVS
COMES SALOPiÆ
AN· ÆTATiS 58
S· H
1580

George Talbot, Sixth Earl of Shrewsbury (*c.* 1528–90). He married 'Bess of Hardwick' in 1568 and became the custodian of Mary Queen of Scots a year later. He built the Hall in 1573 as a safe house to allow the Scottish Queen to take the waters at Buxton. Mary Queen of Scots stayed at the Hall on at least five occasions between 1573 and 1584, usually for several weeks in the summer. She was followed by notable members of the court including Lord Burghley the Lord Treasurer, Sir Thomas Smith Secretary of State, Lord Gilbert and Lady Mary Talbot, and the Earl of Leicester. Catholic supporters of Mary also followed and Buxton became a centre of some plotting and intrigue at this time, occasioning visits by Richard Topcliffe, the Catholic persecutor. [N.T./Courtauld Inst.]

THE WESTERN FRONT OF THE OLD HALL HOTEL, BUILT IN 1670.   DRAWN BY VAN JONES 1927.

The Hall was built by the Sixth Earl of Shrewsbury in 1572–73 to provide a safe house for the visits of Mary Queen of Scots to Buxton. Although enlarged over the years, the original Derbyshire square house construction is still evident. This sketch, made in 1927, shows later additions to the west face. [B.M.A.G.]

respective children of both parties by their previous marriages. Subsequent acquisitions by the Earl and his wife included the chapel, bath and springs at Buxton and several parcels of land.[23] The Sixth Earl of Shrewsbury built the 'New Hall' at Buxton as a secure house to enable Mary Queen of Scots to visit and take the waters. It is likely also that Bess of Hardwick used her considerable business acumen to promote Buxton as a fashionable watering place at a time when this new habit of visiting the baths was becoming an accepted part of the social routine of the wealthy.[24]

The property in Buxton was left by Bess of Hardwick not to her first son Henry, whose behaviour and lifestyle did not meet her standards for an heir, but to her third son Charles Cavendish.[25] His son William became the First Duke of Newcastle in 1628. By 1631 three quarters of the property at Buxton was owned by this Duke, thus the Newcastle Cavendish, not the Devonshire Cavendish, family. The position of land ownership in Buxton by the Newcastle family through the English Civil war and into the eighteenth century is briefly described in Appendix I.2. On the Devonshire side of the family there is a continuing link with Buxton in the ownership of the 'New Hall' at Buxton together with the bathhouse and adjacent land. This property passed from the First Earl of Devonshire (1552–1625) ultimately to the Third Earl who, according to Charles Cotton, rebuilt the Hall from a state of disrepair.

> ... This structure, which in expectation should,
> Ages as many, as't as years have stood;
> Chink'd and decay'd so dangerously fast,
> And near a ruin; till it came at last,
> To be thought worth the noble owners care,
> New to rebuild, what Art could not repair,
> As he has done, and like himself, of late
> Much more commodious and of greater state ...[26]

This description of a rebuilding, which was referred to by a number of later writers, is not entirely supported by recent examination of the structure of the Hall and it may be that Cotton's hyperbole produced an inaccurate account which has been repeated for nearly three hundred years.[27] However, the Third Earl did effect improvements and began again the process of investing in the baths. Further improvements were made to the Hall in 1695/96 by the landlord, Cornelius White and in 1710 William, the Second Duke of Devonshire, commissioned John Barker to reconstruct the baths and other buildings adjacent to the Hall.[28] Through the middle part of the eighteenth century the Devonshire family purchased other land and property in Buxton including the Eagle and Child Inn and about seventy-five acres of land; the enclosure award of 1773/74 showed the Fifth Duke's allocation in Buxton as just over twenty-four acres.[29] The last quarter of the eighteenth century saw the second major promotion of the mineral water baths by the Devonshires, and the consequent acquisition of land and property by the Fifth Duke. Early purchases were the Buxton and Hartington estates of John Edensor Heathcote, bought in 1772 for £6,000 and £2,000 respectively,[30] and the estate of the late William Gould, purchased in 1788.[31] The Duke built the Crescent, the Great Stables (1780–88) and town houses in the Square (1804–6) and Hall Bank (1792–98),[32] and made frequent purchases of further property to provide accommodation and facilities for the visitor. In 1798 the Buxton Estate accounts show a total income of £1574 in rents for the Crescent and Great Stables, and £2376 from 'Buxton lands' The estate, in that year, purchased two farms, including part of the Hall farm, and more than five parcels of land; the surveyor was paid £26 for valuing land at Buxton.[33] Between 1800 and 1807 the average annual rental from the estate was just under £4,000 and major acquisitions included the George Inn and farm lands at £6,000, and the conversion of town houses (including the Duke's) in the

Charles Cotton (1630–87) was born at Beresford Hall in Staffordshire. He is perhaps best remembered for his love of the River Dove and his contribution to Isaak Walton's *The Compleat Angler. The Wonders of the Peak* was first published in 1681; this title page is of the fourth edition of 1699.

Crescent into a new 'Centre Hotel'.[34] Separate rentals for the Buxton and Hartington Estate, taken in 1807 and 1808 give a comprehensive description of the extent of Devonshire holdings in the area that was to be subsequently developed as urban Buxton. The 1807 account shows sixty three rentals totalling £3991 p.a. and including: houses and shops on Hall Bank, the Hall and gardens, three hotels in the Crescent, Great Stables, Eagle Inn, Buxton School land, George Inn and farm, Nithen End public house, the Square (new lodging houses), Shakespeare Inn and gardens, seven shops and seventeen houses in addition to those on Hall Bank, together with drying grounds and gardens, six stable buildings and more than twenty plots of land.[35] The township of Buxton as described by Jewitt in 1811 was largely owned by the Devonshire Estate. In Higher Buxton, Scarsdale Place had been owned by Lord Scarsdale, a beneficiary of the 1773/74 enclosure award for Buxton Manor. This property, which included an Inn known as the 'White Hart', later the 'Scarsdale Arms', had been sold to George Goodwin, proprietor of the St Anne's hotel, some years before 1811.[36] One other significant landowner in Buxton at this time was the Brittlebank family.

In December 1824 the Buxton agent, Phillip Heacock, wrote to H. K. Hemming in the office of Benjamin Currey, solicitor to the Duke of Devonshire:

Dear Sir,   Buxton 24th Dec. 1824.

Herewith I send you a list of all the Houses and other Buildings belonging to his Grace the Duke of Devonshire in the Buxton Collection with a valuation of them and other particulars annexed thereto. A considerable portion of the buildings in question were insured some years ago to the amount of £25,500 but I have not been able to make out from the particulars (of which I sent Mr Currie a copy on 6th April last) the whole of the buildings so insured.

I am Dr. Sir etc.

P. Heacock   H. K. Hemming Esq.[37]

The valuation referred to is extensive, but selective. It lists houses and land in: Buxton (in the parish of Bakewell), Fairfield (in the parish of Hope), and parts of Buxton in the parish of Hartington. In Buxton there are two hotels thirty-four houses, a billiard room, five shops, the Great Stables and five other stables and a theatre. In Fairfield, nine houses, four stables, a smith's shop and a cottage and in the Parish of Hartington seven houses and fourteen cottages. It does not, however, include important other hotels owned by the estate such as the Great, Centre, George, Hall and Shakespeare. The total acreage of land separately listed is: Buxton, 547 acres, Fairfield, 504 acres., and in the Parish of Hartington 1,166 acres. This valuation

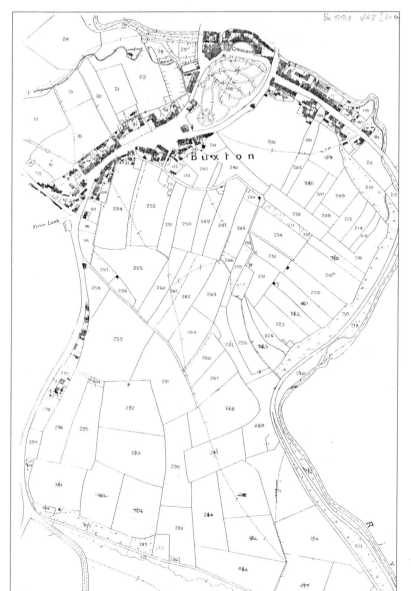

The Tithe Award Map of 1847 shows Buxton as a village or township at that time. Much of the land is owned by the Dukes of Devonshire. [D.R.O.]

covers the area of Buxton which was to form the Victorian town, but includes much more than that specific area. The survey also covers property in the village of Burbage and farms in the outlying areas of Fairfield and Kingsterndale which have not been included here. Whilst it is not possible to delineate precisely the area covered by this survey, it gives some indication of the estate's holding in Buxton and in that area known by the Devonshire Estate as the 'Buxton Collection'.[38] This valuation was, almost certainly, drawn up to identify a set of assets which might be borrowed against to support the Sixth Duke's extravagant lifestyle. The Duke raised a mortgage of £51,000 on portions of the Buxton estate in 1824.[39] Other estates had been sold to support the Duke's finances, including the Wetherby Estate in Yorkshire which realised £160,000 in 1824, the same year as this valuation.[40]

The picture so far is of extensive land holdings by the Devonshire Estate in Buxton township itself but also in a wide area around the town. It is necessary, now, to attempt to delineate that area of land which was to be developed from 1848 into the town of Buxton. The Victorian urban area of Buxton was comprised of the township of Buxton in the parish of Bakewell, part of the township of Fairfield in the parish of Hope and some smaller part of the township and parish of Hartington Upper Quarter. The boundaries can be determined by fieldwork using the Enumerator's descriptions for the 1841 census and these have been employed to show the area which, from 1848, was to be developed into the urban Buxton at the centre of this study. (Appendix I.3). It is necessary, beyond this, to determine the ownership of the land and property under consideration. David Cannadine has calculated that 1848 was the last year in which expenditure on the whole of the Sixth Duke's estates exceeded income

> ... By 1849 the long-hoped-for surplus had at last materialised, and it continued through the early 1850s ...[41]

It is perhaps no coincidence that at this time the Devonshire Buxton Estate had reached its maximum holdings, indeed, plans were already being made for the sales of land for building. The tithe award for Buxton of 1847–48[42] shows that the Duke of Devonshire owned 80 per cent of the township. Seventy-three different property owners made up the remainder, of whom the most significant landowners were: William Brittlebank, of Winster, who owned the Angel Inn, houses and land on Spring Gardens, which was to become the foremost commercial centre in Buxton; George Goodwin with property and land in Higher Buxton; George Hobson, a grocer in Higher Buxton; and the Buxton School Trustees. To this we must add part of the township of Fairfield for which a tithe award was made in 1841.[43] Accounts for the Devonshire Estate are not available between 1841 and 1851 but an analysis of the tithe award shows that the Duke of Devonshire owned two thirds of that part of Fairfield within the boundary given in Appendix I.3 and the rents collected in 1851 suggest that no significant sales had been made up to that time. Sixteen landowners shared the other 33 per cent (about ninety-three acres), the most significant being: William Brittlebank, of Winster, who owned a five-acre plot adjoining his holdings on the Buxton side of the river Wye; Fairfield School Trustees with nearly twenty acres; the incumbent of Fairfield Church, sixteen acres; and Edward White with nearly seventeen acres. The remaining part of what was to become urban Buxton lay in the township of Hartington Upper Quarter for which no tithe award is available. However, from a plan of Buxton held at Chatsworth, dated 1922, which records land sold outright and on lease since 1860, it is possible to determine the Devonshire Estate holdings.[44] With the exception of three acres by the Buxton school trustees, almost all of the rest of the land was owned by the Devonshire Estate.[45]

At the formation the Buxton Local Government Board in 1859 the boundaries of the 'Buxton District' were authorised by the government Home Department as follows:

> ... commencing at Wye Bridge the course of the Wye river was taken
> to the boundary with the Duke's Drive, the Duke's Drive to
> Sherbrook, the Ashbourne Road to the Leek Road, the Leek Road to
> the new school in Burbage, the Macclesfield Road to the lane leading
> to Edgemoor, this lane as far as the bridge, then the course of the
> brook to Gadley Lane, this lane to the Manchester Road then down
> to Corbar Walks which with Corbar Terrace were included, then
> Corbar and Hogshaw Lanes to Fairfield Road and Wye Bridge ...[46]

This follows the boundaries set out in Appendix I.3 but with the addition of a further part of the village of Burbage to the west of Buxton. The Local Government Board's Provisional Orders Confirmation Act of 1873[47] extended the district of Buxton by effectively pushing out the boundaries to take in parts of the adjoining authorities in Chapel-en-le-Frith Rural Sanitary area, Fairfield Local Board, Hartington Upper Quarter and Fernilee townships, adding another 437 acres. The plan of 1922, referred to earlier, shows that most of the additional land encompassed in these Acts was owned by the Devonshire Estate.

CHAPTER ONE

Buxton, 1811–1848

THE INTRODUCTION has set out the acquisition of property in Buxton by the Cavendish family. The real growth of the town begins in 1848. The purpose of this chapter is to set that growth in the context of Buxton as a spa so as to provide a platform for the shaping of the health resort and medical water centre which Buxton was to become. It has been argued that Buxton did not rise to significant national prominence as a fashionable spa:

> … Buxton, despite its elegant late eighteenth-century Crescent, had never rivalled Bath … [it] was developed too late and in too small a scale ever to be really successful as a spa.[1]

Hembry suggests that, after the death of the Fifth Duke in 1811, the spa went into decline.[2] Certainly the immediate years from 1811 were lean; income from the Assembly Room had plummeted from £264 in 1798 to a loss of £36 for the year 1813. In November 1813 the Duke's Buxton agent, Phillip Heacock, wrote to the London Agent, John Heaton explaining that he had allowed the tenants of the hotels in the Crescent to pay their rents in instalments because of the indifferent seasons experienced during the previous four years.[3] This was a time of general unrest, the effects of the war with France were being felt, the serious drain on the revenues of the country were being experienced in the manufacturing districts and this was to have a direct effect on the fortunes of Buxton. The economic dissatisfaction which was to develop, over the longer term, into the political demands of Chartism, first showed in the Luddite riots of 1812. These riots, which began in Nottingham, also affected the manufacturing areas of Lancashire and Yorkshire. Though ostensibly about the introduction of new machinery or changes in trade practices, the unrest was rooted in the harsh living conditions experienced by labourers and artisans. A report of the evidence of a Barnsley weaver to two JPs in 1812 indicates how extensive was the activity in manufacturing towns close to Buxton. There were rumours of 8,000 men in arms in and about Sheffield. Delegates from Manchester and Stockport had attended a secret committee meeting to collect numbers and information. He reported that there were 450 luddites at Holmfirth near Huddersfield and a great number at Halifax. Delegates from Ashton under Lyne spoke of bringing about a revolution. Voluntary contributions were being taken from those

... twisted in from 1d to 1s. per week ...[4]

The authorities responded by coercion, bringing in a severe bill for the purpose, and the army was brought in to quell the insurgence. In Buxton the ducal agent, Phillip Heacock, wrote to John Heaton on 30th July:

> ... I am sorry to say that the whole of the inns and lodging houses, with the exception of the Great Hotel, have hitherto, and indeed are now, very thin of company. I hope that the latter part of the season will be more prosperous but really it can hardly be expected, even if that should be the case, to do so well as on former years. The Lancashire and Yorkshire trades people who used to frequent the place, and spend a great deal of money in it, are now obliged to remain at their own homes. General Maitland, the commander of the troops in the disturbed districts, has made Buxton his headquarters and he has taken up his abode in the Great Hotel which is the reason why Mrs Hall, the tenant, has been so much more fortunate than her neighbours ...[5]

The ever-optimistic Heacock went on to suggest that the consecration of the new church (St John the Baptist) in the following month would bring money and people into the town.

Buxton Market Place in 1849, an oil painting by Godfrey Sykes (fl. 1824–66). This shows the market cross in the centre and to the left a court of shops known as Dunmore Square which was demolished under a local government act of 1873.

To the right may be seen Buxton College between shops and, in the distance, the four-storey Eagle Hotel.
[B.M.A.G.]

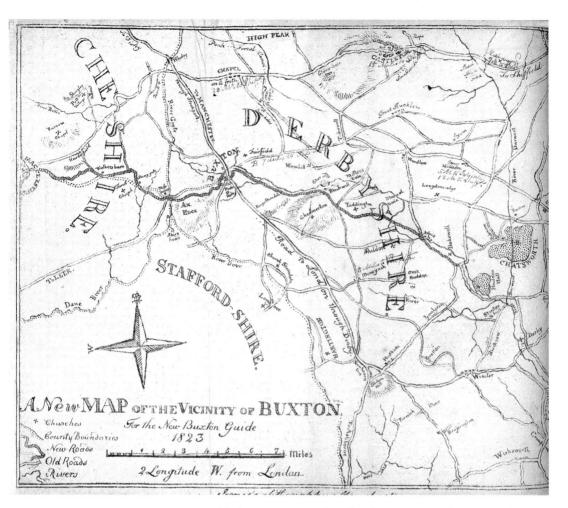

A New MAP OF THE VICINITY OF BUXTON
For the New Buxton Guide
1823

+ Churches
County Boundaries
New Roads
Old Roads
Rivers

2 Longitude W. from London

The map accompanying Daniel Orme's guide book of 1823 shows an area around Buxton suitable for rides and drives for the visitor.

Heacock's letter suggests that, by this time, another type of visitor had become important to the spa, he refers to trades-people with plenty of money to spend. The entertainment in Buxton was based on the successful model for the upper and prosperous middle ranks. Walton has described the

> ... assemblies for dancing and cards, the circulating library and the coffee house ... often regulated by a Master of Ceremonies ... entry into [which] was regulated less by social status in the abstract than by ability to pay the expensive subscriptions and participation fees, although the social perceptions of the Master of Ceremonies, and the elaborate rules of dress, conduct and precedence which governed assemblies, were intended to filter out those 'nouveaux riches' whose manners did not match their financial resources. In practice, however, it was very difficult to shut out the social climber ...[6]

Some of the tradespeople would have subscribed to the Buxton Ballroom, though at one guinea for the season others may have paid only for casual attendance. However, the Assembly Room Subscription Book shows a continuing decline of patronage to the Ballroom; assemblies at Buxton were of decreasing appeal.[7] This decline could be seen as evidence of the more general decline of business to the spa as earlier suggested. The picture is, however, more complex. An analysis of the Ballroom subscriptions shows that through the years 1811 to 1840, whilst absolute numbers decreased, the proportion of titled subscribers remained high, this is particularly noticeable in the later years.[8] To this may be added evidence from an analysis of the net profit taken by the estate from the baths between 1811 and 1842, which shows a much more buoyant picture.[9] It is clear that, whilst attendance at the fashionable Assembly Rooms declined progressively over the years to 1840, attendance by those of the upper class was to some degree maintained. Moreover, business at the baths remained relatively strong over the same period. Why should this be? The answer lies in the changing nature of Buxton's appeal. It may not have made the grade as a fashionable spa, but it was to succeed as a medical water centre, a health resort for the middle classes, and the foundations for this were laid, over a period of nearly fifty years, by Phillip Heacock the Duke's agent. He it was who recognised the changing nature of spa fashion and the unique advantages which could be exploited at Buxton; but he also recognised the need to keep the interest and patronage of the 'opinion formers' both socially and medically, if the town was to preserve its reputation.

Phillip Heacock Esq. – invariably referred to in this manner – came

The Serpentine Walks follows the northern of the two River Wye tributaries and provided delightful walks, as shown here in 1842.

The Crescent and Hot Baths of 1818. Sylvestor's new Hot Baths are the flat roofed building in the right foreground. Part of the Terrace Walks by Jeffry Wyatt may be seen to the left.

from Etwall in Derbyshire and took up residence in the Square at Buxton where he lived as a gentleman. He was the first professional agent of the Devonshire Buxton Estate and his impact was felt from the time of his appointment in 1805. Within two years he had completed a full assessment of rentals resulting in a considerable increase payable by tenants. Thereafter he lost no opportunity in pressing for improvements at Buxton and, although no major new building took place between 1811 and 1848, much work was done to develop the infrastructure of the town. During this period a great number of plantations were laid out around the town, a far sighted policy of the estate which was to transform the town from the barren and desolate aspect viewed by travellers in the late eighteenth century.[10] The estate invested consistently over more than thirty years, employing a nurseryman and laying out plantations at Grin, Brown Edge, Burbage Edge, Staden, Corbar, Cold Springs, Sherbrook, Gadley and Lightwood, effectively encircling the town. The letterbooks of Heacock show annual orders to Derbyshire nurseries for tens of thousands of trees including the varieties of, Larch, Scotch, Spruce, Beech, Sycamore, Mountain ash, Birch and Chestnut.[11]

Having overseen the completion of the Square (1803–6) and St John's Church (1812), Phillip Heacock was anxious to secure further improvements. He wrote to the senior agent, John Heaton, in May of 1813 with several suggestions including the provision of hot baths, some modest housing and a theatre. Heaton was clearly not minded to see any further estate money spent on Buxton and replied in August in that vein.[12] Heacock was not put off. He had already secured a long awaited market charter for the town in 1813 and was pressing for a market house to be built.[13] This he did not see in his lifetime, but other improvements he sought were to be progressively realised.

By 1816 the decision to provide hot baths had been taken and these were built during 1817 in a modest flat roofed structure at the east end of the Crescent. The architect was Charles Sylvester of Derby who had acquired something of a reputation for this kind of installation from his work at the Derbyshire General Infirmary.[14] This was a long awaited development. Dr Denman had advocated hot baths in 1801 and Dr Drever, a seasonal visitor, had called upon John Heaton at his office in London to press the case in 1813.[15] Undoubtedly this investment was of great advantage to the town, not only because a wider range of water treatments could now be offered, but chiefly because it helped to keep the town at the forefront of advances in water medicine. Important promoters of the efficacy of Buxton treatments could be drawn into the town, including Sir Charles Scudamore (1779–1849), a noted London specialist on the treatment of gout, who visited Buxton in the season. Scudamore wrote a treatise on Buxton Water in 1820 which was revised in editions of 1833 and 1839.[16] Undoubtedly his presence at Buxton would have enhanced the medical reputation of the town. Scudamore was joined by Dr William Henry Robertson (1810–97), who arrived in the town in 1835. His impact on the development of the medical centre was to be formative. Of equal importance the new hot baths helped to sustain a good clear profit for the Devonshire Estate. This investment prompted other works, the sloping terrace in front of the Crescent was laid out as a series of graduated walks by Jeffry Wyatt in 1818, the estate spending nearly £1,200 on this facility.[17] Between 1820 and 1822 the estate invested a further £650 in providing soft spring water to the hotels

In 1840 Philip Heacock persuaded the Sixth Duke of Devonshire to provide fresh water for residents in Higher Buxton. The supply, from a reservoir on Manchester Road, was fed to a fountain on the Market Place. From this originated the custom of Well Dressing in Buxton.

Buxton?

An engraving of Lower Buxton in about 1820. The Hot Baths of 1818 are not shown and no illustration of the façade of these baths has come to light, suggesting that the building was of little architectural merit. The low building to the left of the Crescent housed the Natural Baths.

and lodging houses in the Crescent and adjoining Square. This came from a spring in the Manchester Road and its provision was at the instigation of Dr Drever.[18] Water closets were also provided to some of the hotels. In 1840 a water supply was laid to Higher Buxton by the estate which constructed a reservoir on Manchester Road to feed two taps on a fountain in the Market Place. This investment may be seen as laying the foundation for a healthy place. Good air, clean water and sanitary arrangements to those parts of the town that mattered would support the medical reputation and encourage visitors.

In 1828 a new Promenade and Music Room was constructed in the Crescent. This was a modest affair, essentially a conversion of existing property at a cost of about £160. It coincided with some changes in the hotels and lodging houses to offer private room facilities for families and the agent wrote to both national and provincial newspapers advising them of the new facilities at Buxton.[19] The period 1827 to 1830 saw a reduction in business at the baths, and the Assembly Room was costing the estate money to keep open. In 1828 arrears of rent in excess of £7,000 were written off in respect of the three hotels in the Crescent, the Great, St Anne's and the Centre, also the Hall Hotel. It may be noted that the proprietors had been allowed to run with arrears of rent from about 1820, the figure being between £6,000 and £8,000 in total for a given year. It is, perhaps, significant that Heacock decided to regularise the position at a time when the country was suffering the effects of two poor harvests of 1828 and 1829, the resulting poverty leading to greater trade union activity with strikes and violence in the cotton districts, from where the trades-people visitors were drawn to Buxton. In 1830 the Centre Hotel was reduced in size and part of it converted into town houses and shops, in an attempt to maintain the rental income through a larger number of smaller rents. Despite the efforts of Phillip Heacock the proprietor of the Great Hotel, James Muirhead, went bankrupt in 1833, costing the estate in excess of £4,000. By 1842 (the last set of accounts available until 1851), the annual rental income for the prominent properties in the Crescent had dropped to £750 from a high of £1,940 in 1816.

Phillip Heacock was essentially a pragmatic businessman. He was happy to accommodate the tradespeople of Lancashire and Yorkshire because they spent freely, but he was anxious to encourage those from the higher social strata to improve business at the Assembly Room and support the reputation of the spa. These were changing times in the leisure business. Walton has described the growth of the seaside holiday from the beginning of the nineteenth century and the challenge faced by the spas

> ... By the mid 1830s even second rank resorts in the North West such as, Southport, Lytham and Douglas were outpacing Harrogate, the leading northern spa, in visitor numbers ... it was during the 1830s and 40s that the balance of patronage generally tipped towards the seaside, during this time the seaside began increasingly to compete with spas ...[20]

Heacock recognised this trend and was anxious to see that Buxton held its own in attracting the visitor. He was well acquainted with the seaside and sea water bathing, having taken his family to Parkgate for a fortnight's sea bathing on one occasion and to Liverpool on others. He had also recommended a visit to Liverpool for the purpose of bathing and drinking the salt water for medical purposes.[21] He was a strong promoter of the medical advantages of the town but well aware of the need to provide the best of leisure facilities. In 1833 he secured the long awaited new theatre which was built opposite the Hall Hotel.[22] The Devonshire Estate also provided a uniformed band which played in the Assembly and Music Rooms and outside in the Crescent. In August of 1824 Anne Lister visited Buxton for seven weeks with her aunt who was taking water treatment for rheumatism. She recorded in her diary the music of the band playing in the Crescent, on one occasion provoking sad memories, on another providing background to her musing on a love affair.[23] Granville records hearing the

> ... Duke's Band, which seemed to be composed of young lads dressed in a French gray uniform jacket and caps ... playing between eleven and twelve o'clock ...[24]

The Terrace & Hall Bank, Buxton.

The town band played in the Promenade Room and outside in the Crescent, though by 1858 they had been provided with a wooden umbrella, as shown here. The view also shows Jeffry Wyatt's Terrace Walks and to the right may be seen the town houses built between 1792 and 1798 forming Hall Bank.

An important consideration for Heacock was access for visitors to the town. Physically remote, Buxton sits in a bowl at about 1,000 feet above sea level; getting in or out requires a climb over the rim. Despite this it has since Roman times sat on the intersection of a large number of through routes. Roberts, using a compilation by Daniel Paterson, observes that, in 1786, Buxton was listed under no less than eleven cross routes.[25] In the first half of the nineteenth century it was necessary for the Devonshire Estate to see that road access of a reasonable standard was maintained. Buxton was served by a number of turnpike roads in which the Devonshire Estate had a financial interest. Access from the south via the Ashford turnpike required a steep descent at Topley Pike about four miles from the town. Rhodes, writing in 1824 described it thus

> … A very high hill, on the side of which the road is carried along a fearful eminence into the dale below …[26]

He also mapped the route from Ashbourne following, in part, the old Roman road. The route in from Manchester before about 1820 climbed a one in six gradient up Long Hill before descending into the town, after that time the route was altered to reduce the gradient to one in thirty-four.[27] The east–west turnpikes serving the town were the Sheffield–Buxton and Macclesfield–Leek–Buxton. The Buxton Estate carried out some maintenance on these turnpikes, most particularly the Ashford and Sheffield routes in which the Duke had considerable investment. The agent Heacock wrote frequently to

Mathew Frost, the contractor, regarding road repairs and widening. During the difficult years of 1828/29 he used unemployed men to repair the Ashford road near Buxton and to widen the road at

> ... Toplow Pike, as that part of it is so confined as to render it dangerous to the coaches when passing each other and also to carriages of every other description ...[28]

though he found it necessary strongly to urge Frost (a busy man, it seems) to complete the work in a further letter of March 1831. The severe winter experienced in Buxton in 1829/30 may have impeded the work. The estate also maintained and provided internal roads to the town. Examples of work recorded include a junction between the road to Fairfield and that to Ashford, the making of a new road to Fairfield and the diversion of the road from Buxton to the top of Long Hill. The town was served by a wide range of coach and carrier services. In 1835 there were daily services to Manchester, Nottingham, Sheffield, Chesterfield, Macclesfield and more local destinations such as Matlock. Carriers served Chapel-en-le-Frith, Leek, Manchester and Sheffield. Such services changed over time according to the vagaries of business but Buxton, through the period to 1848 and beyond, enjoyed regular and effective road communication.[29]

Buxton could not boast its own railway stations or direct line until 1863, but there was railway activity adjacent to the town from 1824. The inaugural meeting of the Cromford and High Peak Railway Company (CHPR), held at Matlock in June that year, was attended by Phillip Heacock, who was appointed to the committee formed to take the project forward.[30] This proposed railway was to connect the Peak Forest canal at Whaley Bridge with the Cromford canal and thus provide a route for freight between Manchester and Nottingham and the East Midlands. The limestone terrain, a good part of which was at 1,200 feet above sea level, was unsuitable for a canal but could be engineered in a series of inclines and levels to provide a rail link. Such a railway would run within three miles of Buxton at Ladmanlow. The company solicitor was William Brittlebank of Oddo near Winster who was an important landowner in Buxton. Correspondence between Heacock and Brittlebank suggests that the Duke of Devonshire was reluctant to become an original subscriber to the venture and was cautious enough to wait until the promoters were in a position to apply for an Act of Parliament to carry their bill. Meanwhile he was anxious not to stand in the way of the venture and was content for the railway to pass over his land without requiring any remuneration.[31] Heacock also lent the engineer, Josias Jessop, surveys with which to plan the route and had offered to sell lime, limestone and any other type of stone from the estate to the company.[32] By July 1831 this railway was in full operation for freight and in 1833 a passenger service was added which offered a route from Cromford to Whaley Bridge, then via road coach to Manchester.[33] Grin quarry, situated to the south west of Buxton and owned by the Devonshire Estate, was a source of high grade limestone. The proximity of the CHPR offered further business opportunity for the Devonshire Estate though it is not clear how substantial this was, and a branch line into the quarry though planned in 1830, did not materialise until 1857.[34]

Of particular significance in this railway investment was William Brittlebank, the solicitor and clerk, whose son Andrew worked alongside his father in the legal practice at Winster. As we shall see later, it was Andrew who was to lead the serious investment in Buxton with the Royal Hotel which was commenced early in 1849, well before Buxton had its own direct railway service. However, the Manchester, Buxton, Matlock and Midland Junction Railway (MBMMJR) opened their route from Ambergate to Rowsley in the same year and this reduced the travelling time from Buxton to the south. The coach known as the 'Peak Guide', which formerly ran to Ambergate station, now offered a return journey daily from the George Hotel at Buxton, through Ashford and Bakewell, arriving at the Rowsley station to connect with trains to London and Derby. Joseph Paxton was closely concerned with the affairs of the MBMMJR and other board members included the Hon. George Cavendish as Chairman, Sydney Smithers, the Devonshire Estate agent at Chatsworth and Phillip Heacock; very much a Devonshire affair.[35]

In addition to these railway investments, other speculations supported the possibility of the town having its own direct rail link. In 1844 the local newspaper carried articles from the Railway Record describing a line proposed by the Manchester and Birmingham company from Poynton through Disley and near New Mills and Hayfield and through Whaley Bridge, Bugsworth and Chapel-en-le-Frith to terminate in Buxton near the Crescent. This was a length of seventeen miles at a cost of £250,000, but the bill failed to get through Parliament. Further proposals associated with Buxton in this time of 'railway mania' were a junction with the Cromford & High Peak railway at Whaley Bridge,

Sir Joseph Paxton (1801–65) arrived at Chatsworth in 1826 as a young man to become the new head gardener. His influence was to be felt in Buxton in the design and maintenance of tree planting, parks and walks, and in the far-sighted development plans for urban Buxton. [D.C. Chat.]

25

The Sixth Duke of Devonshire, the Bachelor Duke (1790–1858).

a Great Grimsby–Sheffield–Potteries Grand Junction railway, and an east to west line connecting Hull with Holyhead via Sheffield, Leek and Crewe. None of these ventures succeeded but it is of interest to note that the last one had the support of 'The Railway King', George Hudson MP, who was also a supporter of the MBMMJR. The *Buxton Herald* offered a little Parliamentary wit at his expense in its edition of 27 June 1846:

> ... Hudson, it is quite clear said Graham, will not add much to the eloquence of the House. Gad, I don't know said Tom Young, as far as a tone of <u>iron-y</u> goes he ought to be a master and as for <u>railing</u> faith he is near unsurpassable ...[36]

The correspondence of Joseph Paxton in 1846/47 shows that the MBMMJR was pursuing its plans for the Buxton line and he was most optimistic that the Bill would be passed by Parliament at that time, though his ambitions for the company were, ultimately, not to be realised.[37] By 1848 all the coaching services in the town were scheduled to meet trains at the principal cities around Buxton, the

The DUKE of DEVONSHIRE'S Russian Drowski
Pub & Sold N.7 HallBank Buxton. 1826.

Orme del.

services having become so good that remarks had already been made in the local newspaper

> ... Latterly the class of visitors has been of a very different kind, merely visitors, not residents, persons who, having been whirled through the country by railroad have been dropped by the way just to see Buxton and be caught up by the next train ...[38]

The sixth Duke of Devonshire is listed as a patron of the Ballroom from 1806 to 1809 when he was still the Marquis of Hartington.[39] In March 1813, soon after his succession, he visited to inspect the work done under his late father attending divine service at the new church (St John's). This visit must have offered the agent, Phillip Heacock, some optimism for the future since the new Duke, having expressed himself pleased with the church and the layout of the ground around it, indicated that he should like to purchase the Grove Inn and premises opposite which adjoined his own. He was also intending to walk with Heacock to set out ground to be planted and identify an area in front of the Crescent which was to be set out with shrubs and ornamented. Unfortunately, due to very wet weather, this walk did not take place, neither did his plan to return to it the following May.[40] The accounts show no purchase of the properties mentioned or rents taken so we can safely assume that these purchases did not take place. In fact Heacock's optimism was somewhat dampened by John Heaton, the senior agent who, as noted earlier, indicated that it would be inadvisable to lay out any more money on Buxton at that time. Further visits were made by the Duke in 1816 and 1818, the same year in which the Crescent Walks were laid out by Wyatt. Whilst Heacock continued to strive to improve the town the Duke spent a great deal of money in extensions at Chatsworth with a new wing by Wyatt in 1818 followed by twenty further years of work at a house which the Duke, clearly loved.[41] The Bachelor Duke also invested in his other estates in building, furnishings and in horticulture including spectacular garden design. He was also lavish in his entertaining. Great financial outlay was made for the visits of the Princess Victoria to Chatsworth in 1832 and as Queen in 1843 and for his embassy to Russia at the coronation of Tsar Nicholas in 1826. He held many balls at his London houses, Devonshire and Chiswick, huge house parties at his estate at Lismore in County Waterford and at Chatsworth, and shooting parties at Hardwick and Bolton Abbey in the Autumn.[42] The extravagance of his lifestyle culminated in a peak of expenditure in the early 1840s such that, by 1844, he was almost one million pounds in debt. Joseph Paxton, a close confidant of the Duke, whose building and horticultural innovations had contributed to this immense spending, became directly involved in devising and agreeing with the solicitors, Currey & Co., a plan for the sale of estates in Londesborough and Baldersley in Yorkshire. In the same year Paxton was made assistant auditor, my ... grandest triumph ... he wrote to his wife Sarah from the estate at Bolton Abbey in Yorkshire,[43] though, as Chadwick has pointed out, he was wise enough to forego even more complete authority offered by the Duke in 1848, suggesting, instead, that William Currey should suceed his father, Benjamin Currey, who had died in that year.[44]

A number of the Duke's visits to Buxton show the lavish style of his entertaining. In September 1842 his party, conveyed in three carriages with six outriders, consisted of His Royal Highness the Duke of Sussex with his second wife Lady Cecilia the Duchess of Inverness and eleven other of the nobility in addition to the Duke himself and his elder sister, the Countess of Carlisle. The event, which included a tour of all the attractions in the lower town, was reported in detail by the *Buxton Herald*.[45] The visit of 1843 was less splendid but included a party of nine who accompanied the Duke to a concert given by the celebrated violinist Sivori in the Ballroom of the Great Hotel. Again the *Herald* lost no opportunity to report this fully and to pay obsequious respects to one who

> ... has always responded to any proposition ... for the improvement
> of Buxton with princely munificence ...[46]

His visit in September 1847 included a party of twelve, six of whom were titled and they travelled in the state coach and two four-horse barouches. In June of the same year he visited the well dressing ceremonies in Higher Buxton.[47] However in spite of the uniqueness of its water and other attractions, Buxton could only play a small and somewhat formal part in the life of this Bachelor Duke. He recognised the value of its water medicine and came on occasions to take the waters. In June 1844 he was accompanied by his personal physician, Dr Condell, and again in September.[48] But from the mid 1830s a proxy link was provided by Joseph Paxton. In 1835 Paxton accompanied the Duke to take the waters[49] and, given the extensive estate planting underway at this time and subsequent planning by Paxton, it is inconceivable that such a visit would not have included discussion on future development work. Paxton was to modify Wyatt's layout of the Terrace Walks in front of the Crescent in the early 1840s and to carry out other significant work in the early 1850s. He would have been involved in the extensive plantation investment, at the very least in an advisory capacity.

Corbar Walks to the north of the town, laid out by Sir Joseph Paxton and maintained by the Devonshire Estate.

The chapter has so far emphasised the dominance of the Devonshire Estate over the affairs of the town. The estate was to continue strongly to direct and influence the growth of Buxton well after the Local Government Act of 1858 had seen the formation of the Local Board. Before then local democracy had a modest impact on the affairs of the town. There was an open Vestry in Buxton which elected the chapelry and township officers, approved the levying of rates and, occasionally, passed resolutions involving expenditure. The Vestry in Buxton was no different from those found elsewhere in that it was generally attended by the larger rate-payers, the innkeepers, shopkeepers, farmers and professional men who saw themselves as the 'principal inhabitants'. Indeed the minutes show that this precise description was used by the eight or so who signed, particularly in the appointment of assessors and collectors of taxes.[50] The activity of the Buxton Vestry might be said to fall into two distinct areas, first the appointment of officers and, second the provision of certain common services. Buxton appointed one Church-warden only whose main function was to look after the chapelry books and property and pay, from a rate, the parishioners share of the church expenses. He was, ex officio an overseer of the poor, though this responsibility changed somewhat after the Poor Law Amendment Act of 1834 when the Chapel-en-le-Frith Board of

St Anne's Well

The St Anne's Drinking Well, designed by John Carr in 1784, is shown here in 1823. It was administered by the Well Women who were appointed by the Vestry.

Guardians was formed in 1838. The parish clerk was appointed, after 1811, by the Duke of Devonshire but paid by the Vestry. A unique appointment in Buxton was that of the Well Women. The Buxton Enclosure Act of 1772 designated St Anne's Well as public property and required the well and its approach to be kept in good repair. The Vestry was empowered to appoint yearly, in Easter week, a poor person to take care of the well and assist those wishing to take the water. Martha Norton was elected to the post fifteen times between 1775 and 1820. In 1818 the Vestry appointed Peggy Brandreth and set out duties for her and the other women. These included helping the poor women in the Charity Bath, cleaning out the bath and drying mats, bathing gowns and towels. In 1824 there were four well women appointed. The Vestry did not pay these women, who relied on tips for income, but in 1842 a committee of five gentlemen was appointed to ensure that the Well Women did their duties correctly. The management of the well passed, in 1865, to the Local Board and from 1875 it appointed the attendants.

In order to set up arrangements for keeping the peace, Buxton and the adjacent settlements of Staden, Cowdale and King Sterndale formed a township for the appointment of a Headborough, but they joined with Chelmorton, Flagg and Blackwell to appoint a constable to serve the wider area. From 1814 throughout the period covered in this chapter one man, Joseph Vernon, served either as constable or Headborough in these townships and from 1838 as constable of Buxton. Joseph Vernon was a key figure in Buxton's early nineteenth-century

The Bakewell Road forming a southern entrance to Buxton looking towards the Crescent, a watercolour by Thomas Wakeman *c.* 1820. Within forty years this road would become a busy commercial centre. [B.M.A.G.]

local government. In addition to his duties of keeping order he was, at various times, Assistant Overseer of the Poor in Buxton, Surveyor of highways and bye-ways, Assessor and Collector of the King's taxes, Assistant Overseer of Hartington Upper Quarter and Registrar of Births and Deaths, and last appears in the Vestry book in 1857. In the 1830s and 40s an assistant constable was appointed and paid for by an additional rate.[51]

These officers were supported by some limited facilities administered through the Vestry. The township of Buxton had a pinfold for animals, sited in the Cote Heath area and a set of stocks on the market place. In 1829 a lock-up house was built and the Vestry owned three cottages at Cote Heath, ostensibly for use as a workhouse but let at little or no rent to tenants in a destitute state. The 1848 Tithe Award shows the Buxton township owning these properties and the small church, though the cottages and pinfold were sold under an order of the Poor Law Commissioners that year.[52] Some limited work on highways was carried out by the Vestry though, as we have already noted, Buxton was well served by turnpikes and the Devonshire Estate also carried out road maintenance. The effects of legislation were felt to some degree in Buxton local government. Given the pattern of Vestry activity in Buxton it is likely that the Sturgess Bourne Poor Relief Act of 1819 was adopted. This act gave the Vestry power to appoint a poor law committee to manage most of its affairs. The incumbent, churchwardens and overseer were, ex-officio, members of this committee which was also known as a 'Select Vestry'. The first Buxton Vestry Book finishes in 1818 although there are a considerable number of unfilled pages, and from that time onwards there are occasional references to the 'Select Vestry'. In 1838 the Chapel-en-le-Frith Board of Guardians was formed and the Vestry ceased to administer the poor laws. Buxton, Staden, Cowdale and King Sterndale became one township in the Chapel-en-le-Frith Union, paid a contribution to the running of the workhouse, and elected two members to serve on the Board. From this time also the Vestry was concerned only with nominating a constable for Buxton township as described earlier, the final selection being made by the magistrates.

The powers of the Vestry were small and their impact on the town, compared with that exerted by the Devonshire Estate, was very modest. There is no record of the Vestry initiating any important developments and the profound changes brought about by the Public Health Act 1848 did not impact on the Vestry. The attention to drainage, sewerage, water supply, paving and cleansing, and the appointment of a local surveyor to enforce building regulations, with which this act was primarily concerned, was to be ultimately dealt with by the Devonshire Estate.[53] Unlike the neighbouring town of Macclesfield, there was no concerted effort to influence the opinions of rate payers against the provisions of the act. All this kind of thing could be left to the ducal landlord; certainly the motivation for sanitary reform had begun with, and was to continue to come from, his agency.[54] In the leader article of 16 June 1849 the *Buxton Herald*, observed:

> ... The Sanitary Commission with even the keen nose of Mr Chadwick to aid them, could never have detected any corner for their interference in Buxton and, therefore, we have no improvement to record on that score ...[55]

This might have been the case in some areas but taking the town as a whole it was a complacent view; within ten years the Duke's agent, E. W. Wilmot, was strongly arguing the need for substantial investment in sanitary improvements.[56]

When set alongside the rapid expansion thereafter, the period 1811 to 1848 has, on the surface, always appeared to be one of little real growth in the town. This analysis, however, shows that the agent, Phillip Heacock, oversaw the installation of basic sanitary arrangements and water supply, improvements to buildings, road maintenance and railway investment thus laying the foundation upon which Buxton was to grow. These amenities were improved by plantation work and the creation of promenades and walks; a new promenade and music room, the theatre, the band, and the careful management of the hotel leases. He enhanced the medical reputation through the provision of new Hot Baths, the maintenance of the Natural Baths and the Chalybeate (iron bearing water) spring, the encouragement of medical expertise to the town and support for the Buxton Bath Charity. In this period of nearly forty years hard times were experienced. The country as a whole came out of war with France and into social and political upheaval which was to lead to much wanted reforms in working and living conditions and in political enfranchisement. The violent demonstrations of the Luddites, the tragedy of Peterloo and the later Chartist activity in the manufacturing districts around Buxton had a direct impact on the fortunes of the town as a medical resort. Harsh winters were experienced and periods of high unemployment. Collections were taken in Buxton Churches in the early 1840s for distress in the manufacturing districts, the boom years in cotton manufacture were not to be seen for another ten years. In 1842 a correspondent to the newspaper asked why Buxton should be second to any other watering place, why had it not increased its visitors like most other towns similarly situated. Why were the lodging houses not filled with visitors in early spring and continued so until November? The writer recognised the distressed state throughout the country which had affected the last four or five seasons but suggested that, despite this, the advantages of Buxton had not been well promoted and he urged more action and public spirit by the inhabitants.[57] Although there had been much discussion in the local press on the merits and otherwise of the new water medicine of 'hydropathy' promoted in Austria by Vincenz Priessnitz in the early 1840s, the town was slow to take this up.[58]

Phillip Heacock was fighting an uphill battle throughout the period covered by this chapter. Total receipts in the Buxton Collection accounts had seen a progressive fall from £8,889 in 1818 to £7,217 in 1828 to £7,514 in 1834 to £7,120 in 1842.[59] Other spas were doing better. Leamington Spa enjoyed planned growth and royal patronage as did Tunbridge Wells. Bath saw a resurgence of business from about 1810 and Cheltenham enjoyed investment right through the period. Nearer to home Harrogate experienced real growth from 1835 onwards. Nor did Buxton enjoy the patronage of many foreign visitors; a few names only can be found in the weekly list of visitors in the local paper. Three families from Francfort (sic) stayed at the Hall Hotel in 1843 and in the same year the town enjoyed a visit from His Prussian Majesty's Consul General of Hamburg. The King of Saxony made a fleeting visit in June of 1844 as part of his tour of England.[60] In fact the movement was to some degree in the other direction. The *Buxton Herald* observed that:

... of recent years it has been the fashion for invalids to trip off every
Summer or Autumn to the German spas, to the great injury and
detriment of our own watering places ... visitors of rank and
fortune ... are now drained off to the German baths ... who in
former years used to frequent Buxton ...[61]

Buxton's patronage was drawn chiefly from Lancashire and Yorkshire, though there were regular visitors from Ireland and Scotland.
However, despite the difficulties, Heacock's style of approach and
powers of persuasion were effective and this can be gauged from his
correspondence and dealings with all classes of Buxton society. Despite
the serious financial difficulties faced by the Bachelor Duke, and
despite the fact that Buxton was but a minor asset in the estate
portfolio, Heacock managed to hold Buxton's position as a health
resort. Chadwick has suggested that the Sixth Duke was not given
to large-scale planning but carried out improvements to Buxton in
an *ad hoc* fashion.[62] This may appear so, when set alongside the
extensive planning of the town under the Seventh Duke, but it is
clear that Phillip Heacock would have delivered a much more
extensive development plan had the social and economic conditions
of the time allowed and had the Devonshire Estate been in a position
to finance it. The Sixth Duke, in any case, saw the first ten years of
real growth, from 1848 and later chapters will show whether there
was more purposeful planning under the Seventh Duke and the local
authority.

By 1848 Buxton was poised for expansion. Adam's *Gem of the Peak*
offers a good contemporary description of life for the visitor. He
describes the baths and treatments on offer, St Anne's and chalybeate
wells, the Crescent, Great Stables, Assembly and Promenade Rooms,
museums and fancy goods shops, the circulating library, newsroom
and the hotels and public houses together with the many picturesque
attractions, including the Serpentine Walks and St Anne's Cliffe.[63]
Throughout the difficulties of the forty years encompassed by this
chapter, one constant and recurring theme may be found in descriptions of the picturesque scenery in and around Buxton. It has been
suggested that travel writers in the early nineteenth century were apt
to create an image of reality rather than describing reality itself and
there are examples of this in guide books.[64]

... The valley ... through which the meandering and translucent Wye
shapes its course is celebrated for an Arcadian loveliness, heightened
rather than disturbed by the cliff-like Tors and rude precipitous masses
of rock that manifest themselves at intervals along its banks. The
whole vale of Wye, with diversified and romantic features, is
considered to extend from Buxton to its junction with the Derwent at
great Rowsley, and in that space it flows beneath the craggy precipice
known by the name of 'the Lover's Leap,' and the lofty Chee Tor ...

Thomas Allom produced fine engravings for publications on English counties written by Thomas Rose. This view of Chee Tor on the river Wye near Buxton was published in 1833.

but Millers Dale is a particularly picturesque portion of this interesting valley …[65]

Not to be outdone, the local journalist could exhibit a similar selective perception and style of writing to extol the virtues of Buxton during one of the leaner periods of its history.

… [Buxton is] the brightest gem in the coronet of the Duke of Devonshire. It is surrounded by a land of enchantment; the hill, dale, wood and water, the wildest and most cultivated scenery alternately attract the eye …[66]

CHAPTER TWO

The Early Stages of Real Investment

T HE YEAR 1848 was momentous throughout Europe. Revolution began in Paris in February and swept across the Continent. In his analysis '1848 The Opening of an Era', A. J. P. Taylor has described the 'movement' which caused established, but already ruinous, land-marks and old orders, to give way to a new spirit of change

> ... Movement, and a conviction that Utopia could be reached, were the essence of 1848: underlying these was a faith in the limitless goodness of human nature. The revolutionary cry, 'All change!' sounded across Europe ...[1]

England and Russia were the only countries in Europe to escape the revolutions. Thompson has observed that England ...

> ... seemed to have found, in her supple parliamentary institutions and her monarchical traditions, a strange immunity from violent revolution ...[2]

However, the decade to 1848 had seen outbreaks of violence and rioting in England through the movement for parliamentary demo-cracy and constitutional reform. The Chartist convention of 1839 led to mass petitioning in the 1840s, but by 1848 it was a spent force. Insofar as Chartism involved the working classes of the Northern counties, it indirectly affected the fortunes of the resort of Buxton and the local newspaper carried reports of any disturbances in Lan-cashire and Yorkshire. But Buxton was effectively immune from these national and international affairs. Life in the town was governed by the Devonshire Estate and a small number of principal inhabitants exercising power, in part but not wholly, through the Vestry. Further-more, whilst the coal mines above the Goyt Valley and the limestone quarries employed some labourers, many in the town worked as servants and a significant percentage of the population could be described as artisans. In the season everyone who had room augmented their income by taking in visitors. In a population of just less than 1,500 Buxton had eight hotels, eight inns and 110 households providing visitor accommodation.[3] The annual number of visitors to the town was estimated to be at least 13,000.[4] The great cholera scourge of 1848/49, though avidly reported, did not directly affect Buxton people; the habitual cleanliness, and habits of the people combined with the pure air, and high position were felt to be adequate safeguards against

The Royal Hotel in Spring Gardens, built between 1849 and 1852 signalled the start of modern Buxton. Designed by the Sheffield architect, Samuel Worth, for Andrew Brittlebank a solicitor of Winster, it provided a convex curve to balance the concave aspect of the Crescent.

this disease. At a time when resorts such as Southport, Hastings and Margate were suffering badly, no cases were reported in Buxton.[5] In fact, Buxton was an insular town and its people were inclined to look little beyond meeting their own needs for survival. Nevertheless, such survival meant enticing visitors to the delights of the resort and Buxton caught the mood of optimism spreading through England which was to be so brilliantly evinced in the Great Exhibition of 1851. As will be seen later, the town could, in a modest sense, compare its own energy for change with that needed to deliver that great showcase, the Crystal Palace.

In 1848 two significant decisions were made, which were to mark the beginnings of modern Buxton. Andrew Brittlebank, solicitor of Winster and important landowner in Buxton, commissioned the Sheffield architect, Samuel Worth, to design a large new hotel, and the Wesleyan Methodists determined to move from their small chapel, near the Cheshire Cheese Inn to a new chapel and Sunday Schoolroom on a more central site. These two important buildings were under way by early 1849 and the editor of the *Buxton Herald* opened his first edition of the new season with a leader article headed 'Buxton in 1849' as follows:

> ... All history is composed of eras – nations and individuals have, equally, some distinguishing periods from which to date their rise or their fall. The whole world is governed by certain great principles,

which apply to the most extended scale, as well as to the most trivial affairs of life. As a nation we date a certain chain of circumstances from the Reformation, the first French Revolution, the passing of the Reform Bill, the repeal of the Corn Laws &c. while as individuals we connect events with some important portion of our own domestic history ... The same annotation of time applies to localities and every place has some year to which its prosperity can be referred. From all we see going on around us we think that the present year, 1849, will be an important one in its consequences to Buxton ...[6]

He went on to record progress of the railways approaching Buxton from north and south (neither line likely to reach the town for some time) and offered some further observations:

... Since the erection of the Square, never have the sounds of building been so loud and general in Buxton as they are at present. In the upper town the Methodist body are erecting a new chapel which promises to be a great ornament to that part of the town. The style of architecture is handsome and solid and when finished it will be highly creditable to the denomination for whom it is building ... in Spring Gardens, the Angel Inn and the adjoining buildings are raised to the ground, and we understand that in their stead a second crescent is in course of erection. We cannot as yet say what it will be composed of but we know the spirit of the proprietor, Andrew Brittlebank Esq., too well and have seen too many specimens of the taste and talent of the architect, Mr Worth of Sheffield, to doubt that it will be worthy of each and both ... a new era has commenced in Buxton ...[7]

The new hotel, which was to become the Royal, was, indeed another Crescent. Samuel Worth's design, counterbalanced the concave of John Carr's Crescent with an impressive convex building. The fact that Andrew Brittlebank invested significantly in this venture (his day book entries total more than £14,000) suggests that he was expecting the resort to expand considerably.[8] The Methodist Chapel, a small building seating about 350, was designed by James Wilson of Bath and built by J. Ward of Congleton. The cost, exclusive of materials which were obtained locally, was about £1,000.[9] It was sited on the edge of the Market Place in an area formerly used as a cockpit, the irony of which was not lost on the *Herald* editor who wrote:

If progress depends on the substitution of piety and learning for barbarism and ignorance then we are assuredly on the right road for the chapel is on the site of the Buxton cockpit where the great mains between Lancashire and Yorkshire were formerly fought. Let us hope that this metamorphosis is not accidental that it is a mere material illustration of the improved morals and habits of the people.[10]

Andrew Brittlebank was, of course, acquainted with Phillip Heacock; he had traded land with the Devonshire Estate in the 1840s and was

Plan of
BUXTON PARK
The Property of
His Grace The Duke of Devonshire
AS LAID OUT IN BUILDING LOTS BY
Sir Joseph Paxton
1852

24

The original plans for Buxton Park by Sir Joseph Paxton (1852) showed a detailed layout of building plots including two terraces, a crescent and forty-eight substantial houses. Paxton's ambitious urban development also included another crescent, built as the Quadrant, and two further terraces as well as the remodelled baths. Unfortunately these plans were not completed in their original form; a much revised development took place in the 1870s. [B.M.A.G.]

involved in local railway developments, so his speculative investment was not uninformed. He would, undoubtedly, have been aware of the intentions of the Devonshire Estate to develop the town and to sell land for building.

Devonshire Estate work in 1849 included improvements to the Serpentine walks by the river Wye which were open, free of charge, to the public. The chalybeate well was re-sited in the garden adjoining the Great Hotel in the Crescent and covered by an umbrella like structure. The water had previously flowed into a well, on the north side of the river below the George Inn, emerging through a sculptured 'lion's mouth' by which name it was generally known.[11] These improvements were minor, however, compared with the commission given by the Devonshire Estate to Sir Joseph Paxton to design the 'Buxton Park' and other improvements to the town. The Park, set out to the north west overlooking the town, on the north side of the river Wye, was in the township of Fairfield. The most often quoted plan of this development is that of the estate surveyor, William Smith, which was reproduced in the first edition of Robertson's *Buxton Guide* of 1854.[12] Paxton's original plan dated 1852, was more extensive, however, and this research has identified a previously lost copy.[13] This plan shows the detailed layout of building plots and properties which included two terraces and a crescent in the Park itself, together with forty eight substantial houses. The Park included the area known as Corbar Woods, to the north of the Manchester road. This was woodland which had been developed by the Devonshire Estate in the 1840s and offered picturesque walks and commanding views of the town. Paxton's plans for the area of the town known as the 'Quadrant', were also extensive. He proposed the Quadrant itself (another curve or crescent), with a terrace behind and a substantial terrace to the west. Considering the size of Buxton at this time Paxton's proposals were ambitious, an urban plan of 120 acres, much larger than other 'planned' resort towns of the time, and, if carried through fully, would have set Buxton years ahead of its rival watering place Harrogate.[14] However, only parts of the Paxton design were implemented for reasons which will emerge as this chapter proceeds.

Between 1852 and 1853 the Natural and Hot Baths were entirely

The surveyor, William Smith, redrew Paxton's original plan of Buxton Park for the first edition of W. H. Robertson's *Handbook to the Peak of Derbyshire or Buxton* in 1854.

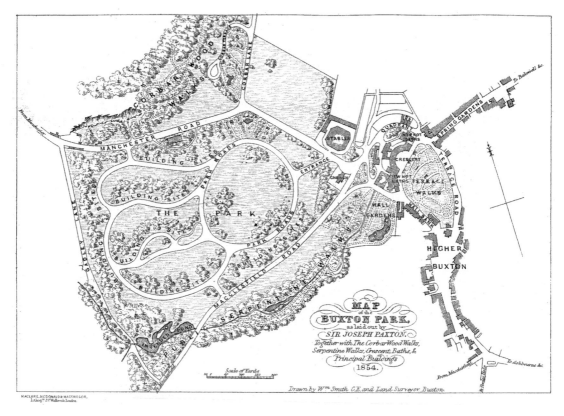

MAP of the BUXTON PARK, as laid out by SIR JOSEPH PAXTON. Together with The Corbar Wood Walks, Serpentine Walks, Crescent, Baths, & Principal Buildings. 1854.

Drawn by Wm Smith, C.E. and Land Surveyor, Buxton.

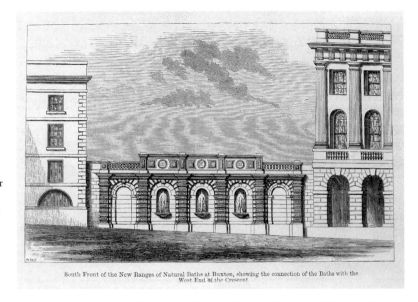

South Front of the New Ranges of Natural Baths at Buxton, showing the connection of the Baths with the West End of the Crescent

The Natural Baths in 1854 after remodelling by Henry Currey. The entrance was through the Crescent arch to the right of the baths. Buxton water emerged from the three fountains set in the arched niches in the façade.

rebuilt to the plans of the architect, Henry Currey. This rebuilding, together with the new Park, constituted a major investment by the Duke of Devonshire whose financial position, by this time, had markedly improved. Two styles of architecture were employed at the baths. The Natural Baths had only one façade which was in stone with three fountains in fluted niches; entry was under cover from the western side of the Crescent. The Hot Baths, situated on the eastern side of the Crescent were built in iron and glass style after the fashion of the Crystal Palace. Both sets of baths, however, had ridge and furrow roofing, a comparatively new process much developed by Paxton in his construction of conservatories.[15] Whilst Henry Currey is very firmly credited with the baths design, there is much circumstantial evidence to suggest the involvement of Sir Joseph Paxton in this work. The ridge and furrow roofing and the glazed eastern side of the Hot Baths were in the style of Paxton's lily house at Chatsworth. Currey and Paxton had worked together on the Princes Park, Liverpool in 1843 and Paxton had advised Currey on his design for the Long Conservatory at Chiswick in 1850, at the request of the Duke.[16] Paxton must have been in Buxton supervising the Park layout at the same time as the baths were being built. Indeed, his plan for the Park included the new baths shaded in pink as were all the other proposed developments. The two architects were in Buxton together in September of 1852 when they toured all the new sites with the Duke of Devonshire.[17] A review of a pamphlet by Dr Robertson, reported in *The Lancet*, in 1852, said,

> ... it appears that Buxton has had, of late years, such an increasing influx of invalids, that the town and baths could not properly accommodate them, and the owner of the baths and adjacent

property, the Duke of Devonshire, has consequently made great improvements to meet the public wants, under the superintendence of Sir Joseph Paxton ...[18]

Currey did not use an iron and glass design in any of the several commissions he subsequently completed in Buxton and he was not responsible for the glass and iron pavilion of 1871, commissioned by the Buxton Improvements Company and designed by Edward Milner. It has been suggested, however, that Currey was involved to some extent in this design and this pavilion is very similar in character to the Pavilion and Floral Hall designed by him at Eastbourne.[19] In essence here is a professional working relationship; Currey, thirty-two years old in 1852, an ARIBA, trained by Decimus Burton (a contemporary of Paxton) and beginning to establish his reputation as an architect; Paxton, seventeen years Currey's senior, now 'Sir Joseph' and a close confidant of the Bachelor Duke. It is likely that Paxton would have had, at least, technical interest in the design of the new baths.[20]

This early development at Buxton coincided with the mounting of the Great Exhibition in London's Hyde Park, an event with which the Buxtonians had a much keener sense of involvement than most other small provincial townspeople. After all Joseph Paxton was known in the town, he had carried out important development work and was to do more, he was a regular visitor, he was the Duke's own man. A meeting in July 1850 chaired by Phillip Heacock cordially resolved to approve of the great industrial exhibition as proposed to HRH Prince Albert and pledge itself to cooperate with the Royal Commission in carrying it to a successful issue. A committee of notable townsmen was formed to further that aim, one of whose members, Dr Carstairs, commented that he was ...

... happy to see the plan for the building in Hyde Park being

A watercolour showing the Hot Baths after remodelling of 1854. The architect Henry Currey used an iron and glass design after the style of the Crystal Palace. The building jutting out to the extreme right housed a cold swimming bath which by 1864 had been converted to a billiard room. [B.M.A.G.]

A view of the eastern end of
the Crescent showing the new
Hot Baths and part of the
Terrace Walks.

commissioned by Mr Paxton, particularly as he is a gentleman so nearly connected with Buxton ...[21]

The Great Exhibition, as an event, has been perceived as ...

... the culmination of the romantic age, displaying the well-known phenomena of the apocalyptic vision, the sense of uniqueness, the conviction that the doors of a new world were opening ...[22]

and this, in a more modest sense, might be applied to Buxton at this point in its history. Certainly the 'doors of a new world' were opening for Buxton. A more prosaic link was provided by those in the town who exhibited at the Great Exhibition. A number of decorative objects in inlaid Derbyshire black marble were exhibited by Buxton spar and marble workers. James Turner, of Spring Gardens, offered two jugs in Ashford Marble, priced at fifty-five guineas; Selim Bright, who had high class showrooms in the Crescent, exhibited tables, chalices, dishes and stands in etched and inlaid black marble receiving an honourable mention by the jury for his vases.[23] Some concern was expressed that the exhibition would affect the number of visitors to Buxton in the season but this did not appear to be the case. It is likely that visitors to the exhibition, from Buxton, would have been the better-off. Whilst the railways allowed provincial working men and their families to pour into London by train, the Buxton working man was not within easy reach of a railway station.[24]

The local press reported on the Great Exhibition, however, and was effusive in its praise for Sir Joseph's Paxton's flair and great skill.

The major investment by the estate at Buxton was accompanied by the sale of land for building. The Quadrant was the first new road to be developed in urban Buxton. The road, itself, was not new. It formed part of the Manchester Road and had been created, in 1780, as part of a diversion under a turnpike renewal Act of 1764.[25] In 1852 the estate paid for the widening including strengthening the bridge over the river Wye. Four plots were set out for building houses and shops and bought by Francis Nielson, a chemist, two plots by John Marples, who was a contractor on the Royal Hotel, and a plot by Samuel Turner, a noted townsman who was to become a sub-agent to the Devonshire Estate.[26] The Quadrant was built progressively between 1853 and 1864, the building land was sold under very reasonable terms by the estate, but the same architectural style was used for each of the nine bays. The style of this impressive curve was set in 1853, undoubtedly by Currey, and the layout appears on Paxton's plan of 1852, another example of their joint work in the town. Though the land was sold freehold, the Devonshire Estate applied a measure of firm building control on the purchasers to maintain the consistent style and this marks the beginning of what was to become a formalised and closely enforced set of planning and building requirements by the Buxton Estate.

Devonshire Villas designed as a pair of substantial houses in Buxton Park in 1853–54 and attributed to Henry Currey. They were built by Messrs Sanders and Woolcott, the main contractors for the remodelled Buxton Baths.

Corbar Hall by Henry Currey, built in 1852 as Corbar Villa for Blackburn brewer Henry Shaw. This and Devonshire Villas are the only remaining properties built as part of Sir Joseph Paxton's original Buxton Park scheme.

In the Buxton Park two substantial plots, costing £300 each, were sold, one to Edmund Buckley, a Manchester businessman, property owner and local magistrate,[27] the other, just over two acres at Corbar side, to Henry Shaw. Shaw, a former brewer from Blackburn, commissioned Henry Currey to design a substantial house known as Corbar Villa, now Corbar Hall. The firm of Sanders & Woolcott who were the main contractors for the baths, built two semi-detached properties known as Devonshire Villas. They paid £125 for the land and arranged a private loan to finance the building. The architect, Henry Currey may also have designed these houses, he certainly supervised their erection to ensure that the restrictive covenants were complied with.[28] They were furnished and let by June 1854. The purchase of two other plots only are recorded. Sarah Eley and her sister, Mary Royston, built on a plot, costing £100, near the reservoir, which they occupied together. Alexander Oliver paid £160 for a plot but no evidence is available to say whether he built. Apart from one or two further developments in the early 1860s this was the extent of the Buxton Park development until a big push was made by the estate to market plots in the late 1870s. The much hoped for and well publicised offer of land for superior development did not take off as expected. Here was an opportunity for the literally rising middle classes to build on a site on elevated ground to the west of the town, away from the noise and smoke; the classic principles of urban layout were met by Paxton's plan,[29] yet the take-up was poor.[30] The reason is that the town was not yet ready for this kind of expansion. It was ahead of its time. While the coaching services were good, a direct railway service (despite the fact that by 1848 there were 5,000 miles of railways in England) would not be seen for another ten years. Thus it was not possible to attract the businessmen from Manchester and elsewhere to settle in the town and travel daily to work. The estate, at this time, was selling land on a freehold basis and it may be that those in the town who could afford to invest felt the price too high. It is noticeable that land in other parts of the town was offered by the estate at a more modest rate. The plots in the Quadrant had sold well at about £60 and in Spring Gardens, a commercial street, at the same rate. Local investors were more likely to pay for centrally situated plots to build substantial lodging houses, which could earn a good income. The top of Hall Bank and Terrace Road (formerly Yeoman's Lane) were both developed from this time with apartments and lodging houses.

The town was beginning to grow but at this stage down-to-earth commercial properties were needed. As Walton has pointed out, land ownership cannot be seen in isolation in resort development. If an elite demand proved insufficient, the landowner might have to lower his sights.[31] The Devonshire Estate did just that. It could afford to wait until the building plots in the Park became more saleable but, in the meantime, raise income from sales of more commercially viable areas. Thus the area close to the successful Quadrant was developed. To the north a new road was laid from the Quadrant to the Great Stables. To the south Terrace Road and Spring Gardens were further developed, in 1857 there were nine lodging house addresses on Terrace road including the newly built Terrace Villas.[32] In 1858 Hardwick

The junction of Hardwick Street and Terrace Road developed 1857–58. The drapery business of J. W. Potter was established in 1860 and continues to this day.

Street was laid out, this led from Spring Gardens on to the rising ground of Terrace Road and provided initially six building plots all of which were quickly sold. It opened up a further area for good quality housing which was to become Hardwick Mount but, more importantly, it provided a new commercial link between the Upper and Lower town. On the opposite side of Terrace Walks, Hall Bank provided a similar link and this was improved at the same time, the estate paying for a new back road to the houses there.[33] Both Hall Bank and Terrace Road led up to the market place where a Market Hall was built in 1857 by the local partnership of Samuel Turner and Robert Rippon Duke to the designs of Henry Currey. The building cost of £1,059 was raised by the issue of £2 10s. shares and the market was run by a committee of sixteen prominent trades-men of the town.[34]

This early building development in the town brought with it a requirement for improved services. The means of sewage disposal was via large, flat-bottomed sewers or cesspools and the river Wye. The layout of the Park had included the formation of main sewers using 'Clayton's Patent Hollow Bricks' though this provided only for local-ised drainage.[35] Throughout the decade the need for improved main and house drainage became increasingly apparent but this was not to be fully realised until 1860. The introduction of gas into the town was not without opposition. The Buxton Gas, Coke & Coal Company was formed in 1850 and established a gasholder and retorts in Bridge Street; the Devonshire Estate paid for a new road to the works. This was a private company, established by prominent townsmen, the same prominent men who were amongst those voting at a Vestry meeting in October 1850 to levy 5d in the pound for lighting the streets of Buxton.[36] It is unlikely that this rate was actually applied for in March 1851 a public meeting was called to determine whether the act for street lighting should be adopted,[37] and in April an Anti-Monopoly Society had been formed. In a pamphlet, this society argued in eloquent terms, against the gas being provided by a profit-making private company and urged ratepayers to defer their decision to pay for a year. At this stage the rate had been reduced to 3d in the pound. This was an unusual challenge to the way in which the affairs of the town were ordered, it was a direct challenge to the oligarchy of prominent townsmen, led by the Duke's agent. Moreover it was, apparently, a challenge by the working class:

> ... The time has passed – become one of the things that have been – when the working class are to fall down and worship a self-created class of aristocrats! ...[38]

though the erudition of the pamphlet, its use of quotations in both English and French and its signature:

Cover of the pamphlet opposing the installation of gas in the town, issued in 1851. [B.M.A.G.]

This engraving of about 1855
shows the Derbyshire village
character of Higher Buxton at
that time. The southern
entrance to the town from
Derby is the London Road
which is joined by the
turnpikes to Leek and
Ashbourne. This is today the
junction of London, West and
Dale Roads and Green Lane.
[B.M.A.G.]

... Vote against 'gas and monopoly' is the advice of ONE OF
YOURSELVES ...

suggests a well educated author. Buxton, as a resort, was not alone
in the opposition to improvements where this meant a liability for
increased rates. At Ilfracombe an anti-improvement party in the 1840s
was able to defeat a campaign for an improvement act. Blackpool,
moving out of parochial and manorial government, experienced similar
opposition and at Bridlington, in the 1850s, the farmers were able to
resist the introduction of gas lighting.[39] Though the movement at
Buxton was short lived its effects were felt for some time. The Vestry
meeting of March 1852 again began by considering whether to adopt
the act at all subsequently agreeing a rate of 4d in the pound and
the appointment of five gas inspectors. Gas was supplied to the baths
and other premises in the Crescent in 1851 but the lighting of streets
more generally in the town did not take place until August 1852. The
rate remained the same up to the end of the decade, though not
without some negotiation between the Vestry and the Gas Company
and it is noticeable that the minutes, unusually, record a two-thirds
majority vote each year on gas provision whilst most other business
was agreed unanimously.[40] The Devonshire Estate continued, however,
to invest in the provision of gas supply and fittings to its chief
properties in the Crescent and elsewhere. The estate also continued
to improve and extend the water supply with a new reservoir at Cold
Springs and a public pump in Spring Gardens near the Shakespeare
Hotel.[41] Those households receiving a piped supply in Buxton compared well against other parts of the country at a time when the
supplies and prices for the supply of water for domestic use differed

❧

markedly.[42] The estate, by 1855, had laid pipes along the commercial street in the lower town, Spring Gardens, and water mains into Higher Buxton. In 1859 nearly £1,000 was spent on the water works, including service pipes, which suggests that much of the town, by this time, had access to piped water. Private house supplies were bought from the estate who maintained the water works and paid for new water closets to be fitted in its own properties.

Throughout the decade to 1860 the Devonshire Estate maintained a firm hold on the provision of services. The Vestry employed the constable but it was to the estate office that he made his request for a greatcoat and trousers. The estate collected and disbursed the annual lighting and police rate for its properties and it maintained the fire engine. When the service offered by the Post Office was felt to be below standard it was the estate office which persuaded the Postmaster General to re-route the mail via Stockport instead of Chesterfield.[43] The Vestry employed a surveyor and carried out maintenance to roads including watering the crushed limestone surfaces in the summer to keep down the dust, but the Devonshire Estate also employed its own surveyor to take care of its extensive properties and to lay out new roads. Very little in the town escaped the attention of the Devonshire Estate office and most amenities were provided by the Duke. The town enjoyed a cricket ground in the Park in 1853 well before the great expansion of cricket from the 1860s, though the gymnasium proposed as part of Sir Joseph Paxton's plan, was not re-alised.[44] In the mid 1850s there were, however, some indications of self-determination by townsmen. The Market House Company was one example, another was the formation of a Mechanics Institute. This was founded in December 1855 by a group of notables, essentially tradesmen, builders, small businessmen and the like. The driving force behind this was Robert Rippon Duke, a builder, who was to rise through the class system to become a successful and respected architect in Buxton. Its formation faced some competition from a Buxton Literary Society formed a few months earlier and promoted by the professional class. Its lectures were typified by the title of one

Handbill of the Buxton, Fairfield and Burbage Mechanics and Literary Institute, founded in 1855. It is signed by Robert Rippon Duke, who was a founder member and president in 1856.

BUXTON, FAIRFIELD, & BURBAGE

Mechanics' and Literary Institute.

The following resolution was passed at a Committee Meeting of the Mechanic's Institute, on the 26th of March last :—

" Feeling ourselves to be under great obligations to Mr. Smithers for repeated kindnesses in receiving our deputations, and especially for the gratuitous use of convenient premises for the Institute, we are desirous to show to Mr. Smithers some expression of our gratitude, and are of opinion that the most acceptable mode of such expression will be to present to him a Stall at the Bazaar, to be held in the Ball Room in August next, in Aid of the Bath Charity Building."

The Committee take this opportunity of calling the attention of the Inhabitants of Buxton, Fairfield, and Burbage to the above, and trust that the Working, Men especially, will exert themselves to contribute articles to furnish the above stall.

Any Member of the Committee will give such information as may be required, on application.

The articles will be received at the Institute, on Saturday, the 26th of July, from 6 to 9 in the evening.

Institute, June 23rd, 1856.

Robert R Duke
President.

Mr Smithers died
8th July 1856.

49

in February 1856 'The philosophy of common things' and its meetings, attended by 'respectable people', were reported in the *Derby Telegraph*. The Mechanics Institute movement was aimed at the working man and artisan wishing to improve himself and this was the case in Buxton. Lectures on popular subjects were well attended suggesting that there were those in the town looking to advance themselves. The two societies could not agree on a merger and it is, perhaps, not surprising that Dr W. H. Robertson, who was asked to arbitrate, wished to see the Mechanics Institute subsumed within the Literary Improvements Society. However, popularity won the day and in May 1856 amalgamation took place resulting in the formation of Buxton, Fairfield and Burbage Mechanics and Literary Institute. It offered a library, reading and newsroom and programmes of lectures on social, scientific and literary subjects. Its list of twenty-eight patrons was impressive and included members of the aristocracy, such as Viscount Combermere and Lord John Manners, together with those of the upper class associated with the town including Sir Joseph Paxton, Henry Shaw and W. P. Shipton the surgeon.[45] The committee and elected officers were all names of burgeoning middle-class families who were to assume political influence over the next fifty years. Arguably the Mechanics Institute in Buxton was most effective in providing the means for advancement in social status for those publicly associated with its management. In common with the movement nationally, it was less effective, over its lifetime of about ten years, in delivering real educational opportunities for the artisan and skilled worker.[46]

Towards the end of the decade Buxton began to feel the effect of the new regime of the Seventh Duke of Devonshire and changes in agents. The agent, Phillip Heacock had managed the affairs of Buxton for nearly fifty years at his death in February 1851. He had overseen the laying of the foundation upon which Buxton was to grow but, sadly, he was not to see the fruits of his labours. He saw the new Buxton Park and the Hot and Natural baths begun but not completed.

Heacock's successor, Sydney Smithers, was agent at Ashford-in-the-Water and handled the Chatsworth estate accounts from 1836 to 1848. The suddenness of Heacock's death meant that the Duke had to find someone quickly to oversee the extensive developments in the town and Smithers was available. His position as agent at Chatsworth during the 1840s had been progressively taken over by Joseph Paxton, who was the agent there between 1849 and 1858.[47] Sydney Smithers was a professional land agent who had held positions on various parts of the Devonshire Estate since 1828. During his time at Buxton he successfully managed the major developments already underway but there is little evidence to suggest that he initiated any significant new work. His experience of managing tenant farming may not have

Photograph by Barrowclough Wright Bentley taken outside his shop at 6 Quadrant in about 1858. B. W. Bentley, an Accrington man, came to Buxton in about 1852 and quickly established his reputation as a fashionable and artistic photographer. He is reputed to be the third commercial photographer in Derbyshire and the first to establish a permanent studio. [J.M.B.]

equipped him for the demands of a growing inland resort. He did, however, promote the town effectively, obtaining good coverage in the *Illustrated London News* on the new baths and in the *Builder* magazine on the baths and new park; he must also be credited with financing, through the estate, the first edition of Dr Robertson's *Buxton Guide* published in 1854, a book which went through more than eleven editions and was a solid advertisement for the town for fifty years.[48] He advertised the new facilities in the major provincial papers, had views of Buxton prepared, arranged for an exhibition of the new park in the Royal Exchange, Manchester, and commissioned an eminent specialist, Dr Lyon Playfair to produce an analysis of the Buxton water which was circulated to 3,500 potential visitors.[49] Nor was he slow at developing himself. He visited Bath and Cheltenham and bought books on cottage architecture.[50] This effort helped Buxton to enjoy, in both 1853 and 1854, the

> ... Very best season ever ... not a bed to be had in the town ... very high demand for accommodation ...[51]

However the 1850s were boom years for the cotton textile trade and between 1850 and 1855 annual money wages rose by 16%, factors which were to support the increase of visitors to the new facilities at

Buxton.[52] In publicity terms, the agent was helped by the town's earliest photographer, Barrowclough W. Bentley, no mean self-publicist. B. W. Bentley had established his business in Buxton in 1852–53 and quickly obtained the patronage of the visiting aristocracy. By 1856 he had moved from a wooden hut at the top of the Terrace walks, to new premises in the Quadrant where he was able to offer the latest portrait technology in a field still in its infancy ...

> ... The beautifully, exquisite Daguerreotype: the large and commanding Calotype; and the singularly cheap Callodiotype ...[53]

He was also able to bring to life the extensive reports carried by the local papers on the Crimean War by offering photographs by Roger Fenton.

Sydney Smithers conducted business from his office in the Crescent but did not involve himself to any degree with public affairs, neither did he actively seek the co-operation of the townspeople. It is apparent that his style of approach failed to recognise the rising expectations of the tradespeople and middle-class for greater involvement in the town's affairs. It is noticeable, also, that he was described in the estate accounts as the 'accountant', taking a salary of £1,025 *per annum* with £100 allowance for a clerk.[54] Smithers was in office for just over five years. He died in July 1856 and the eulogies carried in the local newspapers inevitably suggested that he had been responsible for all the developments in Buxton from 1851 to his death. But Smithers' regime was one of consolidation, he had not enjoyed good health for some time before his death which came after a painful illness; he was, effectively, a caretaker agent.

The new agent, Edward Woollett Wilmot, adopted an entirely different style. He was a man of energy and vision and his appointment, in August 1856, was timely. He was to develop the degree of self-sufficiency and self-determination needed by the townspeople at a time of great change: the new regime of the seventh Duke of Devonshire from January 1858; the introduction of the Local Board of Health in 1859; and the arrival of the railways in 1863. These three major changes were to be seminal in the growth of Buxton as an inland resort and E. W. Wilmot was the right man to represent the estate as they occurred. Wilmot was the sixth son of Sir Robert Wilmot of Chaddesden Hall near Derby. He was a former agent to the Duke of Newcastle with a lucrative practice as a land agent, residing near Congleton in Cheshire.[55] When he came to Buxton at the age of forty-seven, he had already carried out some valuation work locally and would have been familiar with the Buxton Estate.[56] He quickly established positive social and business relationships. In November 1856 he initiated the formation of a savings bank for the 'industrious classes of Buxton',[57] and he subsequently promoted the

The first edition of the *Buxton Advertiser and List of Visitors*, 2 July 1852. Founded by John Cumming Bates, it became the most influential local newspaper and was the first to be printed in the town. J. C. Bates sold the paper to C. F. Wardley in 1882 but continued to run his business of bookseller and stationer in the Hot Baths Colonnade. *The Buxton Advertiser* continues to this day, albeit under different ownership.

formation of agricultural and horticultural clubs. In 1857 he laid the foundation stone of the new market hall and he became chairman of the shareholders of the company. One of his early innovations was to arrange oyster suppers for the gentry and principal residents with the aim of determining how the Duke, his agent and the inhabitants might adopt a policy for the future welfare of Buxton and unite to promote the common good of all. But it was through the elected Local Board that Wilmot was to effect the most fundamental and necessary changes in the town, changes that were wrought against strong opposition by some ratepayers.

At the beginning of 1859 urban Buxton consisted of about 425 houses, a population of just under 2,400 and twenty roads or streets. The decade from 1849 had seen a fifty per cent growth in all three but from 1859 there was a significant increase in the growth pattern. The Seventh Duke of Devonshire had inherited his title in 1858 and added to his own estates in Lancashire and Sussex those of the Sixth Duke giving him 198,667 acres distributed among eleven English and three Irish counties, and a gross rent roll of £180,990. He also inherited debts of £750,000 which, when added to his own £250,000 indebtedness on the Burlington estates, meant he had a consolidated mortgage debt of just under £1 million.[58] He was acquainted with the developments in Buxton having visited the town, as Earl of Burlington, with the Sixth Duke. His policy at Buxton was to be one of self-sufficiency. He would contribute towards new works but not fund these entirely as his predecessor had. He was also to expand considerably the policy of selling estate land for building and from 1859 this policy began to show in the further shaping of the layout of the town. From 1859 local democracy, through the Local Board, also became an important force and, although its impact was slow at first, inevitably tensions arose between the 'owner' through his agent and the townspeople, through their elected Board members. The old order was changing. No longer would the local newspapers refer to the Duke as the 'noble proprietor' not only would the agent Wilmot look for self-sufficiency, the editor of the *Buxton Advertiser*, John Cumming Bates, was pursuing a similar cause. In a July edition 1856 he wrote of the history of Buxton in the last few years being one of rapid improvement and growing fame, but that all of it had been due to the Duke of Devonshire and his agent. He suggested that there was food for thought in all this in that it was inevitable that the future of the place should not depend solely on the agent and the noble Duke but also the efforts of the townspeople themselves.

> ... Hitherto, we fear, the improvements must be considered to have been rather forced upon the inhabitants than to emanate or receive any very active assistance from them. What has been done has been looked upon too exclusively as the Duke's affair; that the inhabitants had nothing to do but look placidly on while their town was beautified, and their business bettered by the developments of others' means, and the energetic exercise of others' brains ... if its owners and inhabitants will but, so to speak, 'dig about it and dung it,' the labours of the husbandman shall not go unrewarded, and instead of being consigned to the limbo of the fruitless and unprofitable, it will grow into increased usefulness, and extend to ever multiplying numbers the healing virtues of its waters, the balmy freshness and purity of its air, and, to the wearied struggler in the busy life of towns, a beautiful and invigorating retreat ...[59]

CHAPTER THREE

Two Decades of Formative Growth

I N T H E T W E N T Y Y E A R S from 1859 Buxton experienced greater
growth than at any other comparable period in the nineteenth
century. The population of the town rose by 146%, houses increased
by 125% and the number of streets doubled to forty-two. An analysis
of lists of visitors to the town shows a significant increase in those
staying and a corresponding increase in the provision of accommodation. Of particular note is the growth in lodging-house and apartment accommodation from 162 premises in 1859 to 356 in 1879, an
increase of 120%. The town grew faster than its northern rival,
Harrogate, and its neighbouring watering place, Matlock.[1] This was
a period of steady rise in house building in Great Britain, with an
increase of just over 100% between 1860 and 1879 but there was a
clear building peak in Buxton beyond the national pattern.[2] In previous
chapters the genesis of this growth has been set out, showing a
thorough preparation for the establishment of Buxton as an important
health resort. It has not previously been recognised, however, just
how pivotal was this twenty-year period and what key factors came
together to stimulate this phenomenal growth.

The policy of the seventh Duke of Devonshire, from 1858, was one
of self-sufficiency and he exercised this through a line of increasingly
professional agents, Edward Woollett Wilmot from 1856 and George
Drewry from 1864, assisted by his son, Frank. Furthermore they were
supported by a small, but active, professional team. Of particular note
are the sub-agents, James Wardley from 1856 and Samuel Turner from
1858, together with Robert Rippon Duke who acted in the part-time
role of architect, surveyor and building inspector for nearly forty years
from 1863.[3] The influence of the Devonshire Estate on the layout,
type and architectural style of buildings in the town in these twenty
years was comprehensive. During this period also local democracy,
from the election of the first Local Government Board (Local Board)
in 1859 was to effect important changes in the way the town was run.
Inevitably the elected members of the Local Board were to find
themselves, from time to time, in disagreement with the policies of
the Devonshire Estate as they sought to establish their own rules and
bye-laws to shape the growth and administration of the town's affairs.
But, undoubtedly, the most significant engine for change was the
long expected arrival of the railways in 1863. The London North
Western (LNWR) and Midland (MR) companies opened adjacent

stations in the same month providing easier access for visitors of all classes, both paying guests and day-trippers. It is the unique interaction of these factors which provides the basis for this chapter.

In December 1859 the Duke's Buxton agent, Edward Woollett Wilmot, gave a lecture to the Buxton & Fairfield Mechanics Institute entitled 'Town Improvements'. It was a persuasive and formative set of arguments for the use of the powers granted in the Local Government Act of 1858 to make comprehensive sanitary arrangements and bye-laws which would materially improve the town. He spoke, in some detail, on systems of effective sewerage and drainage pointing out in graphic terms the shortcomings in Buxton, a description redolent of Chadwick's report more than twenty years before:[4]

> During the last summer our own beautiful river Wye was a miniature Thames; the stench late at night and early in the morning was dreadful ... visitors in walking avoided its banks, and complained bitterly of its condition. In other parts of the town visitors moved from one house to another, to avoid the smell of bad sewers ... Anyone, in hot weather, to stand over, or even pass by the grating at the bottom of the Hall bank, or the one at the top of Yeoman's Lane, will have ample proof of what large flat bottomed sewers can emit in the shape of noxious gas; and, if they will walk from the Dog Leach to the Tonic Bath, they will experience the effect of a surface drainage, assisted by a few cesspools.[5]

In essence, this lecture was a plea to the ratepayers to adopt the best system available and he was at pains to point out that this could be done at a cost less than that faced by other towns of comparative size. He also appealed strongly to the vested interest in a town which relied upon the visitor for most of its growth and economic survival. The timing of this lecture was apposite. At a public meeting in April 1859 it had been agreed to adopt the Local Government Act of 1858 within the boundaries of a district, which had been determined by William Ranger, a local government inspector, to be known as the 'Buxton District'.[6] The newly formed Local Board had met for the first time in June and by October had taken the decision to ask Mr Robert Rawlinson to design a sewerage system for the town. In fact Wilmot had sought advice from Ranger, the inspector. Rawlinson had been recommended, he had visited the town and assessed that a satisfactory system could be had for a rate of sixpence in the pound over thirty years.[7] The choice of Rawlinson was in large part due to Wilmot's connections and his offer of payment by the estate for the cost of the plans and specifications. It was auspicious because Rawlinson was a colleague of Ranger's at the Local Government Act Office where his duties included the inspection of sanitary systems newly installed in towns. Under such circumstances Buxton's system could hardly fail.[8]

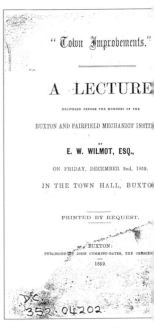

Privately printed pamphlet on town improvements for Buxton by E. W. Wilmot, 1859. [D.C.C. Lib.]

The Buxton Local Board had begun work in earnest, electing as its first chairman E. W. Wilmot, a not unsurprising choice since the Board began with nothing and had to rent its first office from the Devonshire Estate. The first clerk was Josiah Taylor. He was appointed part-time clerk to the Vestry in May 1859 at a salary of £5 *per annum* and in June joined the new Local Board at a salary of £50 in which position he was to be long serving, providing a valuable, indeed remarkable, degree of continuity in the Board's affairs.[9] Early pre-occupations of the Local Board were with the purchase of the water works from the Devonshire Estate, sanitary arrangements, general cleanliness and the provision of certain amenities such as a cattle market, fire brigade and snow plough, but their decisions were at first quite tentative. Robert Rawlinson had observed that the 1858 Local Government Act had given local citizens the power to manage their own affairs for the first time. Under the Public Health Act of 1848 localities had been required to request the General Board in London to apply the provisions of the act, Buxton had not done this. The 1858 Act offered a high degree of decentralisation in that a locality could determine to apply it through a resolution carried by a simple majority of owners and ratepayers. This Buxton had done at a meeting on 9 April 1859, becoming one of the first thirty-five places which adopted the act in 1858/59.[10] The effect of this move to local power meant that towns were for the first time having to frame local legislation, set up systems of finance and manage their own affairs. Buxton was more fortunate than many in having the ducal influence, but the work of the Local Government Act Office (LGAO) under its genial and literary secretary, Tom Taylor, was indispensable in helping embryonic Local Boards get started.[11] Buxton used a model set of bye-laws from the LGAO for the regulation of new streets, sewerage, hackney carriages and slaughter houses, with the addition of three clauses unique to its role as a health resort

1.   No building to be erected on the side of any new street within 10ft of the edge of the footpath.

2.   Bath chairs shall not be drawn on the footpath.

3.   No person shall be allowed to ride or drive a horse on the footpath.[12]

Additional bye-laws were agreed by the LGAO covering the prevention of nuisances, cleaning of footpaths, privies, ash pits and the removal of refuse and it was to Tom Taylor at the LGAO that chairman Wilmot wrote for advice.[13]

From this time the Local Board and the Devonshire Estate worked in harmony for the good of the town, though the agent, Wilmot was clearly the leader, managing affairs to mutual benefit from his position

Josiah Taylor, first Clerk to the Local Board in 1859, Clerk to the Urban District Council formed in 1894, and the first Town Clerk of the Borough of Buxton formed in 1917. His sixty-year record as a chief officer must be largely unparalleled. He was made first freeman of the borough in 1918. [B.M.A.G.]

R. JOSIAH TAYLOR,

as chairman. The Local Board borrowed £3,500 in early 1860 to finance the sewerage system and a further £1,700 in 1861 for street improvements, the provision of hydrants and urinals, and to set out a cattle market. The loans were provided by the Duke of Devonshire secured against the general district rate.[14] The regulation of bath chairs, horse and donkey carriages for hire was an early decision, the Local Board setting out the numbers to be licensed and the fares to be charged. In addition to the clerk the Board employed a full-time surveyor and the part-time services of the Superintendent of Police from the Vestry. The Vestry continued to meet but gradually relinquished its responsibilities in favour of the Local Board, for example, the surveyor in 1859, the gas rate after about 1860 and St Anne's Well in 1865. From 1860 there was a clearer separation between the more secular business and that of the church. Responsibility for the appointment of constables, overseers and guardians of the poor was the last vestige of Vestry affairs which continued up to 1894 when the Local Government Act of that year revoked the powers. The delineation of the boundary between Fairfield and Buxton for Vestry purposes, however, remained as it had been prior to the new Local Board 'Buxton District' of 1859. Indeed, in July 1862 the overseers of Buxton and Fairfield clarified more precisely those boundaries. It has been observed that the propensity of the early Victorians to create a host

In May 1859 the *Buxton Advertiser* carried a short account as follows: 'A small drinking fountain has been erected at the foot of Terrace Road, where every thirsty passer-by may help himself to pure, wholesome, and unadulterated "Adam's Ale".' The fountain may be seen to the right of this photograph.

It is unlikely this was an innovation of the very new Local Board, thus more likely to have been provided by the Devonshire Buxton Estate. It coincides with the development of Hardwick Street opposite, and with investment by the estate in the water works to serve the town. [B.M.A.G.]

of local bodies with particular powers was a recipe for confusion,[15] and so it was in Buxton. In May 1862 the chairman said he had been in touch with Mr Tom Taylor on a point of law which would have implications for the forthcoming and future elections. Any persons paying a poor rate in the townships, any portion of which was included in the Local Government Act district, could vote in the election if they occupied property of a certain rateable value even though they did not reside in the district or pay district rates.[16] However, since this matter did not appear in either Vestry or Local Board minutes subsequently, it would seem that it was satisfactorily resolved.

Typical of the business conducted by the Local Board in its early years was the management of the Market House, postal arrangements, sewers, footpaths, the approval of new house plans, extensions to existing properties and the valuation of properties for rating purposes. The surveyor was kept busy inspecting houses for such things as ash pits, slopstones and adequate drainage. The chairman, recognising the value of harmonious working relationships lost no opportunity to bring people together socially. In addition to his annual 'oyster suppers' for prominent townsmen and tenants, he invited members and officers of the Local Board, the contractors of the sewerage works and the directors of the Buxton Gas, Coke & Coal Co. to the Eagle Hotel one evening where they:

> ... partook of a supper he had liberally provided and afterward spent a few social hours together ...

In turn members of the Local Board organised a well attended public dinner in January 1861 in acknowledgement of Wilmot's

> ... uniform kindness and endeavours to promote the best interests of Buxton ...

and the *Buxton Advertiser* thought fit to devote two full columns to describing the proceedings.[17] The balance sheet for the year 1861/62 shows the modest start which the Local Board had made:

Rateable Value = £8,000: Rate 2s. 6d in the Pound			
Income		*Expenditure*	
£1,000	Interest £160	4s. 4d.	(5d. rate)
	Lighting 139	0s. 0d.	(4d. rate)
	Salaries 115	0s. 0d.	
	Audit 8	17s. 0d.	
	Election 8	0s. 0d.	
	Printing 29	5s. 7d.	(10d. rate in total)
	Stamps 13	5s 4d.	
	Furniture 29	0s. 0d.	
	Highways 335	0s. 0d.[18]	

The harmony between the Devonshire Estate and Local Board was not to last, however. The Board membership was drawn from the group of influential townsmen who had voted, in late 1858, to proceed towards adoption of the Local Government Act and these men were to experience the independence and power in local decision making which the act conferred. It has been pointed out that urban historians might find out more about how decisions were made by identifying key individuals in a city and following up their activities and their membership of societies and organisations.[19] Nowhere could this be more true than in Buxton where the same names crop up repeatedly across the breadth of the town's activities, people who were public-spirited and ready to meet new problems.[20] The challenge to the estate came as early as April 1862 when J. Armitage Pearson, a surgeon, accused Wilmot of trying to force the town to pay 11*d.* per yard for pavement and pavings. Earlier the Local Board had sought to drive too hard a bargain with the Duke over purchase of the water works and in August 1859 he closed the negotiations, resolving to supply the town himself. It was to be another ten years before the town acquired the water works. However, the most significant disagreement occurred in November 1863 on a matter of policy in the provision of sewers. Inevitably Wilmot was seeking the best for the town even if this was to cost more, but the townsmen were carefully watching the rates. Wilmot felt strongly that a sewer should be provided by the town to within 100 feet of every building and

… that the Board should continue the main sewer for the use of every continuous street or row of houses, that should any vacant space intervene between the houses and the sewer, the owner of the land

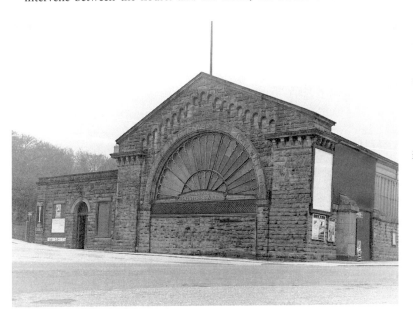

The two stations, opened in June 1863, which stood side by side and had matching façades. The LNWR is on the left and the MR is shown on the facing page. The influence of the Devonshire Estate, through Sir Joseph Paxton, can be seen in this requirement for symmetry in façades, but the stations were by no means identical inside. [J.M.B.]

should put in the sewer but the money should be repaid to him as soon as the land was covered with buildings. This would prevent the necessity of the Board paying for sewers where there were no buildings which would be obviously unfair now a main sewer has been provided for the district . . .[21]

The Local Board's decision was that house owners should be entirely responsible for providing the sewer to their premises. Wilmot appealed to Tom Taylor at the LGAO for legal guidance but the Local Board's decision stood and Wilmot, his position usurped, resigned as member and chairman. No agent of the Devonshire Estate was to stand for election in the following twenty years, from this time the estate exercised influence directly through land ownership and the control of urban development.[22]

The 1861 census includes returns from railway huts for the MR above Bakewell Road and for LNWR at Hogshaw and in June 1863 the, long awaited, railways arrived with both companies officially opening their stations. The LNWR had completed their line from Whaley Bridge to provide a direct link from Manchester to Buxton. The Midland Railway Company had driven and tunnelled their route from Rowsley, through spectacular scenery and over an impressive viaduct at Monsal Head, to Millers Dale. From here a branch line served Buxton. The Midland line was obtained after considerable difficulty and through the direct efforts of Sir Joseph Paxton, a director of the company. He referred to the parliamentary fights needed to secure approval in a number of letters to his wife, Sarah, at Chatsworth.[23] This new form of travel opened up the town to the day tripper and health seeker alike and it has been observed that, whilst

this offered new opportunities to developers it also posed problems. The wider range of income groups who could now visit the town included the working-class excursionists looking for cheap lodgings and amusements. In the mid-Victorian years, however, the best paying and most reliable visitor was still drawn from the wealthy upper and solid middle classes and it was important to protect this clientele. In some seaside towns entrepreneurs seeking to capitalise on the market created by the lower-class visitor could pose a real threat to the longer term economic stability of the resort.[24] This was not to be the case in Buxton where the Devonshire

Estate was uniquely able to influence the growth of the town's amenities and facilities such that the wealthy upper and solid middle classes continued to be the dominant type of visitor. True, some of the facilities in Higher Buxton catered for the working-class visitor, an example being the extension of two large new refreshment rooms at the Seven Stars Inn to cater for the

The Railway Hotel built for the Chesterfield Brewery Company in 1864. The external façade remains remarkably unchanged to this day.

> ... extra numbers who, as excursionists, flock to Buxton ...[25]

and there were lodging houses offering very modest terms in Higher Buxton. The new hotels were decidedly of a higher class, however. Perhaps the most modest was the Railway, opened in the newly developing Bridge Street in 1864, by the Chesterfield Brewery Company. The Leewood, opened in the same year, was situated in Paxton's

The Lee Wood Hotel, built from three private houses and situated in Buxton Park, was opened in 1864 by Brian Bates, wealthy local hotelier.

New Hotel, Buxton

Park and described as large and handsome, converted from three private houses by Brian Bates. The Palace Hotel, opened 1868, had LNWR interests and investment by the Duke of Devonshire. After a shaky beginning it was to become one of Buxton's foremost hotels.[26] The Burlington, built 1874, was another Devonshire Estate investment. The first substantial Hydropathic hotel, the Malvern (opened 1866) was to become the largest hydro in town. The Devonshire Estate sought to capitalise on the medical advantages of the town in order to optimise the return on the baths and on accommodation in which it had an interest. It will be seen that decisions concerning land sales, the management of the baths and the provision of visitor facilities were all taken in order to develop Buxton as a health resort of some repute.[27] The agents of the Duke were well aware of the need to preserve the standards and amenities and were able to plan the layout of the town, determine the location of all classes of housing and to enforce restrictive covenants to ensure that the social tone was maintained in particular areas. The Local Board were partners in this endeavour but, as an embryonic organisation, were inevitably led by the estate.[28]

From 1859 building development continued in the areas of Spring Gardens, the new Hardwick Street and the adjacent Terrace Road (Yeoman's Lane). Despite the expected railways (by 1861 both companies had booking offices in Spring Gardens) development was quite slow. The estate sold land for building in Higher Buxton and at Cote Heath on the southern edge of town. New roads approved by the Local Board were Dale Street, Torr Street, Bridge Street and Sylvan Park where new houses were approved. Hardwick Terrace was an extension of Hardwick Street and a new road was planned from here to Market Street, which would form the beginnings of Hardwick Square. This was an area connecting the more fashionable Lower with the more commercial Higher Buxton and the estate exercised tight building restrictions as they progressively sold the land. In lower Buxton some limited development took place in Buxton Park including Hawthorn Villa for Thomas Marshall, and two buildings designed by Henry Currey – a new parsonage for the incumbent of St John's Church, the Revd Edward Weighall, and a private asylum on Corbar Side.[29] The most important planned development was Broad Walk begun in 1861 as Cavendish Terrace when local wine and spirit merchant, G. F. Barnard, erected the first three houses known as

The Palace Hotel was designed by Henry Currey and built as a speculative investment in 1864–66. After the collapse of the venture in 1867 it was bought back at auction by a consortium composed largely of the original investors. It became Buxton's foremost hotel. The Clerk of Works for the building was R. R. Duke and he subsequently became Company Secretary and architect for the extensions of 1887.

Cavendish Villas on land bought from the estate. This was a wide gravelled walk from opposite the Old Hall Hotel to the Tonic Bath extensively developed between 1861 and 1875 to become one of the most fashionable Victorian terraces in the town in an unrivalled position overlooking the pleasure gardens and, subsequently, the pavilion. Development was rapid; by 1864 there were ten dwellings either built or in the process of erection, all the properties were listed as private lodging houses.[30] Control over the style, value and use of these properties was rigidly enforced by the Devonshire Estate through restrictive covenants. Other development in Lower

Cavendish Terrace Buxton

Buxton included the beginning of Hartington Street adjacent to Hall Bank, and a new road at the Post Office behind the Crescent. At this time the estate were investing in improvements to the baths. New Turkish Baths, designed by Henry Currey, were provided in 1861 and in 1863 the estate capitalised on the baths site by building two arcades of shops known as the Devonshire and Hot Bath Colonnades. The policy of the Duke was clearly demonstrated in the case of these shops. He gave land to the Local Board for a road to the Devonshire Hospital and improvement of the Quadrant, upon which there were building sites, on condition that they carried out the work including making a cab stand. He also received planning approval for his new shops. It was a satisfactory arrangement all round.[31]

The present-day Broad Walk was begun in 1861 and was known as Cavendish Terrace. Earlier work, probably by Henry Currey and later building by Robert Rippon Duke produced examples of fine mid-Victorian villas, most of which were operated as high-class lodging houses in the season. Broad Walk was largely completed by 1876.

In the six years from 1859 the Devonshire Estate accounts for Buxton show a loss in three years and only a small surplus in the other three.[32] Interestingly this coincides with Wilmot's tenure. After his death in 1864 the accounts took on a very different appearance. Wilmot's time as agent coincided with the start of real expansion and a consequent need for the estate to invest in necessary infrastructure. Thus money was spent on the water works, the baths and in setting up a brickworks. Further improvements to the Buxton Estate included work on the pleasure grounds, the new private asylum (total cost £6,500), a new wing to the Old Hall Hotel (£1,329) and the laying out of the new roads already referred to. The brickworks took two or three years to come into profit; thus the 1863 accounts refer to a large stock of bricks unsold and the need to carry the account over to the following year in order to present it in a more settled form. This necessary investment was to bring returns over the medium term and from the time of the agent, George Drewry, Buxton health resort returned a good income for the Duke. In particular the baths were a solid net earner.[33] Up to 1863 a modest amount of land had been sold for building but after this year sales, in general, increased.[34] In the main the land was sold freehold and outright though a few plots were sold on a *Chief Rent*. Drewry introduced a policy of remitting the income from outright sales direct to Currey & Co. as early as 1864 so they did not feature as part of the Buxton accounts. The surveyor, Robert R. Duke, wrote:

> ... Buxton, October 25th 1864 to JP Moore
>
> Dear Sir, When Mr Drewry was here last he told me he wished Mr Currey to receive the purchase money of all land sold here so as to keep it out of our books. I therefore enclose you a cheque £64.8.8d which will pay for Isaac and William Wardle's land £55.0.0 and £9.8.8d Mr Currey's charges. Will you kindly give me a memorandum so that I may show Mr Currey what has been remitted ...[35]

This practice ran up to the late 1870s when outright sales ceased and the use of the 'Chief' or 'Fee Farm Rent' became the more usual land sales arrangement.[36]

The Local Board made impressive progress in its first twenty years of existence and this may be due to its early start in the field of local government and to a stable membership of solid, hard-working townsmen.[37] Elections every three years replaced four members in turn and, though there was a good deal of movement through retirements and deaths, records show a constant line of well-known townsmen, many being re-elected regularly.[38] The press suggested that the Board had missed two early opportunities to acquire the gas and water works defeating the proposals because people did not want to stand the taxation which might ensue.[39] In turn the Board passed early resolutions to try to restrict press reporting, at a meeting in 1862 considerable discussion took place after which it was resolved

> ... that nothing be reported but the actual resolutions as touching the business of the Board ...[40]

This was, of course, not to last. The local press was to prove a stern critic despite the fact that the editor of the *Buxton Advertiser* was an elected member for six years from 1870.[41] The Local Board probably benefited from its procrastination over the purchase of the utilities because the Devonshire Estate made considerable investment in these in the 1860s as will

Hartington Street at its junction with Fountain Street, an engraving of about 1872. On the right are numbers 1 and 2 Prospect Villas which date to about 1865, while the building to the left was part of the well-known Buxton Hydropathic Hotel.

Hartington St & Fountain St Buxton

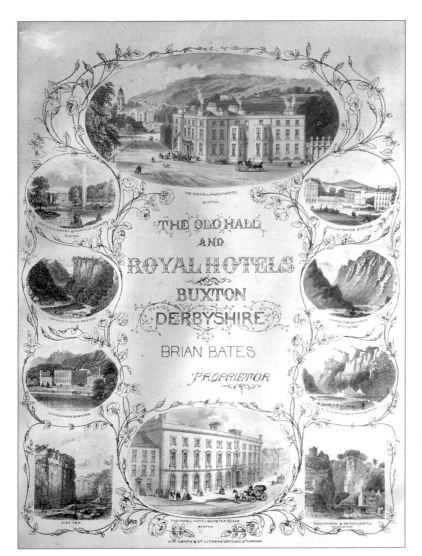

THE OLD HALL FAMILY HOTEL
BUXTON

THE OLD HALL
AND
ROYAL HOTELS
BUXTON
DERBYSHIRE

BRIAN BATES

PROPRIETOR

THE ROYAL HOTEL WINSTER PLACE
BUXTON

In addition to the Lee Wood Hotel Brian Bates ran the Old Hall and Royal together with high-class lodgings at 2 Grosvenor Terrace, Broad Walk. Here he advertises two of his hotels, setting them among the attractions of the Peak District. [B.M.A.G.]

be seen from the accounts at Appendix 3.3. The Local Board, in fact, leased the water works from the estate in January 1868 and had the benefit of the secondment of the estate surveyor, Robert Rippon Duke, for that year to help the smooth transition. R. R. Duke had been the superintendent of the water works for the Devonshire Estate from 1864 and was well versed in the technical aspects of supply. The Local Board raised a loan of £10,000 to purchase the water works outright in 1872.[42] The fairs and market tolls had been in public hands since 1864 and in 1868 the Market House was acquired from its private shareholders. The Buxton Gas Act of 1870[43] had conferred further powers on the company but also indicated that the Local Board should be empowered to purchase the works and in 1872 the shareholders of the gas works sold out to the Local Board. All this

This view of the Hot Baths in about 1870 shows the curve of the Quadrant behind. Originally included in Sir Joseph Paxton's plan of 1852, the Quadrant was completed between 1853 and 1864 with the same external façade for each bay. [B.M.A.G.]

acquisition paved the way for Buxton's first major local government act. The Buxton Local Board Act 1873 [44] marked a significant milestone in the Board's progress, drawing together arrangements for the supply of water and gas, the erection of slaughterhouses and a range of associated powers including financial borrowing, compulsory purchase of property and the regulation of services. At the same time the Local Board obtained approval compulsorily to purchase specific properties in the town which included Dunmore Square on the Market Place and Lawson's Corner.[45] Both were subsequently demolished, Dunmore Square to remove an unsanitary group of buildings and Lawson's Corner, which projected into the main thoroughfare of Spring Gardens.[46] In 1877 the Local Board bought the cattle market outright

Lawson's Corner protruded from the corner of Spring Gardens and effectively narrowed the entrance into Terrace Road and the Crescent. It was demolished under the Buxton Local Board Act of 1873, which gave compulsory purchasing powers. John Lawson's claim for compensation proved to be a lengthy legal case.
This photograph, looking up Terrace Road, shows Lawson's Wine Vaults in the centre before demolition. [B.M.A.G.]

The same order of 1873 allowed
for the demolition of the court
of shops on the Market Place
known as Dunmore Square.
These shops, shown on the left,
had become unsanitary.
[B.M.A.G.]

from the Devonshire Estate together with substantial land in Ashwood
Dale for the siting of new gas works. The analysis of Local Board
borrowing up to 1881 at Appendix 3.5 and the inventory below
show how local democracy in Buxton had established itself in the
provision of direct services and in the regulation of housing and
sanitary affairs.

Buxton Local Board [47]	
7 Horses & Foal & Filly	8 Carts
New Lorry	2 Street Sweeping Machines
3 New Hand Carts	3 Water Carts
7 Sets of Harness	3 Sets of Chain Gears
Harness for Fire Engine Horses	Snow Plough
2 Tumbler Carts	Road Roller
Steam Engine and Stone Crusher	

Much of the social legislation from the 1860s was permissive, in
that local authorities could decide what services, direct works, housing
and public health services they provided. In England this resulted in
an extraordinarily wide variety and variation in the nature and quality
of municipal activities. How much was done depended upon the
influence of individuals and groups in particular towns.[48] The Buxton
Local Board made sound, steady progress at a time when much
legislation attempted to intervene, guided by its competent clerk,
Josiah Taylor, to adopt only those acts which would materially improve
the town.[49] In this it was encouraged and supported by the Devonshire

Estate. The overriding aim was to see the town prosper as a health resort by setting a standard for its visitors.

As the town grew from 1863 the type of property built and the layout of streets and roads were carefully controlled, with the Local Board and Devonshire Estate each exercising influence. At the rent audit dinner in 1863 the estate appointed Robert Rippon Duke as part-time surveyor. He was a conscientious man who took his responsibilities to the estate very seriously and progressively increased his influence. His role was to lay out building plots and roads, deal with land sales and ensure that the requirements of the legal covenants were adhered to, particularly in respect of building design and boundary walls. The Duke owned his land at Buxton in 'fee simple' which meant that he was able to enter into a range of different forms of transaction to sell off land at written-up development value.[50]

Initially most sales were freehold but the use of a 'Chief Rent' or 'Fee Farm Rent' became the more common form of sale. Other variations included sale on Chief Rent with option to purchase within a set number of years, occasional leaseholds, exchanges of land between the Devonshire Estate and others, and plots were also sold at a price with a stipulation that a further sum was payable when the land was built upon.

The estate used these various forms of transaction in order to make land attractive to builders and investors whilst maintaining a degree of control over the value and quality of buildings erected. In R. R. Duke they had a surveyor who could not only ensure this but, when required, could supply designs and supervise building in his other role as the local architect. Sale by Chief Rent was a particularly interesting way of handling building land transactions. The terms 'Chief Rent' and 'Fee Farm Rent' are both used in estate documents to mean the same form of sale.[51]

Using this arrangement the Duke of Devonshire could give a conveyance of freehold but instead of asking for payment of a sale price he would keep a charge or annual rent ie, Chief Rent forever on the land. This was an unusual method. A more common approach by landowners was to use a long lease. In fact a detailed comparison of the two approaches suggests that for all practical purposes there would seem to be little difference between sale of land on a long lease (i.e. 999 years) and on the basis of a Chief Rent. In each case exclusive possession would be transferred to the owner or lessee. Such a person would have the right to exclude all others from occupation, including the landlord. Restrictive covenants used to hold up the value of surrounding land and for other purposes could apply equally in either case. The use of Chief Rents appears to have been a regional convention. It was found in Lancashire, some Northern towns and the West Country.[52] In Barrow land was sold on ordinary freehold and at Eastbourne short leaseholds, with an option to purchase the freehold, were the predominant form of sale.[53]

Why then did the Duke of Devonshire use the Chief Rent in preference to the lease? One reason is that the land could be sold on a freehold basis which made it more attractive to the buyer than leasehold. It is also possible that the Devonshire Estate was able to absolve itself from responsibilities to do with ground works and services which might, in the case of leasehold, be deemed to be the responsibility of the landowner. Also a Chief Rent is like a mortgage in the sense that, if the freeholder defaults on payment the bailiffs can be brought in. There is, however, no power of sale.[54] These advantages, together with the perpetual income, allowed the estate to offer affordable building land whilst still maintaining a degree of control. The purchaser paid the Chief Rent in arrears thus could sell or let the properties once built and apportion this rent to the new occupier before it was due to the estate.

The standard form of conveyance used by the Devonshire Estate included the provisions made in the case of default of payment of the Chief Rent. It also specified a minimum value of the property to be built and the nature of surrounding footpaths and walls in addition to the more usual requirements for drainage and groundwork. Additional restrictions were detailed as follows:

> ... Not to use or suffer to be used without such consent as aforesaid any building for the time being standing upon the premises thereby granted and conveyed or any part thereof for the exercise or carrying on of the trade or business of a catgut spinner, hog skinner, boiler of horseflesh or bones, soap maker, soap boiler, glue or size maker, ale house or tavern keeper or retailer of beer, wine or spirit vaults, slaughterman, butcher, fellmonger, currier or for the purposes of gas works or for any other noxious, noisy or offensive occupation, trade or business whatsoever or which might be or grow to the damage annoyance or injury of the neighbourhood ...[55]

The estate surveyor enforced the requirements assiduously ...

> ... 10th August 1869 to Mr Cotteril

Typical three-storey properties, usually with cellars, built in the 1870s and 1880s for occupation by artisans and small business families. Many would also offer lodgings for visitors in the season.

Dear Sir, I find it is your place to build the wall between your property and the land belonging to Mr Darwin. Will you let it be built at once as there are many complaints about it.

Yours Truly Robt. R. Duke ...[56]

... 17th June 1878 to J. P. Moore at Currey & Co.

Dear Sir, I return your drafts to Broomhead, Perkin and Holmes. Broomhead is to build two houses to the back at a cost of £400 each, they should be used as lodging houses only. He may build a workshop and cottages at the back but the general restrictions as to nuisance as they stand in your drafts should apply to any property in the rear of this land and the other plots north east of it. Perkin is to build one house to the front to cost £500 and workshop at the back. Holmes is to build one house to the front to cost £500 and workshops at the back. The same restrictions apply to these as to Broomhead. In all cases in Hardwick Square South and South street, the front fences must be of coursed stone with tooled ashlar coping. The other fences may be of rubble stone with sanded ashlar coping.

Yours truly, Robert R. Duke ...[57]

The use of restrictive covenants was quite usual where major land-owners wished to exert influence on town planning. There are examples such as the Bedford Estate in Bloomsbury, Bournemouth under Sir George Tapps-Gervis, Robert Grainger in Newcastle upon Tyne and Lord Scarbrough at Skegness.[58] Buxton offers another good example, the practice being usual from the first developments in 1850.

The Local Board surveyor from 1859 was E. Mycock but, upon his resignation early in 1863, the post was advertised at £60 *per annum* and in February J. D. Simpson of Fairfield was recruited from a field of sixteen, which is an indication of how important the position was perceived to be. He remained in post for fourteen years, augmenting his income by also acting as clerk to the Local Board of Fairfield, until he became a sub-agent to the Devonshire Estate, in 1877 at a salary of £200 *per annum*.[59] His duties as surveyor to the Buxton Local Board were set out under section thirty-four of the 1858 Act and included, *inter alia*, inspecting the thickness of walls, structure of party walls, ventilation, space and drainage.[60] The act also specified the requirement for plans of new buildings and any demolition of older buildings to be approved but such requirements were applied gradually at the local level, probably on the basis of expediency. It is noticeable, for example, that the requirement that no building be erected until plans and specifications had been approved came in 1864 as a result of a letter from the coroner regarding the death of a Richard Stubbs who had fallen from a building he was erecting.[61] Professor Burn has asked questions about the quality and competent of key officers in the embryonic Local Boards,[62] and there is no doubt that such officers were feeling their way. Evidence from the minutes

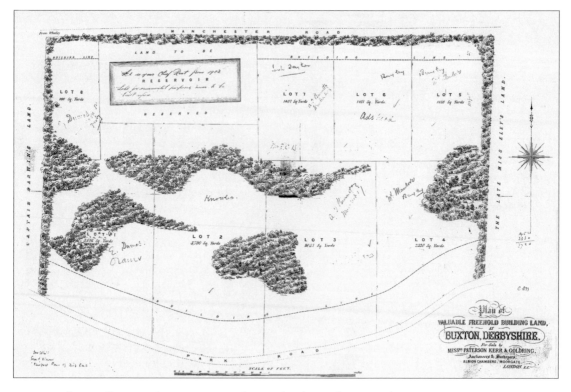

suggests that at Buxton there was a weakness, in the early years, in the technical aspects of building control, but this was balanced by the competence of the Devonshire Estate surveyor. When Simpson took over as surveyor to the Local Board matters improved markedly.[63]

A great deal of work had been put in by E. W. Wilmot in the eight years of his tenure as agent; his approach had been to implement the Duke's policy of involving the town to the fullest extent in its own affairs.[64] In the second half of his tenure, however, investment in Buxton had been such that the accounts showed very little surplus. The Duke was aware of the situation. Wilmot kept in close touch and stayed at Chatsworth to discuss business. The Duke also visited Buxton; on one occasion in April 1864 he had a long talk with Wilmot on business matters observing that

> ... several building schemes are contemplated and Wilmot has much confidence in the place being much enlarged ...[65]

But on 19 May of the same year he observed that

> ... Mr Wilmot has been and still is, I fear, very unwell and I did not stay long ...[66]

In fact Wilmot died on 25 June. Robert Wilmot applied to succeed his father but, despite hearing good reports of him, the Duke appointed George Drewry to the Buxton Estate. A marked improvement in

In 1877 the Devonshire Estate employed a London firm of surveyors and auctioneers to sell eight plots on the east side of Buxton Park. This plan was issued for sale purposes. [D.C. Chat.]

❧

financial performance was rapidly obtained by the new regime. Whilst it may be argued that, initially at least, Drewry reaped what Wilmot had sown (rather as Sydney Smithers had of Heacock) it is noticeable that Drewry managed to finance further investment yet still produce a healthy surplus. He was aided in this by land sales and the increasing popularity of the baths. Sales of building land grew markedly both outright and on Chief Rent but by the late 1870s Chief Rent was the more usual form of transaction.[67]

The sale of Broad Walk was almost all on an outright freehold basis, so was that of Devonshire Park, which was laid out in 1868 and developed for fashionable residential housing between 1870 and 1878. This new park was situated under the lee of Corbar Hill to the north west of the town adjacent to Sir Joseph Paxton's Buxton Park. Unlike Buxton Park, however, the more modest layout of Devonshire Park was immediately successful with nineteen plots sold realising a total of £2,400 for the estate which also built three houses there. The two internal roads, 'Devonshire' and 'Marlborough', were bounded by the main road to Manchester and Corbar Road. Land prices in Buxton varied from 1s. 8d. to 5s. per square yard, building plots in Broad walk typically costing 4s. per square yard, whilst land for artisan three-storey dwellings in Higher Buxton was 3s. to 3s. 6d. and at Hogshaw for workmen's cottages 1s. 10d. Plots for shops in the Quadrant cost just under one pound per square yard.[68] The land valuations were made by the estate surveyor.[69] The estate sold plots of land progressively in the Buxton Park, though many of these were on the boundaries formed by Manchester and St John's Roads. In 1877 the estate employed the London firm of surveyors and auctioneers, Paterson Kerr and Goldring, to sell eight substantial building plots in a bid to see the Buxton Park built upon; this land was sold by Chief Rent.[70] The price of Chief Rents ranged from 1d. to 4d. per square yard through the period. These were modest, certainly compared with those charged by the Sidney Sussex College Estate on a developing Cleethorpes where prices for the same period ranged from 2d. to 8d.[71] The most expensive land was in the new road skirting the Pleasure Garden (Burlington Road) and St John's Road, on the edge of Buxton Park, at 4d. Land in Buxton Park itself was priced at only 2d. and six plots were purchased in 1877 by T. W. Goldring, the auctioneer, at prices ranging from just over 1d. to just under 2d., which suggests that the estate's

St John's Road in about 1875. Robertson's *Buxton Guide* of 1872 has the description 'The Park (St John's Road)' to indicate the new development of substantial villas from St John's Church bordering Buxton Park. St John's Road was earlier referred to as either 'Macclesfield New Road' or 'Burbage' Road.

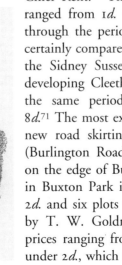

St John's Road Buxton

attempt to sell the Buxton Park were, again, only marginally successful. Land in Higher Buxton ranged from 2*d.* to 3*d.* per sq. yd. and there was no difference in price between the fashionable Hardwick Square and the artisan and working-class streets such as Dale, Hollins, Market and South Streets, though of course the difference in type and density of building meant that in the latter cases the Chief Rent for a plot would be shared among a number of householders.

The developments of Broad Walk, Devonshire and Buxton Parks and the part-developed Burlington Road formed the best residential area of the town and were reserved for villa residences of certainly not less than £500 value usually, but not always, detached.[72] The estate also had to manage the growth of other parts of the town which were much less exclusive. The earlier development of Hardwick Street led to the further expansion of Hardwick Terrace and Mount which in turn connected the more fashionable Lower with Higher Buxton and opened up further residential land. The estate surveyor laid out the impressive Hardwick Square from 1877 which continued the standard of villa property from Hardwick Mount and set a value on the surrounding land in Higher Buxton. The term 'villa', though having its origins in the country estate of the eighteenth century, had become used in the nineteenth century to describe quite substantial middle-class houses of the type built in the developments so far described.[73] In Buxton this also included the semi-detatched houses, usually required by the estate to have the main door on the side so as to present a unified appearance to the front.[74] Some terraces were also built in this style such that Buxton has now a legacy of fine, solid villas. The use of locally quarried stone for building gave rise to finely carved and decorated façades and the Italianate style with

James Salt came to Buxton from the nearby village of Hollinsclough. He became a successful builder, running his business from a yard adjacent to the cattle market. Two of his developments were Hollins and Clough Streets, bordering his yard, which were laid out in the late 1870s for working-class cottages. It is easy to infer the derivation of these street names. Shown here is part of Hollins Street.

exposed woodwork to the eaves is typically found amongst the mid sixties villas. Many of the investors in these properties were the business and professional men of the town; a typical example is the long-serving clerk to the Local Board, Josiah Taylor who joined forces with the surveyor J. D. Simpson to build villa properties on Hartington Street which they then let.[75]

The expansion into Higher Buxton with the substantial villas of Hardwick Square meant that the surrounding streets had to present a good façade, so here are found the three-storey terraces occupied by the artisan and small businessman – all, of course, offering lodgings in the season. The widened South Street, Market, Bath and the new Darwin Streets offered these substantial terrace properties, often built speculatively by local builders. Raymond Villas and Western Terrace on Market Street are good examples. On the western side of town bordering the Pavilion Gardens and Broad Walk, Hartington Street was extended with semi-detached villa residences behind which, adjacent to the Market Place, were built the more artisan terraces and smaller cottage properties of St James Terrace and Torr Street, these built by the local builder James Salt. It is noticeable that even the smaller cottages were built with some degree of style. Where, then, were the real working-class houses to be found? G. P. Davis in studying the Victorian growth of Bath has focused on the relationship between a slum community and the city as a whole and how interests within a health resort, in competing for political control, employed images of the poor and of the slum community that were misrepresentations of existing conditions.[76] Professor Cannadine notes that exclusive resorts such as Bath and Leamington depended for their success and reputation on keeping their considerable population of servants, builders

Much of Bath Street was developed from 1878 with terraces of substantial lodging houses, but this curve, known as Bath Terrace, dates from the mid-1860s. In 1866 it was occupied by three tenants: no. 1 Miss Millington, private lodging house; no. 2. Mr Wardle, grocer; no. 3. Isaac Wardle, a shoemaker who also offered private lodgings.

and beggars at a discreet distance from the dwellings and public buildings constructed for the enjoyment of the 'leisured' classes.[77] Buxton did not have a notable *slum* problem, but it did have the poor and working class who needed housing. The more humble working-class cottages were to be found to the south-east of the town and in the vicinity of the cattle market, where rows of property were built by James Salt on Hollins Street. Dale Street was progressively extended from 1877 opening up further land for modest housing. Some working-class houses were, however, hidden away behind larger

Working-class cottages were often hidden away so the town could present a relatively prosperous front for the *leisured-class* of visitor. These cottages are on Wood's Ginnel, a narrow passage between High Street and the cattle market, which leads to Clough Street. The Derbyshire term 'ginnel' means a narrow passage between two houses. William Wood's grocery shop stood on High Street in the early twentieth century.

houses. There are good examples in Hardwick Square South, St James and High Streets. The area known as Hogshaw, on the boundary between Buxton and Fairfield Local Boards, was also developed in the mid-1860s, the Manchester Villa and Cottage Association planned to build forty cottages known as the Hogshaw estate.[78] The layout of urban Buxton does not, at first sight, appear to have been planned in a coordinated fashion. True there are walks and residential parks, substantial terraces and squares, all dating to the mid Victorian growth, but these do not appear to constitute a grand plan. Yet, on closer examination, it can be seen that the agents and surveyors of the Devonshire Estate worked carefully to maintain their required image of the health resort and managed to site the differing quality and value of property in such a way as to achieve this.

During all this building activity Buxton was developing its expertise as a water medical centre with an advancing medical practice in water treatment.[79] Nor were the spiritual needs of the people, resident and visitor, forgotten. In this period no fewer than eight denominations built new places of worship. The town also had to expand facilities for the visitor with growth in trade and commerce, including retail trades, travel, stables and servants.[80] This chapter will conclude with the major investment by the town in its Pavilion and gardens and the position of the town as a smaller, but nonetheless important, asset in the Duke of Devonshire's investment portfolio during these crucial twenty years to 1881.

The expansion of the town and the greatly increased numbers of visitors brought with it a greater need for entertainment. In the 1860s most of the facilities were provided by the estate which maintained the Hall and Serpentine gardens, Corbar walks and Sylvan Park as well as the Terrace overlooking the Crescent and baths. These facilities were offered free to the public by the Duke who also paid for the

The entrance to the new
Pavilion and Gardens in 1871.

town band which played daily in front of the Crescent and in the
Hall Gardens. There is evidence that he was reluctant to keep funding
the band. As early as 1858 the Duke would offer a subscription of
only £200 to meet the £350 estimate of bandmaster Irving, indicating
that the town could find the rest, and it is noticeable that less money
was offered through the early sixties, the estate paying, on average,
£200 *per annum* in total for the band and expenses at the Ballroom.[81]
At a rent audit dinner in November 1867 it was announced that the
Duke would be prepared to offer £5,000, if a similar sum could be
raised by the town, to provide Winter Gardens – a large summer
house – for the recreation of visitors during cold and wet weather.
This venture, operated commercially, could also provide a venue and
finance for the band. It took the town a little while to move on this
offer but at a public meeting in September 1869 it was resolved to
accept the Duke's offer and proceed to form a joint stock company
to be known as the 'Buxton Improvements Company' The Duke
took some early advice on this from his solicitor, architect and Buxton
agent:

> ... Chatsworth November 3rd 1869. This morning I had a talk with
> Currey and his brother, H. Currey, and Drewry about Buxton
> matters. An enclosed garden with covered promenade is under
> consideration also some bath improvements ...[82]

The Improvements Company aroused great interest and many in the town took shares. In January 1870 a further three acres of ground was given by the Duke together with £1000, the shareholders matching this additional sum. The company moved rapidly to enclose the Hall Gardens commissioning Edward Milner to design a glass and iron 'Crystal Palace' style pavilion and to lay out the gardens.[83] In fact the Devonshire Estate had maintained the Hall gardens with a series of walks, rustic bridges and water effects and, in 1868/69, just before the handover had invested more than £500 to improve the lake and fountain below Broad Walk.[84] The new Pavilion Gardens, officially opened by the Duke in August 1871, were

The Hall Hotel & Fountain Gardens Buxton.

The twelve acres given by the Duke of Devonshire in 1870 to form the Pavilion Gardens were, in fact, the Hall Gardens. These had been maintained by the Devonshire Estate for the benefit of visitors to the town.

This engraving, showing a fountain in the lake with the Old Hall Hotel behind, was made in about 1867 before the Buxton Improvements Company enclosed the gardens.

an instant success – so much so that, by October 1872, the company had to consider enlarging the facilities. A large Concert Hall, designed by Robert Rippon Duke in a style to match the pavilion, was added and opened by the Duke in August 1876. The success of this venture must have been greatly welcomed by the Duke since similar ventures at Eastbourne (Floral Hall and Baths 1874, Pavilion 1876) were not a commercial success.[85] In fact the estate capitalised to some degree on this success for, whilst the Duke had no shares directly in the company, he did sell the rest of the gardens, including what is now known as the Serpentine Walks, in 1875, 1879 and 1890 on Chief Rents which brought in a total of £186 *per annum*. His diary entry for 10 August 1871 is laconic but astute:

> ... Chatsworth August 10th 1871.
> I had to leave Holker this morning in order to open the new gardens etc. at Buxton just completed by the Buxton Improvements Company. I got to Buxton about 3 and proceeded almost immediately to the gardens. The proceedings began by a procession round the gardens, after which an address was presented to me by the directors to which I had, of course, to make a reply. We had afterwards a luncheon in the new pavilion for about 240. It was rather a long affair with a good many toasts. I had to make another speech and very glad I was when the business was over. It is admitted on all hands that the gardens are very successful and it seems to be pretty clear that the undertaking will be financially profitable ...[86]

He also remarked upon the interest shown in the gardens venture in his entry for the opening of the large Concert Hall in 1876.

During the period between 1859 and 1881 the Seventh Duke was much preoccupied with his investments at Barrow and Eastbourne and, in the scheme of things, Buxton came a poor third. The Duke's interests at Barrow had always been

... in a special sense in his own care ...[87]

and from 1840, when still the Earl of Burlington, he had taken a personal interest in its commercial development with investments primarily in iron and steel and shipping but also in milling, ship-building, printing and publishing. By 1871 his investment was substantial. He owned more than a quarter of the share capital of Barrow Shipbuilding Co., the Flax and Jute Mill and Barrow Haematite Steel Co., with a total investment of more than £200,000.[88] However, by 1874–75 difficulties were beginning to be experienced due, in part to foreign competition in haematite ore and a contraction

A rather stylised view of Edward Milner's pavilion of 1871 produced in a contemporary album of views. The interior promenade consisted of two wings with a square central hall. The total length was about 400 feet. Milner also laid out an outside promenade area.

A view of the interior promenade corridor, looking towards the central concert hall.

of the local ore, over-expansion at too high cost and collapse of the American market for Bessemer rail, the main finished product exported from Barrow. Not all of these problems set in at once but in the fifteen years from 1874 substantial resources of the Devonshire Estate were diverted to support the ailing enterprises at Barrow, so much so that in 1886 the Devonshire investment share capital had risen to £1,174,519 and in the case of the shipbuilding and flax mills was more than 95%. If this were not enough the Duke was also investing considerably in the development of Eastbourne. Here, unlike Buxton, neither the local authority nor the local entrepreneurs were able to finance successful ventures and the Duke was drawn, inexorably, into providing amenities on a far larger scale than he would have wished. Thus he invested more than £45,000 into the drainage system, which the Local Board could not finance and he had substantial holdings

Pavilion and Promenade, The Gardens, Buxton

The facilities in the Pavilion Gardens designed by Edward Milner became so busy that more room was needed. The local architect Robert Rippon Duke designed a reading room on the north side and went on to produce a large octagonal concert hall. This hall, which matched Milner's earlier work was opened in 1876 and was an instant success. This view shows Milner's pavilion extended by Duke's concert hall.

The Lake, Buxton Gardens

The Pavilion Gardens offered many attractions for the visitor including the new sport of roller skating in the 1870s. In the winter the lakes were used for ice skating, but here we see boating in the large lake.

DEVONSHIRE HOSPITAL BUXTON. 217.

When Eastbourne erected a bronze statue of the Seventh Duke of Devonshire on the Grand Parade in 1898, the sculptor W. Gascombe-Johns donated its plaster cast to Buxton. It was placed under the dome of the Devonshire Hospital. [E.M. & G.J.B.]

in the water works, parks and baths, college, gas company and pier being the major shareholder of the first three in 1893.[89] The Duke's policy of part-support and self-help did not, it seems, work in Eastbourne as it did in Buxton.

Despite these major preoccupations the Duke still found time to visit Buxton from time to time to discuss developments with George Drewry, but Drewry was the agent for other estates including Holker where he resided so there were opportunities for discussion when the Duke visited Barrow. Day-to-day administration at Buxton was in the capable hands of his sub-agents and surveyor who were in regular correspondence.[90] Buxton was not out of the Duke's mind. Indeed, of his urban development interests, it must have offered him some optimism. Other writers and historians have undersold the contribution which Buxton – the health resort – made to the Devonshire Estate. Grundy Heape has suggested

> ... The Duke of Devonshire was constantly giving, not only to Buxton but elsewhere. Buxton may have yielded him a substantial amount ...[91]

while Leach observes

> ... Eastbourne would have been a seaside village but for his investment. Buxton owes him a similar debt ...[92]

Professor Cannadine has argued that Eastbourne was the most successful of the major forays into urban development which the Devonshires undertook in the eighteenth and nineteenth centuries, larger and more famous than Buxton, better planned and more stable than Barrow. He goes on to say that

... Buxton ... had never revived spectacularly in the nineteenth century however much money the 7th Duke lavished on it ...

and ...

... the 7th Duke's attempts to revive it [Buxton] in the middle of the nineteenth century were only marginally successful ...[93]

Yet, as this chapter has shown, the Devonshire Estate took a good income from Buxton in the twenty or more years from 1859, in the profit on the estate, the baths, in an increasing rental as the number of Chief Rents increased, in capital sums from land sales and in dividends from hotel companies. Far from 'constantly giving' or 'lavishing' money on the town, the Duke enjoyed a steady income from it. Buxton was an asset, small perhaps, but still an asset and no drain on the Devonshire resources.

When Eastbourne erected a bronze statue of the Seventh Duke on the Grand Parade in 1898 Buxton was glad to receive its plaster cast donated by the sculptor W. Gascombe-Johns. It was placed under the dome of the Devonshire Hospital in 1901. Eastbourne got the bronze – Buxton the plaster, it may be wryly observed.[94] As to Buxton's reputation as a spa, it may not have rivalled Bath in the eighteenth century, but it did make itself a name in water medicine, as a Victorian and early twentieth-century health resort as this chapter has begun to illustrate. Chapter four and beyond will develop this argument further.

... A pause, if it pleases you, at Millers Dale where a little crowd of passengers await the train. Here Mr Salford, from Manchester, who has left his rheumatism and crutches behind at Buxton, gets nimbly in the express along with Mrs Salford, and the two Miss Salfords, one a charming symphony in silk, the other a dainty vignette in velvet. Mr Saltley, of Birmingham, very gouty and bound for Buxton, gets out, and there is an interchange of several other passengers ...[95]

People who think Buxton "fast"

People who vote it "slow"

W. G. Baxter published in the *Buxton Advertiser* and sold books of his cartoons which give a humorous slant on life in the town in the last quarter of the nineteenth century. These two cartoons give a fascinating insight into the different classes of people frequenting Buxton in the 1880s.

CHAPTER FOUR

Buxton Comes of Age

Edward Chambers Milligan (1836–1908), who ran the drapery business of J. Milligan & Son, with the main shop on the corner of Hardwick Street and Spring Gardens. John Milligan, his father, was a member of the Local Board and when he died in 1872 E. C. Milligan was elected, thus filling the vacancy occasioned by his father's death. He was chairman for five years from 1885 and again from 1895 until his retirement in 1898.

Mr. E. C. MILLIGAN,

I N THE TWENTY-FIVE YEARS from 1880 Buxton continued to grow, not at the same pace as the previous twenty years, but in a more qualitative manner in physical layout, types of housing, commerce and medical reputation.[1] Furthermore, as a representative unit of local government, the town came of age. The Local Board and its successor, the Urban District Council, experienced remarkable growth.[2] This increase in the power of local government was matched by a corresponding increase in civic pride. The town grew up – came into its own. As the leading local politician, Edward C. Milligan, remarked at the first meeting of the Urban District Council, they had moved a very long way from the time when everything was done by someone he called 'my uncle' and this change had begun with the agent E. W. Wilmot in the 1860s.[3] Long gone was the epoch of the Sixth Duke, the benevolent grandparent providing for the infant Buxton, though the 'sleepy hollow' view of the town indolently waiting for the Duke or someone else to bring about improvements might still remain.[4] But now the 'someone else' was the local authority. In the period 1880 to 1905 most important changes were to be seen. The local authority was to grow in stature and confidence and to take the lead in developing the town's resources. The influence by the Devonshire Estate on the town's affairs was to focus more narrowly and sharply on the commercial return which could be obtained from its management of the urban property and land.

Buxton had reached its apogee as a health resort by 1905. The Devonshire Estate continued to sell land well into the twentieth century, but by 1905 the shape of the twentieth-century town was already determined. The local authority had developed into a significant force and provider of services including sewerage, drainage, refuse, highways, public parks and emergency services but also, by this time it owned the utilities of water works, electricity, gas and the mineral water baths. The Buxton Gardens Company offered a wide mixture of entertainment in the opera house, theatre, pavilion, concert hall and outside facilities of the Pavilion Gardens. Medical treatments in the natural mineral baths and hydropathic hotels combined water and electricity in a plethora of 'new cures' and the health seeker could choose from upwards of twenty doctors for a prognosis. Hotels, hydros, apartments and lodgings catered for more than 4,000 visitors in a week in the high season and, at the same time, Buxton had

become a fashionable residential town. Businessmen from the North West took advantage of the forty-minute rail service to Manchester,[5] employing important regional architects to design large villas in the best parts of town where they might enjoy the benefits of

> ... a bracing climate of absolute purity ... making for the promotion of good health ...[6]

In commercial terms the town of Buxton was geared almost wholly to the provision of the goods and services necessary for a health resort whose season ran from the beginning of March to the end of October. But through the two decades or so of this chapter considerable efforts were made to encourage visitors in the Winter and to compete with its arch-rival Harrogate which also developed an 'all year round season'.[7] Some hotels, particularly the hydros, opened all the year round and the Baths were offered in the winter at half price.[8] The band played each day and the Pavilion, theatres, concert hall and gardens remained open. Publicity material increasingly offered winter sports such as tobogganing, skiing, curling and horse sleigh rides, taking advantage of the regular snowfalls. As an official guide book put it:

> ... In Buxton there are no works or factories. The whole town is

Buxton sold itself as a winter sports venue as well as a summer resort. The long sweep of the Manchester Road, from the junction with Devonshire Road, down to the town was a favourite with youngsters. There were also several prepared toboggan runs.

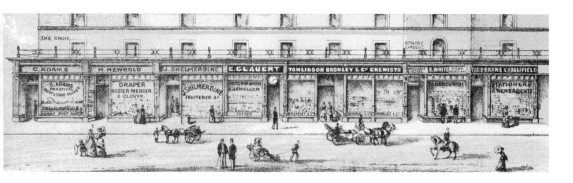

Shops in The Grove and the corner of Spring Gardens in 1887. Spring Gardens was, by this time, a buoyant commercial street and provided the main southern entrance to the town.

given up to the entertainment of the thousands of visitors who come every year for rest andrecreation and health in pure fresh air and amidst charming surroundings ...[9]

with many other health and seaside resorts Buxton relied for its advertising on *ad hoc* arrangements. Between 1885 and 1890 the Devonshire Estate paid W. H. Smith £300 a year to advertise Buxton at 200 railway stations. This coincided with some sizeable new investment at the Baths, but also reflected the interest shown by the Local Board in competing for visitors. Queen Victoria's jubilee year stimulated much promotional activity, Buxton was represented at the Liverpool Exhibition and, in common with the rest of the country, entered into public celebration, seizing the opportunity to lay the foundation stone for the new town hall and library on Jubilee Day, 21 June 1887.[10] Adding its own promotional support the *Buxton Advertiser* produced a magnificent fully illustrated supplement, strongly supported by advertisers, extolling the virtues of the resort and, incidentally, showing how commercially buoyant it was. The Local Board and the Devonshire Estate contributed jointly to promoting the town in periodicals such as the *Pictorial World* until the job of co-ordinating publicity

The cover of Buxton town guide book produced by Charles Smilter *c.* 1899. Later the local authority took on the job of producing a town guide which continued annually up to the 1970s.

was taken on by Charles Smilter, proprietor of the Crescent Hotel. His guide was the first to be produced by the town itself and he was quick to follow. up the Queen's jubilee by sending her a specially bound copy on the occasion of her eightieth birthday.[11] From the early part of the twentieth century the UDC formed a publicity department to promote the attractions of the resort and issue its own guide books.

Despite the assertions of guide books, extensive limestone quarrying in the vicinity and, to a lesser extent, coal mining were an important source of work and income to the town. These two extractive industries took place on the outskirts of urban Buxton and, not surprisingly, drew their work-force from the surrounding villages. Lime workers lived close to the quarries and works in Cowdale, Harpur Hill, Peak Dale and Dove Holes.[12] Coal miners lived predominantly in the Burbage and Ladman-low areas close to the coal fields in Goyt's Moss and Axe Edge.[13] Some lived in urban Buxton, however. The census of 1891 records fifty-three quarry/lime workers and thirteen coal miners. The largest area of employment in Buxton, by far, was that of servant, either in private domestic service or commercially at one of the hotels or lodging houses. In 1891 just over thirty per cent of the working population was in service. In Bath in 1881 one person in nine was a servant, in 1891 in Buxton it was one person in seven.[14] The term 'servant' covers a wide range of roles and carries its own social hierarchy. In Buxton the distinction between working in private service as opposed to commercial establishments was also a status factor.[15] Developing trade in the town stimulated the growth of local businesses and, towards the end of the nineteenth century, Buxton enticed an increasing number of the 'polite' Manchester society to take up residence in the town. This rise in the number of upper-middle and middle-class families increased demand for servants and, although this was a common problem in England, the fact that Buxton was a resort exacerbated the competition.[16] The local architect to the Devonshire Estate, Robert Rippon Duke, and his daughter Sarah Meggitt Smith bemoaned the difficulty in finding good servants and Sarah Meggitt used agencies in Birmingham and Derby, though Buxton had its own servant registry offices.[17] The census describes the occupation for a number of females as 'assists at home': this occurs quite frequently where 'home' is a lodging house. One study has described this in terms of the subordination of the female member of the family working as a servant at home, couching it in terms of the subjection of the female at home, in service and in marriage, suggesting a lifetime of personal subordination in private homes.[18] In Buxton it is clear that the competition for domestic staff would place pressure on the unmarried female to take on domestic duties in the home, particularly where this contributed to income in the family business, but, arguably, she would then have a share in the success of the business.

Commercial activity included the more ubiquitous retailers – the butcher, the baker, the draper, the grocer – but in Buxton work could also be found in a variety of services specific to the medical resort not generally found in other towns of comparable size. Contemporary directories illustrate examples:[19] in 1891 there were seven inlayers of marble offering ornaments in Ashford Black Marble and other stone, four photographers and, more directly medical, ten 'shampooers' or masseurs. In 1895 fourteen bath chair and thirteen cab proprietors

The following is a List of the Fees charg
MRS. MASSEY to Ladies and Gentlemen
ing to her for assistance in procuring Ser

FOR the engagement of a Servant 5/-, unl
wages are under £14, in which case the fee

(If a Servant, for any reason, leaves at or
the end of the first month's service, Mrs. Ma
so desired, will do her best to procure a su
for half fee, or failing to do so will make no
for correspondence.)

For a correspondence not resulting in an e
ment, one shilling is charged to cover posta
other expenses, and no further charge is made
more than one servant is named. In case of
servants being named the fees are as follows

For 2, 3, or 4 names -   -   -   -
  „ 5, 6, or 7   „   -   -   -
etc.

These correspondence fees are only calcul
cover expenses; if therefore accounts of un
have to be sent out more than once, extra
etc. will be charged.

28, King Street

Upper-class households sometimes have difficulty in recruiting good servants, and registries sprang up to introduce servant to mistress for a fee. This shows the fee rates of a Derby agency used by Sarah Meggitt Smith who lived at Gadley, Manchester Road, Buxton.

were listed and by 1904 there were fifteen fancy bazaars and china and glass sellers.[20] Travel to and from the town was catered for in the last quarter of the nineteenth century by a substantial railway network. The LNWR and MR offered fast services to the north and south respectively, London being reached in four hours, but the opening of the Dore and Chinley branch by the Midland Railway gained them through routes between Derby, Sheffield and the North West also. The Act of 1887 amalgamating the Cromford and High Peak Railway Company with LNWR resulted in the Buxton to Ashbourne line connections to the south, a five-hour London service and, more locally, access to the tourist railway in the picturesque Manifold Valley.[21] Increasing rail provision brought about a need for short-distance horse travel and, in Buxton, there was also a good trade to be had in pleasure rides. Not surprisingly there were at least fourteen principal stables in the town in this period.[22]

The extensive house building in this twenty-five years meant that another large employment category in the town was the building trade. Ten per cent of the working population were employed in this trade in 1891. The extent to which house building suffered the peaks and troughs of the industry generally will become clearer as the chapter proceeds as will the influence by the Devonshire Estate on land sales and road making.[23]

This maturing of Buxton as a health resort required considerable investment in infrastructure to maintain its reputation as a healthy and clean town with excellent sanitation. The decade up to 1890 saw investment of just under £6,000 on sewerage and drainage and Buxton was again fortunate in having the advice of an eminent man on the improvement of its sewerage system. In 1885 new precipitating tanks

The Devonshire Steam Laundry on Bridge Street was run by H. Oram and Sons and provided a very necessary service in Buxton. In addition to the larger firms, there were self-employed laundresses who took in washing.

were installed on the advice of Dr J. C. Thresh, a local chemist who became the Medical Officer of Health for the County of Essex.[24] Additional work up to 1905 included the installation of new filter beds, an investment important enough to be described in a pamphlet by the town surveyor. In all £24,000 was invested between 1882 and 1905 on this necessary provision and in 1904 there were 3,500 WCs and 827 baths serving a resident population of 11,500.[25] Buxton was, undoubtedly, advanced in its sanitary arrangements.[26] In 1860 the rateable value in Buxton was about £8,000; by 1882 about £30,000; in 1890 £52,336; and by 1904 just under £90,000.[27] The enormous range of new work undertaken by the Local Board/UDC is set out in Appendix 4.2. Of particular note are the destructor which burned the town's refuse and the electricity generating works built in 1899 with the help of a loan of £24,769. These services, together with gas and sewerage were all sited in Ashwood Dale, a picturesque southern entrance to the town. Whilst acknowledging the spoiling of a beautiful drive into the town the town surveyor, W. H. Grieves, offered a more prosaic view:

> ... the position has its advantages, for here the Council has what might be termed its necessary evils all together ...[28]

A contemporary satirist, Art Hacker, wrote 'Down the Dale – a song with Chorus', which included the following:

> ... Down the Dale – down the Dale, –
> Modern progress leaves destruction in its trail;
> What with sewage, shoot and siding,
> And the mess of man's providing, –
> Oh the UDC want hiding
> Down the Dale! ...[29]

On the high ground overlooking all this the local authority, in 1888/89, built its sanatorium for the treatment of infectious diseases.

The local authority operated through a series of committees including finance, gas and water, general purposes, streets, and of these the last-named was probably the busiest. The streets committee met more times than the others and dealt with a vast range of business including the adoption of roads, drains and sewers, bath chair licences and regulations, new buildings and alterations, slaughter houses, street lamps, gas, fire engine, stone crushing for road making, provision of public lavatories, chimney firing, footpaths. The committee had a judicial role in that it would regularly fine people for setting fire to their chimneys and it also heard and judged cases of misdemeanour by the bathchair men, a unique responsibility –

> ... Divers complaint was made by a solicitor against Jos. Percival the drawer of no 20 Bath chair for recklessly drawing his chair on the

road passing the end of the George Hotel and thereby crushing the complainant against the wall, damaging his umbrella, and throwing a young lady down the steps of the cellar entrance. The man was cautioned and called upon to pay the cost of repairing the umbrella with which the complainant was satisfied ...[30]

The growth of local authority provision was facilitated by a number of local acts of parliament and by the development of bye-laws. Standards were required if the town was to maintain its reputation, speculators could not be allowed to 'jerry' build and Buxton, in line with other towns was anxious to see improvements in the quality of house building.[31] The bye-laws, published in 1886 by the Local Board acting as the Urban Sanitary District, were extensive, containing 101 clauses and repealing the previous streets and buildings bye-laws of 1859 and 1864.[32] Local legislation promoted the power of the local authority. The Act of 1886 increased borrowing limits for the gas undertaking.[33] In 1892 the Local Board used an act, primarily designed to authorise it to accept a new Pump Room from the Duke of Devonshire, to regularise their borrowing powers and to tidy up a number of small pieces of legislation affecting the smooth running of the town.[34] Provisional orders of 1897 and 1901 were used to increase or alter borrowing powers.[35] The Buxton Electric Lighting Order 1894 required distributing mains to be laid in twelve main roads in the urban district and the Urban District Council of Buxton used its Water Act of 1902 to cover a range of purposes such as new streets and buildings, dangerous structures, hackney carriages, sanitary provision, infectious diseases and recreation provision as well as

The Local Board bye-laws regulated a whole range of activities including those which might create a nuisance for others. Some householders would allow their chimney to catch fire on purpose because this had the effect of burning away the soot and avoided the need to pay for a chimney sweep. It was an offence in Buxton and carried a fine. [B.M.A.G.]

CHIMNEY FIRING.

NOTICE IS HEREBY GIVEN that in consequence of the prevailing practice of Firing Chimneys, which is dangerous to buildings, and creates a great nuisance, the Buxton Urban District Council have resolved to adhere to, and enforce, the regulation made some time ago, viz.:

"That all cases of Chimney Firing shall be dealt with by summonses to appear before the Magistrates excepting such as are reported within one week by the person whose chimney has been accidentally fired and who is willing to pay a nominal fine of 3/-."

By Order of the Council,

Town Hall, **JOSIAH TAYLOR, Clerk.**
Buxton, 27th July, 1896.

Printed by the "Herald" Printing Company, South-street, Buxton.

empowerment to construct considerable additional water works at Stanley Moor on the south-western side of the town.[36]

This weight of legislation with consequent increase in power had been taken on by twelve elected Local Board members, the experienced clerk, Josiah Taylor, and an increasing team of professional officers.[37] The elected members were drawn from that group of significant townsmen who had 'character' – were independent, enjoyed decision making and the power of office, who could balance the interests of public life with those of their business, who saw public and private life as being of equal importance.[38] As Offer has pointed out, councillors such as these were effectively proprietors of streets, sewers, buildings, gas, water and electricity, owners of public capital, holding great assets and accepting the financial responsibility of sizeable loans for fixed capital.[39] Some of the members spent many years in public life and had grown with the Local Board, learning by doing, testing the limits of decision-making and shaping the growth of the resort.[40] The Buxton Town Hall was a fitting tribute to this maturing democracy as well as a statement of civic pride. A town hall committee, appointed as early as 1868, had considered a number of ideas for siting and called for preliminary sketches from Robert Rippon Duke.

The Local Board had a town fire brigade by 1879 and the earliest fire station was on Eagle Parade, manned by volunteers. This photograph of 1896 was taken on Eagle Parade and looks to have been an occasion more for the benefit of the photographer or publicity than of a real fire! [B.M.A.G.]

It was not until 1886, however, that the Local Board resolved to offer an architectural competition and a £50 prize for the best design; no opinion was offered as to style of architecture. A Manchester architect, William Pollard, won with an ecclectic design, which might best be described as French Renaisance. The local firm of James Salt won the contract at a tender price of £8,900 and the town hall was built at the top of the slopes on the site of the former market hall.[41] The foundation stone was laid, with due ceremony by E. C. Milligan, Chairman of the Local Board, in June 1887 and the opening, in June 1889, was by the Marquess of Hartington.[42] This was a statement of the progress made by the Local Board who, only thirty years earlier, had rented a small office from the Devonshire Estate. Even so the new town hall was built on land sold by the Duke at a peppercorn Chief Rent.[43] Within the middle quarters of the century the Local Board had progressively moved control from the loose and old-fashioned polity, governed by the aristocratic landowner and the select few townsmen and JPs, to a more actively and democratically regulated community.[44] From this it was a smooth step to assume the title of Urban District Council following the Local Government Act of 1894.[45] At the first meeting of the UDC in January 1895 E. C. Milligan could observe with confidence the continuity and self-assuredness of the membership. At the national level Sir Albert Kay Rollit, president of the Association of Municipal Corporations said in a speech in 1896

> ... The necessary complement of individualism is, for political and social stability and safety, some wise collectivism and municipal channels are best for this purpose ...[46]

The growth of municipal power in Buxton, was not overtly challenged, though there may have been those who favoured private capital and were alarmed at the breadth of investment in utilities.[47] No locally organised opposition can be identified to support the anti-municipal crusade mounted at national level from late 1890s which was led by the banker and Unionist MP Sir John Lubbock (1834–1913).[48] This campaign reached a climax in August–November 1902 when *The Times* published a series of articles under the title 'Municipal Socialism' which evoked strong displeasure in town halls.[49] The lack of interest is not surprising in Buxton which was not overtly political. Seats on the Local Board/UDC were usually contested but the same cannot be said for county or general elections. At the parliamentary level Buxton (part of Derbyshire North Division) largely followed the Liberal persuasion of the Devonshires. From 1832 a Cavendish had taken the seat, the Hon. George being returned no fewer than eleven times between 1834 and 1874, following which his nephew, Lord Edward, took on the seat unopposed in 1880.[50] In fact Derbyshire North was served by two Liberal MPs until the Conservatives managed

The new Town Hall was a statement of civic pride and a mark of the achievement of a local authority only thirty years old. The foundation stone was laid in Jubilee Year, 1887, by chairman E. C. Milligan and the opening ceremony was conducted by the Marquess of Hartington in 1889.

to secure a foothold at the re-division of the county in 1868.[51] The local papers reported from time to time on the activities of the local Liberal Party, where it can be seen that the prime movers of the community, including the Duke's agent, were active in their support and the *Buxton Advertiser* and *High Peak News* were pro-Liberal.[52] In 1880 the town formed a committee of about forty of these worthies to arrange for a portrait of Lord George Cavendish to be commissioned and presented to Lady George Cavendish.[53] The Liberal triumph in April 1880 when Lord Edward Cavendish and J. F. Cheetham took both seats was effusively supported by the *Buxton Advertiser*.[54] A leader article offered the view that since 1868 the Liberal vote for Lord George Cavendish had been cancelled out by the vote for the Conservative member thus effectively disenfranchising the Northern/Peak Division. The paper found an apt quote in Dryden's 'Epilogue to the Duke of Guise':

> ... Damn'd neuters in their middle way of steering,
> Were neither fish, nor flesh, nor good red herring;
> Nor whigs nor tories they; nor this nor that;
> Nor birds nor beasts; but just a kind of bat;
> A twilight animal; true to neither cause
> With tory wings but wiggish teeth and claws ...[55]

All this had now changed with the election of two Liberals, but the euphoria was not to last. Five years later redistribution, following the Third Reform Act, made the High Peak Division one of seven constituencies in Derbyshire and it returned a single member.[56] The Conservative candidate, Captain William Sidebottom, beat J. F. Cheetham by nine votes in a poll of 8,400 out of a possible 9,300. Glossop, with 35,00 votes and a large Catholic vote was against the Liberal.[57] The defeat may also have reflected the increasing urban middle-class Conservative support experienced in England in the last quarter of the century.[58] It is noticeable that Conservative support in Buxton in the 1880 election was drawn from middle-class tradespeople running small businesses and lodging houses. Their press champion was the *Buxton Herald* which saw the *Buxton Advertiser* as a

> ... radical organ ...[59]

This Conservative success was carried through the following three elections. The Liberal support in Buxton and the High Peak was split over Gladstone's policy on Irish home rule. The Duke of Devonshire took a strong and conscientious stance against the Irish Bill and members of the executive committee of the High Peak Liberal Association and the Central Committee at Buxton did the same. They believed that Gladstone's policy would be

> ... injurious to the best interests of Great Britain and Ireland ...[60]

MR. JAMES SALT,

James Salt (1846–1923), whose firm built the Town Hall, was a local politician in late nineteenth- and early twentieth-century Buxton. He built many houses in the town and was responsible for other public buildings including the new theatre or 'Entertainment Stage' designed by W. R. Bryden in 1889. [B.M.A.G.]

In the July 1886 election the supporter of home rule for Ireland, standing as a Gladstonian Liberal, was Herbert Rhodes who lost to the Conservative, (now) Major Sidebottom. The Gladstonian Liberals lost the following elections of 1892 and 1895 to the same Conservative candidate.[61] Liberal tenure in High Peak was not re-secured until after Gladstone's death in 1898, when at the election of 1900 Captain Oswald Partington beat the Conservative Lord Mayor of Sheffield, Mr Samuel Roberts, by 159 votes. The *Buxton Herald,* swift of foot, declared that it had had enough of the

> ... thraldom of toryism ...

for the past fourteen years, and that Liberalism had rehabilitated itself.[62]

The local papers give a good contemporary feel for the degree of interest by the voter in politics. It has already been noted that in Buxton, as with other towns, the townspeople showed a greater interest in the election of local politicians than in the parliamentary contest. The papers were careful not to overface their reading public and at times were decidedly laid-back in their reporting

> ... It was getting on in the afternoon of Monday, the eve of the poll, before anything happened to show that more than a common interest was being taken in the election so far as Buxton was concerned.
> A crowd of a hundred or more children assembled around the shop door of Messrs Oram & Sons Spring Gardens and every now and then they responded to an invitation for cheers to so and so ... they were there because they had been promised handkerchiefs. Mr G. Arden drove up and distributed party colours from the back of his gig – colours too carrying a different political meaning to those already promised – but blue had the same charm as yellow in the eyes of the youngsters and there was great scrambling for them ...[63]

Though the level of interest in the Home Rule affair generated a surfeit of coverage in the 1886 election and the paper thought it fit to apologise for this:

> ... Owing to the press of election news, we offer apologies to our readers – visitors especially – that we are unable to give our usual complete story and items of local news. With thankfulness we contemplate an early finish to electoral work – for the present ...[64]

Nothing approaching the same level of interest was taken in the county elections following the County Councils Act of 1888. The act was brought in after a long legislative process and, together with the Local government Act of 1894, was designed to provide a drastic simplification of the confusing system of counties, parliamentary counties, unions, registration districts and sub-districts and civil parishes which had grown up like topsy.[65] It was passed when Joseph

Chamberlain and the Liberal Unionists held the balance of power.[66] None of this, it seems, impressed the good people of Buxton. The act proposed fifty-three electoral divisions for Derbyshire, one covering Buxton and Hartington Upper Quarter (effectively urban Buxton) and another Fairfield. In Buxton some small measure of interest was shown in the first election in January 1889, when Robert Hulme and G. F. Barnard competed for the seat, Hulme winning by thirty-five votes in a poll of 919. Some time after this the two candidates, both Liberals, must have reached an arrangement for at the second election in 1892 Barnard stood unopposed and at the third in 1895 Hulme did the same. Thereafter the seat was not contested for at least six more elections; Frank Drewry, the Devonshire Buxton Agent, was returned at every election from 1904 to 1913 inclusive.[67] Throughout this time the Fairfield seat was uncontested.[68] The local newspapers reflected the lack of enthusiasm over county council elections. Their coverage was low-key and their copy showed a progressively decreasing lack of interest by the town:

> ... The county council election in Buxton appears to have resolved itself into a walk-over for Mr Barnard, similarly for Mr Hubbersty in Fairfield ... [1892]

> ... The County Council elections have passed off tamely enough. At Buxton and Fairfield the candidates Messrs R. Hulme and J. Beswick have been returned unopposed and will serve the ratepayers for a period of three years ... [1895]

> ... Triennial elections for county council now upon us. It is not probable that there will be any contests for the novelty has worn off and Councillors find that the work of county legislation is incessant and laborious ... [1898] [69]

Dr Keith-Lucas has pointed out that the County Council Bill had envisaged, among other things, a great measure of devolution, but that after the elections about half of the candidates were magistrates and many others were associated with the extant 'county power'. He suggests that county councils must have looked rather like the old Quarter Sessions and that they remained remarkably aristocratic, meeting in the day time and continuing to run affairs in the old 'county' tradition.[70] There are elements of this argument in the Buxton situation, certainly in the neighbouring Fairfield where H. A. Hubbersty JP, a wealthy businessman, became a County Alderman in only his second term of office. His successor, a colleague in the lime business, also became a JP. In Buxton itself the early members Barnard and Hulme represented the established middle-class businessmen but were also long serving local politicians chosen by their colleagues to represent the needs of urban Buxton at county level. Later the established 'county' influence took over when Frank Drewry, the ducal agent, took the seat. Towards the end of the century Buxton was to some degree experiencing what Klopfer has described as a 'petering out' of local democracy. It was difficult for the 'local democrats' to persuade ordinary voters to take up public office, as the newspaper reported:

> ... There seems to be little life in local elections. The county council election in Buxton was a walk-over for Mr Drewry and in Fairfield for Mr Beswick JP. The Guardians elections in Buxton and Fairfield have fizzled out. In the UDC elections there is no contest in Fairfield and the East Ward in Buxton is the only one contested ...[71]

Klopfer has suggested that this was because the ordinary citizen resisted the necessary link between participation in local government and a free and democratic society.[72] In Buxton there were additional reasons. The culture of the town had always been to stand back and see if someone else would take the job on and, despite the considerable achievements of the local authority already described, the old 'ducal' mentality prevailed; if it was no longer the Duke, then it could be someone else. Furthermore, progress and change was driven by a group of 'prime movers' in the town made up of local politicians, the Devonshire Estate representatives and the magistrates, a formidable collective body into which entry and acceptance would not have been easy, particularly for anyone with political views or ideas which did not concur with the vision of this group. This view of 'how things get done in this town' had been developed at least from the beginning of local democracy in 1859, probably from the earlier stages of Buxton's growth in 1848. It was a style developed and supported by the

Members and officials of the Buxton UDC, photographed outside the Town hall on the occasion of the fifty year jubilee of the local authority (1859–1909). Here are some of the 'prime movers' in the development of the town, names include George Smithurst, draper; George Garlick, architect; John Yates, butcher; James Salt, builder; and Robert Lane, proprietor of the Grove Hotel. Officials include the long-serving Josiah Taylor and the respected engineer W. H. Grieves.

continuity of established townsmen; Dr W. H. Robertson, not only the foremost water medical specialist but also a JP for thirty years, the successive Devonshire Buxton Agents, and long serving local politicians such as E. C. Milligan and G. F. Barnard. These and others like them set the standards, the unwritten constitution for governing the town.[73]

As the local authority increased its influence on the town's services and amenities the Devonshire Estate began progressively to consolidate its activities into the management of the land and property forming the 'Buxton Estate'. Sales of land on Chief Rent continued through the period and the expansion of the town took place in three main areas. One was the further development of estate land on the west and south west of the town for substantial upper middle and middle-class housing. A second was the growth of working-class and lower middle-class housing from the cattle market to the south also on Devonshire Estate land and a third was the development of housing for the rising middle class in the areas of Kents Bank Road, Crowstones, Darwin Avenue and Dale road, to the south east of the town, some on privately owned land.

Between 1880 and 1882 no sales of building land by Chief Rent are recorded by the Estate but from 1883 sales begin to increase and there is a pattern of steady growth to the end of the decade. This is in line with the building pattern generally for Great Britain.[74] By 1890, unlike Sheffield, Buxton's house building entered a busy period which was maintained, through the general boom in building, largely to the early part of the twentieth century.[75] By the year 1905 the Buxton Building Estate was delivering nearly 200 Chief Rents worth just under £4,000 *per annum* to the Duke's account at the London and Westminster Bank and the total surplus on the Building Estate business topped £5,000 in the year 1906.[76] Sales of land outright by the Devonshire Estate were at their highest between 1894 and 1898, with steady sales between 1902 and 1906 but these may be more a reflection of the changes in estate policy by the Eighth Duke, described later, than of house building in general. In the last ten years of the Seventh Duke's life the Devonshire Estate continued its policy of handling all land sales on a Chief Rent and Buxton continued to contribute a useful surplus from its rentals and Baths.[77] The Seventh Duke was, by the early 1880s, supporting a massive investment – more than two million pounds – in the very uncertain fortunes of Barrow-in-Furness. The surplus from his estates,

Three-storey artisan housing on Dale Road provided a solid look to the town for the visitor entering from the south. The builder James Salt built many houses of this type on Dale Road and elsewhere in town.

including that at Buxton, had been diverted, through the fifteen years to 1890, to supporting the failing industrial enterprise at Barrow.[78] Professor Burn has observed that the Seventh Duke used his great wealth constructively and it is true that his early development of Barrow involved some shrewd investment bringing a good return. His investments in Eastbourne appear to have been less shrewd and more driven by the desire to set the town up as a principal seaside resort rather like his great uncle the Fifth Duke's attempt to develop Buxton spa as a rival to Bath. His investment in Buxton, the poor relation, was careful enough; and it generally gave a good return. Unfortunately the Barrow industries entered a period of very serious decline and in his own declining years the Duke was forced to divert considerable resources to shoring up this crumbling industrial empire. Professor Pollard offers one theory as to why the Seventh Duke, an intelligent and scholarly man, should have made and lost a fortune in this way:

> ... His approach ... did not greatly differ from that of many of his land owning forebears in other spheres, or of contemporary financiers. Shrewd and enlightened attempts to maximise profits went hand in hand with paternal feelings for his dependants, his shareholders and the inhabitants of the new town, without an understanding of the historical setting or the potentialities of the industries ...[79]

The consequences of all this were that the Eighth Duke, on his accession in late 1891, faced a grave situation where both estate revenue and dividend income were decreasing rapidly yet more than half the current income was needed to service the debt. The speed with which the Eighth Duke grasped the situation and the competent manner in which he placed the Devonshire finances on a firm footing is very well described by David Cannadine and need not be repeated here.[80] However, part of the solution was to sell land in Derbyshire, and the estate policy adopted by the Duke had a direct impact upon Buxton. Although the real scope of the financial problems were not apparent until 1894 when the Seventh Duke's affairs had been sorted out, major changes in the management of the Buxton Estate were made from 1892. It was almost as if Currey & Co., the solicitors and financiers, had anticipated the requirements of the new regime. From 1892 a completely new way of handling the Estate accounts was introduced. Gone were the green ledgers which had recorded accounts on a yearly basis for forty years. They were replaced by pro-forma monthly accounts, each month examined and reconciled in fastidious detail by C. Herbert Currey, the auditor, who would send a list of corrections and suggestions to which Frank Drewry, the Resident Agent was required to respond. Accounts now ran for a calendar year and cash was reconciled at the bank, with surplus remitted every month. The Buxton Building Estate was separately identified and pro-forma accounts were kept, and audited, for the 'Buxton Estate Rentals'. Most importantly, from 1894, the estate began to sell land outright again, as well as by Chief Rent, and the revenue from outright sales was remitted directly to Currey & Co. in Westminster.[81] These changes had a singular impact on the development of Buxton and it is against this background of revised estate management that the continuing growth of Buxton must be viewed.[82]

Between 1890 and the end of the century Buxton Park, the earlier creation of Sir Joseph Paxton, was, at last, extensively developed for building, although the ultimate layout bore little resemblance to Paxton's original grand design. Individual, architect-designed houses were built around a dominant central ring surrounding the cricket ground. The only terrace which corresponds with Paxton's layout is the present Athelstane Terrace, built *c.* 1870. Expansion of the Park took place on the west side with the laying out of Carlisle Road from St John's Road to Manchester Road in 1895 and substantial properties were built along St John's Road itself between 1883 and 1896. The continuation of Burlington Road from St John's Road to Macclesfield Road in 1890 opened up land for substantial detached and semi-detached residences but also allowed the Devonshire Building Estate to be further developed to the south and west of the town.[83] Thus parts of Macclesfield Road near the Tonic or Cold Plunging Bath were developed and several new roads were laid out. College Road from 1892 opened up the area adjacent to the Buxton College (the Grammar School), which itself had been built in 1881. One of the busiest builders in town, G. J. Bagshaw, built at least five of the individual houses on this road between 1892 and 1894, and the architect Barry Parker designed two 'Arts and Crafts' style houses in 1895/96. College Road led to Green Lane (formerly Leek Road) which saw villa development from 1892 to 1900 with the builder G. J. Bagshaw again in evidence. Completing this upper middle- and middle-class estate was Spencer Road in 1894, Robertson Road in 1897, a joint development between the Devonshire Estate and the Buxton Endowed School Governors (Buxton College), and Temple Road completed in 1899. The extension of Compton Road took place between 1887 and 1891 by local builders A. & E. Oakes, and there was further building on this road in 1895–97. This whole layout skirting the south west of the town and consisting of substantial high-class villas and small estates, all architect-designed, is an important feature of late nineteenth-century Buxton. Here the 'polite' Manchester society came to live complementing, undoubtedly raising, the general tone of the health resort. Certainly the standard of house design was raised by important regional architects such as Charles Heathcote of Manchester, Huon A. Matear of Liverpool and the Barry Parker–Raymond Unwin partnership which went on to achieve national prominence. Local

MR. G. J. BAGSHAW,

G. J. Bagshaw, builder and local politician, was one of the busiest builders in town. His work included houses on College Road and extensive developments at Kents Bank, Heath Grove and Crowstones. [B.M.A.G.]

architects such as W. R. Bryden, William Holland and Garlick & Flint also produced some fine designs.[84]

The extension of Dale Road running east–west on the south of the town, in 1891, provided an artery from which which streets for working-class housing could flow. Market Street was extended to the south across Dale Road and a whole 'new estate' of working-class houses was set out. This included New Market Street (1891), Heath Street (1891), Byron Street and Newstead Terrace (1895), The Pies (*c.*1888, but not adopted until 1906), Davenham Avenue (1894) and further extension of Bennet Street (1892–98). London Road, a main southern entrance to the town which skirts this new estate, was also extensively developed in the ten years from 1890. The type of housing varied from lower middle-class style semi-detached or in small terraces, to rows of eight or more working-class cottages. The lower middle-class housing was often three-storey with two substantial rooms on the ground floor and three or four bedrooms, but although these houses look quite imposing from the front they lack depth and most have a very small enclosed back yard. It is noticeable that this type of house is built fronting and near to the two arteries of London and Dale Roads with the smaller cottages further back. Thus the working-class housing is hidden away. New Market Street is an excellent paradigm. It runs south from Dale Road and has on the east side a block of four lower middle-class style houses (including the corner shop), then a pair of three-storey similar style houses. Davenham Avenue runs at right angles from this street and consists of a terrace of eight and one of nine three-storey cottages facing each other across a narrow carriageway. But on either side of the entrance there are two semi-detached three-storey lower middle-class houses, the whole forming a small domain. It was designed by the local architect G. E. Garlick and built for Messrs C. T & J. Hague, almost certainly Joseph Hague the town Surveyor who lived at 22 Market Street. Beyond this are fourteen two-storey cottages including two blocks of six. On the opposite side the pattern is similar except that the area nearest Dale Road was taken up by an Anglican mission chapel opened in 1897. The local builder James Salt was responsible for a number of the properties built in this area and it is noticeable that many simple

The partnership of Alfred and Ernest Oakes bought land and built in Compton Road from 1887. They built a pair of houses for their own occupation in 1889, Alfred lived at no. 1 and Ernest at no. 2 Fern View. [D.C. Chat.]

cottages exhibit a distinctive design feature.[85] As the health resort prospered, all types of housing were needed and the local builders provided employment for all the trades.[86] In 1891 of the ten per cent of the working population employed in the building trades more than forty per cent lived in the area bounded by London Road to the west and Bennet Street to the east. Bennet Street alone could boast seventy-one building workers (almost one per house) including fifteen stonemasons. This was clearly the building workers' quarter. It may also be observed that on the UDC in 1895 and in 1904 two of the elected members ran building companies, and another was an architect. This occupational sector, in addition to changing the topography of the town, made a significant economic contribution given the earnings of building workers and the continuity of work.[87]

The third major area to be developed was to the south east of the town where a small but quite distinct area of middle-class housing was formed. The final phase of the extension of Dale Road to Ashwood Dale, a southern entrance to the town, opened up land on either side of the road for building. G. J. Bagshaw, builder, local politician and member of the Streets Committee of the UDC, and his son William M. Bagshaw developed Recreation Road over ten years from 1899 and built all seventeen houses on Kents Bank Road in 1904.[88] These

Davenham Avenue, off New Market Street, showing cottage elevations and block plan of the complete development. This formed a small domain, it was designed by G. E. Garlick for the town surveyor, Joseph Hague. [D.C. Chat.]

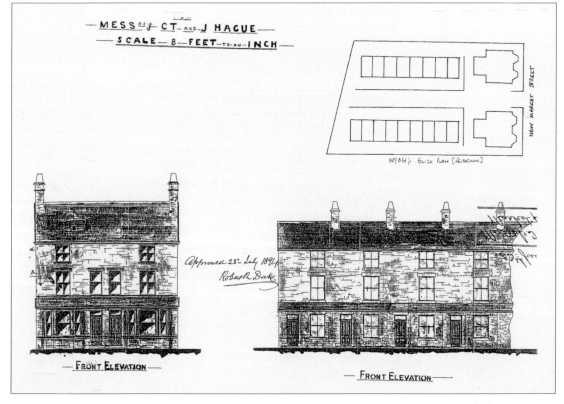

—MESSʳˢ ⸮ CT and J HAGUE—
—SCALE—8—FEET ᴛᴏ ᴀɴ INCH—

Approved 23ʳ July 1891
Robert Duke

— FRONT ELEVATION —

— FRONT ELEVATION —

two roads were on Devonshire Estate land and bordered a recreation field of six acres which the Duke sold to the town in 1896 on a chief rental of one pound *per annum*. It is notable how many of these houses were designed by local architects G. E. Garlick (later Garlick & Flint), and W. R. Bryden. In 1901 G. J. Bagshaw also developed Crowstones with an impressive design of twenty-four houses arranged in terraces of four with each pair sharing a central porch.[89] In 1903 he built two detached villas on the opposite side of the road one, including 'Meilhurst' for himself. This middle-class area was completed by Darwin Avenue which had been formed in 1880 but was partly developed in 1894, and Grange Road which was laid out and built upon from 1891. The continuation of Dale Road under the LNWR bridge opened up land at the south-eastern entrance to the town. Here Messrs Hobson & Sugden built a series of terraces of three and four large houses between 1897 and 1900 which offered the visitor from the south an impressive indication of what the town had to offer.

The juxtaposition of these areas of development representing upper-middle, middle-, lower middle- and working-class housing challenges the idea of class differentiation in housing layout; the notion of a degree of urban planning argued in chapter three, does not neatly fit this situation. Here are upper middle and middle-class properties approaching the working-class area of Higher Buxton (albeit separated by a main road) and those same working-class houses sandwiched by middle-class housing to the east. It is true to say that the working-class cottages were masked by the more substantial looking lower middle-class housing and the eastern middle-class housing was separated by fields. Thus to the casual observation of the visitors passing through from the south on their way to Lower Buxton and the Baths, the buildings must have appeared overwhelmingly middle-class. But the fact remains that the physical separation of the different classes of property was much less discrete in this later development of the town than it had been earlier in the century. The classical view taken by urban geographers on the zoning of towns and cities has been challenged in recent times and an alternative thesis would suggest that the social geography of Victorian towns was very 'weakly defined'. Professor Cannadine has reviewed the arguments and concludes that there are at least two concepts of residential differentiation valid for the nineteenth (and twentieth) centuries:

> ... The first might be labelled 'objective', concerned with criteria such as income, occupation, status, ethnicity and the like. The second is 'subjective' stressing the mental maps drawn by contemporaries the personal space of the actors, rather than the statistical space of the census ...[90]

He goes on to argue that there would be many more mental maps than patterns revealed by analysing the census and to pose the question how is it that, despite their relatively broad social spectrum, certain areas were able to establish and retain a subjective reputation for exclusiveness which the 'objective' analysis of their inhabitants in fact belied. If it is possible for the necessary degree of differentiation to be observed between employer and servant under the same roof, in the smaller houses of the middle class or on the estate of the larger house, then the notion of maintaining this where there is at least a physical separation of housing, such as described in Higher Buxton, can be understood. Moreover, as already noted, some planning effort was made to provide a degree of segregation. Vera Brittain's account of her childhood in Buxton before the Great War describes the social snobbery and unreal values which she perceived, she quotes her father's description of Buxton

... a little box of social strife lying at the bottom of a basin ...

Her 'unreal values' were, of course, the underpinning of the mental maps, the norms supporting the exclusiveness of one particular social stratum over another. But Vera Brittain's description is largely derived from the fact that she found Buxton too restricting for her personal ambition.[91] Not so those who had to make a living in the resort. Many of the people of Buxton were engaged in the common goal of promoting the amenities of the town. Everyone from lowly pot carrier to chairman of the UDC had a part to play in this. Furthermore, the physical isolation of the town, particularly in the winter, gave rise to a culture of interdependency. These factors would also have affected the drawing of mental maps, by the townspeople, in defining the degree of acceptable personal space.

Apart from these three main areas of residential development, between 1880 and 1905 the Devonshire Estate, anxious to release as much land for building as the market could stand, instructed their architect and surveyor, R. R. Duke, to lay out other roads.[92] Holker Road, a very steep gradient laid in 1897, led from the commercial Spring Gardens to Higher Buxton and opened up Victoria Avenue and Sylvan Cliff. This road also provided another route to Silverlands which, from 1895, extended the type of middle-class villas found in Hardwick Square. The working-class area of Hogshaw had seen sporadic development from the 1860s and by 1898 an additional fifty cottages had been approved. Higher value residential

Silverlands, developed from 1895, provided an extension of the substantial middle-class villas in Hardwick Square. Access was improved when Holker Road was driven up in 1897 though this was a very steep gradient.

An interesting way of delineating areas of Edwardian growth in the town is by the siting of Edward VII letter boxes. Since Edward's reign was comparatively short these tend to be rarely seen, but Buxton has several. This one is on White Knowle Road on the southern edge of the town, which was developed with middle-class housing from 1896.

land was made available when the Devonshire Estate laid out Lascelles and Lansdowne Roads to the north east in 1903 but it was some few years before plots on these roads were built upon. Investment was made by the Estate in commercial properties throughout the town, London Road and Spring Gardens being two examples; and a notable architectural addition was made when the Eagle Parade shops on the Market Place were rebuilt, as an impressive crescent, in 1890 to the designs of G. E. Garlick. During this time the Estate worked closely with the local authority and there are good examples of this cooperation to be found in the minutes of meetings and correspondence.[93] By 1905 the shape of the town was complete. This is illustrated in Appendix 4.9 which also shows the major areas of development during the period. Little more new road building would take place until after the Great War when the assisted schemes for building working-class housing began to be implemented. Not only was the town laid out almost wholly on Devonshire land but the Devonshire name was immortalised in many of the street names. The authorities in Buxton did not have the pleasure of choosing street names as other authorities might, though the naming of houses was by personal choice.[94] Devonshire derivatives were used for many streets, for example, Holker, Lascelles, Carlisle, Burlington, Cavendish, Compton, Hardwick, Lismore, Spencer, Lansdowne, Devonshire, all of which remain today. Other names emerge from old existing names such as Heath Grove and Crowstones, while a few carry the names of significant townsmen: Bennet Street after its developer, Dr R. O. G. Bennet, physician, and Robertson Road after Dr W. H. Robertson, Buxton's foremost water medical physician.

In the period from 1882 to 1905 the baths provided a regular and steady income for the Devonshire Estate, an average net profit of just under £2,400 *per annum.* Chapter five explores the developments in water medicine and the throughput of patients but, as an illustration, at the end of the century more than 75,000 baths were being taken in a year.[95] Both wings of the Baths were enlarged between 1886 and 1888 to provide new types of treatment using needle, vapour and massage baths and the Hot Baths were provided with a new water tower, waiting room and shops. In 1894 the Estate built its own laundry in George Street and between 1900 and 1901 the iron and glass colonnading was removed and the front of the Hot Baths entirely remodelled in ashlar stone. This coincided with further massage bath facilities on the first floor to which a hydraulic lift was provided. The designs for this work were by W. R. Bryden.

In 1894 a new Pump Room facing the Crescent was opened. The suggestion that enlarged facilities were needed, where people could drink the thermal water and meet socially, had been made as early as 1881 by the chairman of the Local Board and again in 1883 when

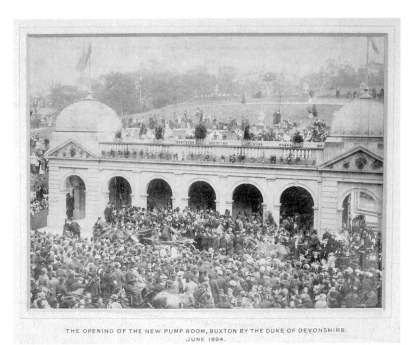

THE OPENING OF THE NEW PUMP ROOM, BUXTON BY THE DUKE OF DEVONSHIRE.
JUNE 1894.

The new Pump Room in the
Crescent, designed by Henry
Currey, was opened in June
1894 by the Eighth Duke of
Devonshire, Spencer Compton.
By 1912 it had been renamed
St Anne's Well and the water,
formerly dispensed by hand
pumps, was ladled from an oval
marble well. The photograph
shows the great crowds who
turned out for this most
important event. [B.M.A.G.]

that ever progressive organ the *Buxton Advertiser* had compared Buxton
unfavourably against Homburg and other continental spas.[96] The
Local Board had managed the Pump Room from 1865 and taken
from the Vestry responsibility for appointing the attendants in 1875.
Since the Duke owned all the land within the area of the springs it
was inevitable that negotiations would take place between the Devonshire Estate and the local authority. From 1887 there were discussions
over plans put forward by J. Hague, the Local Board surveyor, R. R.
Duke, local architect to the Estate and Henry Currey and at least
four sites were considered. The Duke was opposed to siting a building
in front of the Crescent, fearing it would both affect the view and
disturb the water source; the alternative plan, by R. R. Duke, for
enlarging the existing facilities situated in the Natural Baths was
favoured. The Local Government Board became involved because of
possible interference with the terms of the Enclosure Act of 1772
requiring open access to the water. The Duke of Devonshire offered
as early as 1888 to finance the work, which was fortunate because the
Local Board were unable to raise a loan for this purpose. Even so it
was necessary for the Board to promote a bill in parliament to authorise
it to accept the Pump Room as a gift and to safeguard the free access
to the water required under the Enclosure Act. By 1891 a decision to
build an entirely new Pump Room in the centre of the Crescent had
been resolved and Henry Currey would design this, his last work in
Buxton after a career of forty years as principal architect to the
Devonshire Estate.[97] The new Pump Room was opened with due

The optimism with which Buxton greeted the twentieth century is exemplified by the investment of the Buxton Gardens Company in a magnificent Opera House. Designed by the best known theatre architect of his day, Frank Matcham, it opened in 1903.

ceremony by the Eighth Duke, Spencer Compton, on 13 June 1894. At the luncheon following the Duke spoke candidly of the financial difficulties facing him, of the changes this would mean in the management of his estates, and the fact that his difficulties would be compounded by the introduction of death duties on large estates.[98] Ironically, this last gift of the Devonshire Estate to Buxton had been promised by the Seventh Duke but actually given by the Eighth, his name appearing on the act; it is interesting to speculate whether, given the choice, he would have seen fit to donate it to the town.[99]

When it came to the acquisition of the Mineral Water Baths by the town in 1904, no question of a gift arose. In April 1903 when the Duke, through his agent, intimated that he would be prepared to sell the Mineral water baths to the town, the UDC was unanimously in favour of entering into negotiations. This was a time when many resorts were investing in public amenities such as pavilions, piers, baths and municipal orchestras, and Buxton was anxious to match its northern competitor Harrogate and other spas where the baths were municipally owned.[100] The price discussed at this stage was £25,000 in cash and £1,000 *per annum* in Chief Rent, and at a well-attended meeting of ratepayers in January 1904 it was agreed to seek the necessary bill in parliament for the purchase and commercial operation under these terms. The bill met with difficulties in the House of Lords where objection was raised to a Chief Rent in perpetuity and the sale price was renegotiated at £55,000 payable by

half-yearly instalments of £1213 in capital and interest for sixty years from January 1905.[101] The act of 1904 set out the conditions of purchase and operation in some detail and it is notable that a specific clause relieved the Duke from responsibility for any further supply of a pump room or public pump. The Devonshire Estate had now severed all contact with the mineral water treatment.[102]

In these last two major negotiations with the Devonshire Estate the UDC acted in a firm and business-like manner as befits an authority representing its ratepayers in a mature local democracy. The Duke's agent, Frank Drewry, was still an influential figure in the town, but his influence now was chiefly based on rentals and the release of land for development and property speculation. Indeed he had sought and obtained additional influence himself through the democratic process as County Councillor for Buxton from 1904, forty years after his erstwhile colleague E. W. Wilmot had resigned from the Local Board. In his final years the Seventh Duke visited Buxton infrequently but his interest in the medical resort remained, as is seen in his gift of the Pump Room. The Eighth Duke and Duchess visited Buxton in 1893, not too long after his accession, and other visits of a formal nature, such as the opening of the Pump Room or their visit for a week in August 1893 when the town was decorated in their

The provision of a water supply to Higher Buxton by the Duke of Devonshire in 1840 invoked the old Derbyshire custom of well dressing. This pagan festival, appropriated by the Christian Church, involves the decoration of the well with flowers and leaves set into a clay base to provide a tableau, usually religious. The annual custom is depicted here in about 1890 at the Higher Buxton well. [B.M.A.G.]

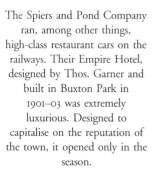

honour, and less formal, such as their visit in January 1893 to inspect the Baths and the new Opera House.

Buxton had every reason to enter the new century in an optimistic mood, despite the pessimism which may have existed in the country after the death of the Queen and the uneasiness of moving from a glorious nineteenth century to an unknown twentieth. Buxton, the health resort, had much to look forward to. The services and utilities were in place, up-to-date and working effectively, electricity was in public buildings and becoming more widely available. The Buxton Improvements Company added a magnificent opera house in 1903 to its other attractions in the theatre, pavilion and gardens.[103] The Terrace walks, Sylvan Park and Corbar crags and woods offered free walks to the public. The Union Club, built in 1886, provided a gentleman's club for guests to the town. Buxton was an attractive residential town with houses to buy or rent to suit all classes. The many annual events included a festival of music and of well dressing, a horse show, bowling, croquet and lawn tennis.[104] The growth up to 1905 had provided apartments and lodging houses in all parts of the town serving all classes of visitor and an extensive range of hotels and hydros. The Empire Hotel built in the Park between 1901 and 1903 is a perfect example of the commercial optimism and buoyancy of the town at the opening of the twentieth century. It was the largest hotel in town, an investment of £150,000 by Messrs Spiers and Pond, the high-class railway caterers, and it opened only in the season providing luxurious accommodation. This confidence, this optimism for the future, was crowned for the townspeople when the Eighth Duke brought his friend and King, Edward VII with Queen Alexandra, to visit the resort in January 1905. The chief purpose of the visit was to inspect the renowned Devonshire Hospital and Buxton Bath

The Spiers and Pond Company ran, among other things, high-class restaurant cars on the railways. Their Empire Hotel, designed by Thos. Garner and built in Buxton Park in 1901–03 was extremely luxurious. Designed to capitalise on the reputation of the town, it opened only in the season.

Charity [105] but the royal party toured the Pavilion Gardens, the Hot and Natural Baths, also the Pump Room where they were introduced to the Chairman of the UDC. The town had received the royal imprimatur.[106]

By 1905 Buxton had reached its peak, it was capitalising on the hard work of the local authority, other prominent townsmen and the Devonshire Estate over the previous sixty years and was poised for an increasingly successful future. Its growth was attributed to them. But there were other prime movers, chief among whom were the water medical doctors whose skills, knowledge and belief in the healing properties of the natural thermal water delivered the successful health resort out of the failing spa. Other key individuals and agencies who influenced or determined the growth of the resort were in estates management, in the underpinning of religious belief and in the architecture of the built environment. These are the subject of the chapters which follow.

... Its climate is all its own.
   Other towns get their weather from America or the morning papers; or, if these last are late, they have to be content with a bit of the Gulf Stream or the fag end of a cyclone.

The size and importance of the Palace Hotel may be gauged from this portrait of the staff taken in about 1905 outside the main entrance.

Buxton received the royal imprimatur when the Eighth Duke brought his friend and King, Edward VII with Queen Alexandra, to visit the resort in January 1905. This photograph shows the royal party outside the Devonshire Hospital.

But Buxton will not be put off by any second-hand goods: it makes a speciality of its climate and defies opposition.

I know of no other place that can cram so much weather into a week, not counting Sundays, as Buxton.

The climate is professionally described as 'salubrious'.

Lugubrious is a better word ...[107]

CHAPTER FIVE

Water Medicine

DURING THE SECOND HALF of the nineteenth century Buxton became a leading water medical centre. The maturing of the town in physical, economic and political terms, described in the previous chapters, shaped an inland health resort which, by the end of the century, could rival any in the British Isles.[1] At the heart of this growth was the unique thermal water emerging from springs at a constant 82°F, and a developing body of knowledge in water medicine. Buxton's reputation was forged, not as a fashionable Victorian spa, nor a centre for day-trippers (though after the railway services in 1863 they were an important part of the economy), nor did it embrace the fashionable hydropathic movement of the 1840s nor the less credible fringe medicines often associated with spas. It developed a clear reputation for the use of hydrotherapy and related methods in the treatment of a specific set of illnesses largely, but not wholly, associated with the systemic inflammatory condition which gives rise to rheumatic disease. The manner in which it did this, while remaining firmly in the orthodox school of nineteenth-century medical practice, is the subject of this chapter.

The development of the Georgian spa at Buxton by John Carr had included four new baths and this, combined with the later work of the architects John White and Son, meant that by 1811 Buxton had a suite of six baths using the natural mineral water at 82°F and a further bath, known as the Matlock Bath, whose temperature of 68°F approximated that of the spring at Matlock.[2] By the early nineteenth century standards of provision were improving and the more ready accessibility of coal led to the installation of artificial hot baths in a number of spas. Leamington Spa had used coal for hot baths as early as 1786 and, though the contemporary view was that hot baths were very expensive, the provision of a complex including hot, tepid and cold waters with high-quality fittings became the vogue.[3] In Buxton artificial hot baths were installed in 1817 with the strong support of Doctors Denman and Drever.[4] Buxton was ahead of the field in this provision and by the time of Dr Augustus Bozzi Granville's tour of the English spas in 1839–40 suites of hot baths were available in other large spas such as Cheltenham, Tunbridge Wells, Harrogate and Scarborough and some smaller centres such as Thorpe Arch and Croft in Yorkshire.[5] Buxton in 1822 had seven tepid baths at the west end of the Crescent (including two for charity patients) and a suite of

Dr W. H. Robertson (1810–1897) Buxton's foremost specialist in water medicine. He was the chairman of the board of management of the Devonshire Hospital from 1866 until his death. A prominent townsman, he was chairman of the Buxton Improvements Company and of the trustees of the Buxton College and among his other public duties he qualified as a magistrate in 1867, remaining a JP until his death.

Hot Baths at the eastern end of the Crescent. It is noticeable that both the cold and the Matlock baths, formerly in the natural baths wing, had been turned to other use by this time, though there was a separate, privately owned, cold bath situated on the road to Macclesfield, some distance from the Crescent and known as the 'Tonic' or 'Cold Plunge Bath'.

It has been observed in chapter one that the facilities in Buxton by 1820 helped to keep the town at the forefront of advances in water medicine and that important specialists in water treatment could be drawn into the town. A medical reputation might be made or enhanced in a place such as Buxton. This was certainly true of the town's two most important nineteenth-century doctors. Sir Charles Scudamore's reputation came before him, that of William Henry Robertson MD, FRCP, was made at Buxton. Both were central figures in the development of Buxton's medical reputation. Sir Charles Scudamore (1779–1849), practised in London and visited Buxton in the season. He was a specialist in the treatment of gout and rheumatism and wrote on these subjects, publishing a seminal work on gout, also chemical and medical reports on several mineral springs including Tunbridge Wells, Cheltenham, Harrogate and Buxton. His treatise on Buxton water published in 1820 was revised in editions of 1833 and 1839; he also carried out an analysis of the Buxton water.[6] He was an honorary physician to the Buxton Bath Charity and practised in Buxton from 1820 to the season of 1848, the year before his death.[7] Dr Robertson (1810–97) came to Buxton in 1835 and was appointed an honorary physician of the Buxton Bath Charity in 1836. From this time his influence grew and he progressed to honorary consulting physician and chairman of the Devonshire Hospital and Buxton Bath Charity in 1865. These appointments placed him in a position of great influence and in a career spanning more than sixty years he became Buxton's foremost water doctor.[8]

These two were most influential in developing the medical reputation of the town: Scudamore in the formative years of the century, and Robertson right through to the end of the century. Robertson lived at number six The Square and Scudamore lodged in the same set of town houses, often at the house of James Boam, a bath man.[9] The young Robertson was fortunate to know such an eminent specialist, possibly Scudamore acted as a mentor, as they worked together for the Bath Charity. Both these men would have accepted the post of honorary medical officer to the Buxton Bath Charity in a spirit of real charity but there is no doubt that, as this body developed into an important hydrotherapeutic hospital, the honorary position could enhance a doctor's reputation.[10] In fact the Devonshire Hospital and Buxton Bath Charity, in common with the hospitals at other centres such as Bath and Harrogate, played a central role in the development of water medicine in Buxton and it is necessary to provide a brief sketch of its history.

The notion of a charitable provision for the sick poor was put forward by Dr John Jones in 1573, but, despite his sound reasoning and later petitioning by residents, no charitable provision was made.[11] The Buxton Bath Charity proper commenced in 1779, in which year it is likely that a bath was specifically designated for the poor. Before this time there had been a second bath, built as part of improvements to the Hall by Cornelius White in 1695/96. This may have been a private charity provided by him but the bath was ultimately used as both a ladies' and a poor bath. A set of resolutions contained in the report of the charity for 1785 set out the rules which, although updated from time to time were to form the basis of the charity. A collection was taken of all those who stayed in hotels and lodging houses and a subscription book kept. Initially no greater sum than one shilling could be subscribed. The funds thus raised were to support sixteen poor patients during the May to October season who were nominated by the gentry of their neighbourhood, certified, if necessary by a church warden or overseer of the poor and verified in writing as a proper case for treatment by a physician or apothecary. The patient received six shillings for board and lodging together with medicines and water treatment for a maximum period of five weeks. Later changes to the rules allowed subscribers to nominate patients, the accommodation, type and length of treatment being dependent upon the amount subscribed.[12] In addition sermons were preached annually by notable clerics to support fund-raising collections. Early reports of the charity have not survived, but in 1811 it was managed by the Duke of Devonshire's agent Phillip Heacock and the local banker, G. Goodwin, about 150 patients being treated annually.[13] In 1822 there were 796 patients admitted and 312 who received medicine and baths but no financial support; the charity had a turnover of £493.[14] By 1854 the balance sheet showed a turnover of £989 with a total of 1,203 patients treated. The question of accommodation was raised in that year. The trustees, concerned that patients had to travel some distance from their lodgings to the baths, wanted a hospital. The Duke of Devonshire gave land and a donation of £100 against the estimated £2,500 required and the trustees set up a public appeal. The architect,

The Square where Sir Charles Scudamore lodged and Dr Robertson lived for most of his time in Buxton. Robertson came to Buxton in 1835 and was able to lease no. 6 from the Devonshire Estate. In this view of the west face it is the most distant bay.

The charity rules allowed subscribers to nominate their patients and the hospital would advise the subscriber of the patient's progress upon discharge. Later in the century pre-printed and stamped postcards were used for this purpose, as can be seen here.

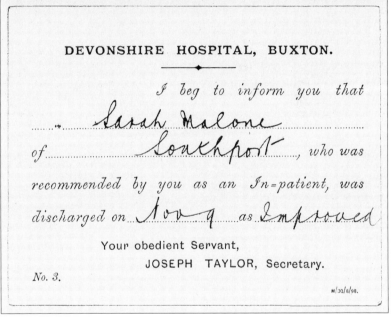

DEVONSHIRE HOSPITAL, BUXTON.

I beg to inform you that

Sarah Malone

of *Southport* *, who was*

recommended by you as an In=patient, was

discharged on *Nov 9* *as* *Improved*

Your obedient Servant,
JOSEPH TAYLOR, Secretary.

No. 3.

M/30/8/98.

Henry Currey designed a hospital for sixty patients which was to be sited on Sylvan Park but the Duke's agent, E. W. Wilmot, declared the site unsuitable and, against a degree of opposition, persuaded the Duke to allow a half of John Carr's Great Stables to be converted for use by the charity. This conversion took place in 1859 and the charity became 'The Devonshire Hospital and Buxton Bath Charity' a hospital specialising in hydrotherapeutic medicine.[15] Although Currey's conversion provided 120 beds and a small number for accident cases, the arrangement was not satisfactory; part of the ground-floor was still in use as stabling.[16] From this time Dr Robertson led a number of delegations to the agent but it was to be nearly twenty years before the whole of the building was acquired from the

Devonshire Estate. In 1877 an agreement was, at last reached, new stables were built for the Duke on land to the north of the railway stations, and the trustees were able to draw up plans for the full conversion of the Great Stables into a hospital. Between 1879 and 1882 a new 300-bed hospital emerged from the stable building, designed by Robert Rippon Duke and featuring a magnificent slated domed roof.[17] The total cost of just over £26,000 was provided by a grant from the Cotton Districts Convalescent Fund with an agreement that 150 of the beds would have preferential use for patients from the cotton districts.[18]

The Devonshire Hospital and Buxton Bath Charity thus sits at the heart of Victorian medical development in the town. Many doctors were drawn to offer their services gratuitously in support of its work and it became a centre of excellence for diseases described as of the 'locomotor' and 'nervous' systems.[19] The practice of citing and describing 'cures' effected through water treatment was greatly helped by the numbers of patients treated at the hospital. While some doctors used their own patients as case histories of success, it was more usual for the Buxton doctors to cite successes at the Devonshire Hospital. In this they had a ready set of case histories and useful statistics. Furthermore, because the patients came from poor living and working conditions, they were likely to benefit from several weeks of rest, change of air and a reasonable diet.[20]

Between 1820 and the early 1850s no further investment was made at the Natural baths but provision at the Hot Baths was doubled in 1836/37 to two baths each for ladies and gentlemen, complete with vapour and shower bath.[21] Buxton could offer hot and natural tepid baths, a cold plunging bath, resident and seasonal doctors with the support of shampooers or those skilled in medical rubbing.[22] Apart from Scudamore and Robertson there were six other doctors in the period up to the refurbishment of the baths in 1851, all of whom were on the staff of the Buxton Bath Charity.[23] These medical men were assisted by medical rubbers, the forerunners of modern-day hydrotherapists, who were either seasonal

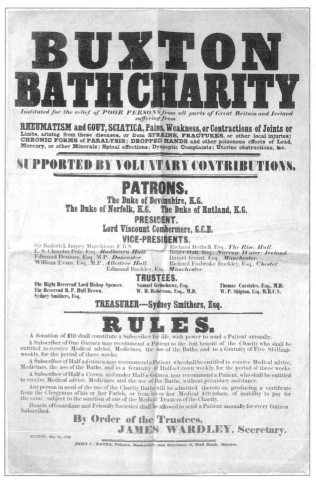

A large linen-backed poster printed by J. C. Bates for the Buxton Bath Charity in 1853 to advertise their work.

The Devonshire Hospital. Buxton.

Devonshire Hospital before the conversion of 1879–82. In this engraving of about 1865 the building is in use as part stables/part hospital. The hospital occupied the upper floor. It was to take the trustees of the charity twenty years from 1859 to persuade the Duke of Devonshire to allow them to take over the whole of the building for medical purposes.

visitors or resident in the town. Mrs Ainley from Sheffield practised in the s-eason from 1826 and J. Whalley and Son of Salford similarly from 1835 but Joseph Miller built up a resident business. They advertised recommendations from the local doctors amongst others.[24] The popularity of the baths was steadily increasing and the agent to the Devonshire Buxton Estate, Phillip Heacock, was anxious to maintain a good flow of business into the town.[25]

Given this situation it is very surprising that Buxton was not one of the first centres to take advantage of hydropathy and the hydropathic movement which developed in Britain from the early 1840s and had a significant impact on water medicine, indeed, the medical profession as a whole.[26] The term 'hydropathy' as used in this chapter has a specific meaning. It refers to a method of cold water cure popularised by Vincent Priessnitz (1799–1851) of Graefenberg in Austrian Silesia. A degree of legend surrounds the origins of Priessnitz's methods. The son of a small farmer, he undertook no formal medical training yet his charismatic personality led to tales recounted by his followers. It was said that he had observed animals bathing and massaging their muscles in the springs flowing from the mountains above his home and had, himself, used a wet compress to cure a broken rib. The legends are repeated today.[27] His cold water cure was based on the belief that health is the natural condition of the body and that only water can separate

In 1879 the trustees of the Bath Charity began the conversion of John Carr's Georgian stables into a 300-bed hospital. The architect for the project was R. R. Duke, notable townsman who, himself suffered from a form of rheumatic disease and in later life used a wheelchair. It was completed in 1882. R. R. Duke was, for fifty years, a trustee of the Bath Charity.

Devonshire Hospital.

115

Patients receiving their
prescribed Buxton water under
the central dome at the
Devonshire Hospital

and carry off the foreign matter in the system causing illness. His procedures consisted largely of wet and dry packs to induce sweating, cold baths, and the douche or water spray. He combined this with the drinking of pure water, exercise, outdoor work and diet in a regime which barred the use of any form of drugs.[28] A contractor in asphalt, Captain R. T. Claridge, is credited with being the first person to publicise the regime of hydropathy, or the water cure, in England. His book, published in 1842, described the treatment in detail and set out the wide range of ailments, from gout to lockjaw, which could be cured. He also charted the phenomenal growth of Priessnitz's establishment from forty-five patients in 1829 to 1,576 in 1840. It was a highly enthusiastic and successful publication; in the third edition (also published in 1842) he noted in the foreword that an abstract was to be published as a cheaper version to reach all classes.[29] From this time hydropathy gained prominence in the medical world. Claridge's book was followed up by others in quick succession and hydropathic establishments began to spring up, the earliest being Stansteadbury in Hertfordshire, Harrow-on-the-Hill, Great Malvern and Ramsgate.[30] At the same time a number of publications challenged hydropathy both as a 'cure-all' and as another form of quackery. Remarkably, a water practitioner named James Culverwell, published a critical book only one month after that of Claridge's.[31]

Hydropathy was not new. It was not sophisticated in medical terms. It did not represent a particular medical advance.[32] Why, then, did it become so popular and how did Buxton feature in this movement? Hydropathy arrived at a time when medicine seemed to be lagging behind other sciences and was driven to make claims it could not substantiate.[33] The Pharmacy Act of 1852 and the Medical Act of 1858 had yet to arrive. The former would require druggists to be qualified; the latter would provide a General Council of Medical Education and Representation to set and regulate standards. Meanwhile doctors,

Elements of the Cold Water
Cure taken from R. T.
Claridge's book *Hydropathy,*
1842.
1. half bath; 2. head bath;
3. sitting bath; 4. douche bath;
5. sweating; 6. going to the
bath after sweating. These give
some impression of how
rigorous the treatment was.
[Wellcome]

THE SHALLOW BATH.
" Your true life preserver."

First morning at the Water Cure.
(Bathman brings the Wet sheet.)
" But I am sure I shall get my death
of cold."

Hydropathy was fertile ground for the cartoonist. Here are two examples. However, when compared with some of the contemporary books on hydropathy these do not look too far removed from reality!

whose level of income was dependent upon the sale of drugs, prescribed reckless quantities which could be toxic just a little in excess of the therapeutic dose. The early nineteenth century saw a developing pharmacopoeia including drugs such as morphine, colchicum, quinine, acetate of lead, sulphur, digitalis, tobacco as well as the older mercury and its derivatives. The application of leeches and bleeding was still used excessively as a therapy.[34] Hydropathy came along with other medical movements such as homoeopathy, naturopathy, phrenology and mesmerism which blossomed in the early Victorian age and challenged the orthodox medicine of the time offering alternatives to the potentially poisonous drugging.[35] Hydropathy, in common with some of these other movements, was holistic, it offered natural forms of treatment and focused on the contribution which the individual could make towards curing themselves. The established medical profession challenged hydropathy on three major counts: that Priessnitz had discovered nothing new since the origins of water treatments could be seen in antiquity; that hydropathy was for hypochondriacs; and that the treatment was non-specific. James Culverwell said that Priessnitz's combination of cold bathing, sweating, cold water drinking, fresh air and exercise was a buckshot rather than a specific aim and concluded that Graefenberg patients would get well despite

… the good services of the mountain professor …[36]

Paradoxically, the strength of opposition to hydropathy may have served to reinforce its value in the public eye. It was at one and the same time damned as the 'water death' by *The Lancet* and extolled as a valuable cure by such luminaries as Edward Bulwer Lytton from literature and Charles Darwin from science.[37] The medical establishment was particularly vociferous in its opposition. An early article in *The Lancet* described a lecture given by Dr Wilson from Graefenberg at the new Hydropathic Society in these terms,

> ... a more miserable failure, a more wretched display of ignorance, it was never our lot to witness ...[38]

and ammunition was provided by the deaths of patients under treatment, widely reported amongst them Sir Francis Burdett in 1843 and Mr Richard Dresser three years later.[39] The *British and Foreign Medico-Chirurgical Review* used a book review to mount a virulent attack on both the author and Dr Macleod of the hydropathic[40] at Ilkley which they described as

> ... Ben Rhydding Hotel and Boarding-house ... [who] has identified himself with the aqueous and globulistic quacks ...[41]

This hydropathic notoriety was balanced by the approbation of notable figures. The medically respected Sir John Forbes, founder/editor of the widely read and respected *British and Foreign Medical Review*, wrote two reviews in support of hydropathy in 1846. The celebrated author, Edward Bulwer Lytton (1803–73)

Dr. Francis Kennedy Dickson, F.R.C.P., F.R.C.S.,

was treated by Dr Wilson at Malvern, Dr Weiss in Petersham and in Germany under Dr Schmidt at his hydro at Boppart. In an influential book he described the wet sheet packing treatment:

Dr F. K. Dickson ran the Wye House Asylum in Buxton which advertised itself as: 'An establishment for the care and treatment of the insane of the higher and middle-classes'. He was a Hon. Medical Adviser to the Buxton Bath Charity.

> ... the first momentary chill is promptly succeeded by a gradual and vivifying warmth, perfectly free from the irritation of dry heat – a delicious sense of ease is usually followed by a sleep more agreeable than anodynes ever produced ...[42]

Charles Darwin took treatment at Malvern under Dr James Manby Gully in 1849 and continued the treatment at home in an outdoor douche and bath in his garden. He returned to Malvern four more times and despite the death of his daughter Anne from some form of wasting disease in 1851 while she was being treated by Gully, he did not lose faith. He subsequently used hydros at Moor Park in Surrey and at Ilkley. The fashion of hydropathy spread through literary and intellectual society in the 1840s and 1850s, and by 1850 ʡ

there were about thirty establishments vying to be the 'dernier resort' in England.[43]

It might be argued that Buxton should have been among this first group. It had a long history of water medicine and, indeed, could offer a cold water treatment in the Tonic Bath on Macclesfield Road. Furthermore, one of its most eminent specialists, Sir Charles Scudamore, had visited Graefenberg in April and May 1843 and, being an open-minded practitioner, gave Priessnitz's water cure measured support in a book published in the same year.[44] The town was well appraised of the controversy surrounding the water cure through its seasonal paper, the *Buxton Herald and Gazette of Fashion*. During 1843 and 1844 it kept up a lively correspondence on the pros and cons and reviewed the earliest books. Editorially the paper was refreshingly down to earth, reflecting the pragmatic nature of the mountain resort. Priessnitz was awarded full merit for *not* discovering that a rest from business, fresh air and a plain diet are good for health as has been known as long as Adam. It was suggested that fashions were fickle but the advantages of Buxton water depended neither on fashion nor the fame of any celebrated physician but were written on the grateful memories of hundreds who have suffered. Buxton water would do as much good in weeks as the cold water cure did in months. Nevertheless, the newspaper suggested that hydropathy should not be condemned without a trial and that the townspeople should think about the possibility of establishing a cold water treatment establishment.[45] Add to all this the presence in town in 1854 of Sir Edward Bulwer Lytton MP as chairman of the Buxton Bath Charity for that year, a man who had done much to publicise hydropathy, and it is clear that there have to be significant reasons why Buxton was not in the first phase of the hydropathic movement.[46]

In fact there was a hydropathic in Buxton by 1855. In April Mr Joseph Miller placed a large advertisement thanking those who had, for many years, patronised him as a shampooer and professor of the cold water cure and indicating that he had erected a commodious house at Hall Bank extensively fitted up as a hydro. This venture did not enjoy the success of hydros developing elsewhere at this time, such as Matlock or Ilkley even though Mr Miller ran his advertisement for some time and operated his business well into the 1870s. It was not recognised as a significant medical facility and the fortunes of Mr Miller's hydro sit right at the heart of Buxton's reticence to

---

BUXTON AND THE WATER CURE.

Mr. MILLER

BEGS to return his sincere thanks to those Ladies and Gentlemen who have for many years past patronized him as a SHAMPOOER and PROFESSOR of the COLD WATER CURE, at his former residence, and to inform them that he has recently erected a commodious house at HALL BANK, which has been constructed and fitted up specially for the accommodation and home comfort of patients as an HYDROPATHIC and LODGING ESTABLISHMENT. Mr M. begs also to intimate to the ladies and gentlemen visiting Buxton that he has had for many years an extensive practice, both as a Shampooer and Professor of the Water Cure, and can therefore confidently promise great relief and benefit to persons afflicted with gout, rheumatism, nervous complaints, and kindred disorders, having successfully treated innumerable patients suffering under such diseases, and can refer to many ladies and gentlemen of the highest respectability who have been benefited by his treatment.

N.B. VAPOUR BATHS, on the most scientific principle, and a large quantity of new Blankets and Sheets for the treatment.

Hall Bank, Buxton, April 16, 1855.

Joseph Miller, a shampooer, advertised his premises on Hall Bank as a Hydro in 1855 and although he continued in business well into the 1870s his establishment was not recognised by the Buxton medical profession as a significant medical facility. Dr W. H. Robertson in his influential *Buxton Guide* described Miller's premises as a lodging house and his expertise as a shampooer or masseur only.

embrace the movement in its early phase. Buxton in the 1840s was a town with a substantial and growing medical reputation. This reputation was based upon the natural tepid mineral water and a range of treatments developed around that resource. The nature of the cure at Buxton, it was asserted by the doctors, arose from the efficacy of the natural minerals and the nitrous gasses which issued from the thermal springs. These two properties, they would avow, placed the Buxton waters in a class of their own and the practising doctors remained firmly part of the medical establishment. Dr W. H. Robertson was referred to in *The Lancet* as

> ... well and favourably known to the profession by his previous writings ...[47]

Many analyses were conducted on the water to demonstrate the mineral contents from which its medical properties were derived.[48] Great emphasis was also placed on the gaseous content of the water, in particular the nitrogen gas where Buxton water was compared with that of the German spa Wildbad.[49] A clear example of the importance attached by Robertson to the efficacy of the gasses and the tepid heat of the water may be seen in his protracted negotiations with the Devonshire estate over the siting of the new Charity Natural bath in the 1870s.[50] A number of the doctors at Buxton published on the medical use of the Buxton waters and all stayed within the established medical practice in respect of treatments.[51] It is notable that no edition of Robertson's books mentioned hydropathics and, of particular significance, Mr Miller's Hydro was not included in the directory of any edition of Robertson's handbook, Miller was referred to only as 'Shampooer and Private Lodgings, Hall Bank'.[52] The importance of the stance taken by different members of the medical profession in the early advance of hydropathy cannot be underestimated. A contrast may be made, for example, between Matlock, Malvern and Ilkley, three of the leading hydropathic resorts, and Buxton, Bath and Harrogate. The first three resorts had developed only a weak reputation for their natural mineral water in the early nineteenth century but they could offer a hilly, wooded and scenic setting akin to that of Graefenberg and their development was supported by resident doctors and others zealous in their application of the water cure techniques.[53] Matlock developed hydros from the early 1850s and, at the height of its popularity, had at least thirteen including John Smedley's magnificent hydro capable

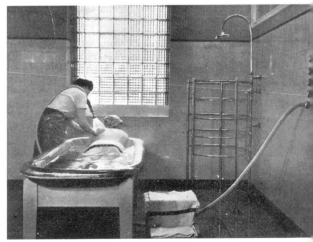

The Buxton Douche massage was, as the name suggests, particular to the town. The patient lay in a shallow bath of copper coated with white metal. The water depth was 7 or 8 inches (20cm) and at a different temperature from the douche body spray. There were variations of treatment but all included massage. On the right of this picture can be seen a needle jet shower.

Patient being lowered into a small treatment bath. The large common bath of earlier in the century gave way to individual private baths as medical fashions and treatments changed.

of treating 2,000 cases in a year.[54] Ilkley and Malvern grew similarly, Malvern enjoying the patronage of famous patients including Gladstone, Macaulay, Tennyson and Florence Nightingale as well as Darwin.[55] The resorts of Bath, Buxton and Harrogate were, on the other hand, already established medical centres by the time Priessnitz arrived on the scene and their regimes were firmly held by medical practitioners who were disinclined to accept the efficacy of ordinary cold water and a system devised by a Silesian peasant.[56] For these reasons, Buxton did not enter the first phase of the hydropathic movement. Its resident doctors, most influentially W. H. Robertson, did not need or choose to recognise it.[57]

Though hydropathics continued into the early part of the twentieth century, the first phase of hydropathy could be said to be over by 1870. By this time important developments were already taking place in water medicine. Through the eighteen fifties and sixties the medical regimes administered under the term hydropathy had begun to broaden out from the simple system advocated by Priessnitz. As early as 1847 Dr Gully at Malvern was using hot as well as cold water treatments, and his colleague James Wilson was pressing for the general acceptance of hydropathy as part of rational medicine.[58] In 1856 Dr Macleod had constructed a compressed air bath, a type of pressure vessel, used for relief from deafness, dyspepsia and sterility, but chiefly for pulmonary functions and lung problems. He also added a Roman or Turkish Bath and medical gymnastics to his medical armamentarium.[59] John Smedley at Matlock used tepid water to avoid the shock or possible 'crisis' brought on by very cold water.[60] Other practitioners, anxious to develop more illness-specific approaches, simply added the cold water techniques to their medical repertoire.[61] In addition to this broadening out, the medical profession gradually took hold of hydropathy as it passed its first flush of popularity. In a polemical review of books by Smedley and Gully *The Lancet* argued strongly for sanatoria and properly staffed water medical centres.[62] As specialisation grew, through the hospital movement, the notion of spa practitioner as a specialist alongside general practitioner and consultant was voiced.[63]

Whilst Buxton passed largely un-touched by the first phase of hydropathy, from the mid-1860s with the rise of the sanatorium movement, and with hydropathic establishments gradually becoming part of the medical establishment, hydros began to appear in the town.[64] An Anglican minister, Revd James Shore, came to Buxton to open the first of these, Malvern House Hydro, in 1866. He was a Devon man who had become involved in homoeopathic and hydropathic medicine at Smedley's Hydro and his own, Matlock House Hydro in Matlock. The Malvern House became Buxton's most successful Hydro, with accommodation in 1867 for forty patients. By 1884 it could take 180 and by 1905 it had become the Buxton Hydro advertising 260 rooms. But in general the development of hydropathics in Buxton was both modest and slow. In 1870 Shore leased the Royal Hotel to run as a hydro, but this was short-lived.[65] In 1880 Dr Hyde formed a company to develop Buxton House on Terrace Road into the Peak Hydro to accommodate 150 guests. The other establishments were smaller. The Corbar Hill Hydro, Manchester Road, was converted from the Clarendon private lodging house in 1890s and there were two hydros on London Road, the Haddon House (later known as Haddon Grove and as Olivers), from 1883 and the Haddon Hall, built in 1903.[66] These hydros offered a range of water therapies and, latterly, electro and electro-water treatments as new techniques

Malvern House Hydropathic Establishment, Buxton

Malvern House Hydropathic opened in 1866 by Revd James Shore. He had previously run Matlock House Hydro at Matlock. Malvern House was the first real hydropathic Hotel in Buxton and became the most successful.

In 1899 large extensions were made to extend the accommodation to 260 rooms and Malvern House Hydro became known as The Buxton Hydropathic. It was run very successfully by James Shore's nephew, H. R. P. Lomas and, from 1931, as the Spa Hotel by A. W. H. Lomas. The hydro had its own farm at Pomeroy just outside Buxton to supply fresh food. This photograph also shows some aspects of Victorian building practice.

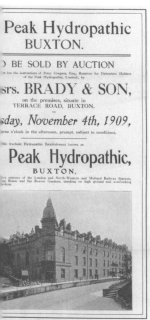

The Buxton House
Hydropathic on Terrace Road
was developed into the Peak
Hydro by Dr Samuel Hyde
(d. 1900) in about 1880.
Despite Dr Hyde's reputation
in water treatment and the new
medicine of balneology, the
Peak Hydro had a chequered
career as a business. Hyde
probably overreached himself
with ambitious plans and,
certainly the building was
extended to provide extensive
facilities including a ballroom.
This illustration is from auction
particulars of 1909.

The Haddon Hall
Hydropathic, London Road
was opened in 1903. It had a
full suite of baths including
vapour, douche, spray, hot air,
medicated and electric bath
treatments together with 50
bedrooms and spacious public
rooms.

developed. Most were attended by qualified doctors and all combined their treatment with rest, bracing air and sensible diet.

The Buxton Baths continued to be developed from the major redesign of 1851–54. In 1861 a suite of Turkish Baths was built in the Hot Baths wing, no doubt to take advantage of the perceived popularity of such treatment, but this was not successful and the Devonshire Estate closed them in 1865 after several years in which income failed to cover costs. The commercial potential of the baths was fully exploited by the Devonshire Estate which also kept maintenance (a constant need with steam and condensation) up to a high standard. From the early 1860s shops and colonnading were put round the Hot Baths and both sets of baths were re-roofed (Paxton's ridge and furrow being by then prone to leaking). A significant expansion of facilities was obtained in 1875–76 when the Charity Baths, formerly occupying a suite at each of the Hot and Natural Baths, were removed to new sites allowing expansion for more paying guests.[67] Changes in the baths reflected the medical trend towards individual treatments and a wide range of techniques; thus the Hot Baths by 1875 was composed entirely of private baths. Ladies' and gentlemen's corridors ran from the entrance leading in each case to ten private baths complete with dressing room, douche equipment and shower bath. By 1891 the Natural Baths also had five private baths each for men and women together with the larger public baths, two for men and one for women. The Hot Baths had fourteen private baths for women and ten for men. Treatments included Russian, needle, vapour, massage and Sitz in addition to the long established 'Buxton Douche'.[68] Electro, air, radiant and electric-hydro treatments were to follow.[69] In the decade

100   HYDROPATHICS.

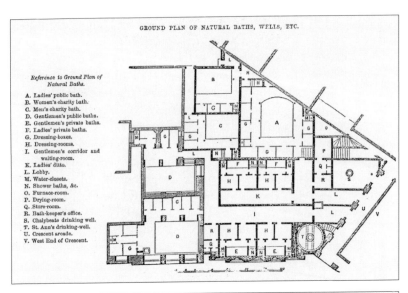

GROUND PLAN OF NATURAL BATHS, WELLS, ETC.

Reference to Ground Plan of
Natural Baths.

A. Ladies' public bath.
B. Women's charity bath.
C. Men's charity bath.
D. Gentlemen's public baths.
E. Gentlemen's private baths.
F. Ladies' private baths.
G. Dressing-boxes.
H. Dressing-rooms.
I. Gentlemen's corridor and
waiting-room.
K. Ladies' ditto.
L. Lobby.
M. Water-closets.
N. Shower baths, &c.
O. Furnace-room.
P. Drying-room.
Q. Store-room.
R. Bath-keeper's office.
S. Chalybeate drinking well.
T. St Ann's drinking-well.
U. Crescent arcade.
V. West End of Crescent.

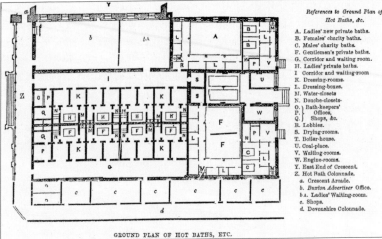

References to Ground Plan of
Hot Baths, &c.

A. Ladies' new private baths.
B. Females' charity baths.
C. Males' charity baths.
F. Gentlemen's private baths.
G. Corridor and waiting room.
H. Ladies' private baths.
I Corridor and waiting-room
K. Dressing-rooms.
L. Dressing-boxes.
M. Water-closets.
N. Douche-closets.
O. } Bath-keepers'
P. } Offices.
Q. } Shops, &c.
R. Lobbies.
S. Drying-rooms.
T. Boiler-house.
U. Coal-place.
V. Waiting-rooms.
W. Engine-rooms.
Y. East End of Crescent.
Z. Hot Bath Colonnade.
a. Crescent Arcade.
b. Buxton Advertiser Office.
bA. Ladies' Waiting-room.
c. Shops.
d. Devonshire Colonnade.

GROUND PLAN OF HOT BATHS, ETC.

Plans taken from Dr Robertson's *Buxton Guide* showing the layout of the Hot and Natural Baths in 1872. The baths were impeccably maintained by the Devonshire Estate and a number of changes in layout took place during the century to reflect developments in medical techniques.

The Corbar Hill Hydro stood on the corner of Manchester and Marlborough Roads. It was converted from the Clarendon Private Lodging House in the 1890s. The Haddon Grove, also known as Oliver's Hydro, was situated behind the Haddon Hall Hydro on London Road.

HYDROPATHICS.

THE CLARENDON (Corbar Hill

Near Mineral Baths, Pavilion, Opera House and Railway
South-west Aspect.
Lounge, Billiard, Smoking, and Drawing Rooms.
Electric Light.   Small Tables.   Every Mod
Nat. Tel. No. 3.   Apply MANAG

THE HADDON GROVE HYDRO

Stands in its Ow
Free from Croq
Tennis and Croq
Good Stabling & M
Full Suite of L
Gentlemen's
Heated Throughout.
Perfect Sanitary
Table d'Hote
Terms from 12 ft. swe
Week-end Terms on
All Arrangements und
Supervisio
For Illustrated
Apply C. OLIVER

Haddon Grove

from 1894 an average of 75,000 baths *per annum* were given at Buxton, a figure largely comparable with Harrogate and Bath.[70]

In making great claims for the climate and the air at Buxton it was necessary for the local authority and the Devonshire Buxton Estate to ensure that the resort could offer the very best in sanitary arrangements.[71] The range of sanitary acts after 1858 is of itself an indication of the huge amount of work needed to bring clean water and drains and to remove air and other pollution in the increasing urban development in England. Healthy Buxton must rise above this; no 'miasma' could be allowed in the town.[72] It is unsurprising, therefore, that Buxton lost no time in appointing its own Medical Officer of Health (MOH) who quickly became effective, facing little of the difficulties experienced by these professionals in some of the larger urban areas.[73] Following the Public Health act of 1872, Frederick

Turner was appointed for the Buxton Urban District by 1874. He had been appointed the MOH for Buxton District within the Chapel-en-le-Frith Union and he held both appointments until 1888 when the growing urban district required him to concentrate solely on Buxton.[74] Turner had the distinct advantage of being a born-and-bred townsman and he was able to join the Buxton Bath Charity as an honorary medical officer in 1866 whilst newly qualified.[75] An important comparative measure for Buxton was the rate of mortality. From the time of the installation of the first sanitary system in 1859 Buxton could boast a far lower death rate than England and Wales as a whole and lower than that of its rivals such as Bath and Cheltenham. Buxton's rate progressively decreased from seventeen per thousand in 1861 to the lowest of any watering place at nine per thousand in 1884, remaining between nine and ten per thousand at the end of the century despite the increase in population.[76] The resident doctors invariably set out the mortality figures in their publications since these served to enhance their reputation, Dr Robertson being careful to point out that some adjustment should be made for the deaths amongst the annual influx of visitors.[77] At the provincial summer meeting of the Institute of Sanitary Engineers held in Buxton in June 1902 the chairman Dr Wilkinson said that Buxton, because of its low death rate, was in the category of the few towns where it might be said that

Dr Frederick Turner (d. 1914) was the son of Samuel Turner, noted townsman. He was Medical Officer of Health at Buxton from 1874 to about 1905 and also ran his own practice from Grafton House in the Quadrant. In common with many other of the town's doctors he was a medical adviser to the Devonshire Hospital and Buxton Bath Charity.

> ... the Doctor neither lived nor died – did not live because he had no patients, and did not die because the place was so healthy ...[78]

As water medicine progressed in the last quarter of the century, some of the long-held beliefs about the efficacy of Buxton's tepid mineral water began to be redefined by the resident specialists. Dr Robertson was firm in the view that the nitrogen and carbonic acid gases aid the absorption of the water through the skin:

> ... The greater the amount of friction of the surface of the body, and of exercise of the trunk and limbs, while in the bath, the greater is the probable amount of absorption of the water ...[79]

... it is admitted to be still difficult to determine the precise nature or extent of the effects of uncombined nitrogen, when introduced into the human system, whether by absorption through the skin, or through the mucous membrane of the stomach ...[80]

... Carbonic acid is chiefly valuable in mineral waters as a solvent for more powerful ingredients, and as a means by which the more rapid absorption of the waters, either through the skin or through the stomach is secured ...[81]

He recognised that the minerals contained in the water and identified through successive analyses were not in a sufficient quantity to be effective if administered individually as drugs, nevertheless, in combination and as part of the water treatment, they significantly aided the cure. He developed an important specialism in the treatment of rheumatism, gout, neuralgia and forms of spinal, uterine and dyspeptic affections all of which could be treated with some degree of success by various water regimes. The other doctors held similar views and followed very similar approaches.[82]

As the range of treatments developed, however, a greater differentiation of ailments which could be treated was made and doctors began to offer 'contra indications' suggesting illnesses for which the water treatment was not effective. By the end of the century Robertson's views could be challenged. In 1898, a year after Robertson's death, Dr Samuel Hyde of the Peak Hydro, said that no scientific explanation could be made for the value of the nitrogen gas; that absorption through the skin was one of the greatest fallacies of balno-therapeutics; and that science had not advanced enough to analyse fully the value of Buxton mineral water.[83] Traditional water medicine, influenced by hydropathy and an ever developing range of treatments, had given way to water regimes better described collectively as hydrotherapy. But Buxton, in common with its northern rival Harrogate, together with Bath, Droitwich, Leamington and other centres offered an even wider range of treatments, which included the use of electricity, for which the general term 'balneology' was used.

Hydrotherapy, with its origins in medical rubbing, runs as a theme through Buxton's maturing health resort. Traditionally doctors had always seen the value of massage or rubbing of the skin during bathing. The shampooers of the 1840s had turned, by the end of the century, into 'masseurs' and in Buxton as with other health resorts electrotherapy ran alongside massage.[84] The Devonshire Hospital, in 1904, had three hon. masseurs and two hon. masseuses as well as a hon. consulting electrical engineer.[85] Electric baths, massage and electromassage were available, several different forms of massage were used in Buxton and the town had at least one electrical engineer specialising

Dr W. H. Robertson was Buxton's foremost medical doctor in the nineteenth century and did much to develop the reputation of the town as a health resort within the recognised medical establishment. His funeral in 1897 was a large public occasion and all businesses were closed during the afternoon of the day as a mark of respect.

To the Inhabitants, Magistrates, and Clergy of Buxt[o]
District.

Dear Sirs,

     The sad death of Dr. Robertson took pla[ce]
Thursday morning.

We feel sure that the Inhabitants of Buxton and Ne[ighbourhood]
will be desirous of expressing their sympathy with the [family of]
Dr. Robertson in their bereavement, and of the great [loss]
the Town has sustained in the removal by death of o[ne who]
devoted so much of his valued time, services, and goo[d counsel]
in connection with all that has been done for the Inte[rest of the]
Town.

We therefore desire that there shall be a Public [holiday on]
Monday next, and that all shops and places of busine[ss be closed]
from 2.0 to 4.30 on that day.

The Funeral will take place at Burbage, at 3.0. [We will]
meet in the Crescent at 2.30.

    E. C. MILLIGAN, J.P.,
        Chairman Urban District Counci[l]

    H. SHAW, J.P., D.L.

    H. A. HUBBERSTY, J.P.,
        On behalf of the Petty Sessional

BUXTON,
  16th July, 1897.

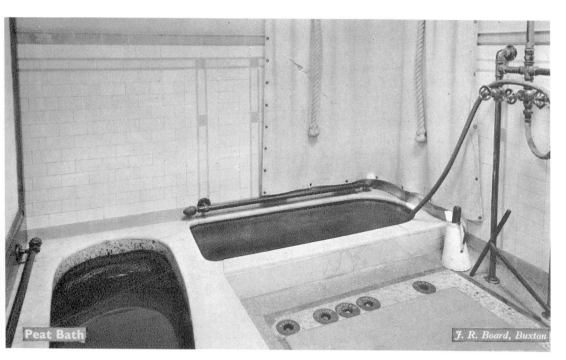

Peat Bath   *J. R. Board, Buxton*

The Peat or Moor Bath used peat from the hills surrounding the town. In the Natural Baths this treatment consisted of peat mixed with steamed thermal water in a wooden truck on rails under the bath building. The truck was then wheeled up a slope to lock under the bath side, as seen here, and the client stepped into what they thought was a fixed bath. The treatment remained popular as a tonic right up to the 1950s.

in electromedical apparatus and several private masseurs and masseuses.[86] By the end of the century hydrotherapy in health resorts was part of a wider movement of balneology and climatology. Some attempts were made to link water medicine with sanatoria in the treatment of phthisis (Tuberculosis – the largest single killer disease of the time) but not many sanatoria used water medicine in the treatment of this disease. The practice was more prevalent in Germany.[87]

The Society of Balneology and Climatology, founded in about 1895 with headquarters and library in Cavendish Square, was influential in drawing together and providing professional recognition to all the medical practitioners working in this 'specialist' field. Dr Hyde of Buxton was an early, if not founder member, a Vice-President and Chairman of Council. In 1905 the society had 400 Fellows and, in the same year, Buxton had nine Fellows all practising in the town, some associated with hydropathic establishments, others hon. medical officers to the Devonshire Hospital. Harrogate, in that year had sixteen Fellows as did Bath, Droitwich six, Leamington five, Malvern five, Ilkley three and Matlock one; the pattern was similar for 1906.[88] This suggests that the most successful health resorts were those which had a natural mineral water of some repute and which had developed traditional water treatments supported by a specialist hospital. Buxton was one such resort.

In May 1906 the president of the Balneological and Climatological Society, Frederick Roberts MD, gave an address entitled 'Some general comments on Balneology and associated methods: and on Spas' in which he presented a perfect summary of the wide range of treatments and therapies offered in this specialism:

... (1) Ordinary baths of different kinds and at varying temperatures

(2) Swimming baths either of fresh or sea water including ocean or sea bathing

Interior Views. Thermal Baths and Wells

The Buxton Guides often showed photographs of the corridors and treatment rooms in the Hot and Natural Baths. On the bottom right can be seen the interior of St Anne's Well after 1912 when the water was served for drinking from an oval marble well fed from the main spring.

128

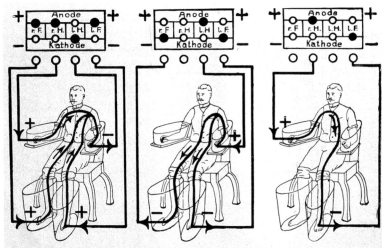

VARIOUS METHODS OF DIRECTING THE CURRENT IN THE FOUR-CELL BATH.

An electric-hydro treatment known as Dr Schnee's four-cell bath. The four baths contained water and the diagram shows the various methods of directing the current. It was used for general treatment or for local applications and claimed many advantages over the immersion bath.

(3) Affusion, douche, shower bath, needle bath etc. of general or local application using ordinary water at different temperatures

(4) The general wet pack or sheet; the blanket bath; wet sponging of the skin

(5) Local applications of cold, by means of the ice bag or wet appliances; impermeable wet compresses; heat and moisture by fomentations, poultices, spongiopiline etc.

(6) Vapour or steam bath or douche, general or local and either simple or impregnated with pine, balsams or various aromatics

(7) Air baths – general exposure to hot or cold air; the solarium or sun bath; local application of superheated air by Tallerman, Greville or Dowsing methods; composite air baths, the body generally or a limb or other region being fumigated with sulphurous anhydride from burning sulphur, or with mercurial vapours

(8) Complex baths, Russian, Turkish, light and ozone baths

(9) Natural thermal or mineral waters used as baths, douches or in other ways

(10) Artificially prepared mineral waters intended to imitate the composition of certain natural waters, and used in similar ways. Medicated baths containing special ingredients in solution

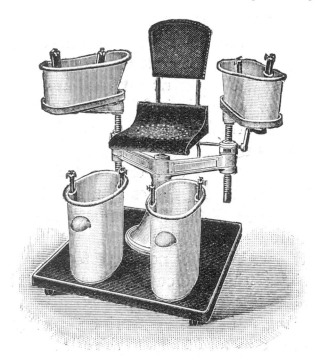

DR. SCHNEE'S FOUR-CELL BATH.

(11) Mud baths and the like. Pine peat, moor, Fango or Italian mud

(12) Baths to which particular materials are added – mustard, bran, gelatine, nutrient baths

(13) Applications of dry heat – sand bath; local application by means of hot bottles, bags containing heated salt or sand or other well-known methods

(14) Lubrication of the surface with oily materials; inunction through the skin

Continuing a line of public access to St Anne's Well, John Carr designed a new well in 1783 to meet the terms of the Enclosure Act (1773–74). Henry Currey's new pump of 1852 provided the thermal water on one side and a cold on the other. In 1895 a new pump issuing only thermal water was erected close to the new Pump Room and in 1940 this was replaced by the present St Anne's Well. John Carr's well is shown in chapter one, here can be seen the double pump of 1852, its single pump replacement of 1895 and the present St Anne's Well.
[R.Mc.L.S.]

PUBLIC PUMP, ST. ANN'S WELL

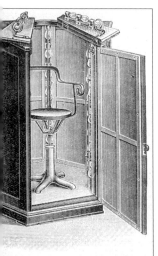

THE FULL ELECTRIC-LIGHT BATH.

The Electric Light Bath was a form of radiant heat treatment. The patient sat in this cabinet which had rows of light bulbs on its inner surfaces. In some cases a spray douche might also be applied. Variations of this bath were made to treat particular parts of the body, for example the spine or the legs and feet.

(15) Physical methods – ordinary friction after a bath; gymnastics or other special exercises; dry massage, general or regional; the Aix-le-Bains or Vichy Douche, massage douche or wet massage; vibratory massage or mechanical vibration; Arthromotor exercises for joints by means of special apparatus; Swedish exercises; Nauheim and other exercises for cardiac cases

(16) Applications of electricity – ordinary electrical treatment by Galvanisation, Faradisation, high frequency current, auto induction; electric massage; the use of electric light and radiant heat, general or local; electrical baths or douches; hydro-electrical baths

(17) Special treatment by Rontgen rays; coloured light (incandescent and arc baths)and other light-cure methods

(18) Respiratory methods, systematic deep respiration; treatment by compressed or rarefied air in pneumatic salons or chambers; inhalations of oxygen, pine oil etc. in inhalation chambers; the use of sprays of different mineral waters …

Any or all of these treatments may be aided by air, climate and diet, sunshine, exercise, time in a peaceful environment away from the urgency of business …[89]

Almost all of these treatments were on offer at Buxton. This plethora of treatments is a measure of how far Buxton had come from Sylvester's Hot Baths of 1817, but also an indication of how far the medical profession had to go in treating rheumatic disease of which there are upwards of two hundred different forms and which is, today, still clinically difficult to manage.

> … The large mass of clinical evidence, derived from the vast experience in gout, rheumatism, and arthritic diseases which the Devonshire Hospital supplies, furnishes conclusive evidence of the therapeutic value of the Buxton Mineral Waters …[90]

131

CHAPTER SIX

Agents of Change

T HE ROLE OF THE AGENT was both central and important in the management of landed estates.[1] This was no less true in Buxton. The work of the agent to the Devonshire Buxton Estate was pivotal in the pace of growth, the physical shape, and the provision of amenities in the town.

The ownership by the Duke of Devonshire of most of the land which formed nineteenth-century urban Buxton placed his agent in a powerful and influential position. Nothing moved without the approval of the agent.[2] This was certainly the case in the first half of the century, perhaps less so in the second half, but the estate office remained influential into the early twentieth century. Though not strictly landed, the agents at Buxton could be considered part of the gentry on the basis of their perceived position in the town, the influence of their office, and their public roles such as Commissioner of the Peace or administrator of the Poor Law.[3] The Agent was supported by a staff, some of whom became of importance in their own right, carrying a good deal of formal and sapiential authority as servants of the Duke of Devonshire.

The Buxton office grew in staff numbers as the town grew.[4] Phillip Heacock, agent from 1805, employed only a clerk and the part-time services of specialists such as a surveyor. By the time of George Drewry's death in 1896 the office staff numbered eight, only one of whom was part-time. The influence of the Agents has been described in earlier chapters in the context of Buxton's urban growth. In this chapter the character, style and competence of the agents and the staff of the agency office is examined in some detail to identify just how formative their impact was.

Between 1848 and 1905 there were five agents at Buxton. All were trained by experience as land agents, none was formally qualified, nor were any of them members of professional bodies such as the Land Agents Society or Institution of Surveyors.[5] They had followed the nineteenth-century pattern of learning from experience in different positions in estate management, acquiring both practical and theoretical knowledge. In some cases this was under the guidance of the agent on a large estate; in others, perhaps, it was closer to Caleb Garth's way

... my business is of many sorts my boy. A good deal of what I know can only come from experience: you can't learn it off as you learn things out of a book …[6]

It would, nevertheless, be reasonable to expect that, on an estate with substantial commercial potential, the particular skills and competence of successive agents would match the developing opportunities in the health resort. In other words, that commercial acumen in urban estate management, particularly that of an inland resort, might be sought in order to optimise the Duke's investments. This is not borne out in reality, however. George Drewry (agent 1864–96) was no less an agrarian agent than Phillip Heacock (agent 1805–51), probably more so, since he had a more extensive portfolio of rural estates in his control. Drewry's son, Frank, though employed in the Buxton office from 1877 did not concentrate on the urban development; he was as much concerned with the tenant farms in the Buxton Estate as the building and commercial lettings in the town of Buxton. The effect of the agent taking this breadth of focus was that significant authority for the built environment had to be delegated to key subordinates in the estate office, the sub-agents, surveyor, and architect. So, from an agency point of view, the development of urban Buxton took place within the management of the wider Buxton Estate portfolio which included extensive tenant farms, plantations, limestone quarrying and coal and lead mining, with turnpikes and railways earlier in the century. This is not to say, however, that agents did not seek to inform and update themselves on the exigencies of a developing inland resort, and later agents undoubtedly reaped the reward of good groundwork by their earlier colleagues in a time of rising urban land values through the nineteenth century.

Phillip Heacock (1778–1851) moved to Buxton from Etwall but continued for some time to handle the Devonshire estates at nearby Tutbury.[7] His portfolio included the Buxton, Hartington, Peak Forest and Edale collections and his annual salary, in 1805, was £560 rising to £640 in 1817 to £705 at the time of his death in 1851. He lived and worked in a new town house in the Square (built 1803–6) in the manner of a gentleman, driving out in a barouche drawn by two fat brown horses and driven by a postillion.[8] He wielded great power and his style, befitting the time, was autocratic. He took a firm hold on the property rentals from the time of his appointment and thereafter organised the Buxton Estate in a professional manner.[9] Heacock's range of work did not, perhaps, rival that of some earlier 'professional' agents such as John and Thomas Gilbert on the Bridgewater Estate, but he could count himself among the new breed of professional land agents which developed in the eighteenth century.[10] His salary may be compared with that of Francis Blaikie, the agent for the First Earl of Leicester at Holkham in Norfolk who earned £650 in

1822.[11] Francis Blaikie was a recognised professional land agent who had worked his way up in the business and was able to put Thomas Coke of Norfolk's affairs on a regular and systematic footing.[12] Phillip Heacock did similarly at Buxton. In addition to the improvements obtained in the spa of Buxton described in chapter one, Heacock managed turnpike and railway investments, coal and lead mining and lime production in the surrounding area as well as extensive tenant farms.[13] His knowledge of the tenantry is reflected in the different manner in which he treated different tenants:

> ... Buxton 9 August 1824 to Geo. Wood
>
> Mr Heacock begs his compliments to Mr Geo. Wood and will feel particularly obliged if he will favour him with his half years rent to Mich's. last on the 31st inst ...
>
> ... Buxton 9 August 1824 to Mr Wm. Keelins
>
> I will thank you to oblige me the balance of your half years rent to Mich's last namely £46.10.0. on 31st of this month ...
>
> ... Buxton 9 August 1824 to Mr Edw. Jackson
>
> If the rent due from you to the Duke of Devonshire to Michs. last (namely £57.10.0) should not be paid on or before the 10th of next month I shall be under the very unpleasant necessity of enforcing the payment thereof ...
>
> ... Buxton 9 August 1824 to Rich'd Lomas
>
> If you wish to retain your tenement under the Duke of Devonshire you will not fail to pay your half yearly rent into my hands on 31st of this month ...[14]

Heacock, in common with many agents of his time, acted as a substitute for the owner.[15] He was the ducal equivalent of a Lord Lieutenant, acting for a Duke who made only occasional 'state' visits to Buxton, and representing the Cavendish family on all public occasions. This included activity in the political arena, regular entries in his accounts show canvas expenses for Lord Cavendish and the Hon. George Cavendish who stood in the Northern Division of Derbyshire, and for travel to other constituencies in support of the Duke's interest. Politically Heacock hedged his bets, voting for G. H. Cavendish but also for his Conservative opponent in the two seat constituency.[16] He travelled at least annually to London on estate business, in the early

A pistol used by Philip Heacock, no doubt carried by him as he rode out to inspect farms and other Devonshire Buxton Estate property. [B.M.A.G.]

years to see the chief agent John Heaton who served the Fifth Duke, but from the accession of the Sixth, Heaton's replacement, the 'dour' Scot, James Abercromby.[17] From 1827 Benjamin Currey became solicitor and financial adviser to the Sixth Duke.

In forty-six years as agent, through the agricultural depression following the French wars, through Chartism and despite the Sixth Duke of Devonshire's profligacy and precarious financial position, Phillip Heacock whose

... urbane manners made him a great favourite in Buxton ...[18]

laid a solid foundation for the growth of the inland resort. As the *Buxton Herald* put it:

... He applied himself so assiduously to every scheme calculated to add to its prosperity ...[19]

Memorial to Phillip Heacock in St John's Churchyard. It was designed by Camden Society architect Alexander Beresford-Hope (1820–87) and erected in 1851 by the stonemason John Mowbray under the supervision of Robert R. Duke.

Robert R. Duke's papers contain this account from John Mowbray, stonemason, for work on the Heacock memorial. Addressed to Mr Duke, Mowbray asks for ten pounds on account for carved work at Mr Heacock's monument.

and a measure of the esteem with which he was held may be gauged from his impressive memorial in St John's Churchyard, designed by the amateur architect, Alexander Beresford-Hope.[20] The Devonshire estate was entirely unprepared for his death, despite the fact that he had been complaining of difficulty in breathing for some months. He died on 9 February 1851 from heart disease after being confined at home for three weeks.[21] His son, to whom he was devoted, died from consumption two weeks later.[22]

In the mid century, despite a growing professionalism, land agents were still drawn from the provincial middle class as respectable, practical men.[23] It was not surprising that at least one such candidate should apply for the vacancy. Simon Ivery, the farm manager son of Sir H. Ivery Bt. of Quarndon near Derby, wrote a speculative letter on 17 February 1851.[24] He was not successful, however, for the estate played safe and appointed an existing agent, Sydney Smithers, to the Buxton Agency. Sydney Smithers (1795–1856) was a career agent with the Devonshire estate; in 1828 he held the agency at Staveley and from 1836 to 1848 managed the Chatsworth estate.[25] In 1851, when he took on the Buxton Estate, his portfolio was already extensive, based on Ashford but covering estates as far east as Dore, north to Edale and west, through Hartington, to parts of Staffordshire.[26] His yearly salary of £1,025 reflected this wide responsibility. He brought with him a clerk, James Wardley, who was paid £70 p.a. and he employed a surveyor, William Smith at £100 *per annum*. Smithers' impact on urban Buxton has been described in chapter two. His legacy was the effective way

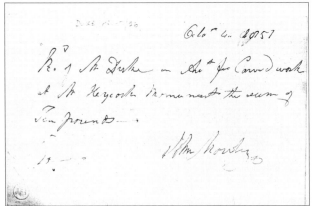

in which he brought to fruition the major developments in baths, amenities and urban layout, begun by his predecessor. He set up an office in the Crescent and was considered to stand aloof from the affairs of the town but this is, perhaps, not surprising given his extensive estate responsibilities. Smithers was essentially a land agent. His knowledge and skills were those of practical and scientific farming, law and accounts as set out by Caird in 1850–51 or MacDonald in 1865, though he was referred to as the 'accountant' in the Devonshire Buxton accounts.[27] However, Smithers, as already noted, did take steps to acquaint himself with the development of inland resorts through visits and reading. He was a driving force behind the provision of charity hospital facilities in the town and helped to raise money for this purpose, though he did not live to see the Devonshire Hospital provision of 1858. Sydney Smithers died in July 1856 at the age of sixty-one after a painful illness. The Devonshire estate had maintained tradition and played safe in appointing, in him, a solid land agent. Would his successor's experience and training reflect the emerging needs of a growing inland resort, a centre of water medicine? [28]

At first sight Edward Woollett Wilmot (1809–64) was out of a similar 'land agent' mould to his two predecessors. The sixth son of Sir Robert Wilmot, Third Baronet of Chaddesden, Edward Woollett Wilmot had worked as agent on the Fourth Duke of Newcastle's estates at Worksop. He moved to manage the extensive estates of Edward Davies Davenport of Capesthorne Hall and lived at Hulme Walfield near Congleton.[29] He was described as enjoying an extensive and lucrative practice as a land agent and being well known as a skilful and enterprising agriculturalist.[30] He clearly had a career grounded in agrarian estate management. How would he match up to the needs of urban Buxton? In fact E. W. Wilmot proved to be exactly the right choice. His business training showed immediately upon appointment and his ready grasp of urban estate management was impressive. But above all his understanding of people, of the lifestyle and motivation of the town, of how to get things done in this insular community high in the Derbyshire hills, was by far his greatest asset. His may be described as the keystone agency of the five. A number of factors contributed to this. First Wilmot was clearly gentry, his family connections were impeccable.[31] Secondly, his manner was urbane but he demonstrated powerful leadership skills and his belief in 'self-help', a philosophy akin to that of Samuel Smiles, closely matched the needs of the Seventh Duke who succeeded two years into Wilmot's agency.[32] Thirdly, though no longer working for that estate, he would undoubtedly have followed the setting out of the Nottingham Park, an important urban development by the Fifth Duke of Newcastle from 1854.[33] Finally, the range of estate management, previously undertaken by Smithers, was reduced from ten estates

⁊

An example of one of the many initiatives of agent E. W. Wilmot, this handbill refers to the formation of a Rifle Corps. Wilmot has drawn together a formidable committee of townsmen to promote the cause.

to six which enabled Wilmot, a hard-working man, to spend more time on Buxton.[34]

Wilmot's achievements in the context of Buxton's urban growth are set out in chapter two. His thorough attention to detail may be seen in his introduction of a ledger to record all visits to the estate office and business transacted, a sort of day-book. The earliest entries were in his own hand and the ledger provides evidence of estate business and how it was transacted.[35] E. W. Wilmot, in common with agents of other large estates, showed particular concern for the living conditions of the tenants, in part as guardian of parochial morality but also for the more hard-nosed reason of safeguarding estate property.[36] In 1857 he made a complete inventory of the properties in the township of Buxton including nearby hamlets Kingsterndale, Cowdale and Staden. This was comprehensive and included comments on the moral standing and probity of the tenants as these examples show …

… George Buxton 9 acres of land £23 p.a. [comment] land lies well and cheap, lives in the weighing machine house, a widower five young children, rather slovenly and drunken, family sadly neglected, stable turned into a dwelling house in 1858 …

… Buxton School trustees, house, yard, school & playground, rent 1/-. [comment] … School in Higher Buxton, bad situation, rooms small and inconvenient. School land should be sold and new schools built …

… Mary Glaizbrook, house in the Square, rent £40. [comment] House in very dirty condition, drainage very bad, tenant slovenly and ill tempered …

… but shrewd business observations were also recorded …

… William Dennis Sutton, the new billiard room, rent £25. [comment] situated near the Hot Baths, some shops might be made in the corridor …[37]

His involvement in the affairs of the town was wholehearted but purposeful, he sought to bring about unity of purpose amongst the townspeople. In addition to his annual oyster suppers, designed to stimulate proactive ideas for the development of the resort, he and Mrs Wilmot held an annual New Year's Ball in the Assembly Room for about two hundred of the professional people, hoteliers, lodging house keepers and tradesmen in the town. He gave dinners and suppers to the estate workers, lime workers, coal miners and navvies, also childrens' parties at Christmas. He held positions in many public bodies and societies, a number of which he had initiated, including: President of the Agricultural and Horticultural clubs and the Burbage Building Society, Chairman of the Rifle Corps, Market Hall and Gas Companies, Church warden of St John's and Burbage Church, and he was, of course, the first chairman of the Buxton Local Board. He lived at 'Wyelands' in Burbage in some style, employing a cook, three maids, a nurse, gardener and groom.[38] He was an important benefactor to the village of Burbage and his work included obtaining a new church, built in 1861 and designed by the architect Henry Currey.[39] The marriage, in 1861, of his eldest son to the daughter of Dr W. H. Robertson, Buxton's foremost water specialist, further strengthened the agent's bond with Buxton. During his eight-year term of office E. W. Wilmot reinforced the staffing of the estate office. His thorough review of the estate's assets in the early part of his time is reflected in the use of a number of part-time surveyors in addition to William Smith, the resident surveyor. By 1864, the year of his death, the staff at the estate office were: James Wardley, Clerk £151 p.a., Samuel Turner, Sub-Agent, £130 and Robert R. Duke, surveyor and Architect, part-time £78, Wilmot himself received an annual salary of £1,125 throughout his tenure.[40] These three staff became a formidable and highly professional team. Definitive in the urban development, they provided an important degree of continuity in the management of the estate.

E. W. Wilmot died of inflammation of the liver at the early age of fifty-five. He had been ill for more than two months and died in Harrogate which he had visited for a change of air and recuperation. Wilmot's prominence was reflected in his eulogies and the reputed 2,000 mourners at his funeral in Burbage. Monuments to his life are to be found in Christ Church Burbage and St John's Buxton.[41] His sudden death was a serious blow for the Duke of Devonshire. The man who had most clearly understood the needs of the growing resort, who had shaped the introduction of local democracy, who had begun the physical layout of Buxton the town, was gone. A replacement out of a similar mould was needed, Wlmot's son Robert (who had applied) or someone like George Ambrose Wallace, agent at the Devonshire estate at Eastbourne perhaps.[42]

The man selected was, however, again primarily an agrarian land agent, though he had probably acquired some experience in urban development. George Drewry (1816–96) was already managing the Devonshire estates at Holker in Cumberland and Keighley in Yorkshire when he was appointed to the Buxton agency. He was a Cumbrian, the son of George Drewry of Weary Hall, Wigton, and a land agent in the traditional mould. Educated in Cumberland, he joined the Duke of Bedford's estate office at Tavistock in 1838 under the agent J. Benson and began training in land management, learning by experience and guidance, on a large estate. Some of the great estate offices became training grounds for young men employed initially as clerks or juniors in a manner similar to the solicitor's articled clerk.[43] Drewry was fortunate to work in the Tavistock estate; not only was he working for an important and progressive landowner, but the estate included the town of Tavistock itself and may have offered some urban management experience.[44] After two years he moved to become agent for Sir Anthony Buller's estate at Pound near Plymouth, supervising the home farm for five years before taking the Holker agency in October 1845.[45] He was appointed to the Keighley estate in 1846 and agent for the Lancashire property of Lord Chesham in 1865.[46]

So, essentially, George Drewry was a land man. He was described as a 'noteworthy agriculturalist' supervising an enormous acreage and agricultural capital. But his responsibilities also included towns, villages and hamlets in the four substantial estates. He was noted for his agricultural advances, the wide use of steam power, for example, and for his sound knowledge of land management. He won a national reputation for breeding pedigree shorthorn cattle, winning many prizes for the Duke and earning substantial sums from sales. He was a long-time member of the Royal Agricultural Society, frequently judging at shows including the Royal Show held at Windsor in Jubilee year.[47] He resided at Holker Hall and became a close personal friend and confidential adviser to the Seventh Duke of Devonshire and one in whom the Cavendish family could put implicit trust and confidence.[48] The Seventh Duke shared this interest in shorthorn cattle visiting Holker, his favourite country house, to inspect the herd as a diversion from his many business dealings at

George Drewry (1816–96), agent to the Buxton Estate from 1864 to 1896. During his agency at Buxton he managed three other estates and operated as an absentee agent as far as Buxton was concerned. He resided at Holker but spent much time travelling between est ates.

Barrow and elsewhere.[49] George Drewry was obviously very hard working. His vast portfolio meant that he needed to travel a good deal and work long days. In this he was not unlike the Chelmsford Parkers, a father and son firm of commercial land agents who took commissions to transact estate business for various owners and travelled extensively in Essex. The range of work detailed in their diaries between 1826 and 1875 offers a picture of the busy land agent.[50] Such a man was Drewry who took over the role, described from his predecessor's time as 'receiver' at Buxton at a crucial point in the town's development. A man of stature and obvious sound judgment but with little experience in the commercial vagaries of a popular resort. Furthermore, he was an absentee agent, appearing in town generally only for several days twice each year at rent audits in the spring and autumn. The *Buxton Advertiser*, in its typically direct fashion, observed:

> ... [He] lived at Holker and paid but occasional visits to Buxton. He was disadvantaged in knowing the needs of an improved building estate and of Buxton in the front rank of watering places. His methods did not always commend themselves to the townspeople but his decisions were honest and of genuine regard to the trust imposed on him as agent ...[51]

He was not present at some of the more conspicuous occasions such as the foundation stone laying at the large concert hall in the Pavilion Gardens or the opening of the new Charity Baths. How, then, was the town managed in a period which saw the scale of growth outlined in chapter three, extensive land sales, assiduous building and an emerging local democracy? The answer lies in the Buxton Estate office and a team of three who became very influential in the town – James Wardley, Samuel Turner and Robert R. Duke.

James Wardley (1829–91) came to Buxton in 1851 as Sydney Smithers' clerk and remained at the office for thirty-eight years, retiring on a pension in 1889. He became the chief clerk, a man indispensable to Drewry in handling all the administration of the busy office.[52] He lived in Spring Gardens, moving to a newly built estate house, 'The Knoll', Devonshire Park in 1876.[53] He was a careful man, straight in his dealings and making few enemies. He was responsible for the immaculately prepared accounts ledgers and office records which survive now in the muniments room at Chatsworth. While his colleagues were out and about negotiating rentals, dealing in land sales and so on, he was the lynch pin at the estate office in George Street.

Samuel Turner (180–76) was one of the most respected men in Buxton.[54] He was born in Buxton and spent much of his early career running his own building and joinery business. His association with the Devonshire Estate began in the time of Phillip Heacock when he took up a part-time appointment as building adviser. In his partnerships with James Turner and with Robert R. Duke he carried out much building work on estate farms and properties. He bought land in the new Quadrant in 1853, living in Grove Cottage

🏃

Samuel Turner (1803–76), sub-agent to the Buxton Estate, 1857–76. He was, in his time, one of the most respected men in Buxton and became involved in a wide range of activities in the church, the Devonshire Buxton Estate, in politics, in the Buxton Bath Charity and in commercial developments such as the Buxton Improvements Co.

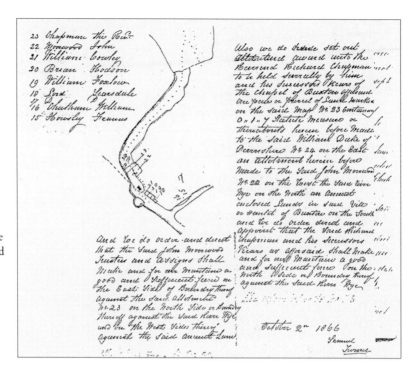

Samuel Turner was an effective sub-agent who could built good working relationships with tenants of the estate. His notebook shows his grasp of land law, finance, cartography and draughtsmanship required in the position. [D.C. Chat.]

there, subsequently moving to a new property in Sylvan Park. Turner was recruited into the Buxton office, by E. W. Wilmot, as a full-time sub-agent in 1857. His work was not confined to Buxton; he was concerned with the management of estates at Hartington, Peak Forest, Tideswell and Wetton, but all were within the Buxton Collection. Samuel Turner was greatly experienced in estate business and took a fair and even-handed approach to negotiations. He was a good-natured and cordial man who could respond to personal banter with wit and a twinkle in his eye and was well respected by tenants.[55] His notebook shows a detailed grasp of the law, finance, cartography and draughts-manship required in the work.[56] So influential was Turner that, when he died suddenly in October 1876, a replacement of some considerable ability was needed.

Samuel Turner's death was both sudden and tragic. He had been out to visit a farm some ten to twelve miles from Buxton in a horse trap and got very wet, neglecting to put on the mackintosh he had with him. He was taken seriously ill with pneumonia and his son, Frederick, a doctor, was unable to save him.[57] As a townsman, Samuel Turner was extremely public spirited, serving as churchwarden, over-seer of the poor, returning officer, elected member of the Local Board, Treasurer to the Devonshire Hospital and Buxton Bath Charity, Director and shareholder of the Palace Hotel and the Buxton Improve-ments Companies. His standing in the town is well demonstrated by two memorials. On the north wall of St John's Church is a marble memorial similar to those of the agents Smithers and Wilmot and 'Turner's Memorial' an impressive drinking fountain designed by Robert Rippon Duke, standing outside the Hot Baths, is a fine statement of his worth.

The third member of the trio, Robert Rippon Duke (1817–1909), was a truly remarkable man, a man so well qualified and so well suited to manage the estate's interests in the absence of a resident agent that it is difficult to conjecture what shape the town might have been without him.[58] R. R. Duke came to Buxton from Hull in 1849 to supervise the building of the Royal Hotel under the Sheffield architect, Samuel Worth. He subsequently formed the partnership of Turner and Duke, builders, with Samuel Turner, continuing the business himself, after Turner had joined the estate office. In 1863 he replaced the surveyor James Scott at the estate office as part-time surveyor on an initial salary of £78 *per annum*. R. R. Duke was a time-served joiner and self-taught draughtsman who worked his way up through supervisor, clerk of works and builder to surveyor and, ultimately, architect. He combined his position at the Buxton Estate with a developing private practice as architect and surveyor and was responsible for the design of many houses and public buildings, notably the Large Concert Hall of 1876 and the Devonshire Hospital extensions of 1879–82. He was, like Arthur Davies on the Calthorpe Edgbaston Estate and George Ambrose Wallis

at Devonshire's Eastbourne, responsible for the layout, style and building standards of all new building, and he personally vetted all plans.[59] He exerted a significant influence on the actual shape of the town, proposing to Drewry where roads and building plots should be laid out. He was required to seek policy decisions from the agent but, in the matter of enforcement of covenants, he wielded considerable power:

> … Buxton 18th July 1893 to Mr Alfred Mycock 41 Temple View Higher Buxton.
>
> Dear Sir, Your plans are approved subject to the gable end next to Mr Webster's being faced with rippings. I understand that it is being built with rubble only, if that be so be good enough not to proceed further with that gable as it will have to be taken down. I have not

The memorial to Samuel Turner which stands in front of the Hot Baths was designed by his friend Robert Rippon Duke, who raised £224 from 354 people in town to pay for it. The memorial was unveiled on 1 January 1879 by Dr W. H. Robertson with Turner's son Frederick in attendance. The memorial was rebuilt in 1994.

🦡

seen how you are building the front elevation but hope you are careful to see that it is as shown on the amended elevation drawing which was approved, otherwise I must have it set right. Yours truly Robert R Duke ...[60]

... Buxton 30th July 1886 to Mr Booth Millward Spring Gardens

Dear Sir, I enclose your plans for completion and send herewith a plan of your land showing the building lines from which please have a block plan made on which should be shown the fences, drains etc. That part coloured green is not to be built upon so that all the buildings must be upon that part coloured pink.

As I explained to Mr Millward the back road is to be 24 feet wide half the width to be on your land. The fences to the back and the two sides to be of rubble stone built in mortar with three courses of rippings or two courses of wallstone at the top and covered with half-round ashlar coping the whole to be 4½ ft out of the ground when finished. Yours Truly, Robert R. Duke ...[61]

It was necessary for R. R. Duke to correspond regularly with George Drewry at Holker. An analysis of one of the letterbooks shows that of the 450 letters written by him between August 1866 and June 1871 almost two hundred were to George Drewry.[62] Often letters would cover more than one subject and points of business would be saved to await the next visit of Drewry to Buxton.[63] Visits would then be an extremely busy time for the office ...

... Buxton 10 Oct 1866 to Mr Moore

Dear Sir, I enclose bankers draft ... Mr Drewry is here but is very much engaged today, Mr Wardley will ask for a cheque the very first opportunity. [yours truly Robert R. Duke] ...[64]

Inevitably delays would occur where the surveyor was waiting for replies from the agent. This could potentially affect the efficient management of the estate:

... 27 March 1865 to Mr Moore

Dear Sir, Sale to Thos Gregory

It is the same Thos Gregory, a butcher, and the same piece of land that has been waiting so long until several little matters tho' important could be accomplished. The terms are the same as before viz. to build 3 houses at a cost of £150 each to fence the land on all sides except the east which is already fenced by the Duke. There are no restrictions to prevent the Duke building on the land at the back. [yours truly Robert R. Duke] ...[65]

... 31 Spring Gardens 24 Jany 1868 to Dr Dickson Wye House

Dear Sir, In reference to the land in Devonshire Park, I cannot stake

Robert Rippon Duke at the age of about 55. He was surveyor and architect to the Buxton Estate from 1863 to 1908 but he also ran a very successful architectural practice in town and designed notable buildings including the Burlington Hotel (1874), the Large Concert Hall (1875) and the Devonshire Hospital conversions (1879–82). He was a prime mover in the town.

it out until I have Mr Drewry's instructions to do so – I clearly
understood from the conversation that passed between yourself and
Mr Drewry that it was left for Mr Drewry's further consideration.
I am Dear Sir, Yours truly, Robt R Duke ...[66]

It is apparent, however, that R. R. Duke would use delays to his
own advantage where it suited and that he would also stretch the
limits of his responsibility where he felt this was expedient for both
the estate and himself.[67] On the question of policy George Drewry
was very firm but prepared to take professional advice from his
surveyor:

... Buxton 28 Jany 1868 to Geo Drewry [at Holker]

Dear Sir, At present Mr Taylor and Mr Wellings have taken no
further steps.

Plot no. 34 in Devonshire Park is intended for two houses. Will you
sell it on Chief rent with the option of purchasing in, say, seven years,
and of building one or two houses as the purchaser may decide. If
one house is built it should cost from £700 to £800 if two say £1200.
I am sir Yours truly Robt R Duke ...

This is a good example of two facets of their relationship; the
surveyor needs Drewry's decision but offers firm professional advice
concerning it; there is clearly an understanding based on mutual
respect. The correspondence reveals other aspects of Drewry's direction
from a distance. In 1877 there was a marked increase of land sales
through Chief Rent. R. R. Duke wrote to Drewry:

... 7th February 1877 to Geo Drewry Holker

I have had interviews today with Messrs Clayton, Allen and Turner
and have arranged the decision of the land behind Buxton House to
their satisfaction. Mr Allen wanted the piece behind Clayton's property
to be made freehold but I told him that you had decided to sell all
land on Chief without exception ...[68]

In this way George Drewry, the absentee agent, managed the urban
growth of Buxton, inevitably delegating extensively and leaving his
Buxton Estate office team of professionals with considerable authority
to implement his policies on behalf of the Duke. The absence of the
agent meant that others had to take the lead in promoting the town;
the oyster suppers of Wilmot were no more. In the mid-1870s attempts
were made to engage interest in advertising the inland resort to keep
it ahead of its rival Harrogate. Robert R. Duke, always public-spirited,
chaired a meeting at the Shakespeare Hotel in 1877 at which an
attempt was made to raise an advertising fund.[69] Progress was slow,
however, and it took some time for the town fully to embrace the
need for self-promotion.

ᎧᏋ

Frank Drewry (b. 1853).
He came to Buxton at the age
of twenty-four to become
sub-agent to the Buxton Estate,
a position he held from 1877 to
1896. At the death of his father
in 1896, Frank was promoted
to the agency. He retired in
1919. [B.M.A.G.]

The nature of this arrangement and the key part played by each of the three professionals meant that a replacement had to be found rapidly when Samuel Turner died. The choice of George Drewry's son Francis, who joined the estate office in January 1877, was not on the surface ideal, but it was safe. Frank Drewry (1853 – retired 1919) was only twenty-four and still learning by experience which meant that a greater load was inevitably placed on Wardley and R. R. Duke. However, now George had a member of his family in a key position at Buxton. Frank Drewry came in January 1877 and moved straight into the role of sub-agent on a salary of £220 *per annum*. At the same time a full-time surveyor, J. D. Simpson, joined the office from the Buxton Local Board where he had been surveyor for fourteen years.[70] In this way the estate office was strengthened with local authority expertise at a time when there was increasing negotiation of land and building arrangements with the Local Board.[71] George Drewry now had a strong team at Buxton and his workload was eased to a marked degree. Early correspondence shows that Frank Drewry took responsibility over the whole of the estate business leaving R. R. Duke to handle land sales and new building at Buxton.[72] R. R. Duke's correspondence with George Drewry reduced markedly, in 300 letters sent between 1877 and 1883 fewer than 100 were to George Drewry, but ninety were to Frank Drewry.[73] Though needing to seek decisions from his father, business was speeded up by Frank Drewry's use of the new communication medium, the telegraph.[74]

Frank Drewry initially took lodgings with John Rodgers at the 'Laurels', Marlborough Road, but shortly after his marriage in January 1881 he moved to an estate house known as 'Court Heath' on the southern edge of the town. In 1891 he was employing a cook/servant, a nurse and a servant to look after his wife and family of two daughters and a son.[75] He progressively took control of the Buxton Estate transacting the full range of business, farm tenancy and repairs, estate maintenance, leases and lettings and he became increasingly conversant with the management of the urban estate. He was referred to as the 'Resident Agent' as early as 1881 but this title was not used in the accounts for another ten years.[76] By 1890 he had a good knowledge of the affairs of the town as well as the wider estate. His style of approach and grasp of detail is illustrated in the following exchange:

... 13 July 1894.

A deputation appointed to see Mr Drewry re getting better access from Market Place to Hardwick Square South. Deputation consisted of G. F. Barnard; R. Hulme; E. C. Milligan; F. Rowland; J. W. Willoughby; W. Woodruffe. Drewry said that no promise had been made since he came in 1877 and he was not aware of any arrangement made previously with the purchasers of land in Hardwick Square

South. The cottages which belonged to the Duke in Concert Place had been pulled down and the new property built to an improved building line as far as they could control it ...[77]

The size and importance of members of the delegation indicate the degree of influence exerted by the estate on planning matters; these are all members of the Local Board. Frank Drewry's command of the affairs over twenty years meant that by the time of his father's death in 1896 he was the obvious successor. (This was, perhaps, the only piece of succession planning seen at the Devonshire Buxton Estate.) Robert R. Duke, by this time the architect to the estate, was bereft at hearing of George Drewry's death. He wrote to Frank who was at Holker:

... Buxton 14th April 1896

My regret and sorrow on hearing of the sad and sudden termination of your dear father's illness is more than I can describe, and was, when told of it yesterday, rather suddenly, a sense of shock to me. Being the only one left of the three connected with the Buxton Estate when your father succeeded to the Agency over 30 years ago, I do feel the severance most keenly, and all the more so as during the long time that I have endeavoured to do my duty in my position under your father, I do not remember an unkind word from him. Kindly express my sincere sympathy with the family.

Yours very truly, Robert R. Duke ...[78]

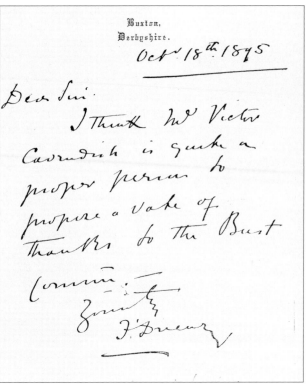

R. R. Duke, not an obsequious man but one who knew his place, described George Drewry as the best and most businesslike agent, having a straightforward and honourable way of dealing with difficult subjects and individuals, even-handed and decisive.

Frank Drewry's accession to the agency was well received in the town. It was recognised that, in twenty years, he had become closely associated with all aspects of the estate and its tenants. He had lived long enough in the town to be a part of its progress and growth, and, as the local paper said:

... he is in a unique position to keep that [progress] going. He has control of the baths, which are Buxton's pride, and building land

Typical of the correspondence between Frank Drewry and R. R. Duke, this letter refers to the unveiling of a bust of the Seventh Duke of Devonshire which was placed in the new Pump Room. The bust was by sculptor William Day Keyworth Jnr (1843–1902) of Hull and was unveiled Dr W. H. Robertson. Drewry suggests that Mr Victor Cavendish (later the Ninth Duke of Devonshire) should give the vote of thanks.

which is Buxton's hope for the future, and of the many beauty spots, the lungs of Buxton …[79]

and added that he would need to work closely with the Buxton UDC in the mutual interests of the town and the Duke. Frank Drewry was able to do this. In his forty-two-year career with the Buxton Estate he was the loyal guardian of the Duke's interests in the development of the inland resort to its height in 1905 and beyond.[80] He experienced the changes being brought about in aristocratic land ownership from the end of the century. Agricultural depression was undermining confidence, rentals and values. Wealth and income through land holdings was giving way to new forms of investment which carried fewer management burdens. At the same time urban land values were rising. The policies of the Eighth and Ninth Dukes were, broadly, reflecting these changes and the estate which Frank Drewry left on retirement in 1919 was far removed from the optimism of its height in 1905.[81] The *Buxton Guide* in 1925 carried a full-page advertisement for building sites on the Devonshire Buxton Estates; it is inconceivable that such a thing would have been necessary twenty years before.[82]

The agent was always a key figure in the growth of urban Buxton. But some agents were, clearly, more focused in their policies and interventions than others. The expectation that successive agents would be carefully selected to further the commercial potential of the inland resort is not borne out by this research. Undoubtedly the commitment and sheer energy of key support figures in the estate office was an indispensable constituent of urban growth. Many of these support staff were long serving. Samuel Turner was associated with the estate for more than twenty-five years before his untimely death. James Wardley served forty-eight years and Robert R. Duke for more than forty years, ostensibly retiring in 1901 aged eighty-four, but still receiving a salary in 1908. In 1897 he prepared for Frank Drewry a description of the duties of architect to the Buxton Estate, an indication of the increasing formalisation of estates management.[83] The cost of the agency at Buxton was not above 5% of estate turnover throughout the period of nineteenth-century growth; this would compare favourably with costs on other well managed estates.[84]

F. M. L. Thompson has observed that it would be wrong to conclude that landowners confined themselves purely to the proper expenditure of their incomes, leaving the procuring of the money entirely in the hands of their agents. Equally it would be misleading to suppose that the main decisions on the development and running of estates were taken by the landowner leaving the agent simply to execute orders.[85] The study of urban Buxton shows, in microcosm, the complex interaction of relationships, power and authority at work in the estate office to optimise income for the owner but also to determine the most effective reinvestment. Thompson goes on to say that it is hard to disentangle the parts which owner and agent might play in, say, the development of a town. This is only partly true of Buxton. As this chapter – indeed book – shows, the agent was a very powerful initiator, a generator of ideas, a persuasive force looking to develop the estates for which he was responsible. When the Duke of Devonshire visited Buxton it was usually either to inspect some new investment or discuss an idea for development. Almost invariably those new initiatives were not his but those of his agent. Furthermore, in Buxton it is more than probable that those new initiatives originated with a sub-agent or surveyor, the support staff in the estate office. This was more particularly the case during George Drewry's absentee agency. The influence of such support can easily be underestimated for they were not there simply to execute orders. The role of key support staff in estate management, more generally, is worthy of further detailed study.

The five agents and their staff at the estate office in Buxton lived and worked through a time of great investment by landed aristocracy; investment, not only in crops and cattle, but in iron and steel, coal, minerals transport and communications and extensive urban development.[86] The decisions of these landowners had a material effect upon thousands of families dependent for work, home and livelihood. In Derbyshire in 1872/73 six peers and twenty-one great landowners between them owned just under half the 630,000 acres. Ownership of the other half was shared between almost 20,000 others. A version of Bateman's record of great landowners would look very different today from his publication of 1876.[87] The five agents and agency staff at Buxton were central to these decisions of policy. They were not simply carrying out decisions; they were often formulating ideas and policy which had profound implications for the fortune of the town, its growth and physical shape as an inland resort. Furthermore, whilst the earlier agents, directing affairs on the spot, can be likened to their counterparts on other estates, there was a period of twelve years, during George Drewry's agency, when the absence of the agent placed great influence in the hands of the sub-agency team. The Dukes of Devonshire were not only fortunate in having competent and loyal agents; they also had in Buxton a strong and equally loyal supporting staff.

> ... as Agent to the Estate at Buxton Mr George Drewry was the best and most businesslike. I always admired his straightforward and honourable way of dealing with difficult subjects and individuals ...[88]

> ... I hold it the most honourable work that is ...[89]

CHAPTER SEVEN

Religious Belief – the Mortar Between the Stone

GREAT CHANGES in religious life and worship were to be seen in Buxton in the sixty years from 1848. These reflected the changes in England, with all branches of the Christian Church seeking to find new ways of maintaining a spiritual foundation in the life of the people, but also included initiatives unique to the needs of the inland resort.[1] This was a period of expansion in religious sects, denominations and churches bringing a significant increase in religious building.[2] Between 1840 and 1876 the Anglican Church built 1,727 new churches in England and Wales and restored or rebuilt 7,144 at a total cost of £25 million.[3] Membership of the main Nonconformist bodies grew at a rate greater than the population up to the 1840s and at about the same rate as the population up to 1880.[4] In Buxton these changes had an impact on the social fabric of the town and on its topography; no fewer than eleven new places of worship, representing eight different denominations, were built and considerable church extension took place.

Religious belief was at the heart of everyday life in Buxton as elswhere. As McLeod succinctly puts it:

> ... For Roman Catholics, every Sunday was a 'feast of obligation' and those who failed to attend mass were in mortal sin; for High Anglicans weekly communion was de rigueur; for Evangelical Protestants, church attendance, preferably twice, was part of the proper observance of the Lord's Day; Liberal Protestants, though they had no rules of this sort, would still have felt pretty uncomfortable if they did not attend some sort of service; and for respectable people generally church-going was simply among the 'recognised proprieties' of life ...[5]

Membership of the church or chapel reinforced the notion of 'respectability' amongst working- and lower middle-class people and was a means of social mobility in a society concerned with self-improvement and self-help.[6] The 'respectable grocer' went to church because this was a natural part of his everyday life.[7] The middle classes went to church or chapel and accepted the doctrines preached, though in many cases their belief was pragmatic and for many untested, in that no conversion had been experienced. It was, however, a socially required Sunday activity at the least, and one in which the sermon was often at once a prime source of intellectual stimulus and a reinforcement of the particular beliefs and moral standing of the church or chapel goer.[8]

Not all working-class people practised religion, Beatrice Webb may have been impressed with the 'depth and realism' of religious faith amongst East Lancashire mill-hands, but the typical northern working man was likely to be vaguely Nonconformist or vaguely Anglican and apathetic towards Sunday worship.[9] This was despite the growth of such movements as Primitive Methodists earlier in the century or the later Salvation Army, which more strongly appealed to the working-class family.[10] Some working men thought religion to be unpractical, bearing no relation to a hard working life. Where the aspiring lower middle class saw membership of church or chapel as a practical means to an end, the middle-class employer took an equally practical view in its maintenance of values associated with the work ethic.[11] The growth of religious following in Buxton may be set against the framework used by Derek Fraser to describe the role of religion in urban politics. He argues that religion provided three essential functions. First it operated as a focus of association, a means of entering an appropriate level of urban society. Second it provided the citizen with an almost ready-packaged set of behavioural norms with which to meet the new demands of urban living. Third it offered a set of political objectives as part of church membership, objectives which differed between denominations but which, essentially, reflected the values of the individual member whether Anglican or Nonconformist.[12] In an insular and fairly close-knit community such as Buxton the social pressure to belong would have been strong; as would the influence of employers. Religion was part of the essential fabric of the town – the mortar between the stone – cementing the growth of the inland resort. The extent to which Fraser's three essential functions are borne out may be examined as Buxton's religious growth is described.

The tensions which characterised Victorian religious growth within and between churches, denominations and sects are reflected in Buxton. Tensions such as those between Anglican and Nonconformist growth, the effects of the Oxford Movement, perceptions of 'High' and 'Low Church', formal and evangelical forms of worship, differences in liturgy and litany, all played themselves out. The Wesleyan– Primitive schism of Methodism is to be seen, Congregationalist and Unitarian differences, an early example of Roman Catholic renascence and, quite separate from the more ubiquitous denominations, a Catholic Apostolic following. Add to this the foundation of Buxton's fortune, its unique thermal water and the strong connections through history between the holy well, religious belief and the water-cure, and David Thomson's words remain apposite to this study:

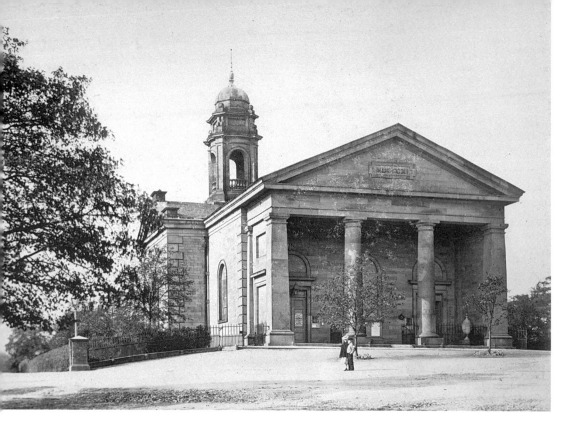

The Church of St John the Baptist built by the Fifth Duke of Devonshire and dedicated in 1812. It remained for the most part the only Anglican provision for worship until the church of St James was opened in 1871. This photograph shows the original east-end entrances before the remodelling of 1896–97.

... No interpretation of [mid] Victorianism would be sound which did not place religious faith and observance in the very centre of the picture ...[13]

In 1848 the embryonic town had six places of worship for its 1,500 inhabitants. Two of the six were Anglican: St John the Baptist, a substantial church funded by the Fifth Duke of Devonshire under the Buxton Church Act of 1811 and designed by John White and Son, and the small church in Higher Buxton which bears the date 1625 carved in the porch.[14] Paradoxically the large church of St John, built in a Neo-Classical Tuscan style, was a chapel-of-ease to the Parish of Bakewell and actually stood in the Parish of Fairfield. Not until the boundary changes of 1859 did the church sit within urban Buxton and it was to be 1898 before the church acquired its own parish.[15] Though a chapel-of-ease, St John's was to all intents and purposes the parish church of Buxton from its dedication in 1812.[16] From this time the old church in Higher Buxton was closed and, apart from its brief re-opening for worship in 1841, St John's remained the only Anglican provision for nearly sixty years. By the mid-1860s the Anglican church in Buxton was falling behind other denominations in providing for the visitors and in making its presence felt. Others, Nonconformist and Roman Catholic, were publicly demonstrating a greater glory to God by their neo-gothic offerings – their towers and spires and lancet windows. The incumbent of St John's,

St James the Great, Bath Road
was designed by Manchester
architects J. Medland & Henry
Taylor who were known for
their somewhat unusual church
designs. It opened in 1871 but
by 1896 required substantial
repair work to render it safe.
[J.M.B.]

Rev. S. Ray Eddy, raised the question of accommodation in his preamble to the churchwardens' accounts of 1868, pointing out that provision was needed for some hundreds of visitors as well as an increasing resident congregation.[17] In September and October 1866 he issued advertisements in the local papers and succeeded in raising sufficient funds (the Duke of Devonshire gave £1,000) to propose a large new church, St James the Great on Bath Road. The projected cost of £5,000 included tower and spire, and seating for 750 worshippers. Designed by the prolific Manchester architects J. Medland & Henry Taylor, it opened in 1871.[18]

The Anglican churches in Buxton offered an increasingly ritualistic form of worship, centred on the 1662 Book of Common Prayer but with lighted altar candles, rich vestments worn by the celebrant for holy communion and a robed choir.[19] The old church in Higher Buxton had been used as a school and a mortuary chapel but after re-dedication as the Church of St Anne by the incumbent of St John's, the Revd William Malam in 1885, it became a centre for high Anglicanism in the town.[20] An average of fifteen services each week were held there by the priest-in-charge, the Revd William Lear. Richly embroidered stoles were worn by the clergy, the altar cross and candlesticks were flanked by ten vesper lights and twenty vases of fresh flowers. In 1891 a sanctuary lamp was introduced and the sanctus bell was rung at holy communion. In introducing incense the church became directly involved in the controversy between the evangelical and high church fuelling fears that Romanism, under the guise of

The Mortar Between the Stone

ritualism, was making marked advances in Buxton as elswhere in England.[21] An old Buxtonian revisiting the town wrote:

> ... At the Established Churches in the town I find there is a great tendency to be 'high', the plain old fashioned Church Service of my boyhood seems to be a thing of the past, this I think is to be greatly deplored, and must tend to alienate very many devout Evangelical Churchmen. Still the desire seems to be to get the people; ornate services, elaborate ritual, high-class music abound, these may certainly be aids to worship, but I am afraid do not make for righteousness ...[22]

Thomas Shepherd, former secretary to the Buxton Protestant Electoral Association, observed in a letter:

> ... The Church of England is sadly losing ground both as regards the preachers and the congregations. How different in former times when the preaching of Christ and Him crucified was the principal theme – where now we have young and unfledged essayists in the pulpit. Recently we had an instance of one who began 'In the name of the Father' etc. and then read from a newspaper cutting a speech of the late Bishop Moorhouse without any reference to the scriptures. Doubtless many of his hearers had already read it in the daily papers. Well may the congregations of young people and women be prevalent and lack the attendance of men! ...[23]

Others held the opposite view:

> ... There is also cause for rejoicing in the improvements which have been affected in the churches and their services. The Oxford Movement is evident in its effects on the church throughout the land, but not least in the good old town of Buxton: may it all tend to the glory of God; and to the present and eternal welfare of mankind ...[24]

The high church traditions in Buxton were supported by membership of the English Church Union. Succeeding John Baker JP of the Gables, Manchester Road, Dr W. H. Robertson, churchwarden at St John's for thirty years, became chairman of the Buxton branch and was a vice president of the county union. Special services of the branch, such as anniversaries, received the support of sympathetic members of the Anglican hierarchy.[25] The high church tradition was carried into the cemetery which was designed by the town surveyor, Joseph Hague, and built by the local firm of G. J. Bagshaw. The building was Gothic in style with a central archway

On 'Hospital Sundays' a sermon was preached, usually by an eminent cleric, and a collection taken to support the Devonshire Hospital and Buxton Bath Charity. Here the cartoonist W. G. Baxter gently pokes fun at the congregation of St James Church.

Hospital Sunday at St. James'—"Standing room only."

153

and a mortuary chapel on either side with a caretaker's house and registrar's office. The chapel on the north side was for various denominations, that on the south was Anglican and was furnished at the time of dedication in 1896, with an altar from St John's Church, Latin cross and mortuary lights. The altar front and the walls were hung with violet cloth and candles were used.[26]

By 1885 the Anglican church was providing pews for almost two thousand worshippers in the three churches of St John, St James the Great and St Anne. This was, however, soon felt to be insufficient for the growing town. In particular the new area of housing branching off from the extended Dale Street was felt to be in need of a mission chapel and in 1891 Miss E. Mirilees gave £500 for the erection of a temporary mission church and payment of a priest for four years.[27] The new incumbent at St John's, Rev. Charles C. Nation, arriving in 1893, found that all of his churches were making demands on the slim financial resources of the local Anglican establishment. He assessed that St John's had insufficient accommodation and the internal layout was such that the altar could not easily be seen from the west end.[28] A restoration committee appointed Sir Arthur William Blomfield & Sons of St Marylebone as architects for extensions. But the mission chapel on Dale Road was put on hold and redevelopment at St John's modified in scope because St James in Bath Road was found to need urgent repairs. Within little more than twenty years

The Cemetery on Ashbourne Road was dedicated in 1896. It had two mortuary chapels: the south chapel was for the Anglicans and the north for other denominations. It was built by the local firm of G. J. Bagshaw to the designs of the town surveyor, Joseph Hague.

of opening, serious defects were found in the stonework of the west end and a partial collapse of the spire required immediate work. The local architect W. R. Bryden was employed and Charles Heathcote, the Manchester architect who resided in Buxton, was a member of the building committee.[29] Work to the value of £2,150 proceeded through 1896 and included the rebuilding of the west end clerestory and aisle walls. Some enlargement of the west end took place but the proposed rebuilding of the spire, after necessary demolition, did not take place.[30] At St John's Church exploratory borings on the north side had shown the foundation soil to be soft and muddy and Sir Arthur Blomfield concluded that his original plans were impracticable. He could see no way of expanding the present building without interfering with its architectural character and spoiling some of its best features. Also the work would be much more expensive.[31] A new scheme was drawn up and a faculty obtained for major changes which included a new chancel necessitating the closure and resiting of the entrances on either side of the east end. Due to the work at St James and other demands on funds, this work was spread over fifteen years, though the chancel and a new organ were dedicated in August 1897.[32]

In 1885 long-awaited Sunday schools were built at the top of Bath Road on land provided by the Devonshire Estate. These were extended in 1895 and in the same year a new parsonage, designed by W. R. Bryden, was completed on Lismore Road.[33] This intensity of Anglican growth was capped by the erection of the mission chapel in Dale Street. St Mary the Virgin, dedicated in February 1897, grew slowly; only 386 communicants were recorded for the year 1900, rising to 517 in 1904.[34] In St Mary's the Anglican church had an answer to the evangelism of the Wesleyans who ran missions in Dale Street. The single most important occurrence, one which marked the *fin de siecle* for the Anglican Church, was the creation of a separate parish of Buxton, a status for which St John's had yearned throughout the century. In 1898 the Eighth Duke of Devonshire surrendered St John's to the Ecclesiastical Commissioners and, after some adjustment of boundaries with the adjacent parish of Fairfield, Buxton's four Anglican churches stood, for the first time, in their own parish.[35]

The High Church tradition was appropriate for many of the middle-class professionals and substantial businessmen in town, many of whom were also Tory and candidates for the Local Authority.[36] One professional was not, however, enamoured with this tradition. Joseph William Taylor (1837–1923), Buxton's first 'modern' solicitor, was strongly opposed to the Buxton high church practice in litany and liturgy which he saw developing out of the second phase of the Oxford Movement.[37] He desired a form of worship within the established church one in which, nonetheless,

... the simple truths of God's word, unalloyed by superstition on the one hand or scepticism on the other, shall be faithfully exhibited ...[38]

He convened a meeting in 1865 to promote the erection of a new church. His aim was to obtain a church in a central position in town which would offer a plain and evangelical form of Anglican worship. Taylor's small committee, which included Dr Thomas Dickson of Wye House Asylum (Taylor's father-in-law), F. K. Dickson, Dr W. H. Flint, Aaron Plant, bath proprietor and R. K. Batt, lodging house keeper, raised funds and were able to purchase land on Hardwick Mount in October 1868. Over the following two years they met with a number of difficulties, mainly to do with the lack of an endowment for the church, but also because Taylor, by his actions, was forcing the pace of growth in the Anglican establishment in town. These difficulties brought Taylor's plans to a halt but, being unable to sell their land, his committee sought permission from the Bishop of Lichfield to form a new district within which to build a new church. Dr Selwyn, the bishop, meeting with Taylor's committee and the incumbent of St John's and his sidesmen, exhibited the judgment of Solomon in turning down the request and advising J. W. Taylor to wait to see how well the new St James was able to satisfy the needs of the locality. If it was still decided to go ahead, his committee should erect a chapel-of-ease. For Taylor, the issue was not simply a question of satisfying numbers of worshippers; it was much more a question of satisfying the need for a low-church, congregationally-inclusive form of worship. This was to become his most important mission in life; he was to be founder-trustee of Trinity Church for fifty years. His decision, 'after mature consideration',[39] was to assume full responsibility for the cost of the land and to underwrite the investment in a new church. On Easter Monday 1872, Mrs Janet

The mission chapel of St Mary the Virgin was erected in 1896–97 on Dale Street. It competed with the Wesley Methodists who ran missions in the Dale Street area which was being developed with lower middle- and working-class housing.

156

❧

Trinity Episcopal Chapel, Hardwick Mount was designed by Robert R. Duke to seat 200 in 1872–73. It was completely funded by solicitor J. W. Taylor who subsequently funded many of its extensions. In Trinity Chapel he fulfilled his desire for a church offering a plain and evangelical form of worship.

Taylor turned the first sod for a small building, Trinity Episcopal Chapel, designed by the local architect Robert Rippon Duke to seat 200 and built at a cost of £614 by Messrs Hinch & Bennett. The chapel formed the southern part of the present building and was opened in 1873. Trinity Chapel proved popular with townspeople and visitors and by the early 1880s funds were raised for enlargements. These included a schoolroom beneath the church, and transepts, built in 1883 on land given by J. W. Taylor, the total cost being nearly £2,000. In 1885 a parsonage fund was set up, raising £1,561 in two years, to enable the trust to acquire a detached house in Hardwick Square East which became the Parsonage House. The church was further enlarged by the provision of a tower, partially built in 1893 and completed in 1903 to mark twenty-five years' service by Rev. C. S. Green. Other significant gifts by Taylor were an organ in 1906 and a set of tubular bells in 1909. For more than ten years from its inception J. W. Taylor was the single most important benefactor of Trinity Chapel. He was personally responsible for the stipend of the incumbent, which reached £200 p.a., until at least 1884. Because of this, and the difficulty of finding others who could share the burden, a trust was not formed until 1880 when Taylor was joined by one other only, Mr John Headington, a grocer in Fairfield. A strengthening of membership in 1882 saw three additional trustees, all of whom were from out of town. Effectively J. W. Taylor owned and ran Trinity Church. As befitted a solicitor his requirements were expressed very precisely in the trust deed: all seats to be free; there were to be no pew rents; the incumbent was to be appointed by the trustees, in concurrence with the bishop of the diocese, and was to be

> ... a clergyman of the Church of England, of blameless life and character, honestly attached to the Protestant Evangelical Standards of

the Church of England; who shall, before his appointment, give an assurance in writing to the trustees that he will conduct the services of the said chapel with simplicity, and particularly that he will not discard the use of the Geneva or academical gown in the pulpit of the said chapel, but will preach therein, and that he will not directly or indirectly introduce an intoned service or surpliced choir into the chapel ... no reredos or communion table, other than a movable one of wood, shall at any time be introduced into the said chapel ...[40]

In his beliefs Taylor was no latitudinarian; his was no weak church-manship or liberal stance. As an evangelical he was very clear about his form of worship. Not for him the 'Church and stage' fashionable at the time.[41]

J. W. Taylor was a member of the professional aristocracy of the town, an Anglican occupying a position bearing both the responsibility and the power of a patron by choice. Trinity Chapel, which rivalled the Anglican church as well as the Nonconformists, would not have existed without Taylor, who was both zealous and wealthy. Hugh McLeod offers examples of similar patronage among both Anglican and Nonconformity in London. In Lewisham the Congregational chapel in the High Street was said to have been built largely with the money of Henry Wood, a gentleman of independent means living nearby. The building of St George's, Catford, was said to have been financed single-handedly by George Parker, a solicitor and a JP living in Lewisham House, and in North London, Greville Place Congregational Church, Kilburn, formed in 1858, depended heavily on the support of the Callard confectionery family. Other such examples can be reiterated and from earlier in the century but among Dissenters the private individual's generosity gave way to a proper exercise of democratized polity. These were not private chapels; they were for public worship. McLeod, in his study, could not identify examples where a single individual has used his power to influence the style of worship.[42] In J. W. Taylor can be seen as such an individual and he was prepared to go to any lengths to maintain the requirements of the trust. In 1895 he entered into a long controversy, fought out publicly through the correspondence pages of the local newspaper, with C. S. Green, the incumbent of Trinity Chapel for thirty-two years from 1882. Outwardly the disagreement centred upon the nature of services, the wearing

W. G. Baxter pokes fun at the divisions between the high and low church movements found in Buxton.

Broad and Low Church.

St Anne's Roman Catholic Church was supported by Samuel Grimshawe, wealthy land and mill owner of Errwood Hall in the Goyt Valley. Designed by J. J. Scholes, it was built by the firm of Robert R. Duke in 1861. Monsignor Manning (later Archbishop of Westminster and a Cardinal) preached at the opening mass.

of a surplice and issues to do with the choir, but in reality it was about power in the management of the church. Green challenged the right of the trustees to interfere in the manner of church services so long as the minister did not contravene the words of the trust deed. He described Taylor's behaviour as dictatorship and set up a church council of twelve members expressly against Taylor's wishes. Matters reached the issuing of writs for libel before the dispute was uneasily resolved. Relationships between them remained formal if not cool, though Green had the confidence of the congregation and continued his ministry there until 1913.[43]

Another challenge to establishment Anglicanism in town came from the Roman Catholics, who opened their new church on Terrace Road in July 1861. This was an earlier example of patronage from a single wealthy family, the Grimshawes of Errwood. From modest beginnings the renascence of Roman Catholicism in Buxton had reached an important milestone. After the emancipation of the Roman Catholics in 1829 visiting priests were known to have travelled from Leek to say mass but twenty years later the prime movers in obtaining a permanent priest were Francis Anzani, proprietor of a fancy goods bazaar in Spring Gardens, and Robert Nall, lodging house keeper of High Street. Anzani brought the first priest, Father Edward McGreevey, into Buxton in about 1850 and mass was celebrated in the houses of Nall and Anzani and in a room in the Old Courthouse until a chapel for about sixty hearers was created in Scarsdale Place.[44] Samuel Grimshawe, wealthy land and mill owner of Errwood Hall, was the principal benefactor for the new church, the foundation stone for which was laid in July 1860, on the Feast of St Anne, by the Bishop of Nottingham, with Grimshawe's seven-year-old daughter,

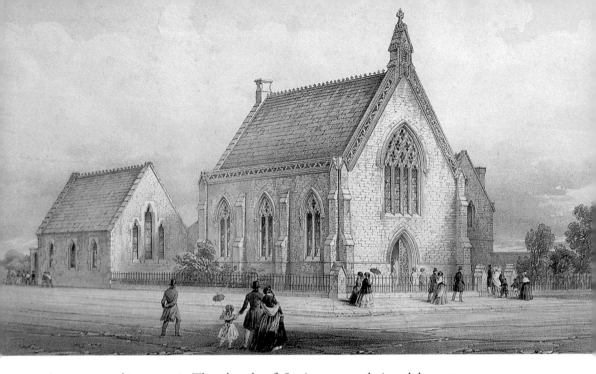

Genevieve, taking part.[45] The church of St Anne was designed by J. J. Scholes in the Lancet style, to accommodate 400 and built by the firm of Robert Rippon Duke.[46] It was opened with pontifical high mass by R. B. Roskell, Bishop of Nottingham, the choir was directed by Mrs Grimshawe from the harmonium and, the sermon given by, her husband's friend Manning, then Provost of Westminster, to a largely Protestant congregation, was in strong support of the pontificate of Pius IX. Using the newly declared dogma of the immaculate conception, his words on the infallible voice of the pope as the vicar incarnate of the Son of God were unequivocal.[47] The origins of the Roman Catholic church in Buxton are notable for a number of reasons. This was a church in the early phase of the restoration; in 1861 there were 798 churches, in 1901 twice that number.[48] It was built soon after Pope Pius IX restored the English Hierarchy in 1850 and established the Metropolitan See at Westminster and twelve Suffragan Sees which included Nottingham.[49] But the attendance of Monsignor Manning at the opening mass was a coup for the church and for the town. It is little wonder the occasion was advertised in the local press. Manning, a founder member of the Oxford Movement, had been Archdeacon of Chichester until converting to Roman Catholicism in 1851. He became Archbishop of Westminster in 1865 and Cardinal from 1875. Together with John Henry Newman (Cardinal 1879–90) he exerted a definitive influence on the Catholic revival in England.[50]

Successive parish priests increased the church facilities. John Power, parish priest for ten years from 1875, bought land from the Devonshire Estate and built a presbytery and his successor, J. T. Hoeben, built

The Wesley Methodist Chapel and Schoolroom, Market Place, were completed between 1849 and 1851 to the designs of James Wilson of Bath. [B.M.A.G.]

the school behind the church and invited three sisters of the Presentation Order to organise the teaching.[51] Obligatory attendance at Mass on Sundays and holy days ensured the visible disciplined growth of 'Catholicity' in Victorian Buxton.

Nonconformity in Buxton provided a second, most important, focus of association. The Wesleyan Methodists were particularly influential and included prominent townsmen in a solid way of business. In common with the Anglicans, they provided a third of the elected members of the local authority.[52] In 1849 they opened a new church on the Market Place to replace their former small and structurally unsound building.[53] It was noted in chapter two that this new church coincided with other major investments in the town though there is little evidence to suggest that it was built to cater for an increasing membership, more likely because the old chapel was falling down. Furthermore its opening coincided with a serious drop in Wesleyan church membership nationally. Between 1849 and 1855, due to a serious dispute with the leadership, the Wesleyans lost a third of their members.[54] The decline in membership in Buxton was equally serious, requiring much investment of time and money from those who remained. Fortunately these included such stalwarts as John Milligan the draper, Charles Raynor, grocer, James Clayton, baker and Samuel Fiddler, saddler and the church was opened with great ceremony, services taking place over three Sundays attended by several of the movement's luminaries including the Revds. Robert Newton, Jabez Bunting, John Hannah, Jonathan Crowther.[55] This says much for the standing of the Buxton Wesleyan Methodist Circuit as does the fact that the new Church and adjacent free-standing schoolroom (built 1851) were designed by the respected architect James Wilson of Bath.[56]

Recovery in membership from the setback of 1849–55 was not helped by the breakaway from the Buxton circuit of the townships of Chapel-en-le-Frith and Whaley Bridge to the north of Buxton in 1867. Numbers fell from 429 leaving a circuit of 116 members in the Buxton society and six other preaching places in villages around the town. However, over the following twenty years membership rose to 352 with the Buxton Wesley Society having 125 members alone.[57] During this time church facilities were expanded including the acquisition of a manse in 1865, a new school building in 1879 and extensive enlargements in 1880, to the plans of Robert Rippon Duke, when the church became cruciform in shape to seat 460.[58] In 1873 a Wesley chapel was built in the newly developed, fashionable, Devonshire Park. Designed by Mellor and Sutton of Southport, in the Gothic style, it had a tower and an octagonal spire; inside there was a rear gallery with the nave leading to an apsidal chancel and a sculptured stone pulpit.[59] It is difficult to ascertain just why this chapel, which would seat 800, was built. There was no previously established society to

A Wesley Methodist Chapel was built in the newly developed, fashionable Devonshire Park in 1873. In Gothic style, it had a tower, an octagonal spire and an apsidal chancel, and could seat 800.

back it and the Buxton Wesley circuit minutes are not revealing. The town at this time was, of course, busy as a health resort and the decision to build this chapel would seem to have been based on the perceived need to cater for visitors, but may reflect also the desire of the middle-class members for a presence in a fashionable part of town.[60] Added weight may be given to this suggestion in that the services were described as very liturgical, Woodhead quotes what may be an apocryphal story, nevertheless indicative:

> ... Sir Robert Perks and his family were staying at the Palace Hotel; on the Sunday morning when Sir Robert asked the hall-porter where the Wesleyan chapel was, the porter replied, 'There's one up the road', pointing towards Devonshire Park, 'But if you want the real thing you'll have to go to Higher Buxton' ...[61]

The Devonshire Park chapel was small in membership (only fourteen in 1889) but had some success after it was reorganised as a mission, separate from the circuit, in 1897. The missioners drew a congregation from the working class of Higher Buxton and by 1905 when it returned to the circuit the membership numbered eighty.[62] The Wesley movement enjoyed successful missions in Buxton holding open air and cottage meetings including a mission in the developing area of Dale Road, Ash and Bennet Streets.[63]

Despite being within a few miles of the origins of the movement, Buxton was not an early centre of Primitive Methodism.[64] Cottage services were being held in 1840 and by 1842 services were advertised at a room fitted up for preaching in Hobson's Yard.[65] By 1857 a chapel in Back lane, behind the Queen's Inn, was in use and was still listed in 1860 though the cause may have become moribund for it was revived in that year by Mr Henry Prime a watchmaker from

PRIMITIVE METHODIST CHURCH AND MANSE, BUXTON.

An enlarged Primitive Chapel was built in 1890 on the site of the former chapel (1869) on London Road. The Primitive Methodist domain was completed by a manse named 'Bourne House', after the founder of the movement Hugh Bourne, adjacent to the chapel and schoolroom behind.

the nearby village of Flagg who began to hold services in his house in West Street.[66] Services were then held in the Independent chapel in Spring Gardens and the houses of several members until a site was acquired in 1868 on London Road to build a chapel and manse. Earlier attempts to purchase land from the Devonshire Estate had been unsuccessful, the agent E. W. Wilmot being reluctant to sell for Nonconformist development. His successor, George Drewry, was more amenable. It will be seen later in the chapter that Wilmot was equally reluctant to sell land to the Congregationalists; contemporary accounts suggest he was influenced by the Anglican clergy.[67] The architect for the chapel, opened in 1869, was John Simpson, surveyor to the Buxton Local Board. The Primitive Methodist Buxton circuit was established in 1868 and the movement grew such that a schoolroom was added in 1876–77 by which time six class leaders were organising regular gospel bands. Strong support for the Buxton circuit came from the meetings of the wider Primitive Methodist Connexion enjoying the attractions of the inland resort.[68] In 1880 the Nottingham District, which covered the East Midlands, met for services, open-air rallies and processions over two months and a similar rally occurred in 1886 when Buxton was in the Manchester district. Such was the growth of this movement that, within twenty years of building their first chapel, the trustees were obliged to consider enlarging their facilities. Although predominantly working-class, the Primitive Methodists, as with every other religious movement in town, were strongly supported by prominent townsmen. R. R. Duke, the architect and a sometime methodist, had persuaded them to take the risk of buying extra land from the Devonshire Estate in 1868 which enabled a new chapel to be built on the site of the old.[69] F. A. Holmes, tailor and outfitter, was an influential and active member of the London Road chapel; he founded a society library in 1895.[70] The local architect, G. E. Garlick, worked closely with the trustees to design a new chapel in the Gothic style to seat 500 and remodel the manse which was named 'Bourne House' after the founder of the movement. It is a further measure of the buoyancy of the Buxton circuit that fifteen commemorative stones were laid at the start of building, in May 1890, by friends and trustees who contributed £430 towards the tender price of £1,455. The design included a side entrance with porch for bath chairs.[71]

It was a feature of both branches of Methodism that missions, open-air and camp meetings drew people from the heavy industrial areas around Stockport and Manchester – the cotton manufacturing districts – to the mountain air and countryside of the inland resort. In this sense the church was not only catering for those who visited but actively encouraging parties to travel to the town. Such evangelism gathered its own congregation.

A close parallel to the Primitive Methodists, the Salvation Army was a social and religious movement with a strong evangelical out-reach.[72] In 1878 Derbyshire had no corps but by 1883 there were sixteen and by 1905 seventeen.[73] Following evangelical work in 1886 a corps was established in Buxton and by 1891 a much travelled Captain Samuel Coupe and his family were in charge of a barracks in Torr Street capable of seating 400.[74] The movement carried on a small mission with four Sunday services and four week-night evening meetings, but, unlike other denominations, little is reported of their activities, due undoubtedly to the competition – probable opposition – in a town of High Anglicanism and powerful establishment Noncon-formity.[75]

Other denominations were less evangelical in approach but, never-theless, desired to offer visitors of their persuasion a place to worship. Indeed, it is apparent that decisions taken by a faithful few in a particular denomination to build a new place of worship were based on an untested belief that such a facility would encourage an increase in local membership and meet the needs of visitors. In some cases the level of local support at the start of major building investment was so modest that pure faith in God to provide must have been the motivation. The growth of the Congregationalist presence demon-strates this and provides a further example of a single benefactor assuming responsibility for the establishment of a significant church building programme. From an earlier presence in town the Inde-pendent Congregationalism movement grew substantially after 1848.[76] The Revd T. G. Potter of Marple Bridge came to Buxton for his health in that year and found the chapel on Spring Gardens closed. He conducted services and formed a committee who petitioned the County Union for funds. His committee contained no Buxton resident. By 1855 he had, however, gathered a group of six residents to form the church. One of these, Henry Shaw, a brewer from Blackburn, had recently moved to a house at Corbar designed by Henry Currey as part of the Buxton Park development. He made an initial donation of £25 and pew letting in the old chapel commenced but, in his subsequent promise of £500, Shaw became the major benefactor and prime mover in establishing the new church.[77] Negotia-tions with the Devonshire Buxton Estate agent, E. W. Wilmot, proved difficult. T. G. Potter recorded that the agent refused every site applied for and, in so doing, was acting in accord with the clergymen of the day. This was a case of Anglican opposition to developing Noncon-formity in a town which was now growing rapidly and could foresee an imminent railway link. It was to be fifteen years before the Anglicans would increase their accommodation. The Congregationalists might not be numerous but, with Shaw leading, they were seen to be influential. Unlike the Primitive Methodists, they did not wait for a

The chapel shown on the left of this picture was opened in about 1810 and used by a number of prominent preachers of the Independent Congregational movement who visited the town, including James Alexander Haldane and Thomas Wilson, both evangelical enthusiasts. The land for the chapel was purchased by Wilson's father-in-law, Arthur Clegg. The Revd T. G. Potter of Marple revived the chapel in 1848 and promoted the following which ultimately built the new church on Hardwick Mount.

change of agent and delay their building programme. In January 1857 Henry Shaw sought the intervention of Sir Joseph Paxton and proposed four possible sites. Wilmot was opposed to three but reluctantly agreed to sell the fourth site which was on the newly developed Hardwick Street.[78] The resulting church, designed by Henry Currey and built by Robert Rippon Duke, was large and imposing, described in the press as early pointed architecture with a nave and aisles, two vestries, porch, tower, spire with school room under a gallery. Sixty feet by forty with a height of thirty-eight feet and a tower and spire one hundred feet high, it was the most impressive sacred building since the Anglican St John's of 1811. The preacher at the opening service in July 1861 was Rev. T. Raffles, an eminent Independent minister, who took as his text Isaiah 60, v. 13,

... and I will make the place of my feet glorious ...

his message portraying the invisible God, yet always among us, and greater than any building, statue or man-made artifact.[79] At the luncheon in the Royal Hotel Henry Shaw said he was not ashamed of Congregationalism; he was thankful that they had the Church of

England with two faithful, noble and kind hearted men to minister the gospel there, together with Wesleyans and other Christian people but also Congregationalism. Here was Shaw, confident in his own class and in the standing of his church, extolling harmony towards the Anglican opposition and other denominations in town.[80] In Henry Shaw can be seen another example of the Congregational businessman, typical of many throughout the country, who learned that the pursuit of free trade must be tempered with improvement – the moral precondition for unfettered commerce. Perhaps the best known was the younger Edward Baines, newspaper proprietor of Leeds, but William and Charles Bradbury Robinson, pill box and bandage manufacturers, invested time and money in the Congregational church in Chesterfield and in so doing emulated their forerunner, Thomas Wilson, also a manufacturer of gauze.[81]

Congregational Church, Buxton.

The Congregationalists built their church on the newly developing Hardwick Mount in 1861. Designed by Henry Currey and built by the firm of Robert R. Duke, it was, at the time, the most imposing church to be built after St John the Baptist in 1812.

The Congregational church depended heavily upon a single individual for patronage because the membership could not collectively support such a building programme. The influence of Shaw, 'a solid Nonconformist' was dominant and when he died in 1861 his son Henry junior took on the role, providing a new organ in 1867 and assuming leadership for the nine months in 1878 between a retiring T. G. Potter and a new pastor J. W. Blore.[82] The movement grew steadily, and between 1855 and 1878 almost 150 members were registered. A number of these were well-respected business people such as John Hobbis, the photographer, Dodds the drapers, and James Wardley, chief clerk in the Devonshire Estate office who was, for some time, church secretary. In all cases wives became members in their own right in common with other Nonconformist denominations.[83] In 1881 a Sunday school was opened, built on land on Hardwick Square East, bought from the Devonshire Estate, and by the early part of this century the church had 110 seat-holding families divided into seven districts in the town. Notable among these were Manchester Congregationalist families who had moved into town including the McDougal flour millers, Vickery the metal dealer and the Seebohms of shipping firm Schill Seebohm & Co.[84]

The Henry Shaws, father and son, and J. W. Taylor epitomise the influence of commercial and professional middle-class wealth shaping a particular style of worship. But these two families pose an interesting question. How comfortable would each have been attending the other's

In 1881 a Congregational Sunday School was opened in Hardwick Square East.

service? J. W. Taylor insisted on the academic gown and Geneva bands, a form of dress worn by some Congregational Ministers and some of the statelier Dissenters. He would presumably have been at home with the Te Deum and the psalm amongst the liturgy of the Congregational opening service, and he would have surely warmed to the way in which these were sung to God by all those attending:

> ... Psalms and hymns and spiritual songs should ever ascend from the lips and hearts of a thankful people to their God. Singing should be the best of its kind, but never let us forget that to be acceptable to the Almighty it must be *congregational* ...[85]

The great divide between them was to do with conformity, yet they could both be described as dissenters and both sought a form of worship far removed from the ritualism of the High Anglican churches in Buxton. These were men of great self-assurance who could move in and out of areas of public life as they wished.[86]

The diversity of religious movements in the growing health resort was completed by two other churches, the Unitarian and Catholic Apostolic, whose following was smaller than those already examined but who, nevertheless, were able to consolidate their presence in lasting stone and mortar.

The Unitarian church was the earliest Nonconformist movement in the town. The noted local historian, Ernest Axon,[87] traces the origins of the Buxton Chapel to Dr James Clegg, physician, farmer and Presbyterian minister, who had a personal interest in the healing properties of Buxton water and founded a chapel and a manse in 1725.[88] In common with others the movement had a chequered history and the chapel remained poorly used right up to 1873 when the minister, John Thomas Cooper, left it in a ruinous state with but a small congregation to go the Diss in Norfolk.[89] Indeed, the fortunes of this chapel were so precarious that it is difficult to see why the trustees, none of whom lived in the town, resolved to start a building fund in 1869.[90] In the appeal for funds they admitted that the congregation was small and likely to remain so for some time.[91] The answer lies, to some degree, in the strong Unitarian movement in Manchester (where most of the trustees resided) and the resurgence of Unitarian building taking place at that time.[92] The trustees were also anxious to provide for the visitors to the town. But the main reason was because the old chapel and the Kings Head were again in need of repair; in fact the Local Board had given trustees notice that two principal external walls were a danger to the public and must be rebuilt. The estimated cost of £1,000 to rebuild a chapel of no particular architectural merit at a time when a new and splendid chapel, to match those being built around Manchester, might be had for about £3,000 acted as a powerful incentive. The trustees had an offer for the old chapel and manse, so appealed to the Unitarian public for funds, raising all but £500 of the £3,000 total cost of the new chapel and schoolroom, which was built on land in Hartington Street obtained at a favourable cost from the Devonshire Estate. The architect was a Unitarian, Thomas Worthington and the builders Messrs Clay and Sons who were jointly responsible for many of the Unitarian churches built at this time.[93] The chapel and schoolroom were not outstanding architecturally. It was constructed of gritstone with ashlar dressings and a slate-covered deep pitched roof. The windows were of Lancet form, grouped and in singles; a feature of the interior furnishings was the entrance from the vestry, built on rising ground, to the pulpit.[94] Again the largest proportion of the

The Hartington Street (Unitarian) Chapel was built in 1874–75, funded in part from the sale of the old Presbyterian Chapel and Manse (The King's Head) on the Market Place. Thomas Worthington, a Unitarian, and Manchester architect was the designer and the church included a schoolroom. A manse was added in 1890–91 designed by W. R. Bryden of Buxton.

funds came from outside Buxton; only two local subscribers can be identified, B. W. Bentley, the photographer and Charles Wilkinson, a shopkeeper, who gave £5 each. Wilkinson became a trustee in 1876 when a new trust deed was drawn up, the first time for a century that a Buxton resident had held such office.

At the opening service on 15 May 1875 the preacher, the Revd Charles Beard, made an eloquent plea for casting aside all fetters that might have come from Presbyterianism of the past and loyally holding to an unsectarian religious life and work in the spirit of Christ. At the dinner, held at the Palace Hotel, Mr William Jevons, the senior trustee said there never was such a time when the Unitarian body needed eloquent preachers such as Beard to set forth the value of free worship against the assumption of the infallibility of the Pope on the one hand and the evangelical orthodox revival teaching on the other. Dr Beard, in response, mentioned his twenty years' association with the town and spoke of his difficulty with the spread of ritualistic sacerdotalism which he felt they could not look upon without concern, a clear reference to the Anglican High Church movement in town.[95] Great emphasis was laid upon fact that the chapel stood for the maintenance of religious services without sectarian intention, supporting the prevalent Unitarian idea that their chapels should not be bound by a creed.

So the Unitarian movement in Buxton faltered its way through the century. In 1883 the first minister of the new chapel, Andrew Macreight Creery, resigned because he had ceased to be a Unitarian minister.[96] Trustee Charles Wilkinson kept services going helped by preachers from the East Cheshire Christian Union. Perhaps the most successful minister at Buxton in the nineteenth century as both preacher and organiser, was Richard Cowley Smith who came in 1884. He was able to keep the chapel open and to gather a congregation as a personal following. He established a Sunday school, a young men's debating society and raised enough money to build a manse. This was designed by the local architect W. R. Bryden and built by the local firm of James Jones for £920 on adjacent land, completing a neat grouping of chapel, schoolroom and manse. Cowley Smith, in true Unitarian tradition, undertook practical work in the town and was prominent as a religious and educational worker and a Liberal politician. His personal following drained away at his death in 1897 and after six months of supply ministers, George Street was persuaded by clergy trustees to accept the vacancy. He succeeded in building a genuine church life with a modest congregation. The Unitarian church in Buxton did not establish itself fully in any sense in the period of this study; local support was not strong, but it did meet the need of

… an influential portion of our visitors …[97]

who provided comparatively high seasonal collections. It was driven predominantly by the strong movement in the Manchester and Cheshire associations.[98] Nevertheless, the ability of Unitarianism to embrace scientific developments was in tune with the new water medicine appearing in the health resort; their doctrine, summarised by McLeod

> ... of duty without sin, self-development without hedonism, progress through public service ...[99]

is mirrored in Revd H. E. Dowson's anniversary sermon to the Hartington Road chapel in 1896. He spoke of personal purity against the disorganisations which exist in all branches of life. The scattered churches of Unitarianism, he said, tried to work not by large close associations but by individual effort, a more practical than denominational effort to purify the hearts of men, rather than undue proselytism.[100]

Perhaps the most selective religious movement in Buxton was the Catholic Apostolic Church which largely appealed to the well-to-do and had a small membership.[101] The movement represented an attempt to return to the fundamental tenets of the early Christian church; it combined Adventist, charismatic, apostolic and ecumenical beliefs and offered two aspects of a revived apostolic teaching, charismatic on the one hand and traditional, formal worship on the other. The church in Buxton was referred to locally as 'for the use of the Irvingites' after one of the founders Edward Irving (1792–1834).[102] The dual philosophy of charismatic and traditional worship was reflected in the organisation of a 'Particular Church'. The 'Angel' (or Bishop) was the chief pastor, supported by 'Elders' in the rule of the church. Other 'Pastors' attended to individual needs and heard confessions.

Undoubtedly the most unusual religious movement in nineteenth-century Buxton was the Catholic Apostolic Church. The church had a dual philosophy of charismatic and traditional worship which led to early difficulties among its elders. But the major limitation was a belief in the imminent second coming of Christ which caused the church to make no preparation for succession among its senior officiates. Thus the movement ultimately went into decline. The following began in Buxton in about 1875 but it was not until 1896 that a permanent church was built. This is on Hardwick Square South and was designed by W. R. Bryden.

'Prophets' interpreted the scriptures and might speak as the Holy Spirit directed them and 'Evangelists' kept the first principles of the Gospel and its truth before the people.[103] In this dual philosophy lay one of the two major limitations to the survival of this movement. At the highest level the authority of the Apostle might be undermined by a Prophet who, speaking through the Holy Spirit, had to be heard. If a prophetic utterance was overruled, this would have the effect of subjecting the pronouncement to human interpretation thus undermining the authority of the Prophet. In this competition for power the formal authority of the church, supported by Apostles such as Henry Drummond and John Bate Cardale, assumed greater dominance when the authority of the Apostles over Angel-Prophets was asserted by letter in 1840. The Apostles were decreed to be the supreme head of a complex formal hierarchy.[104] This led to the second, and major, limitation affecting the tenure of the Catholic Apostolic Church. The church held a fundamental belief in the imminent second coming which was evinced by the appointment of twelve Apostles for life but with no plans for their succession. Thus, the death of the last Apostle in 1901 foresaw the ultimate demise of the movement and, despite the survival of Angels and others, it was recognised that the apostolic work on earth had come to an end.[105]

In its early growth the church was joined by converts from all the major denominations, both Anglican and Nonconformist, and by 1835 there were seven churches in London. A number of the early leaders had been deposed from their respective churches through doctrinal disagreement as happened to Edward Irving in 1833.[106] Congregations were formed in major towns; by 1836 there were thirty-six in the British Isles, and evangelistic work established churches abroad including Switzerland, France and a considerable strength in Germany. By the end of the century this minority religious group was organised and settled in its rules and liturgy.[107] The church at Buxton was a late development. Although land was purchased in 1875 the earliest services were conducted by ministers from Manchester on Wednesday evenings in the school room on Hartington Street (the Hartington Road Chapel) until 1885 when a corrugated iron chapel was erected in Hardwick Square South.[108] Dr Flegg's recent authoritative thesis suggests that less is known about the Catholic Apostolic than any other religious group or movement due partly to the fact that it has ceased to exist for all practical purposes as an organised church and because records have been withheld and in some cases destroyed.[109] This exacerbates the difficulty of piecing together a history of the Buxton church as an outlier of the mother church at Stretford Road in Manchester.[110] It is likely that it owes its existence, as with others in Buxton, largely to a single benefactor and to the continuing support of his two daughters who were present at the foundation stone laying service in 1896.[111] Services were held in the small chapel from 1885 with morning prayers and Holy Eucharist and evening prayers with sermon each Sunday provided by ministers from Manchester.[112] By 1891 the church had its own minister, Richard Leadham, who originated from Southwark and in 1895 he had been succeeded by Thomas Livesley. Plans were approved for a new church by the Local Board in 1896 though not without some controversy.[113] The foundation stone was laid in August by the Angel of the mother church attended by his deacons. Among the items buried beneath the stone in a tin box were a copy of the great testimony which had been sent to all heads of churches and crowned heads of the world in 1836 and a parchment with a brief history of the foundation work in Buxton. The chief minister spoke of the fourfold ministry of the church and stressed that the building was not to be erected in a spirit of sectarianism.[114] He emphasised their wish to be at one with the Christian church in town but his homily supported the paradox of a movement which was separate and exclusive, wishing to be seen as a special force for change within the whole Catholic Church, seeking to unify the church, not to add to its divisions.[115] The church was designed by W. R. Bryden and was laid out in a style to suit the particular form of worship with steps leading through a decorated stone arch to the altar, which stood in an apsidal chancel. The roof of the chancel was painted with stars of different sizes and the east window was three lancet-style stained-glass lights. Other windows were of similar style and the stained-glass portrayed symbolism rather than explicit biblical scenes.[116] Today the building is used for worship by a movement known as 'The Church of God' but some furniture and artifacts remain which show the nature of Catholic Apostolic worship. There are holy water stoups in the vestry and by the north porch, a carved pulpit, four elaborately carved chairs and small lecterns for use by the Deacons, and a collection box in three divisions for 'poor', 'tithe' and other 'offerings'.[117] The new church was consecrated in March 1899 by an Angel from Leeds assisted by others from Manchester and Newcastle upon Tyne in an impressive service.[118] The Catholic Apostolic church was a minority denomination in Buxton commanding little attention; few reports appear in the local press, although by 1905 the church was buoyant holding two services on Sundays, including the Holy Eucharist and a Thursday and Saturday evening service with teaching and instruction.[119]

The Catholic Apostolic Church appealed to the upper class wishing to maintain the existing social order in religion at a time when this was being challenged by the growth of new movements. They were unworldly in their belief that social order was of divine making, that there will never be perfect social order until Christ returns in power to rule. Because of this they opposed all individuals and bodies who promoted political or social change.[120] Though the church in Buxton, in common with others of the movement, struggled on, it could not last. By 1947 it had closed.[121] Professor Horton Davies offers a wonderful summary of the inevitable demise of the movement:

> ... the church became so wrapped up in its own interior life that it had no message for the teeming millions of an industrial society.
> It hugged itself to death. It was conspicuously the church of one race and of one class in society, through the absence of missionary concern. To this extent it lacked the Catholicity in its social composition that it sought in its worship ...[122]

As Buxton developed into a leading health resort, a rich ecclesiastical body emerged to meet the needs of a growing resident and visitor population.[123] The extensive range of denominations on offer meant that people from all classes and persuasions might find their place in the right pew. Furthermore, it can be seen that association with a particular church was a means of increasing one's perceived status in town. Charles Wilkinson, the Unitarian trustee, was more than the 'shopkeeper' as described on the legal document; he became a man of some stature who served on the Local Board for two terms and ran a glass and fancy goods 'warehouse'. Many others reinforced their position by active membership of their church. Wealthy townsmen, already influential, ensured that their particular beliefs were represented by founding their own church or strongly supporting the expansion of an existing denomination. In Congregationalism, for example, the foundation work of the Shaws was continued by incoming families such as the McDougals and Seebohms. Even the denominations appealing mainly to the working class had leading townsmen managing their affairs, F. A. Holmes, well-off tailor, was a prime mover in the Primitive Methodists. It was a mutually satisfying arrangement. It is also noticeable that townsmen of one persuasion would subscribe to the building funds of other denominations. This was due in part to the recognition that the church would provide some stability in the social order of the town, but also because of the need to conform and support one's self-image, since subscriber lists were published in the local press.

In Buxton also can be seen the paradox of Nonconformist divisiveness – their need for separateness – yet desire for cohesion and harmony. It ran as a thread through Buxton Nonconformist middle-class society, it was expressed publicly by Congregationalists and Unitarians but also clearly demonstrated by them and Methodists in their strong political and other associations in the town.[124] Whilst membership of a particular church might provide a moral underpinning of particular political values, at the local level those of different denominations worked together to achieve common goals in the expanding health resort. The church and chapel were an essential mortar in public affairs.[125]

Undoubtedly religion, an integral part of the fabric, acted to support the decisions of the prime movers in the town, but such prime movers were themselves supporters of the fabric of the church. Buxton, it may be said, was parochial in more ways than one.

> ... my father had finally established himself as the senior sidesman of St James-the Least-of-All. Conferring the right of leading the other sidesmen up the central aisle at the end of the collection, this was the more gratifying since my father had only obtained it as the result of a prolonged and determined struggle, in which his chief opponent had been a retired fishmonger known as Alexander Carkeek ... now a sleeping partner in the firm of Carkeek and Carkeek, fishmongers and poulterers ...[126]

CHAPTER EIGHT

Shape and Style: the Influence of Architects

Take a perambulation, in the manner of Professor Pevsner,[1] to the top of the Terrace Walks, laid out in 1818 by Jeffry Wyatt with later modifications by Joseph Paxton. Looking down at Lower Buxton, the view of the Georgian Crescent (1780–84) by John Carr of York is interrupted by Henry Currey's Pump Room of 1894. Beyond this the townscape is dominated by Victorian architecture; the Palace Hotel (1864–66) by Henry Currey, R. R. Duke's Devonshire Hospital Dome (1879–82) and the Quadrant (1854–61) by Currey/Paxton. Beyond these are the Buxton and Devonshire Parks containing substantial mid- and later Victorian villas. To the west is Broad Walk (1861–75), beyond which Burlington Road, a boulevard of later Victorian houses, leads to a further park of Victorian and Edwardian housing in Spencer and Robertson Roads and Green Lane. Turn one hundred and eighty degrees to face the head of the Terrace Walks and the Town Hall by William Pollard of Manchester (1889); Higher Buxton, grouped around the Market Place, with a few, not particularly prominent architectural exceptions, is wholly Victorian. To the south and east much of the housing is lower-middle and working-class with some middle-class small estates, notably Hardwick Square, Kents Bank and Crowstones. Slightly further out, to take advantage of more pastoral settings, are the Arts and Crafts houses of the early twentieth century at Lightwood, St Johns, Carlisle and Temple Roads.

The reason for this growth is now clear. Earlier chapters have charted the ascendance of the health resort through aristocratic land ownership and the emergence of power in the local authority. Prominent movers in this growth have been identified: the medical profession – promoting the natural resource; land agents – affecting geography and layout; religious movements underpinning influence and power structures within the town. In this scheme of things architects do not feature as initiators; essentially they follow, yet their legacy is the built environment; theirs is the physical shape of the resort, the lasting statements of art and creativity – shape and style. The purpose of this chapter is to identify those architects, to look at who commissioned the buildings and, where possible, to relate the architectural style of a particular building to its function.

Cecil Stewart has suggested that Victorian architecture, viewed by the later observer, is the architecture of revivals and he argues that its study should, consequently, be of architects as well as of styles.[2] Writers classifying Victorian architecture have used terms such as: 'Classical', 'Romanesque', 'Neo-Gothic', 'Queen Anne', but the sheer breadth of creativity employed as the century progressed, coupled with increasing professionalism, has required the classifier to find further descriptors for later in the century.[3] One writer uses the term 'In Search of New Architectural Forms' which fails to grasp the richness of development through exploration of the vernacular into what became the Arts and Crafts movement.[4] Certainly, in the rapid urban growth and the need for new estates, many unknown architects emerged who remain to be identified in studies such as this – architects who were not wedded to a particular style. New forms of building were used but standard architectural patterns might be adopted by speculative builders. Betjeman suggests that one of the more notable contributions to the architectural world was the introduction of cast iron and sheet glass into building construction, a form used often in developing resorts, certainly in Buxton.[5] But predominantly Victorian architectural styles were drawn from earlier eras and different countries. The Gothic revival can be seen in the context of a search for a style which was quintessentially English. As the revival acquired its full strength architects became divided into the two camps of Gothicist and Classisist.[6] Ruskin argued powerfully for the exclusive adoption of the Gothic style but, ironically, in promoting this his advice …

> … Do not be afraid of incongruities – do think of unities of effect. Introduce your Gothic line by line and stone by stone; never mind mixing it with your present architecture; your existing houses will be none the worse for having little bits of better work fitted to them … the vault, arch, spire, pinnacle, battlement, barbican, porch and myriads of others of Gothic architecture everlastingly poetical and powerful whenever they occur …[7]

… could ultimately be interpreted by architects to mean a mix of a variety of styles. From about 1860 until the turn of the century many architects felt free to vary their choice and combination of styles from building to building. Eclecticism might be the term to describe this, though Pevsner has pointed out that the term 'historicism' is more precise. This is because architects were not really creating a style out of the best of existing styles, rather they were allocating different styles to different buildings and mixing elements of various styles in one building.[8] This eclecticism or 'historicism' is to be readily found in Buxton. Local architect W. R. Bryden could mix 'shaped' gables with Classical pedimented window hoods and carved, decorated stone-work on his theatre (1899); R. R. Duke designed a Greek Portico entrance flanked by two Italianate lodges to his wrought-iron domed

Henry Currey (1820–1900) was articled to Decimus Burton and in the office of William Cubitt. He designed a number of buildings in London, including the London Bridge Railway Terminus Hotel (1861), before becoming architect for St Thomas's Hospital in 1865–66, a position which he retained through his lifetime. He designed the Long Conservatory at Chiswick House and the Baths at Buxton (1851–54) for the Sixth Duke of Devonshire, going on to complete much work at Eastbourne and at Buxton for the Seventh Duke. [N.P.G.]

Devonshire Hospital (1879–82). Many other examples will be found in this chapter and it is for this reason that a 'chronology of design' is relevant in only a broad sense to describe Buxton's architectural growth. Attempting to label the predominant style of a building might be useful but could also prove restrictive, lose perhaps some of the richness in the idiosyncrasies of the architect's design. In Buxton there may be seen fine examples of particular styles of architecture from the mid-Victorian period as well as outstanding designs reflecting the creative movements of later in the century.

Two phases of design may be proposed, the forty years from the late 1840s dominated by the predominant landowner and to a marked degree provider of public buildings; and a later phase from about 1890 to the start of the First World War when intensive land sales saw the rising fortunes of local speculative builders and incoming moneyed people, who wished their new houses to reflect what had made them successful. Their particular aspirations of taste, style and value-for-money were met by the local and well-known regional architects whom they commissioned to design private houses and small estates.

The domination of the town by the Devonshire Estate meant that most of the early architecture was influenced by the Duke of Devonshire's architects. Joseph Paxton laid out the Buxton Park, which was not completed fully to his design. He influenced the re-modelling of the Baths in 1851–54, most particularly in the iron and glass of the Hot Baths roof, façade and eastern side. He may have designed the façade of the Quadrant which maintained uniformity despite being built over seven years for individual purchasers. It was located on his ambitious town plan of 1852 but its architecture is more likely to be by Henry Currey; the two were working in town at the same time. Dr W. H. Robertson credits R. R. Duke with supervising its building after his successful job as clerk of works for the Sheffield architect, Samuel Worth's Classically styled Royal Hotel (1849–52).[9] Beyond this it is difficult to attribute any building design in Buxton to Paxton. By 1851 he had been knighted and subsequently he became a busy politician. His great legacy, apart from Buxton Park, is the layout of plantations and walks around the town which he supervised while chief gardener at Chatsworth. He remained attached to the town, however, and was an active

MR HENRY CURREY, *Architect of St. Thomas's Hospital.*

promoter of the Midland Railway line to Buxton. Henry Currey's influence on the built environment was much more pervasive. He became architect to the Seventh Duke of Devonshire in 1858, having earlier completed the Long Conservatory at Chiswick House and the Baths at Buxton for the Sixth Duke.[10] Currey also took commissions for other clients at Buxton. Among his earliest work was 'Corbar Villa' for the Blackburn brewer Henry Shaw and Devonshire Villas for Sanders & Woolcott, the main contractors for the Baths. These, of local stone, show something of the Italianate style which was to be his forte, in particular his use of Romanesque (fully rounded) arches to windows and doors, featured keystones, fluting, bracketed sills and overhanging roof with decorative eaves. These stylistic forms can be seen in the Quadrant and in some of the earlier houses in Broad Walk, described as Italianate, which may be attributed to him for this reason.[11] This style was carried through to the Pump Room of 1894 with its round-arched arcading. Currey also used sequences of narrow hipped roofs to form a façade; examples may be seen in the Congregational Church and Wye House Asylum of 1856.[12] This style of architecture may also be seen in numbers four to six Cavendish Villas (1864) on Broad Walk but further evidence is needed to attribute this building firmly to Currey.[13] Retention as Devonshire Estate architect meant that Henry Currey was responsible for modifications to existing buildings as well as designing new. He designed a dining room addition to the Old Hall Hotel and extensions to the Shakespeare Hotel in 1860, new Turkish Baths in 1863 and regular improvements to the Baths up to the end of the century.[14] Perhaps his most important building, certainly the most prominent, was the Palace Hotel commissioned by a joint stock company in 1864 at a cost of nearly £50,000. Currey was himself an investor in this venture and he designed the 105-room hotel in a French château style, with a central tower, on an elevated site adjacent to the railway stations.[15]

Henry Currey carried an extensive portfolio. He was architect to the St Thomas Hospital Trustees, designing the new hospital (1868–71) in the Italianate style and laid out as a series of pavilions on the

This design by Henry Currey in 1856 was for a Charity Hospital which was not built due to the perceived unsuitability of the site in Sylvan Park. The design was subsequently used for the Wye House Asylum (1859–60) run by the Dickson family. It became the Cavendish Girls School in 1912.

south bank of the river Thames. He had other clients in London and was kept busy by the expansion of Eastbourne; professionally he served on the council of RIBA and was vice president for a total of seven years as well as retaining membership of related professional bodies and trusts.[16] Fortunately in Buxton he had a well-qualified surveyor to provide local supervision of works – the 'Pooh Bah' of Victorian Buxton – Robert R. Duke. R. R. Duke has walked through most of the chapters of this study but, in the context of the present chapter, he is best described as a builder-architect. During the time of aristocratic direction he was to be found implementing Currey's plans; but he ultimately became a local architect of some stature and his influence links the two periods of this chapter. Though responsible for much supervision, he progressively built up his architectural practice from 31 Spring Gardens through extensive networks in town.

Pub by J.C. Bates, Buxton.

Eng by Newman & Co 48 Watling St London

Entrance to Poole Cavern, Buxton.

Poole's Cavern lodge by R. R. Duke in 1852 exhibits the 'Old English' style of J. C. Loudon with steep pitched roofs, ornate barge boards and patterned roof tiling.

179

He was not using the title 'architect' when he designed, as early as 1852, a lodge at the entrance to Poole's cavern for the Buxton agent Sydney Smithers. The style was 'Old English', imitative of the work of John Claudius Loudon, with steep pitched roofs, ornate barge-boards and patterned roof tiling, highly appropriate for the entrance to a show cave.[17] From this time until 1863 he was fully engaged in running his own building business, at one point employing 105 men, and it is likely that he was offering architectural design to his clients. He may have designed 'Burbage House', a small mansion built of brick by his firm for Robert Broome in 1861, and he certainly designed and built 'Thorncliffe' for his friend J. C. Bates. This is a very interesting Old English style design entirely symmetrical at the front such that it appears to be two dwellings. It had tall chimney stacks, ground-floor bays and highly decorative barge-boards to steeply pitched roofs. It was a statement of J. C. Bates' achievement in the ten years since he had founded the *Buxton Advertiser*. R. R. Duke's building business collapsed in 1862 but the following year he was appointed surveyor to the Devonshire Buxton Estate.[18] He was free, however, to develop his architectural knowledge which he did, in part, by observation and travel, in England and on the Continent, but mainly by reading; his library contained many books on building design and runs of periodicals such as *British Architect* and *Architect's Journal*.[19]

R. R. Duke took on assignments large and small: two refreshment rooms at the Seven Stars Inn in 1864, a printing works for J. C. Bates in the same year, the Fairfield Wesleyan Chapel in an Early English style in 1868. He may have been responsible for 'Stanley', 'Lake' and 'Cambridge' Villas (1866–68) on Broad Walk but this attribution is based on style and the fact that he was supervising the building on behalf of the Buxton Estate. He designed properties on building plots he had bought 'Argyle Villas' on Broad Walk in about 1875 and his own residence, 'Park House' on Manchester Road, built by the firm of George Myers with whom he had worked in Hull.[20] The latter is a detached Italianate double bay-fronted house with much decoration to the stone-work. He used segmented arches to the centre door and over each window, though those to the first floor double-sash windows are decorative rather than functional.[21] Due, perhaps, to Henry Currey's preoccupation with Eastbourne, R. R. Duke was directly commissioned by the Devonshire Buxton Estate. He designed

'Thorncliffe' (seen in the far right background of this engraving) on Hartington Street, designed and built by R. R. Duke, in 1861, for John Cumming Bates, founder of the *Buxton Advertiser*. J. C. Bates had opened his printing business and published his first edition of the newspaper in 1852 and it is a mark of his progress that, within ten years, he could commission his own house.

Cavendish Villas, Buxton.

The Burlington Hotel, built by the Devonshire Estate in 1874 on the site of an old house at the bottom of Hall Bank. R. R. Duke was paid a fee of £193 for its design, which is just under 5% of the total cost of £4,520. The building features different stone carving designs to each of the four floors.

the Burlington Hotel on Hall Bank in 1874, using a different treatment for each of the four floors, which incorporated stone carving. He could have found his inspiration for this in such Manchester warehouses as that designed by Edward Walters for James Brown Son & Company in 1851, though he did not aspire to the classical façade of Walters since he was required to build in keeping with the Georgian town houses adjacent.[22] In Devonshire Park, which R. R. Duke entirely laid out for building, he designed three villas for the Estate, perhaps others. These are 'Hamilton' and 'Arnside' on Devonshire Road (1873), in a Gothic-style, three-storey with bay windows and a dormer. Very decorative barge-boards are used, and there is much variation to the shape of windows which are embellished with stone carvings over the window hoods and decoration to the façade. The doors are at the sides giving an uninterrupted façade facing the road. 'The Knoll' on Marlborough Road, built 1874, exhibits similar characteristics but is plainer.[23] Duke was undoubtedly responsible for much other domestic design but his major achievements were the large concert hall in the Pavilion Gardens and his domed conversion of the Devonshire Hospital. The client for the large concert hall was the Buxton Improvements Company which had engaged Edward Milner to design the glass and iron pavilion in 1871. Milner's work completed the influence of the of Currey–Paxton–Milner triad in town.[24] Milner's pavilion was so successful that, within eighteen months the directors were being pressed to extend the facilities, but Milner was not retained for the work, nor was his son, Henry Ernest, who was to do later work on the gardens layout. The Improvements Company asked their fellow director, R. R. Duke, whose plan for a large octagonal concert hall of iron and glass with all the necessary offices was accepted. This was by far the most ambitious project undertaken by Duke so far in his career and, as Dr W. H. Robertson explained at the foundation stone laying in 1875, without established patterns the design had to be made from scratch, resulting in some miscalculation and subsequent delays.[25]

Despite the challenges of working in what was for him a new medium R. R. Duke completed his concert hall to be opened in 1876 to great acclaim. He had managed to produce a seamless join between his work and that of Milner to provide Buxton with an enviable amenity. The question which arises is why did he select an octagonal roof, a difficult form to design and construct? This question may also be posed of his Devonshire Hospital conversion, an even more difficult and ambitious project, which incorporated what was described at the time as one of the largest dome-shaped roofs in this country or abroad,[26] Two reasons may be offered. First R. R. Duke was a man of some courage, entirely self-taught in draughtsmanship and design; he was not a member of the RIBA. Pevsner has suggested that, in Victorian England, iron and glass remained the domain of the engineer, stone and brick that of the architect.[27] R. R. Duke was a draughtsman, a competent builder and an architect, and he established a strong working relationship with Messrs Henry Rankin of Seacombe

Plans for 'Hamilton' and 'Arnside' (1873) in Devonshire Park. These are by Robert R. Duke who also designed 'The Knoll' a detached house in Marlborough Road nearby. These were investments by the Devonshire Estate. R. R. Duke's liking for decorated barge-boards may be seen, also stone carving and variation of window shapes. [D.C. Chat.]

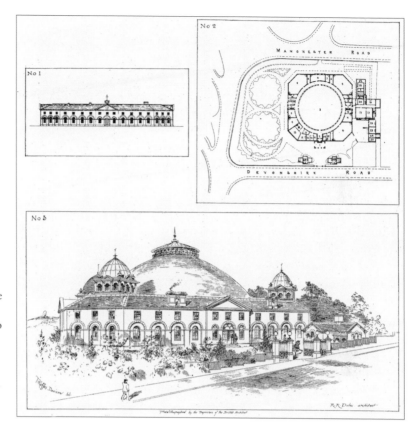

Part of R. R. Duke's original prospectus for the Devonshire Hospital conversion (1879–82). Drawing no. 1 shows the hospital before conversion. The ground plan no. 2 shows two lodges and an extended portico to the main entrance but his drawing no. 3 shows only one Italianate lodge and a scaled down portico as actually built. A clock tower not shown on these drawings was added.

Iron Works, Liverpool who produced the cast and wrought iron for both the concert hall and the Devonshire Hospital conversion. Second, although the dome construction was unusual in Victorian England there were a number of examples of which Robert Duke would have been aware. His erstwhile Hull stonemason, George Myers, provided a domed building for a model of the earth's surface by the MP and geographer James Wyld (1812–87). Wyld's dome, sixty-five feet in diameter, was displayed in Leicester Square in 1851.[28] Of the two hundred or more designs for the Great Exhibition one which was reported in the *Illustrated London News* proposed a dome 190 feet in diameter. Sydney Smirke designed the Reading Room in the British Museum with a domed roof, 140 feet in diameter, in 1852–54 and the International Exhibition of 1862 was housed in a building designed by Captain Francis Fowke which featured a 160 feet diameter glass dome at each end.[29] This building was re-erected at Alexandra Palace, opened in May 1873, and had burned down within sixteen days.[30] So R. R. Duke was in elevated company when he chose his roof design for the Concert Hall and, most clearly so, when he insisted upon a domed roof for the Devonshire Hospital conversion against powerful opposition from some trustees.[31]

This last great project of his, a functional hospital for 300 patients

A view of the interior of the
Devonshire Hospital dome
with an inset portrait of R. R.
Duke. The image is burnt on
china to give a brown or sepia
tone, probably by H. Hedgfield
Stella, 1882. This gives some
idea of the ironwork ribs bolted
onto an iron ring on the
supporting pillars.

with portico entrance, Italianate lodge (only one was built), Gothic
clock tower and miniature domed roof lights, crowned by a slated
dome of 138 feet in diameter rising 118 feet from floor to the top of
the finial, was to bring him to his knees. The project ran over cost
– the ubiquitous 'builder's extras' – and two years of arbitration took
a serious toll on R. R. Duke's health; he retired and sold his business
to W. R. Bryden.[32]

The development of a large and successful practice in Buxton by
William Radford Bryden FSA, FRIBA and member of the British
Society of Architects coincides with the extensive residential growth
in the town through speculative building with local and incoming
investment. By about 1880 the Devonshire Estate had settled to the
business of land sales and management, its central influence on the
town's affairs diminishing. Local businessmen were investing in
property and a number of local builders were becoming well established. The efficient railway service attracted residential wealth. It
was the right time for an ambitious young architect to build on the
practice of the only substantial architect in town and there was
little competition. William Pollard of Manchester had opened an
office briefly in the Quadrant but this was during the building of the
new Buxton College (1880–81) which he had designed in a Gothic
style. His later work on the Town Hall (1887–89) did not cause him
to establish a practice in the town.[33] There were no others of note,
and W. R. Bryden could see the potential. He came to Buxton in
1883 from Bideford in Devon where he had conducted a successful
practice since 1877. Bryden was well qualified. He had been articled
to Edward Middleton Barry RA (1830–80) and had trained in the

The letterhead of the architect
William Radford Bryden
(fl. 1877–1915) shows his
qualifications and uses a stylish
name board which reflects his
eclectic designs.

One of Bryden's earlier works in Buxton, The Union Club of 1886, which takes advantage of the sloping ground with its interior layout.

offices of R. W. Edis RSA and W. H. Crossland, becoming ARIBA in 1876.[34]

Contrary to his own assertion, R. R. Duke did not retire when he sold his business; indeed, he worked with Bryden on extensions to the Palace Hotel. A new west wing to match Currey's façade was completed in 1887–88 and an iron and glass dining room using R. R. Duke's usual ironman Rankin of Liverpool. But Bryden and Duke had serious disagreements. It would seem that, at times, the younger man was too modern, too fast perhaps for R. R. Duke, Bryden was a young man with ambition, whose business methods were not always those of the long-established townsman.[35]

W. R. Bryden moved directly into major projects. He designed the Union Club in 1886, a ballroom for the Buxton Hydropathic in 1887 and a new theatre (called 'Entertainment Stage') for the Buxton Gardens Company in 1889.[36] The first of these was built on rising ground which Bryden used to good effect in the internal layout, featuring cast-iron roof supports. In the other two he used a form of Dutch or Shaped gabling as part of the façade, a 'Queen Anne' stylistic feature he much favoured. The 850-seat theatre, built behind the Pavilion, has a single façade onto St John's Road; here he designed pedimented windows, decorative pinnacles and shaped gables carved with the theatrical masks of comedy and tragedy, making the best of a restricted site. Other public buildings where he used a Shaped gable façade include 'Marlborough Mansions' on Marlborough Road (1891) and the 'Milnthorpe Homes' on Macclesfield Road (1905) and the style may be found on private houses – an example of 1898 is that situated in the Buxton Park Ring built for the Misses Hannah and Mary Jane Barker.[37]

The Entertainment Stage, 1889, by W. R. Bryden features shaped gables carved with the theatrical masks of comedy and tragedy, pedimented windows and decorative pinnacles.

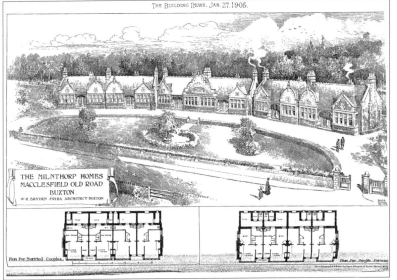

THE BUILDING NEWS. JAN. 27. 1905.

THE MILNTHORP HOMES
MACCLESFIELD OLD ROAD
BUXTON.
W·R·BRYDEN·F·R·I·B·A·ARCHITECT·BUXTON

Plan for Married Couples.

The Milnthorpe Homes, Macclesfield Road (1904–05). It is reputed that Mr Joseph Milnthorpe gave £10,000 in cash to build 12 houses on land owned by the Duke of Devonshire at Wye Head to be occupied by four old women, four old men and four old married couples. W. R. Bryden designed them featuring his shaped gables and the builder was G. J. Bagshaw.

W. R. Bryden derived much business from the later development of the Buxton Park and the new roads of high-class housing to the west of the town. He was responsible for all but one of the houses on the new extension of Burlington Road laid out in 1890, nine detached and semi-detached substantial houses standing in extensive grounds opposite the Pavilion Gardens and adjacent to the two feeder tributaries of the River Wye.[38] His style can be described as Vernacular; he mixed a range of informal features, shaped gables, towers, pinnacles, crenellations and a variety of window treatments to form an impressive whole. 'The Hawthorns', built for Mr David Sherratt of Chester, is a fine example, but the houses on Burlington Road differ in style reflecting the commissioning brief. Two pairs, known as 'Elmwood', 'Riverside', 'Glenbrook' and 'Elmbank', built for the local grocer

William Wood were much plainer, one pair featuring Bryden's shaped gables.[39]

Bryden's office was kept very busy and much more work can be attributed to him, as will be seen, but he provided the town with two other architects, both of whom established successful practices: George Edwin Garlick (*c.* 1863–*c.* 1932) and William Holland (b. 1861). Both worked in Bryden's office and had worked under R. R. Duke.[40] They set up offices in about 1890, G. E. Garlick at number 5 and William Holland at 9a Terrace Road, and each took on a breadth of assignments from a simple cottage to an upper middle-class detached house with all offices. Of the two, Garlick developed the larger practice, but he was also a local politician, a member of the UDC from 1895. Neither architect designed much public building; Garlick produced the curve of shops in Eagle Parade (1890) seven double bays with bay windows to the first floor, carved stonework and dormer windows with highly decorated pediments and 'Bryden' style Shaped gables with a broken pediment. He was also responsible for the new 'Grinlow Tower' (a landmark known locally as 'Solomon's Temple' standing at 1,436 feet above sea level) which was opened by Victor Cavendish in September 1896.[41] His design for the Primitive Methodist Chapel and manse (1889–95) has been noted in chapter seven. George Garlick

'The Hawthorns', Burlington Road (1891–92) designed for Mr David Sherratt of Chester by W. R. Bryden. This shows Bryden at his eclectic best, mixing shaped gables, towers, pinnacles, crenellations and a variety of window styles to create an impressive whole.

took a younger man, Charles Flint (b. *c.* 1873) into partnership from 1896 for some years and was later joined by his son G. W. Garlick (1890–1962). Garlick's work can be seen on at least thirty streets in town, a solid contribution to late Victorian and Edwardian Buxton.[42] William Holland has provided a similar legacy: a few larger villas but chiefly cottages and lower middle-class houses. He was responsible for the Oddfellows' Hall of 1895 in Market Street and his work may be seen in sixteen other streets. Much of this work is stone-built houses in pairs or small terraces with plain sashes; some working-class cottages have ground-floor bays, some lower midddle-class have bays to the ground and first floors.[43]

Both of these architects, together with W. R. Bryden, worked closely with the builders in town on commissions and more speculative ventures. The work of James Salt, who had premises known as Devonshire Works on Market Street, is described in chapter three and some of G. J. Bagshaw's in chapter four. As the fashionable area to the south-west of the town opened up George Garlick designed semi-detached and detached villas on Compton Road in 1897 for G. J. Bagshaw, who had taken several plots from the Devonshire Estate. The estate at Hogshaw, developed by Frederick W. Booth between 1896 and 1899, consisted of forty-two cottages and a house all designed by George Garlick.[44] George Brocklehurst commissioned Garlick for his houses in Robertson Road and South Street, and builder John Henry Holmes of South Street worked with both Garlick and Holland to develop his land in Robertson and Spencer Roads and with Bryden on Sylvan Cliff. When Farrow and Brindley opened up Lightwood Road in 1903–5 with impressively large semi-detached houses they used W. R. Bryden designs.[45]

The practices of Bryden, Garlick and Holland dominated the local architectural provision in this period. There were other architects' offices. John Simpson, surveyor to the Devonshire Buxton Estate, carried out some private commissions and another chartered surveyor, John L. Strain, designed 'Delrow Terrace' in Darwin Avenue, houses in Robertson Road and cottages at Silverlands. Strain lived at 'Braeside', the Park, a detached house of the early 1890s, Vernacular with corner turret and spire. Samuel Gladwin, who had premises in Hardwick Street, designed investment property for the owner of the Buxton Hydropathic, H. R. P. Lomas. These included 'Rochester Terrace' a block of four-storey town houses with Italianate features to the first floor and extensive use of dormers and plain sash windows, and four cottages in Torr Street, but little further work of his has been identified in Buxton. William Perry designed his own house 'Southleigh' in newly developing Spencer Road in 1894 and it was praised particularly for its internal design by the *Building News*, though externally it is unpretentious.[46] His only other known design was two villa residences

MR. GEO. E. GARLIC

George Edwin Garlick
(*c.* 1863–*c.* 1932). A pupil of
W. R. Bryden he designed
many shops and private houses
in the town. In 1895 he was
elected to the Buxton UDC.
[B.M.A.G.]

also in Spencer Road, in 1898, for Simpson Bros. the fishmongers, Scarsdale Place. The period from 1890, however, saw notable regional architects undertaking commissions, Charles Heathcote came to live in town; so did Barry Parker who opened an office with Raymond Unwin, others, such as Huon Matear, Thomas Garner, Frank Matcham and Larner Sugden visited to design buildings. All have left their mark on the town.

Charles Henry Heathcote FRIBA (1851–1938) trained under Charles Hansom, the noted church architect of Bristol, and he spent a year in the offices of Lockwood and Mawson before setting up his practice in Manchester in 1873. He designed many important commercial buildings in Manchester, including twenty or more banks, a similar number of insurance offices and about half the factories on Trafford Park.[47] He came to live in St John's Road, Buxton, in about 1893 in a house which he had designed in Arts and Crafts style and named 'Wychwood'.[48] His family settled into life in the town and the two sons who were to join his practice were brought up at 'Wychwood'.[49] Heathcote took an active part in the Anglican community; his involvement in architectural aspects of St James Church are noted in chapter seven. He took commissions in Buxton, becoming one of the many architects involved in extensions to the Peak Hydropathic and he designed several houses in addition to his own.[50] 'Southcroft' in Carlisle Road, designed for F. Baden Benger in 1896, was illustrated in the *Building News* after completion in January 1897.[51] It was in Arts and Crafts style reviving the Cheshire half timber with Tudor in the treatment of gable ends and small pane windows. Close by he designed, in 1899, 'Thornwood' for Mr John Seebohm, a member of the firm Schill, Seebohm & Co., Shipping Merchants of Portland

An example of the work of Manchester architect Charles Heathcote (1851–1938) who came to live in Buxton in about 1893. This house 'Southcroft' on Carlisle Road was built in 1896 in the Arts and Crafts style reviving the Cheshire half timbers with Tudor treatment to the gable ends and small pane windows. It was built for F. Baden Benger.

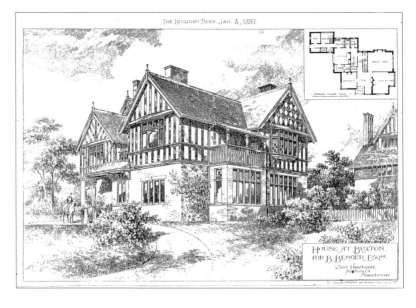

THE BUILDING NEWS, JAN. 8, 1897.

HOUSE AT BUXTON.
FOR B. BENGER, ESQRE.
Chas Heathcote,
Architect
Manchester

Street, Manchester.[52] His design for Miss Emily Mothersill's house in the Park was more restrained, in stone with some hung tiling and string-courses in smooth stone. It had two ground-floor windows set at right angles, separated by a narrow corner pier which was a feature of all his Buxton houses.[53]

Mr Digby Johnson, General Manager of the Lancashire Insurance Company, and a much travelled man, bought more than two and a half acres of land from the Devonshire Estate in 1893 at a Chief Rent of £70 *per annum*. He commissioned Huon Matear of Liverpool to build him a substantial house, called the 'Branksome', in an idyllic setting, adjacent to the River Wye tributary.[54] Matear, who had achieved FRIBA in 1892, designed a quite exquisite house and stabling in the Cheshire half-timber style; the walls were of Yorkshire stone parpoints and the half-timbering in solid English oak. His tall Tudor style chimney stacks were in brick and the roof tiles green. Inside the floors were of maple, the joinery in oak and yellow pine, and Matear designed a number of features including a full height smooth sandstone fireplace to the hall. Digby Johnson's estate was completed by two staff houses on Gadley Lane, one by Charles Heathcote (1898), the other, a coachman's house, by W. R. Bryden in 1902.[55] It is not known whether Matear set the pace of the Tudor brick and Cheshire half-timber revival in Buxton. Barry Parker was in town at this time and designed 'Faringford' and 'Somersby', in 1896–97, on land bought by his father, Robert.[56] This pair of houses, situated on the newly developing middle-class area of College Road are prime examples of the richly eclectic Northern Arts and Crafts style with extensive use of timber framing in the gables and much external woodwork. Others were to follow including several by W. R. Bryden.

Robert Parker, father of Barry was a manager with the Crompton & Evans Union Bank Ltd who moved to Buxton in the late 1880s. He bought a plot of land in the Buxton Park in 1891 agreeing to build three properties of not less than £1,500 each in value.[57] These

Frederick Baden Benger owned the Grange at Knutsford and ran the nationally known business of Benger's Foods specialising in baby and invalid foods. This advertisement of 1883 shows the origins of his company.

'The Branksome', St John's Road designed in 1894 by the Liverpool architect Architect Huon A. Matear. It was designed in the Cheshire half-timber style with Yorkshire stone, brick Tudor style chimneys and green roof tiles. The interior features were also carefully designed by the architect and included a full-length smooth sandstone fireplace to the hall.
[B.G.P.L.C.]

were 'Longford Lodge', 'Moorlands' and 'Strachur' reputedly designed by Barry Parker but local architect, G. E. Garlick, was involved.[58] Barry Parker and Raymond Unwin, who were half-cousins and brothers-in-law, began working together in 1894. Moorlands became the Parker family home and, when Raymond Unwin (1863–1940) moved to Bank Hall Lodge, Chapel-en-le-Frith, in 1896 he was able to travel by train to work in the Buxton office which they opened

A photograph of the south facing front of 'The Branksome', St John's Road. It was built for Mr Digby Johnson, General Manager of the Lancashire Insurance Company.

191

"MAISON ROUGE" at BUXTON for FREDERICK SMALLMAN Esq

SOUTH ELEVATION.

"MAISON ROUGE." BUXTON — Mr. LARNER SUGDEN, F.R.I.B.A., ARCHITECT.

at 6 & 7 the Quadrant.[59] Between 1889 and 1892 Richard Barry Parker (1867–1947) had been articled to George Faulkner Armitage (1849–1937) who is credited with the Domestic Revival of Tudor brick and Cheshire half-timber.

Armitage was a skilled woodcarver and an interior designer and he ran a Manchester agency for the firm of William Morris.[60] His influence on Parker was formative and lasting. Here the links with Armitage, Morris and architects in Buxton take on a further dimension. Larner Sugden (1850–1901), the Leek architect, came to Buxton to design one house only, the 'Maison Rouge' on Park Road, in 1897 for the vegetarian caterer, Frederick Smallman.[61] William Morris studied the art of dyeing at Thomas Wardle's works in Leek between 1875 and 1877, during which time he and Sugden met. Sugden subsequently became one of the first members of Morris's Society for the Protection of Ancient Buildings, a Socialist and member of the Co-operative movement. He was a good friend of Raymond Unwin, himself strongly influenced by Ruskin and Morris, being secretary of a Manchester branch of Morris's Socialist League in 1885.[62] So here in Buxton may be found a coterie of architects in the Northern Arts and Crafts mould. Larner Sugden's Maison Rouge, now sadly demolished, was outstanding. It had a central pitched roof with roughcast upper stories and a bold decoration in the centre of the gable, either side were round towers with conical roofs. The roof was covered with hand-made red clay tiles, but the most marked feature were the verandahs to both the ground and first floors. This dominated the entire front of the house.[63] Sugden could not, however, escape the watchful eye of the Devonshire Estate, for a note on the plan reads:

Larner Sugden (1850–1901) and his father William Sugden (1820/21–1892) were prolific architects in Leek, Staffordshire, and much of their work can be seen there. The 'Maison Rouge', or Red House on Park Road is the only example of Larner Sugden's work so far identified in Buxton. It was built in 1897 for Frederick Smallman, a vegetarian caterer in Manchester. [B.G.P.L.C. and D.C. Chat.]

... N.B. It was agreed 6 Feb 1897 between the architect and Mr R. Duke of the Devonshire Estate Office Buxton that in lieu of red brick facing to the ground stores and yard walls Dunford Bridge stone parpoints should be used. Also that all exposed wood covering oriels, veranda etc. shall be executed in teak or greenheart ...[64]

Parker and Unwin designed five further houses. They were 'Greenmoor' on Carlisle Road (1898/9) and two pairs on Lightwood Road at the extreme northern edge of the town, known as 'Cavanleck', 'Overlaw', 'Lightwood Ridge', and 'Woodlea' (*c.* 1901). They also designed extensions to the 'Towers' on College Road (1901) and a conservatory for Dr William Tweed Hannah at no. 1 Broad walk in 1901/2. But their most outstanding house is 'Greenmoor', which has a continuous oak-framed window curving round the corners of the first floor and is of three storeys with steep overhanging roof and

Barry Parker's father built three houses in the Buxton Park, one of which – 'Moorlands' – became the family home. Barry Parker designed two houses on land bought by his father in the newly developing College Road. 'Farringford' and 'Somersby', of 1895–96. These are prime examples of the richly eclectic Northern Arts and Crafts style and were the first of several to be designed in this mode in Buxton by the partnership of Parker and Unwin.

A view of College Road in about 1900. 'Farringford' and 'Somersby' can be seen on the near left and beyond them 'The Towers' designed in 1896 by Garlick & Flint with alterations and additions by Parker and Unwin in 1901.

Preliminary Sketch for the Hall for a House at Buxton.

Whilst in Buxton Barry Parker published a paper 'Our Homes' which was serialised in *The Builder* and *Building News*. Parker and Unwin also published a collection of lectures and illustrations in a book, *The Art of Building a Home*, in 1901. These publications featured their designs for houses at Buxton. Here is a preliminary sketch for a hall at Buxton. [L.G. & Co.]

neat dormer windows, the chimneys are tall and of brick. Pevsner describes this house as eclectic and Miller suggests they were influenced in their earlier work by published designs of Voysey and Baillie Scott.[65] Parker and Unwin worked in Buxton until moving to Baldock, Hertfordshire, in about 1906 to complete Letchworth Garden City. In fact the plans for Letchworth were drawn at Buxton and two other major projects, New Earswick, for Rowntrees of York and Starbeck near Harrogate were also under way.[66]

These were formative years for the partnership, for these three projects were influential in shaping new approaches to housing design and layout. Though he was also designing middle-class housing, Unwin's beliefs in the social purpose of the Arts and Crafts movement led to designs for artisan housing and forms of co-operative living. Both sought publicity, giving lectures at conferences advancing the Fabian Society's aims of municipal socialism and advocating standards for the basic principles of shelter, comfort and privacy. Whilst in Buxton Barry Parker's paper 'Our Homes' was serialised in *The Building News* and a number of articles and sketch designs appeared in that journal and *The Builder*.[67] The significance of the presence of Parker and Unwin in Buxton has not, until now, been fully appreciated. They ran an office for ten years in the Quadrant during which time they were doing work which would lead them out into the Garden City movement through Letchworth and Hampstead Garden Suburb to achieve national recognition in the newly emerging discipline of town planning. In Buxton they left fine examples of their earlier and formative work but, more than this, they appear to have inspired at least one other architect, W. R. Bryden. Bryden took

Photograph of a living room in
Buxton by Barry Parker and
Raymond Unwin. [L.G. & Co.]

his Vernacular designs into a pair of large semi-detatched houses,
'Lakenham' and 'Inglethorpe' at the end of Burlington Road with
half-timbered gables and crenellated ground-floor bays in 1898 and
Lakenham became his own residence. He crossed the road to design
semi-detached houses known as the 'Alison' (1904), on a plot between
College and Temple Roads, in half timber and red tiling to match
'Farringford' and 'Somersby' opposite, but restrained with none of
the 'restless detail' [68] seen in Parker's work. He took the style up a
pastoral Temple Road, under the lee of Grin Low, to design 'Lerryn'
in 1908 for Robert McDougal, of the flour millers, Arthur McDougal,
and 'Heatherton' in 1910 for stockbroker Henry Lancashire.[69]

When Manchester textile merchant Richard Henry Brooks decided
to build 'Brooklands' next door to 'Heatherton' in the same year he
commissioned the Manchester firm of John Bowden to design in a
similar style.[70] Temple Road and the entrances to it became a
treasure-house of the Arts and Crafts and particularly Cheshire Half-
Timber revival in domestic housing, with the addition of two further
houses. These were 'Filleigh' built for Manchester metal dealer, James
H. Vickery in 1906 and 'Brantwood' for the Misses Taylor of Nottingham in 1907.[71] The architect was Charles Swain of Manchester and
his designs were a feast of exposed timber with first- and second-floor
bays featuring stained-glass windows. 'Brantwood' has massive wooden
shaped brackets to support the roof to the curved bay; 'Filleigh'
featured a central turret and spire to the front elevation.[72]

W. R. Bryden used the Vernacular style in the last house he designed
for his own occupation in Buxton. The plans for 'Heathfield' in the
Buxton Park were approved in 1905. The house has an abundance of
features in stone, red clay tiles and half-timbering which its modern
additions cannot hope to emulate.

So the families of the wealthy could enjoy the pure air and semi-rural
ambience of the resort and could find many of their own kind with

Bryden built 'Heathfield' in
Park Road in about 1905 for his
own occupation. The house
featured his Vernacular style in
an abundance of features of
stone, red clay tiles and
half-timbering.

whom to mix. The correspondence of Sarah Meggitt Smith, wife of Aston W. Smith the Railway Contractor shows this family 'etiquette'. She was in touch socially with many families including Margaret Orme at 'Glenwood', St John's Road,[73] Mary Heathcote at 'Wychwood', Ann Williamson at 'Overdale', Maria Shaw at 'Whitehall', and the Brydens at their various addresses.[74] The Smiths had moved to 'Gadley' on Manchester Road in 1893, a house which A. W. Smith designed for himself. Miss Lucy Gibbs used her family connection for her house 'Villette' on Green Lane which was designed in 1897 by the Sheffield firm of Flockton Gibbs & Flockton.[75] The style is unusual: two-storey square bays and narrow mullioned windows reminiscent of the seventeenth-century Hall at Hartington which has three- to five-light mullioned windows with hood moulds.[76] Richard Mason Esplin, chairman of E. Goodall, Lamb & Heighway Ltd, a substantial Manchester firm dealing in carpets, floor coverings and furnishing lived in 'Farringford' on College Road. John Hampden Beckett of the Manchester manufacturing chemists, J. M. Beckett & Son, bought 'Corbar Hall' in 1897, the Shaws having moved to 'Whitehall', Manchester Road, where Henry Shaw's grandson Arthur Pilkington Shaw, a barrister, raised his family.[77] The house, 'Melrose', in Buxton Park, later the home of Vera Brittain, was in 1899 occupied by George Hicks, an insurance underwriter who had been a prime mover and investor in the Manchester Ship Canal.[78] William Righton, who ran a cloth and dress wholesaling business on the Stretford Road, lived in the Parker house, 'Strachur', in Buxton Park for some years until he commissioned W. R. Bryden to design his new house

'Parkfield' on Carlisle Road in 1910.[79] Such families as these brought wealth into the town and helped to raise its cachet as a resort. It is easy to see why the railway catering firm of Spiers and Pond should chose to build a high-class hotel right at the beginning of the twentieth century. They commissioned Thomas Garner (1839–1906) who designed a 300-room hotel in an 8½-acre prime site in the Buxton Park.[80] Designed in 1898, it embodies much of the Queen Anne style, built round two quadrangles with five bays to the front and Dutch Gables to all faces, tall chimneys and a central cupola – it might be compared in some respects to 'Betteshanger' in East Kent, a large country house remodelled between 1856 and 1882 by George Devey.[81] The Empire Hotel, opened in 1901, provided luxurious accommodation in the season but closed in the winter months.[82] To add sparkle to the town the new century was greeted with a magnificent bijou opera house, designed by the prolific theatre architect, Frank Matcham (1854–1920), and opened in 1903. Noting it as a surviving provincial theatre of architectural importance the *Architectural Review*'s description in 1976 was:

> ... a real gem, inside and out, of Edwardian architecture ...[83]

Buxton the health resort was an epitome of good, solid, and some outstanding, Victorian and Edwardian architecture. Earlier the Devonshire Estate had dominated the shape of the built environment through their own architects. Later, shape and style owed more to local authority and private investment. All was for and because of the 4,000 or so visitors each week in the season and the wealthy putting down roots in the town. The buoyancy so generated in the local economy meant that architects local and regional could indulge their clients, and themselves, in the fashionable, the different, the daring. Buxton could be *fast* socially but also architecturally. In 1905 the view from Solomon's Temple was over a townscape laid out and built with optimism for the future.

> ... Buxton has many advantages as a residential town. As a
> fashionable health resort it offers the attractions of first-class concerts
> and plays, excellent shops and well-kept streets, pleasant society and
> good schools, a fast train service and many of the advantages of a
> large city. On the other hand, the disadvantages of town life are
> absent, and in their place we have pure, bracing air, charming scenery,
> and delightful gardens, quietness and rest. In a word, the best features
> of city and country life are combined ...[84]

CHAPTER NINE

Buxton: An Estate Resort ...
Poised for Constant Re-invention ...

T HE STUDY of Victorian and Edwardian Buxton is one of impressive provincial development. It is a story in which the growth and shaping of an inland health resort by an aristocratic landowner gives way to mature and assured control by the local authority. In order to set this story in context the first chapter has described some of the conditions which contributed to this growth and shaping. Now the story is completed by an examination of how the seminal growth shaped physical and social aspects of the town beyond the Great War of 1914–18. This chapter therefore has the two-fold aim of drawing together the main themes of the book and taking the story on to explain and explore Buxton – the inland resort – in the twentieth century.

Between 1848 and 1905 the town reached its highest point in medical reputation, economic performance, and physical growth: a pinnacle of conspicuous prosperity in its history not reached before or since. Other health resorts grew and prospered at this time, some promoting their natural mineral water, some the regime of hydropathy. But

Cheltenham Spa showing the Town Hall, Central Spa and Winter Gardens in the 1920s. [B.S.F.]

Buxton was different from other health resorts in that it was developed as an estate-town. This was to have important implications for the way in which it grew. Many health resorts were developed by a combination of public and private investment and, after the Limited Liability Acts of 1856 and 1862, private syndicates were formed to exploit a natural water resource. The Corporation of Bath controlled the pumps as early as 1823 and progressively its income from land, baths, pump rooms, water works and market tolls was spent in the modernisation of sanitary and other services, including house building. This meant that by the 1880s it was managing an increasingly complex business. Leamington Spa, extensively developed by two landowners, Edward Willes and Mathew Wise, as a Regency town, gave way to the middle-class property owners and business people who monopolised the Local Board from its establishment in 1852. The local authority acquired the Royal Pump Room and baths in 1868 and made progressive improvements to the town, obtaining borough status in 1875. The large town hall of 1883–84 by J. Cundall, a Tudor-Baroque design, is an impressive statement of civic progress. At Cheltenham developments up to the 1840s by Joseph Pitt with his Pittville Estate, Pearson Thompson's Lansdown Estate, Robert and Charles Jearrads' spa developments, including an immense and expensive Queen's Hotel, were only marginally successful as was the Bayshill Estate

The saline waters and brine baths of Droitwich were developed by John Corbett who had built a virtual monopoly of the medical resort facilities by the end of the nineteenth century. St Andrew's Brine Baths of about 1890 are built in a free style with much use of exposed timber. [B.S.F.]

Company's attempt to develop the Old Well area with classical-style residences of a 'superior grade' including a Royal Crescent to rival Bath. The town went through a period of stagnation as a spa but its fortunes were revived in the 1860s by syndicate finance. Incorporation as a borough in 1876 saw increasing investment by the local authority as the century proceeded, though private syndicate finance remained significant. Harrogate rivalled Buxton as a genteel and fashionable resort for the affluent visitor from Lancashire and Yorkshire. Development at Harrogate from the 1860s was by public and private enterprise and some joint work, private money generally providing residential and commercial building. Public ownership of springs and baths at Harrogate, like Bath, began earlier in the century. The Board of Commissioners, set up in 1841, had acquired the Royal (over the old sulphur well), the Tewitt and John's Well pump-rooms and, after the Local Government Act of 1858, the town progressively bought the baths and promenade facilities, completing public control of all the known eighty-seven springs and baths by the early 1870s. So Harrogate's local authority-led development was very differently shaped from that of Buxton, a difference not always recognised by the respective local newspapers in their comparisons of performance. Smaller resorts were often developed by a single promoter, Llandrindod Wells owed its resurgence into a large and fashionable resort to the investment of Sir Richard Price Green from 1862; neighbouring Builth Wells had no such investor and failed to blossom as a Victorian resort, suffering from the competition of its neighbour and the lack of rail communication. The saline waters and brine baths of Droitwich were largely developed by John Corbett, owner of a prosperous canal boat fleet, who exploited the salt commercially as well as building up an extensive empire in foundries, sawmills and brick-making. Corbett used his wealth to promote Droitwich, laying out the town and baths so that by the end of the century he had built up a virtual monopoly of the medical resort facilities. The iodine waters of Woodhall Spa in Lincolnshire, opened up by the lord of the manor Thomas Hotchkin, were further exploited by a syndicate which bought the estate in 1886. Early hydropathic centres relied for their *raison d'être* on promotion by members of the medical profession and Hydropathic Hotels were competitively commercial. Ben Rhydding at Ilkley had the inventive Dr William Macleod. At Malvern Doctors James Manby Gully and James Wilson developed formidable reputations counting among their patients some well-known literary and intellectual figures. At Matlock the wealthy hosiery manufacturer John Smedley and his wife assumed their own medical expertise, both publishing text-books on practical hydropathy.[1]

The development of Buxton as an inland resort was significantly different from these other resorts. It was owned and exploited during the first three-quarters of the nineteenth century by the Devonshire Estate. As an estate-town Buxton was not unique. Other estate-towns have been described, such as Bournemouth, developed by Sir George Tapps-Gervis, and Skegness by Lord Scarborough. Investment by the Devonshires' neighbour, the Duke of Rutland, in the Derbyshire towns of Bakewell and Ilkeston was modest and never likely to rival the size and reputation of Buxton.[2] Both Eastbourne and Barrow-in-Furness were similarly developed; indeed, this account of Buxton can be seen as completing a trilogy of studies into three principal investments by the Seventh Duke of Devonshire.[3] But Buxton's development was comprehensively controlled by the estate as the principal land-owner, unlike for example Eastbourne where, in addition to the Devonshires, the Gilbert family owned a significant if lesser acreage.[4] Little private investment of note is to be seen in Buxton. The Palace Hotel, a joint stock company, which might be regarded as the most conspicuous example, and the Buxton Improvements Company, with

Woodhall Spa, The Pump Room showing the rural setting of this small iodine water resort in Lincolnshire. [B.S.F.]

its local shareholders, were both directly influenced by Devonshire Estate investment. Even the Market House of 1857, funded by townsmen, was designed by the Devonshire architect Henry Currey and its foundation stone laid by the duke's agent.

In this comparison two things stand out. First, in its monopoly development of an estate-town becoming a leading inland health resort, Buxton may be said to be unique. Second, the earlier dominant influence of the estate gave way to control through the local authority, progressively but with increasing rapidity as urban land values rose and the estate sought new forms of investment which carried fewer management burdens. Thus Buxton was also unusual in the way in which domination by the estate changed rapidly at the turn of the century to comprehensive control by the local authority.

The domination by the Devonshire Estate permeated all facets of the developing resort, in the provision of utilities, public health standards, street layout, size and architecture of buildings, provision of hotels and, not least, the class of visitor to be encouraged. By the time the local authority was in a position to exert a comparable degree of influence the tone had already been set. The ground was firmly laid by Phillip Heacock, agent for nearly fifty years to 1851. Though struggling to secure real financial investment he transformed the environs of the town with his tree planting programme and he began from an early stage to influence public health by the provision of piped water to the main areas of habitation and spring water to the estate's hotels. He it was who recognised the changing nature of visitors to the town and the estate's emphasis in attracting solid middle-class spenders may be said to issue from his agency. During Heacock's time and beyond the influence of (Sir) Joseph Paxton was seen, principally in plantations and gardens but also in the Buxton Park. This was a serious investment by the estate to develop urban Buxton but it did not work as expected, for not even the Devonshire Estate was immune to the vagaries of the land market. As a new and exclusively middle-class residential area the Buxton Park could be described as 'suburban' both in its position on the western edge of the town and in the provision of substantial building plots for villas and crescents of large houses.[5] The layout and style of the Park clearly intended it for an upper middle- and middle-class clientele at a time when such differentiation in residential location was increasingly to be seen. Unfortunately for the estate there was little immediate demand from within or outside the town. It required the arrival of the railways in 1863 to stimulate greater expansion. Later developments by the Devonshire Estate in terms of plot size, position and exclusivity exhibit the nature of suburban development though the resort of Buxton had, as part of its amenities, expectations of quality and standards in housing akin to those of suburbia. The Devonshire Park is a good

Examples of decorative stonework much favoured by architect Robert Rippon Duke. The detail of Chiswick House, Marlborough Road, may be attributed to R. R. Duke and his own house on Manchester Road (1870–71) has attractive stone carving to window and door surrounds. [B.M.A.G.]

example, it was much more immediately successful, indicating the willingness of prosperous townspeople and outsiders to build property for private occupation or for investment once communications had improved. A number of other locations were developed by the estate in a suburban style as one of the ways in which the desirable class of visitor and new resident were drawn to the town. The direction of the estate may also be seen in the placing and masking of working-class housing. To the south and east are a number of streets, in the higher town, which are fronted by three-storey terraces. These present a good façade but lack depth, having a small yard and service road to the rear. They were occupied in the main by lower middle-class families, often with seasonal letting rooms. Behind such houses were placed the working-class cottages. By virtue of its predominance in land ownership the estate was able to influence the type and size of housing in particular areas and the use of Chief Rents within a regime of restrictive covenants allowed the value and quality of house building to be carefully controlled. The earlier architecture was dominated by the estate, and Buxton has a legacy of mid-Victorian buildings designed by Henry Currey in his preferred Italianate style. Under no particular pressure to change his last public building, the Pump Room of 1892–93, exhibits features of this style. Apart from Currey the only architect of note up to about 1885 was Robert Rippon Duke who was more eclectic and adventurous, particularly in his large public buildings, though he too, whilst favouring decorative stonework, delivered solid family villas.

The mark of the estate is also to be seen in the provision of utilities and in public health. The prime mover in this was the Agent Edward Woollett Wilmot, chairman of the first Local Board. He was instrumental in obtaining the services of Robert Rawlinson, an eminent engineer who became chief inspector, in designing the first sewage system and this placed Buxton ahead of other towns. It set the tone in standards and it is notable that the Local Board used the services of another sanitary specialist, Dr J. C. Thresh, in its updating and expansion of facilities in the 1880s. The estate ran the water works until 1868 and gave the services of its surveyor for a year to ease the transition of the service to the Local Board. Here are clear examples of the local authority learning from the Devonshire estate.

It has been noted that the estate, while to some degree operating in a paternalistic style, maintained a commercial hard nose in its Buxton dealings. It was necessary to optimise earnings from the baths, maximise earnings from land sales and draw the right kinds of visitors to the town to fill the hotels in which it had a pecuniary interest. Surpluses from Buxton might well have been used in investment-hungry Eastbourne, and later in the century were needed to shore up the ailing Barrow. Through the time of the study, Buxton was a net earner for the estate and, indeed, revenue from some land sales by-passed the accounts and were remitted directly to Currey & Co. at 14 Great George Street, Westminster. The use of the Chief Rent was an unusual way of handling land sales and providing a perpetual income for the duke since ordinary freeholds or leaseholds were more usual arrangements. Estate business was conducted through agents who were resident in Buxton up to 1864 when George Drewry, who lived at Holker, added the Buxton agency to his existing portfolio in Lancashire and Yorkshire. For more than twelve years the Buxton Estate was managed on a day-to-day basis by three local staff. This was unusual; absentee landlords were fairly common and smaller estates were often managed on a part-time basis by professional land agency firms but Buxton, which included a large agricultural tenancy and a growing urban estate now found itself with an absentee agent.

"Trippers"

A lovely cartoon by W. G. Baxter showing a motley assortment of trippers in the Pavilion Gardens.

The effect was to place considerable authority in the hands of the three sub-agents who were themselves part of the group of prominent townsmen ruling affairs in the resort. They enjoyed decision-making and saw public and private life as of equal importance; they were the group from which the local politicians were drawn. Opportunities to progress business would be sought through various associations in town. Thus, all three were church members, two as Anglicans, the third as a Nonconformist, and Turner and R. R. Duke served for periods on the Local Board. These two featured in many public areas of town life and were active in such associations as Freemasonry, Oddfellows and Foresters. Both were also closely concerned with the management of the Devonshire Hospital. Clearly one way of getting a favourable decision would be to cultivate these agency staff. Another effect of the absentee agent is seen in the assiduous way in which restrictive covenants and building standards were enforced. This shows today in the quality and layout of housing and in such details as the stone ground-floor bay windows and in the uniform nature of property walls and gateposts where half-round ashlar coping, smooth-bevelled coping and uniform pattern gateposts are ubiquitous. R. Grundy-Heape claimed that if Phillip Heacock was presented with a proposal of which he did not approve he would tell the proposer that it would be submitted to the Duke, which meant Mr Heacock's wastepaper basket. When Robert R. Duke said about some aspect of a builder or architect's plan that His Grace would not approve what he really meant was that Robert Duke did not approve and the plans would have to be changed.[6]

The rationale for all this estate activity were the visitors to the town. The numbers of visitors in a typical week in the high season increased by four hundred per cent between 1859 and 1905. But who were these visitors? It was in the interest of the Devonshire Estate to attract the reasonably well-off or at least respectable visitor and to draw from as wide a catchment area as possible. A typical indication taken from the *Buxton Herald and Visitors' Gazette* for Wednesday 16 July 1902 reveals many from Lancashire and Yorkshire but also significant numbers from London, Scotland and the Midlands. The titled and better-off are in the large hotels and hydropathics; many of these families are from London. Others are in lodging-houses from the modest establishment on West or Market Street to the private hotels and more up-market lodging-houses skirting the Parks and baths. Many are families where perhaps one member of the family is in town to undergo medical treatment at the baths and the rest to provide support and companionship and take a holiday. These patients have usually been referred by their own doctor to a water medical doctor at Buxton who would undertake his own examination and prescribe particular courses of hydrotherapeutic treatment. This was the protocol agreed between the Buxton health resort profession and the referring doctor. The patient was of course required to pay both for consultations and the courses of treatment at the baths. The establishment medical men kept up a reputation for the efficacy of the water treatment. It was in their own interests and that of the Devonshire Estate and the local authority to develop the medical reputation. Hence Buxton became one of the foremost health resorts by the end of the nineteenth century. Of course the town also had its excursionists and day-trippers, and there were refreshment rooms and other facilities for them in Higher Buxton. Contemporary accounts and the publications of cartoonists such as Baxter showed some of the less desirable effects of a crowded concert hall in the Pavilion Gardens or the bustling Pump Room in the morning but in the main the direction of the estate, the medical profession and the local authority combined to keep the class of visitor genteel or at least respectable.[7]

Patients at the Devonshire Hospital were, of course, in town through charity arrangements and were drawn mainly from the working class in Lancashire and Yorkshire but also from places to the south and west including Derby, Nottingham, Burton-on-Trent and as far as London. An analysis by Dr John Pearson in 1861 gives a cross-section of one hundred patients, examples of occupations being file-smith, labourer, washerwoman, gardener's wife, knife-maker and silk weaver. The annual reports of the hospital listed trades and occupations of patients from 1875, from which it can be seen that many were cotton operatives, both male and female, including carders, but others worked in occupations ranging from char-woman to seamstress, to engine driver, stoker, collier and miner.[8] These patients were largely segregated from the paying patients and Buxton visitors. Whilst exercise was deemed to be part of the

For eight years from 1879 conductor Carl Meyder presented very popular concerts in the Large Concert Hall and seats were at a premium. In the midst of this altercation the third gentleman might just secure the chair!

The evening Concerts—rush for the last chair.

treatment, shortly after the first conversion of the hospital the Devon-shire Estate gave land to the front of the hospital on a low Chief Rent on the understanding that ornamental gardens were laid out for such purposes. The trustees used the services of Adam Hogg, the curator of the Buxton Gardens. Until 1875 the charity patients had their own suites of baths in the Natural and Hot sides of the Crescent approached by rear entrances. From the early 1870s the baths became very busy and the agent began to look for ways of providing for charity baths elsewhere so as to release more space for the paying patient. Dr Robertson's disagreement with the estate over the siting of these baths is one of the rare occurrences where medical and estate opinions clashed. Robertson staked his medical reputation on his belief that the Natural water treatment must be taken close to the source if the properties of the water and its constituent gasses were not to be lost. A neat compromise resulted in new Hot and Natural Baths for charity patients but, in the case of the latter, a much reduced provision. When the hospital grew to 300 beds with the major conversion of 1879–82 a new pump room was built for patients. Again this was as a result of pressure in the press and from townspeople who complained of the overcrowding in the drinking well at the Natural Baths, which was used by both charity and paying patients. The charity patients were an 'inconvenience'.

"No seat can be considered engaged, unless personally occupied."
Rather a shame. He had only risen from it for a moment, and never knew it had been removed till——

W. G. Baxter's caption says it all!

The siting of working-class housing has already been referred to and it is clear that throughout the century actions were taken to keep the working class, both visitor and resident, in their place. In this the estate was supported by the medical establishment, and the policy was continued by a local authority which was as anxious to retain a good quality free-spending visitor. The layout of housing did not materially change as the local authority assumed greater influence over planning, nor did the Local Board or UDC seek to challenge the location of new roads proposed by the estate. It would not be until after the Great War that the local authority would take the lead in town planning and the provision of working-class housing.

The need to provide for the spiritual needs of visitors forms part of the reason why the town saw so many new places of worship built during the period. In a number of cases, decisions taken to build a church or chapel were not based on a large local congregation, more likely on the need to provide for the visitor; indeed some, such as the Unitarians, survived because of a well-supported visitor collection plate. The range of denominations on offer meant that visitors of a particular class or persuasion might find a place in the right pew. The Devonshire Estate showed its Anglican stance quite clearly in blocking progress in Nonconformity, though where a particular church had a wealthy promoter the way could be eased. The estate position may be seen as one of supporting the middle-class expansion. Certainly the Unitarians and the Catholic Apostolics had no difficulty in obtaining land for their respective churches, unlike the Primitive Methodists.

The dominant Anglicans locally were high church. This caused one wealthy solicitor to build Trinity Church for low Anglicans. The high churchman Dr Robertson could never bring himself to mention this in his influential *Buxton Guide*. However, Anglicanism and Nonconformity managed to work together for the good of the town. Each would give to the other's building fund and each was equally represented on the Local Board and other groups tending to promote the benefits of the inland resort.

In water medicine Buxton developed a precise reputation. Unlike its neighbour and rival Matlock, it did not embrace the fashionable hydropathic movement. It retained, like its other rival Harrogate, a treatment regime based upon its natural mineral water. Many inland resorts took up the use of water in medical treatment devised by Vincenz Priessnitz at Graefenberg and hydropathic hotels sprang up in existing and new centres such as Malvern, Liverpool, Stanstead Bury, Ramsgate and Ilkley. The 'new medicine' was, at one and the same time, heralded as a cure for all, or most, ailments and as a piece of quackery no better than the mesmerism or phrenology also common at the time. Buxton stayed in the mainstream of established medicine because its reputation was carefully controlled by Dr Robertson, its foremost medical man, and others of note in town such as Ottiwell Gifford-Bennet, F. K. Dickson, George Lorrimer and W. P. Shipton. Robertson's proficiency in water medicine was well recognised by *The Lancet*. This firm hold on the medical regime and the efficacy of the natural mineral water helped to sustain a medical clientele of the right sort and in this the medical establishment in town supported the efforts of the Devonshire Estate and the local authority. An important comparison can be made between Buxton, Harrogate and Bath, which all remained part of the formal medical establishment with their natural mineral water supported by a charity hospital, and other centres which relied upon the growth of hydropathics from which to build a reputation. As the century proceeded doctors selected from a wider range of treatments, some of which had originated in hydropathy, but as techniques developed the science of balneology became part of the medical establishment and water doctors saw themselves on a par with consultants in other branches of medicine. Undoubtedly the value of hydrotherapy in the treatment of rheumatic disease was recognised.

The earlier domination by the estate gave way progressively to local authority direction, though it must be remembered that the layout of the town up to the early part of the twentieth century was still very much influenced by the estate as the principal landowner. While the estate did not seek directly to influence local politics by having a nominee on the Local Board after the resignation of Woollett Wilmot, it is noticeable that John. D. Simpson was recruited as surveyor in 1877, a man with fourteen years in similar service with the Local Board. In this appointment the agent was preparing for more equally balanced negotiations: the principal landowner would need to find an accommodation with the local democratic processes if it was to achieve its desired land sales. Progressively, the estate found that it had to seek approval from the local authority to complete its proposed new roads and building plots and to ensure adoption. Robert R. Duke was to be seen frequently supporting the estate's case at Local Board fortnightly meetings.

Relations between the two were generally amicable and there are many examples of constructive co-operation. These can most readily be seen between the respective surveyors over road layout or building standards. Disagreements arose most usually over who was to pay for a particular investment. A notable early split occurred over the sanitary arrangements and was the cause of Edward Woollett Wilmot's resignation as chairman of the Local Board. Later disagreements were over who should pay for the bridges spanning the Wye tributaries on the Burlington Road extension, the siting of the cemetery, the extension of Dale Street and the layout of Hardwick Square North. The Local Board progressively found its feet as the estate gradually relinquished power. Services such as gas, water, street sweeping and watering, fire service and refuse collection were provided, and regulation of community behaviour through bye-laws increased to meet the standards needed in an inland resort.

The year 1886 can be seen as a watershed for the Local Board and the town. In this year, as the Urban Sanitary Authority, the Board gathered all the earlier bye-laws into a new set containing 101 clauses. From this time up to 1905 an exponential growth may be seen in local authority investment. No fewer than 101 loans were sanctioned, amounting to just over £400,000 of actual borrowing for improvements to the town's services and capital investment in plant and machinery to provide this.[9] The town hall, begun in 1887 overlooking the Higher and Lower towns, was a 'citadel' for the Local Board which now had its own council chambers and could move from the small offices rented from the Devonshire Estate in George Street.

'Ravensworth', Carlisle Road
(1912), a good example of
W. R. Bryden's eclectic design
incorporating many features,
including Cheshire revival
half-timbering, oriel window,
square and round bays and
variation in gables and roof
shapes.

The year 1886 was significant in another respect: the architect
William Radford Bryden began to leave his mark on public and
private buildings. Before this Buxton's architecture had been dominated by the estate architect Henry Currey and the associate Robert
Rippon Duke, leaving little opportunity for others. Few buildings
had little or no Devonshire estate involvement (the Town Hall and
Buxton College by Pollard of Manchester are notable exceptions).
But from 1886 the field began to open out and this may be seen as
another example of the loosening of the estate's hold on town development. W. R. Bryden came in 1883 to purchase the business of Robert
R. Duke. He brought an eclectic approach learned, no doubt, from
his experience as a pupil to E. M. Barry who was for a time professor
of architecture at Kings College, London. Bryden had a singular
impact on Buxton architecture, not only through his own work but
in his training of two pupils, George E. Garlick and William Holland,
who each worked extensively in the town. Bryden was a man of his
time; free style in architecture allowed him to exercise his penchant
for the Vernacular and a clever mix of different styles on the one
building. Many of his clients were well off and discerning. They came
from Manchester and the North West to set up a family home or
second house in the clear bracing air and climate of the health resort,
taking advantage of an efficient and speedy rail service. In common
with others Bryden's work as primarily a local architect has, until this
study, been largely unrecognised and certainly underrated. To some
extent the same might be said of the Arts and Crafts and Cheshire

Domestic Revival work in the town. Of course the work of Parker and Unwin has been well researched by others, and that of such notables as Faulkner Armitage is documented, but the presence in town of a select group of architects designing in the Northern Arts and Crafts style has not previously been recognised. In addition to Parker and Unwin the work of Larner Sugden of Leek, Charles Heathcote, Huon Matear and Charles Swain is now known. Much of it remains, although some can now only seen in the form of plans and drawings. This study has identified a period of great artistic activity, a time when the town was not only bustling with visitors but was welcoming wealthy business families who, through their commissions, were allowing architects the creative freedom to develop distinctive and quite outstanding houses. The buoyancy of the time might be gauged, in visitor and resident numbers, by the bold decision of the Spiers and Pond Company to build a high-class 300-guest Empire Hotel in Buxton Park and of the Buxton Gardens Company in commissioning Frank Matcham to design a magnificent Opera House capable of seating 1,200.

While the wealthy continued to commission architects, creative free-style work ensued, particularly in Cheshire Domestic Revival architecture. Good work in this style continued up to the end of the 1920s and examples can be seen into the inter-war years although they become progressively poor imitations. Bryden and Walton completed plans for 'Ravensworth' on Carlisle Road for Mr Charles Dent in 1912, another eclectic design by Bryden, who in the same year designed the Burbage Institute and Buxton's Cottage Hospital. They had been responsible in 1909 for the replacement of the Hot Baths' colonnading in iron and glass, lit by electric light, and for the conversion of Robert R. Duke's Post Office on Cavendish Circus into five shops featuring stylish exterior glazed tiling. Their dark mahogany banking hall for Williams & Glyns Bank at 1 Cavendish Circus remains today. The last work identified by them is the new baths for patients at the Devonshire Hospital built on the south front in 1914. W. R. Bryden retired to the south of England in 1915 but this was not before he had complained publicly about losing the contract for a new St Mary's Church on Dale Road. The Bryden and Walton designs for a church, in a Perpendicular style, to seat 400 were published in the *Buxton Advertiser* in 1913 followed by a letter from Bryden bemoaning the fact that the selection committee had ignored local talent and sent the work out of town. However this turned out to be a wise decision for the architects commissioned, P. H. Currey and C. C. Thompson of Derby, produced a quite outstanding Arts and Crafts design which included interior furnishings, in the style of the Northern Art Workers Guild.[10] St Mary the Virgin is described by Pevsner as very attractive, in stone with a steep undulating roof spanning the nave and very low aisles. It has what he calls 'eyebrow dormers' instead of clerestory windows; the east, west and transept windows are lancet style and it has a small central belfry with a single office bell.[11] St Mary's has been underrated architecturally perhaps because of its location; it stands in the middle of a late nineteenth-century estate of working- and lower middle-class houses. Had it been built in Temple or Carlisle Road it would have been seen as a natural complement to the domestic Arts and Crafts architecture and more readily recognised for the gem it is.

After the First World War architecture in the free-style tradition was carried on by Charles Swain of Manchester who had acquired the old office of Bryden and Walton at no. 3 George Street in 1921. He designed several houses in a Vernacular style, often using Cheshire half-timber features. These included a six-bedroom house with servants' rooms on Carlisle Road for Mr A. Parker in 1923 and several houses in Green Lane including 'Poole Croft' and 'Cove Side' and a pair, typical of his creative style, which have an open porch under a half-curved lintel and circular window to the side of the front door with uneven length of eaves in the roof treatment over the door. In the post-war expansion of Temple Road his work is in evidence at 'Canavan' built for J. A. Jackson in 1922 somewhat after the style of C. F. A. Voysey with wide round arch doors, small pane windows and extensive variations to roof shapes which are covered in green tiles. Temple Road became one of the most fashionable roads in town. It was completed by 1927 with substantial free-style houses by regional architects such as Lumb & Walton of Blackpool; Lockwood, Abercrombie & Saxon of Chester; Norman Jones of Southport, and the Alderley Edge firm of Isaac Massey & Sons Ltd. John Yates Potter,

The quite stunning Arts and Crafts church of St Mary the Virgin, Dale Road (1914–15) by Derby architects P. H. Currey and C. C. Thompson. It is described by Pevsner as very attractive, in stone with a steep undulating roof spanning the nave and very low aisles.

owner of the long-established drapers and outfitters in town commissioned a little known Stockport architect, P. Oakes (who lived in the nearby village of Dove Holes), to design a five-bedroom house known as 'Garth' at the entrance to Temple Road in 1927. Close by, Buxton College was extended in 1928–29 with a three-sided quadrangle of 'veranda' style classrooms by George Widdows, the Derbyshire County architect.[12] The local architects Charles Flint and William Holland were still in evidence, designing individual but modest houses in the fashionable areas including Mosley Road, one of the few immediate post-war roads, which was developed in the mid-1930s. Houses on this road were designed by Flint for builder William M. Bagshaw, continuing the business of his father George, the local politician whose firm had built extensively from the later part of the nineteenth century. Another old established firm, James Salt were still building in Wye Grove, off the Macclesfield Road which they had opened up in 1911.

The Devonshire Estate continued to sell building plots, more frequently now to speculative builders who were inclined to imitate and produce less refined designs. Of these the local firm of James Brindley, which built on Macclesfield Road, to the fashionable west of town, and the newer Lansdowne Road amongst other areas, carried a good reputation and chiefly worked to architect designs. The developer Thomas Hidderley of Hale in Cheshire who built also on Macclesfield Road and later on St John's Road was not viewed in the same light by at least one influential individual. Sarah Meggitt Smith, daughter of Robert R. Duke described his houses as 'gimcrack' and had little time for his actions as a speculator.[13] More modest housing was provided by the developer James Boon who constructed Curzon and Kedleston Roads off Sylvan Cliff and extended Heath Park and Brown Edge Roads largely with three-bedroom semi-detached houses.[14]

Early in 1917 Buxton and adjoining Fairfield Urban District Councils were officially incorporated into a newly formed Buxton Borough Council. The incorporation was a long drawn-out process with strong and organised opposition from Fairfield residents. The question had been under consideration since at least 1891. The Privy Council recommended a Charter of Incorporation in 1913 and the details were settled through four war years. This increased the population and rateable value of Buxton from 12,300 to 17,000 and £91,111 to £104,583 respectively but, more importantly, promoted self-assurance and energy for change through the new unitary authority. Changes in town planning and housing provision came quickly and they further weakened the influence of the Devonshire Buxton Estate.[15] Very soon after the end of the war house building was stimulated by a conference held in Buxton on 5 December 1918 between the inspector from the Local Government Board and the borough authority. The subject was arrangements for working-class housing and from this the Housing

After the Great War (1914–18) the Devonshire Buxton Estate continued to sell land for building, as this advertisement from a Buxton Town Guide of 1928 shows.

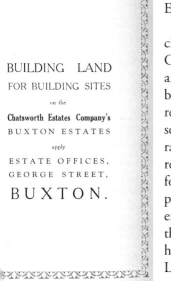

BUILDING   LAND

FOR BUILDING SITES

on the

Chatsworth Estates Company's
BUXTON ESTATES

apply

ESTATE OFFICES,

GEORGE STREET,

BUXTON.

98

The Market Place and Town
Hall in 1928 is depicted here in
a watercolour by Stewart.
Contemporary photographs
show that many trees had been
planted on the Market Place at
that time. [B.M.A.G.]

and Town Planning Committee of the Buxton Borough Council was
formed. The expense of building in the district was acknowledged to
be high, but the deficit borne locally was not to exceed a one penny
rate and national grants were available for this type of provision. Plans
for housing in the Heath Grove area and in Fairfield on Cliff, Queens
and Kings Roads were put forward. Actual building was slow. The
assisted scheme got under way on Cliff and Kings Road in 1921 and
Queens Road and Heath Grove in 1924 and working-class housing
of a good standard was built, but it was some distance from the main
attractions of the resort.[16] The new science of town planning was
now to reduce the Devonshire Buxton Estate's role in the town to
that of land and property management and sales, a far remove from
the days when Robert R. Duke determined the positioning of new
roads, the layout and the standards of building. Now the advice of
an external consultant was to be sought.[17] In 1925 the Town Clerk
reported that Mr Allen, the expert recommended by the President of
the Town Planning Institute, had recently visited Buxton to meet
Devonshire Estate Office and corporation officials. He had inspected
portions of the Devonshire Estate which were likely to be developed
in the near future and would let the council have his observations

on layout.[18] The estate continued to manage its land and property through the earlier twentieth century until the sale of Buxton properties and Chief Rents to pay death duties in 1951 severed any remaining influence by the estate on the town's affairs.

During the Great War Buxton had provided hospital facilities for the military. Vera Brittain has recounted her time as a VAD nurse in the Devonshire Hospital during the early part of the war.[19] A number of hotels became hospitals. The largest of the hydros, the 'Buxton', became the Granville Military Hospital and the Palace and Empire Hotels were annexed to it. Companies of soldiers were billeted in Buxton and the Pavilion Gardens lakes provided a good training ground for Royal Engineers. Towards the end of the war the town was designated a discharge centre for Canadian troops who used a number of the hotels. In 1921 Princess Mary laid the foundation stone of a new wing at the Devonshire Hospital which commemorated its work during the Great War. Despite its wartime activity a measure of the devastation experienced by the resort may be gauged from the number of hotels and business properties which subsequently came up for auction; these included the Peak Hydropathic, the Empire, Savoy and Shakespeare Hotels.[20]

Buxton was not slow to recover; the official guide book for 1921 was as handsomely produced as that of 1914 and gave an extensive picture of what the town had to offer: from treatments at the baths through annual sporting and musical events to more than twenty different amusements from badminton, croquet and bowls to boating, walking and rock-climbing.[21]

Water medical treatments continued to be popular and to draw the well-off client into town and while treatments were still prescribed for a range of illnesses the notion of an 'annual cure' – a visit to the baths for a physical overhaul as a means of preventive medicine – began to be promoted.[22] This showed in the 'three week' cure advocated from the late 1920s when the borough offered an all-inclusive ticket which included free daily admission to the Gardens and Pavilion. In 1935 a group of businessmen set up the Buxton Clinic in the east wing of the Crescent using the adjacent Hot Baths. They offered a three-week cure including treatment and board and residence for a modest four to six guineas weekly, thus opening up the facilities of the resort, and the idea of water treatment as a tonic or for convalescence, to a wider market. The resort would now have to appeal to the widest possible range of client if it was to remain competitive, with medical resorts at home and on the Continent. Inclusive period tickets remained available up to the 1950s when football teams were regular visitors. Well-known teams such as Manchester United and City, Nottingham Forest and Southampton would stay at the Palace

Hotel and take a short course of tonic aeration and Buxton Douche baths to tone players up for matches.

The Borough continued to invest in new treatments at the baths. A Ministry of Health loan allowed for a major upgrading of the Natural Baths in 1924 to include an impressive array of electro-water treatments as well as other most up-to-date forms of balneology. Such treatments as the Electric Water bath, four-cell Schnee bath, D'Arsonval High Frequency and the Dowsing Radiant Light & Heat Treatments and Electro-vibratory massage were available and Fango mud treatments were given using mud specially imported from Fango, Italy.[23] A new addition to the treatment list in 1924 was the Whirlpool Bath which was specially adapted for limbs affected by gunshot wounds. A popular treatment, which remained until the 1950s, was the 'peat' or 'moor bath' which used peat brought from the moors above Buxton. The patient lay in a steam-heated bath of peat and this was reckoned to be a very refreshing tonic. Buxton's reputation into the 1930s was supported by the British Spas federation which described its facilities and treatments in regular publications, and in 1938 the bathing facilities received a very satisfactory report from the British Health Resorts Association.[24] Despite this apparent level of interest income from the baths began an irreversible decline from the late 1930s and the failure of the National Health Service to include water treatments at health resorts meant that from 1948 the decline became terminal. Attempts to maintain interest with new treatments using physiotherapy and hydrotherapy in remedial and fitness regimes kept the baths going until the early 1960s when the Hot Baths closed; the Natural Baths, converted for public swimming, remained open until 1972. The sixty-year mortgage taken out by the UDC to buy the baths in 1904 was just long enough to last their life as a commercial enterprise.

The Devonshire Hospital became known in 1935 as the Devonshire Royal Hospital in recognition by King George V of its continuing contribution to health care. From the early 1930s the Hospital Management Committee began to acquire properties around the hospital for expansion of services. Thus Corbar Hall became a maternity hospital in 1946.[25] Plans to extend the Thermal Department with additional bathing accommodation, new wards for the treatment and study of cases of arthritis, together with reception and consulting rooms, were put forward in 1937. An appeal for funds went out but this extension, which would have changed the south front, did not materialise.[26] Some modernisation did, however, take place within the National Health Service, when the Devonshire Royal Hospital offered Physical Medicine and Orthopaedic Surgery and became a specialist centre for rheumatology. Towards the end of the twentieth century the hospital had 142 beds and a number of departments offering

Delegates entering a conference
ball at the Pavillion Gardens in
the 1930s

services for both in- and out-patients in radiography, pathology,
physiotherapy, occupational, speech and education therapies, chiro-
pody and dentistry. When the hospital closed in July 2000
hydrotherapy pools, using the natural mineral water, were still in use.
After nearly 2,000 years the use of Buxton water for therapeutic
bathing had come to an end.

During the late 1920s and 1930s the town became a centre for
high-class conferences. Business at the baths could not match the
halcyon days before the First World War and both the Borough
Council and hoteliers had to optimise their investments. The acquisition of the Pavilion Gardens and large Concert Hall from the Buxton
Gardens Company in 1927 meant that the Buxton Borough had
control of all the town's important amenities and a direct incentive
to optimise their use. The larger hotels could offer all types of function
rooms as well as some magnificent ballrooms and, of course, good-
quality accommodation. In the marketing efforts, which included fine
sepia brochures, can be seen a continuation of the old policy of
drawing the better-off visitor to the town, and this was reasonably
successful. The attractions offered by the town were enhanced when
Lilian Baylis, manager of the Old Vic Theatre, brought her company
to present a three-week play festival in August and September 1937.
So successful was this that the festival continued as an annual event
up to 1942, though during the war years it was reduced in length.
Famous actors appearing included Constance Cummings, Stewart
Grainger, Alec Guinness and Andrew Cruickshank. The 1937 town
brochure advertised the first festival, produced by Tyrone Guthrie,

217

and a measure of business in the resort during this period may be gauged from the thirty-one substantial hotels and more than forty private apartments and lodgings listed.[27]

The conference trade continued after the Second World War, though investment in this type of business by the local authority did not match the bold decisions taken by its old rival Harrogate in providing modern purpose-built facilities. In the late 1950s the town became more of an entertainments centre and may have attempted to rival Matlock Bath as a centre for day-trippers with annual illuminations and a wide range of shows at the Pavilion Gardens including concerts by many of the famous 'big bands' and pop groups. Repertory companies, including those of Anthony Hawtrey and the Penguin Players, provided annual programmes of plays in the 1940s and 1950s.[28]

Town guides into the 1960s and 1970s concentrated on sporting facilities and shopping, the Pavilion Gardens remaining the main centre of entertainment. Greater emphasis was also placed on such attractions as stately homes, picturesque towns and villages, show caves, ancient monuments and scenic dales which could be reached in a short drive from the town. A more recent resurgence has come from the refurbishment and re-opening of the Opera House in 1979 which led to an annual opera festival with its fringe activities, and other events such as the annual Gilbert and Sullivan Festival. The Opera House was reborn as a fully functioning theatre with an all-year round programme of entertainment and the town was now reputed for its antique, craft, book and similar fairs. Buxton still hosts conferences and draws in holidaymakers, for many of whom it serves as a base to explore the magnificent Peak District National Park. While new uses await John Carr's Georgian Crescent and Robert R. Duke's Devonshire Royal Hospital, it is hoped that the plans of the University of Derby, itself a newly formed foundation with a reputation to make,

A Conference in session in the Large Concert Hall in the 1930s. This view was used in the high-quality sepia brochures of the time to give an impression of the size of the Octagon Hall for conference organisers.

to establish schools of tourism and leisure and hotel and catering will breathe new life into these buildings and the rest of the town.

For its own part the local authority has embarked in recent years on a programme of modification and refurbishment to enhance and maintain the attractive heritage of the town. In 1987/88 a new road to relieve the very congested Spring Gardens was built. This necessitated the removal of the old Midland Railway station, which had closed in 1967, but paved the way for the main commercial street to be pedestrianised in 1997 and for the Spring Gardens Shopping Centre to be built. The modern glass barrel-vaulted design incorporates a tubular steel and glass external colonnade which, unfortunately, now mars the view of Samuel Worth's curved façade to the Royal Hotel (1849–52), but this building still fits neatly into its commercial environment.

In 1985–86 the Hot Baths were converted into a retail centre called the Cavendish Arcade by architects Derek Latham, incorporating a barrel-vaulted roof in stained-glass by the architect Brian Clarke. This centre retains original tiling and two of the small plunge baths together with an illustrated history of the Victorian baths. The terraced slopes in front of the Crescent, by Jeffry Wyatt in 1818, modified by Joseph Paxton in 1840s were again refurbished in 1993–94, and this work included the replacement of Turner's Memorial in its original position in front of the Hot Baths.

The Pavilion Gardens, a must for the Victorian visitor, is still a popular venue and will be enhanced by the restoration taking place between 1997 and 2003 at a cost of £4.7m to which the Heritage Lottery Fund has contributed £3.5m. This work includes a new bandstand after the style of Milner but larger to accommodate today's brass bands, the restoration of the lakes and Broad Walk, many new facilities for children and extensive new planting. The engine pulling the new railway ride for children has been named 'Edward Milner'. Adjacent to the entrance to the Pavilion Gardens, the Opera House external front and auditorium was refurbished in 2000 at a cost of £2m. Plans for the Grade 1 listed Crescent are dependent, in 2001, upon a £17m application to the Heritage Lottery Fund and include a 69-bed four-star hotel, ten retail units, a visitor centre allowing public access to some of the historic rooms in the Crescent, and extensive enhancement work to the front of the building. The Natural Baths, which still retain some of the old facilities including Henry Currey's Ladies Bath, are planned to become a new spa facility and the Pump Room of 1894 would be used as a new Tourist Information Centre. In Higher Buxton the High Peak Borough Council launched a regeneration scheme in 1999 to enhance the frontage of business premises, and in 2001 plans for a new layout to the Market Place itself were under active consideration. In these ways Buxton continues

to re-invent itself and re-present its appeal, as a modern resort built on rich historical foundations, to the wider world.

In some respects the sixty-years heyday determined the direction to be taken, but so did the withdrawal of the Devonshire dominance and its eventual total departure; Buxton became as vulnerable as any other resort both in its immediate control and to wider and larger influences and trends. Greater Manchester and the Peak National Park, communication, and developments in holiday patterns, health regimes, conference arrangements, cultural changes, have all contrived to mean that Buxton has had to re-invent itself constantly. It continues today, yet what is remarkable is the extent to which such re-invention is still determined by the legacy of the sixty years of Victorian and Edwardian growth, buoyancy and economic prosperity: hence the focus of this book.

> ... No English health resort surpasses Buxton in the salubrity of its situation; the beauty of its surrounding scenery; the extent, comfort, and luxury of its baths; the music and other charms of its Pavilion

Aerial view of Lower Buxton in the 1930s. The centre foreground is dominated by the Crescent with the Quadrant curving behind and the two railway stations beyond. In the centre is the Palace Hotel with the Devonshire Hospital to the left and behind these spreads Devonshire Park, fashionable housing built from the late 1860s. [B.M.A.G.]

An Estate Resort ...
Poised for Constant
Re-invention ...

Gardens; its opportunities for every form of indoor and outdoor recreation; its magnificent hotels and lodging houses; its cleanly roads and well-lighted streets; its ample supply of the purest water; its complete and efficient system of drainage and sewage disposal; its easy accessibility and splendid railway services from all parts of the kingdom. These and many other advantages, the origin and result of steady growth and development, have won for Buxton a foremost position amongst the health resorts of Europe ...[29] [Dr Samuel Hyde in 1898]

INTRODUCTION, APPENDIX 1: *Genealogical Table of the Cavendish Family*

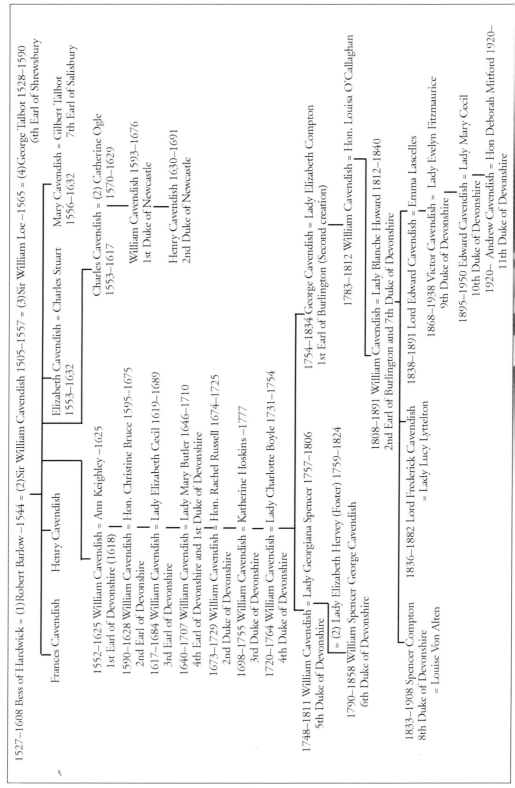

Buxton and the Newcastle Cavendish Family[48]

THE BUXTON PROPERTY owned by Bess of Hardwick was left to her third son, Charles Cavendish. His son, William, became Baron Cavendish and the Earl of Newcastle in 1628.[49] He was appointed governor to the Prince of Wales, the future King Charles I, and travelled widely, using his vast estates to support a lavish lifestyle. Early in the reign of Charles I the Earl may have acquired more land at Buxton, which was one of the purlieus of the Royal Forest of Peak. At this time certain wastes decreed to the freeholders and inclosures thereon were sold to them. A map of 1631, drawn by the Cavendish family surveyor, William Senior, shows the Earl of Newcastle owning about three quarters of Buxton at that time.[50]

In the economic and political crisis before the English Civil War, the Earl became heavily in debt and was deeply committed in support of the king. He placed parts of his estate in the hands of trustees to lease or sell in order to raise money for his children and to satisfy his debts, but none of the Buxton estate was sold for these purposes. During the Civil War the Earl of Newcastle saw much action as a leader in the Royalist cause and after fighting under Prince Rupert at Marston Moor, he fled to Europe with his wife and children. During the Commonwealth the government raised finance by confiscating and selling land belonging to the Church, the Crown and leading Royalists. The Earl lost most of his estates through sequestration and attempts to 'compound' for them, or obtain land back by paying a substantial fine, were not very successful. The Countess of Newcastle and her brother-in-law, Sir Charles Cavendish had returned to England for this purpose with little success. The Parliamentarians raised £111,593 from the Newcastle estates. Following the Restoration, the Earl returned to England in May 1660 but, although he had lost the huge sum of £950,000 during the war, he received back former lands worth only £759 *per annum* from an estate which should have returned more than £5,000 *per annum*. There followed lengthy and costly law suits when the Earl attempted to sue for lost rents for the years 1642 to 1660; he also sold land in order to pay debts and retain selected properties. The estate at Buxton had passed into the hands of former tenants and the second Duke of Newcastle, Henry (1630–91) entered into a lawsuit with thirteen local landowners for arrears of rent in property at Bakewell, Blackwell and Buxton. A long and complicated case, between 1674 and 1678, proved the eventual ownership of the Buxton lands by these landowners, the principal owners at Buxton being a yeoman, Michael Heathcote, possibly of an early Buxton family, and Andrew Morewood a descendent of the Morewoods of Bradfield and the Oaks, a well established family in Derbyshire. The link between the Newcastle Cavendish family and Buxton was thus lost.

Map Showing the Area of Urban Buxton, c. 1848

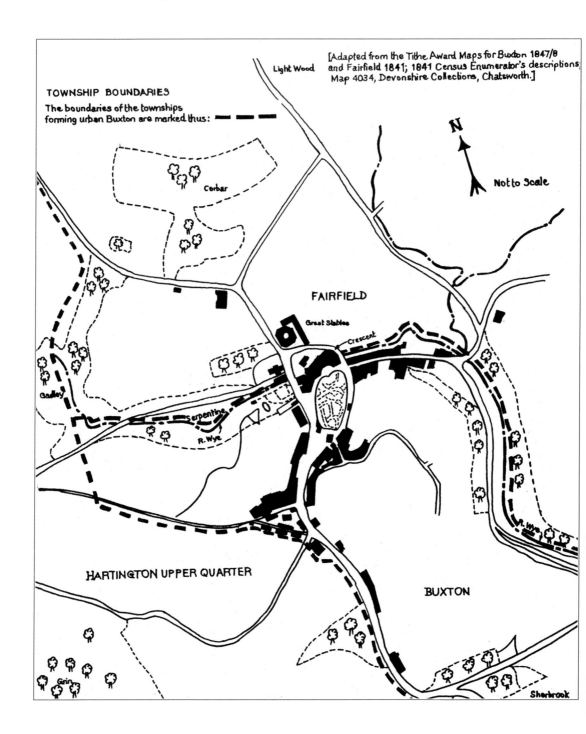

Light Wood

[Adapted from the Tithe Award Maps for Buxton 1847/8 and Fairfield 1841; 1841 Census Enumerator's descriptions, Map 4034, Devonshire Collections, Chatsworth.]

TOWNSHIP BOUNDARIES

The boundaries of the townships forming urban Buxton are marked thus: ▬ ▬ ▬

N

Not to Scale

Corbar

FAIRFIELD

Great Stables

Crescent

Cadley

Serpentine

R. Wye

HARTINGTON UPPER QUARTER

R. Wye

BUXTON

Grin

Sherbrook

Land Ownership in Urban Buxton, c. 1850

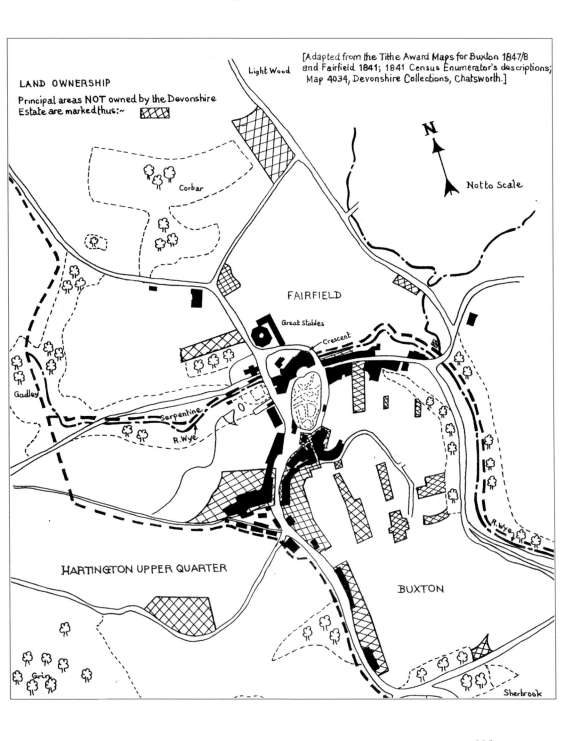

[Adapted from the Tithe Award Maps for Buxton 1847/8 and Fairfield 1841; 1841 Census Enumerator's descriptions; Map 4034, Devonshire Collections, Chatsworth.]

Light Wood

LAND OWNERSHIP

Principal areas NOT owned by the Devonshire Estate are marked thus:~

N

Not to Scale

Corbar

FAIRFIELD

Great Stables

Crescent

Gadley

Serpentine

R. Wye

HARTINGTON UPPER QUARTER

BUXTON

R. Wye

Grin

Sherbrook

Graph Showing Subscriptions to the Ballroom, 1788–1840

Devonshire Buxton Estate – Clear Profit on Natural and Hot Baths

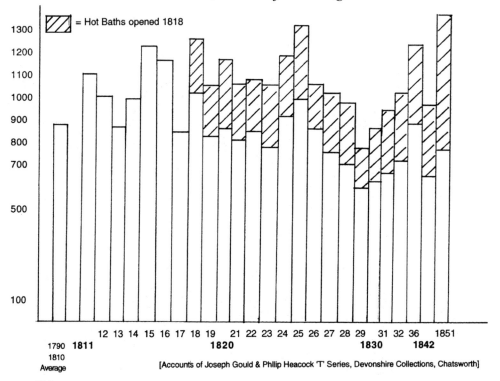

= Hot Baths opened 1818

[Accounts of Joseph Gould & Philip Heacock 'T' Series, Devonshire Collections, Chatsworth]

Devonshire Buxton Estate – Expenditure on Plantations, 1811–1842

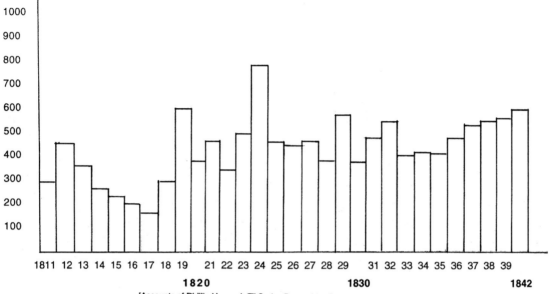

[Accounts of Phillip Heacock 'T' Series Devonshire Collections, Chatsworth]

Map of Principal Areas of Development, 1848–1859

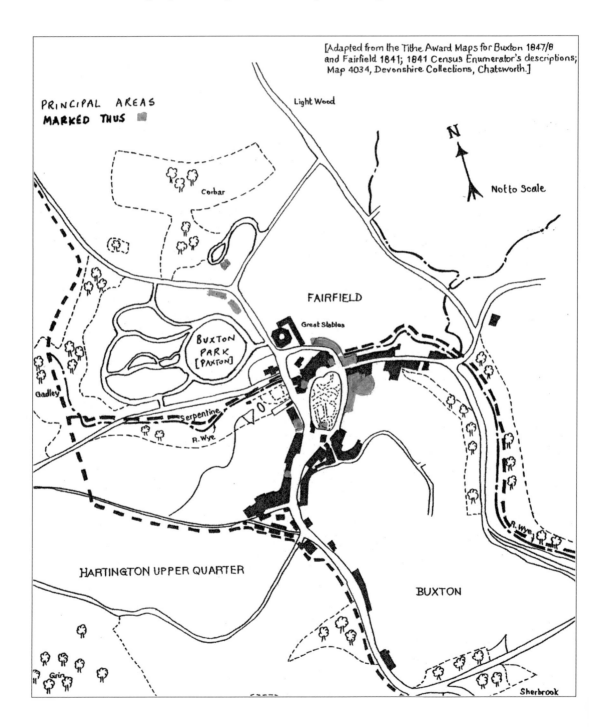

[Adapted from the Tithe Award Maps for Buxton 1847/8
and Fairfield 1841; 1841 Census Enumerator's descriptions;
Map 4034, Devonshire Collections, Chatsworth.]

PRINCIPAL AREAS
MARKED THUS ▓

Light Wood

N

Not to Scale

Corbar

FAIRFIELD

Great Stables

BUXTON
PARK
[PAXTON]

Gadley

serpentine

R. Wye

R. Wye

HARTINGTON UPPER QUARTER

BUXTON

Grin

Sherbrook

The Comparative Growth of Urban Buxton, 1859–1881

1. Population [96]

	1861	1881	% increase
BUXTON	2,450	6,025	146
Harrogate	4,563	9,482 [97]	108
Matlock	4252	6,093 [98]	43
All urban towns of 2,500-10,000 population	1,959,700	2,730,600	39

2. Houses

1861	1881	% increase
458	1,030	125

3. Number of Roads [99]

1859	1879	% increase
20	42	110

4. Visitors [100] [Typical week in the high season]

1859	1879	% increase
1,280	3,021	136

5. Hotels/Inns/Hydros

1859	1879	% increase
14	22	57

6. Lodging Houses/Apartments

1859	1879	% increase
162	356	120

Some Prominent Buxton Townsmen, 1858

List of those voting for the resolution for a new 'District of Buxton' under the Local Government Act 1858 with details of their status [101]

* John Acton — Chemist & Druggist the Quadrant [102]
* Francis Anzani — Rocking Horse Bazaar proprietor, Spring Gardens
* Brian Bates — Hotelier proprietor of The Old Hall & Leewood Hotels amongst others.
* John Cumming Bate — Founding editor of the *Buxton Advertiser* printer and publisher.
* Joseph Bates — Bookseller, stationer, newsagent,
* G.F. Barnard — Wine & Spirit Merchant, Spring Gardens
* James Bradbury — Proprietor the Shakespeare Hotel, Spring, Gardens
* Selim Bright — Silversmith & jeweller, The Crescent
* William E. Clayton — Private lodging house keeper, the Square
* Dr Thomas Dickson — Founder and resident physician, Wye House Asylum
* Robert Rippon Duke — Builder & surveyor, Spring Gardens
* Samuel Fidler — Proprietor of the livery stables at the Great Stables.
* George Hobson — Proprietor, Queen's Head Inn, Higher Buxton
* John Lawson — Proprietor, private lodging house and wine, vaults, Terrace Road
* William Lees — Proprietor of the George Hotel and other lodging houses

* Joseph Mortin	Joiner & builder, Higher Buxton
* John Milligan	Draper, Spring Gardens
* Robert Nall	Private lodging house keeper, Spring Gardens
* John Naughton (Norton)	Private lodging house keeper, Spring Gardens
* J. Armitage Pearson FRCS	Surgeon, the Quadrant
* Charles Raynor	Provision dealer, Higher Buxton
* John Smilter	Post Office and private lodging house keeper, The Crescent
* James Smith	Proprietor, The Seven Stars Inn, Higher Buxton
* George Smith	Manager of the Gentlemen's Hot Baths and lodging house keeper, Market Place
* W.D. Sutton	Proprietor of the *Buxton Herald & Gazette of Fashion*
* Thomas Swann	Farmer, corn & cheese factor, Cote Heath
* Samuel Turner	Sub-Agent in the Buxton Office of the Devonshire Estate, very respected townsman
* Dr W.H. Robertson	Consultant physician, Buxton Bath Charity and Devonshire Hospital. Foremost water medical doctor in Buxton
* Thomas Woodruff	Spa museum & marble ornament manufacturer and private lodging house keeper, The Quadrant
* Edward Woollett Wilmot	The Duke of Devonshire's Buxton Agent 1856–1864

CHAPTER THREE, APPENDIX III

Devonshire Buxton Estate Income and Expenditure for Urban Buxton, 1859–1881 [103]

Year ending 31 December - Agent E.W. Wilmot

Year	Income – £	Expenditure – £	Balance – £
1859	8,582	8,531	51
1860	8,323	8,321	2
1861	8,804	10,554	–1,750 [104]
1862	9,633	11,937	–2,304 [105]
1863	11,269	10,397	872 [106]

Half year 1 January-25 June 1864: Agent E.W. Wilmot

1864	3,361	5,417	–2,056

Year ending 30 June: Agent G. Drewry

1865	11,795	12,653	–858
1866	12,283	7,652	4,631 [107]
1867	12,285	7,407	4,878
1868	13,111	7,514	5,597
1869	12,341	6,676	5,665
1870	12,665	6,241	6,424
1871	12,889	9,940	2,949 [108]
1872	13,335	10,381	2,954 [109]
1873	14,086	7,570	6,516
1874	13,867	8,305	5,562
1875	14,884	6,435	8,449
1876	15,116	9,030	6,086 [110]
1877	14,956	11,884	3,072 [111]
1878	20,412 [112]	11,441	8,971
1879	15,146	9,096	6,050
1880	15,657	8,132	7,525
1881	15,961	7,487	8,474

The Baths at Buxton – Financial Performance, 1859–1881 [113]

Year	Income £	Expenditure £[114]	Balance £
1859	3,625	1,414	2,211
1860	3,308	1,725	1,583
1861	3,426	2,257	1,169 [115]
1862	3,217	2,226	991 [116]
1863	4,339	1,713	2,626
1864	1,075	429	646 [117]
1865	4,744	2,956	1,788 [118]
1866	4,995	2,411	2,584
1867	5,361	1,394	3,967
1868	5,760	2,403	3,357 [119]
1869	5,368	2,231	3,137
1870	5,682	2,461	3,221 [120]
1871	5,981	3,030	2,951
1872	6,233	1,626	4,607
1873	6,136	1,970	41
1874	6,602	2,151	4,451
1875	7,149	2,138	4,911
1876	6,978	4,464	2,514 [121]
1877	6,771	7,635	-864
1878	6,655	2,562	4,093
1879	6,205	2,292	3,913
1880	5,823	2,277	3,546
1881	6,324	2,360	3,964

TOTAL **£65,532**

Note: from 1860 the Estate also owned a cold water bath known as
the 'Tonic Bath' which earned very little and was leased in 1869.
The figures are not included here.

Buxton Local Board Statement of Loans Sanctioned, 1860–1881 [122]

For what purpose	Date of Sanction	Period (years)	Amount Sanctioned	Amount Borrowed
Sewerage Works	28.2.1860	30	3,500	3,500
Street improvements, Cattle Market, Hydrants and Urinals	21.10.61	20	1,700	1,700
Purchase of Buxton Fairs and Market Tolls	20.4.64	30	500	500
Purchase and extension of Market Hall	17.5.67	30	2,700	2,700
Sewerage Works and Public lamps	17.5.67	30	600	600
Extension of Market Hall, Sewerage Works, Cattle Market sheds and pens	15.6.69	30	1,200	1,200
Purchase and extension of Gas Undertaking	Bx. Gas Act 1870	50	20,000	20,000
Purchase of Water Works	21.11.72	30	10,000	10,000
Expenses incidental to above	13.8.73	50	15,000	15,000
Roads and Bridges	B.L.B. Act 1873	10	1,000	1,000
Sewerage Works	—do—	35	2,775	2,775
Gas works	B.L.B. Act 1873	50	1,500	1,500
Erection of Schools Hardwick Square	c. 1875	50	6,527	6,527
Street Improvements and Cattle Market	24.2.76	50	9,479	9,479
Slaughterhouses and Markets	24.2.76	30	2,000	2,000
Street Improvements and Mud Carts	24.2.76	20	575	575
Street Improvements etc.	13.2.78	50	1,860	1,860

For what purpose	Date of Sanction	Period (years)	Amount Sanctioned	Amount Borrowed
Erection of Stables	13.2.78	30	470	470
Surface Drainage	13.2.78	30	200	200
Water Works	13.2.78	30	200	200
Surface Drainage	3.5.78	30	2,550	2,550
Gas Works	P.O.Con. Act 1878	50	23,500	23,500
Gas Works	13.2.78	50	5,000	5,000
Water Works	18.4.79	50	2,500	2,500
Purchase of Stone Crusher, Fire Engine, Fire Escape, Horses and Carts	1.5.80	10	1,370	1,370
Water Works	1.5.80	30	920	920
Street Improvements erection of Stables, Urinals, Engine House and other Buildings	15.8.81	20	2,000	2,000
Water Works	15.8.81	30	1,000	1,000
Gas Works	25.8.81	50	4,500	45,004
Sewerage and sewage Disposal	13.9.81	30	3,000	370

CHAPTER THREE, APPENDIX VI

Freehold Building Land Sales in Buxton by the Devonshire Buxton Estate, 1859–1881

Freehold land sales recorded in the Devonshire Buxton Estate accounts in pounds rounded up [123]

Year ending 31 December		Approximate number of plots
1859	£1,418	15
1860	1,575	10
1861	456	9
1862	834	9
1863	611	8
Half year 1 January - 25 June		
1864	226	2
Year ending 30th June		
1865	82	2
* 30 April 1864 – 30 June 1866		
	5,408 [124]	29
1 July – 31 December 1866		
	1,940	11
1867	2,308	12
1868 to 1870 [125]		
	5,132	29
* 1871	2,234	12
* 1872	1,246	8
* 1873	1,861	16
* 1874	1,685	10
* 1875	3,341	13
* 1876	1,146	7
* 1877	8,997 [126]	11+
* 1878	8,827	7
1879	228	3
1880	26	1
1881	No entries in the accounts	

Total remitted to William Currey = £26,745

Total included in accounts and plan records = £14,836

Grand total 1859-81 = **£41,581**

Building Land Sales by Chief Rent in Buxton by the Devonshire Buxton Estate, 1859–1881 [127]

Year [128]	No of Total Rent p.a.	Price per sq. yard	Transactions(in £s rounded up)
1859	4	12	1.1/2d–3d
1860	1	10	1d
1861	1	5	–
1863	2	9	2d
1864	2	3	2d
1866	1	2	1/2d [129]
1868	1	1 [130]	–
1870	1	23	1d
1875	2	42	4d
1876	2	132	2d
1877	14	298	1.1/2d–3d
1878	26	363	2d–4d
1879	6	212	2d–4d
Totals	**63**	**1,112**	

Buxton: The Main Areas of New Residential Growth, 1859–1881

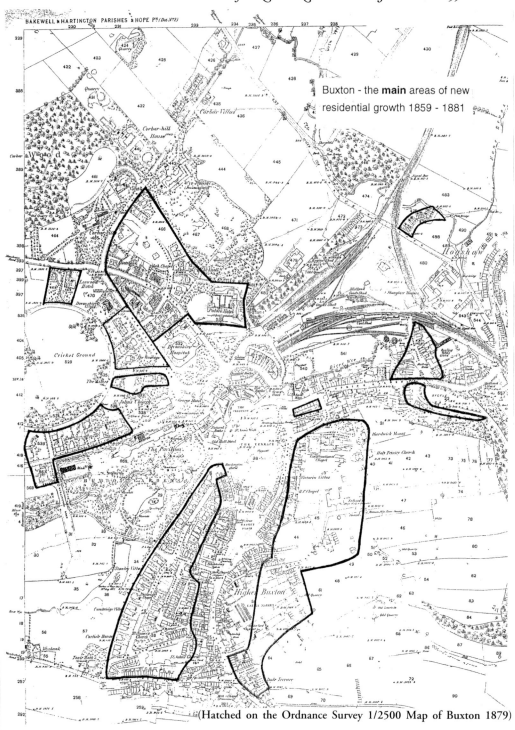

Buxton - the **main** areas of new
residential growth 1859 - 1881

(Hatched on the Ordnance Survey 1/2500 Map of Buxton 1879)

The Comparative Growth of Urban Buxton, 1881–1905

1. Population [108]	1881	1891	1901	% increase 1881–1901
BUXTON [109]	6,025	7,540	10,181 [110]	69
Harrogate [111]	9,482	13,917	15,712 [112]	66
Matlock [113]	6,093	7,131	7,798	28
All towns of 2,500-10,000	2,730,600	2,970,400	2,883,100	6

2. Houses	1881	1891	1901	% increase 1881–1901
	1,030	1,274	1,771	72

3. Number of Roads [114]	1879	1905	% increase 1881–1901
	42	84	100

Comparison of visitors and accommodation in selected years 1879–1905 [115]

4. Visitors [Typical week in the high season]	1879	1889	1895	1905	% increase 1879–1905
	3,021	3,473	3,956	4,296	42

5. Hotels/Inns/Hydros, +	1879	1889	1895	1905	% increase 1879–1905
	22	23	24	27	23

6. Lodging Houses/Apartments	1879	1889	1895	1905	% increase 1879–1905
	356	295	343	322	-10

Buxton Local Board/UDC Statement of Loans Sanctioned, 1882–1905 [116]

For what purpose	Date of Sanction	Period (years)	Amount sanctioned	Amount Borrowed
Works of Paving	1.11.1883	20	2,240	2,240
Works of Sewage Disposal	17.1.84	30	3,000	3,000
Disposal of Sewage	8.9.85	30	1,714	1,714
Disposal of Refuse	8.9.85	20	1,000	1000
Water Works	8.9.85	30	700	700
Providing Furniture & Fittings for Offices	29.4.87	10	500	500
Providing Offices	29.4.87	30	3,620	3,620
Public Library, Erection of Building	29.4.87	30	1,730	1,730
Public Library, Furniture and Fittings	29.4.87	20	250	250
Water Works, Land and Springs	26.5.87	50	1,385	1,385
Re-lining &c. Lightwood Reservoir	26.5.87	15	8,000	8,000
Hogshaw Bridge	22.9.87	30	488	488
Town Hall	12.12.87	30	2,000	2,000
Works of Sewerage	8.3.88	30	70	70
Otter Hole Pumping Station	8.3.88	5	400	400
Water Works	8.3.88	30	240	240
Sanatorium Buildings	18.9.88	30	800	800
Sanatorium Furnishing	18.9.88	10	260	260
Sanatorium Building	18.9.88	30	1,365	1,365

For what purpose	Date of Sanction	Period (years)	Amount sanctioned	Amount Borrowed
Sanatorium Furnishing	18.9.88	10	175	175
Hardwick Square School, Enlargements	c.1890	30	900	900
Works of Sewerage Ashwood Dale	18.8.90	30	1,060	1,060
Water Works	17.3.91	35	4,800	4,800
Sewerage and Surface Drainage	3.3.92	30	463	463
Water Van	3.3.92	10	82	82
Steam Roller	3.3.92	10	350	350
Street Improvements	30.3.92	10	2,000	2,000
Public Walks & Pleasure Gardens	30.3.92	18	485	485
Sewage Works and River Arching	30.3.92	30	350	350
Street Improvements, St John's Road	30.3.92	20	190	190
Cost of B.L.B. Act 1892	B.L.B. Act 1892	10	1,067	1,067
Works of Sewage Disposal	30.3.92	30	1,900	1,900
Gas Lamps	30.3.92	10	444	444
Gas Mains & Services	30.3.92	30	312	312
Water Works	24.8.92	30	630	630
Burbage, New Reservoir	6.6.93	30	10,600	10,600
Street Improvements, Crescent Road	11.10.94	20	350	350
Provision of Public Convenience, Terrace Rd	8.5.95	8	250	250
Cemetery	14.8.94	50	1,300	1,300
Cemetery	14.8.94	25	3,700	3,700
Destructor	9.12.96	20	500	500
Stables	9.12.96	10	800	187
Pleasure Grounds, Recreation Ground	9.12.96	17	1,500	1,500
Gas Machinery, Mains, Meters & Stoves	9.12.96	15	2,639	2,639
Burbage, New Reservoir	9.12.96	30	8,745	8,745
Sewage Works Reconstruction	8.7.98	30	836	836
St John's Road Bridge	8.7.98	27	500	500
Street Improvements, Green Lane	8.7.98	17	184	184
Cemetery	13.3.98	25	560	560
Street Improvements	3.9.98	10	69	69
Concert Place	3.9.98	50	431	431
Scavenging and Highways	12.12.98	9	255	255
Ambulance Carriage	20.12.98	10	120	120
Electricity Works	4.5.99	25	24,769	24,769
Street Improvements, Back London Road	28.10.99	12	180	180
Street Improvements, Macclesfield Road	28.10.99	12	1,010	1,010
Hardwick Square School, Enlargements	c.1900	30	787	787
Burbage, New Reservoir	16.1.1900	30	4,647	4,647
Purchase of Horses	11.7.00	5	293	293
Stone Crusher	6.6.00	5	130	130
Steam Fire Engine &c.	6.6.00	10	346	346
Burbage Reservoir	14.8.00	30	1,400	1,400
Street Improvements	14.8.00	31	112	112
Street and Bridge Improvements, St John's Rd	16.10.00	19	608	608
Street Improvements	16.10.00	20	111	111
Purchase of Land, Ashwood Dale	6.6.00	50	350	350
Purchase of Land for Sewage	1.1.01	50	2,000	2,000
Reconstruction of Gas works	4.7.01	30	5,534	5,534
Fire Brigade Purposes	26.7.01	13	220	220
Band Stand	29.7.01	20	375	375
Water Works	29.7.01	21	675	675
Scavenging, &c., Plant	16.8.01	6	500	500
Sewerage Works	24.8.01	30	170	170
Street Improvements	24.8.01	17	350	350
Electricity Works	28.8.01	25	16,520	16,520

For what purpose	Date of Sanction	Period (years)	Amount sanctioned	Amount Borrowed
Park Road sewer	18.11.01	20	115	115
Street Improvements, Irwin Rd, London Rd Footpath	4.12.01	20	528	528
Town Hall Electric Fittings,	4.12.01	10	525	525
Expenses of Act	B.U.D.C.	5	5,500	5,500
Expenses of Act	Water Act 1902	5	1,530	1,530
Water Works	Water Act 1902	56		20,000
Water Works	Water Act 1902	58		10,000
Water Works	Water Act 1902	57		10,000
Water Works	Water Act 1902	55		20,000
Water Works	Water Act 1902	57		10,000
Reservoir	Water Act 1902	60	171,000	8,000
Water Mains	Water Act 1902	40		4,000
Water Works	Water Act 1902	54		15,000
Water Works	Water Act 1902	54		15,000
Water Works	Water Act 1902	53		15,000
Water Works	Water Act 1902	45		23,000
Water, London Road	Water Act 1902	23		2,000
Reconstruction of Gas Works	14.1.02	16	13,000	13,000
Street Improvements, Charles St	16.8.02	15	500	500
Street Improvements, Macclesfield Road	28.5.02	12	430	430
Cab Stand	10.6.02	15	300	300
Street Improvements, Terrace Road	5.8.02	30	300	300
Fire Brigade Appliances	14.5.02	9	100	100
Sewage Filter Beds	24.7.02	30	11,700	11,700
Sewerage Works	15.12.03	30	1,000	1,000
Purchase of Baths & Wells	Buxton UDC Act 1904	60	55,000	55,000
Cost of 1904 Act	Buxton UDC Act 1904	9	1,152	1,152
Baths Purchase of Fittings	Buxton UDC Act 1904	30	4,000	4,000
Ladies' Lavatory	30.5.04	8	600	160
Cattle Market Pens	29.7.04	26	824	824
Street Improvements	6.6.04	17	1,020	1,020
Street Improvements	6.6.04	17	1,020	1,020

It will be seen that, in addition to the wide range of common services provided during this period the local authority also ran the utilities; water, gas and electricity.

CHAPTER FOUR, APPENDIX III

Members Attending the First Meeting of the Buxton Urban District, 4 January 1895 [117]

Ward [118]	Member	Occupation
North	GF Barnard	Wine & Spirits Merchant
	JE Harrison	Joint Proprietor, St Anne's Hotel
	J Willoughby	Secretary to Bx Gardens Co.
South	T Cooper	Pork Butcher
	G Smithurst	Draper
	J Salt	Builder
East	EC Milligan	Draper
	R Hulme	Farmer and Butcher
	J Gladwin	Builder
West	JH Lawson	Proprietor, Old Hall Hotel
	F Rowland	Grocer
	GE Garlick	Architect

Members of the Buxton UDC in 1904 [119]

Ward	Member	Occupation
North	Abraham Brown	Retired Naval Officer
	Charles F. Wardley	Printer, Propr. of *Buxton Advertiser*
	William F. Mill	Proprietor, George Hotel
South	George Smithurst	Draper
	John Wm. Yates	Butcher
	James Salt	Builder
East	John Banks	Boot and Shoe Maker
	Robert Lane	Proprietor, Grove Hotel
	Robert Hulme	Butcher and Farmer
West	Frederick Rowland	Grocer
	Geo. E. Garlick	Architect
	Geo. J. Bagshaw	Builder

CHAPTER FOUR, APPENDIX IV

Building Land Sales by Chief Rent in Buxton by the Devonshire Buxton Estate, 1883–1905 [120]

Year	No of Transactions	Total rent p.a. (in £s rounded up)	Price per sq. yard (highest-lowest in pence)
1883	1	31	3d
1884	2	6	1d,
1885	4	115	2d–2.½d
1886	6	65	2.½–3d
1887	4	54	2d
1888	4	65	2d–4d
1889	5	65	2–18d [121]
1890	13	186	2–18d
1891	13	311	2–3d
1892	3	41	—
1893	7	141	2d
1894	10	184	2–3d
1895	10	199	2–3d
1896	13	276	2–3d
1897	6	176	1.½–2d
1898	7	235	2d
1899	3	115	2d
1900 to 1905 [122]	23	490	
Totals	**13**	**£2,755**	

238

Chief Rents 1859–1905 A Comparison

In order to reconcile sales of land by Chief Rent with annual income, the sales from 1859–1879 (Appendix 3.7) and 1883–1905 (Appendix 4.4) are compared here with the account for the 'Buxton Building Estate' in 1905/6

Chief rents sold 1859–1879	63	Value	£1,112
Chief rents sold 1883–1905	134	Value	£2,755
Totals	**197**		**£3,867**

Buxton Building Estate Accounts, Ladyday 1905 to Ladyday 1906, Total Chief Rents [124]

Buxton	88	Value	£1,727
Fairfield	56	Value	£1,331
Hartington Upper Quarter	55	Value	£735
Totals For Urban Buxton	**199**		**£3,793**

Devonshire Buxton Estate Income and Expenditure for 'Buxton Building Estate', 1892–1906 and Land Sales, 1894–1906 [125]

Year	Income £ [126]	Payments £ [127]	Balance	Land sold outright £ [128]
1892	3,160	1,335	1,825	No sales
1893	3,148	1,305	1,843	No sales
1894	3,626	1,017	2,609	15,584
1895	3,910	1,124	2,786	11,965
1896	3,698	1,471	2,227	8,149
1897	4,922	2,025	2,897	1,197
1898	5,900	1,513	4,387	6,434
1899	5,371	2,052	3,319	181
1900	5,492	623 [129]	4,869	2,671
1901	5,263	489	4,774	No sales
1902	5,262	597	4,665	3,968
1903	5,263	2,040	3,223	4,211
1904	5,749	1,429	4,320	839
1905	5,645	1,403	4,242	6,555
1906	6,022	670	5,352	3,035
Totals	**£72,431**	**£19,093**	**£53,338**	**64,789**

Note: Between 1882 and 1891 no record can be found of outright land sales in the accounts.

Devonshire Buxton Estate Income and Expenditure for Urban Buxton, 1882–1891 [130]

Year	Income £	Expenditure £	Balance £
Year ending 30th June: Agent G. Drewry			
1882	15,962	6,441	9,521
1883	16,519	6,312	10,207
1884	16,073	8,032 [131]	8,041
1885	16,483	6,734	9,749
1886	15,440	7,050	8,390
1887	14,910	8,834 [132]	6,076
1888	15,542	8,172	7,370
1889	14,651	6,921	7,730
1890	15,819	7,918	7,901
1891	15,271	5,551 [133]	9,720
Half year 30 June–31 December 1,891: Agent G. Drewry			
1891	8,736	5,131	3,605

Total Surplus [10.1/2 years] £88,310

Note: From January 1892 the accounts are presented in a much revised form. It is not possible to extract the income and expenditure for urban Buxton from the wider collection which includes significant rentals from Hartington, Peak Forest, Tideswell and Wetton. The accounts do, however, allow for the extraction of income and expenditure for the 'Buxton Building Estate' which reflects the physical growth of urban Buxton. An analysis is given at appendix 4.6

The Baths at Buxton – Financial Performance, 1882–1905 [134]

Year	Income £	Expenditure £	Balance £
1882	6,550	2,220	4,330
1883	6,580	2,621	3,959
1884	6,420	2,476	3,944
1885	6,626	2,445	4,181
1886	5,722	2,499	3,223
1887	5,208	5,036 [135]	172
1888	5,453	4,116	1,337
1889	5,095	2,852	2,243
1890	5,025	2,513	2,512
1891	4,808	2,290	2,518
1891 (July to December)	3,486 [136]	1,579	1,907
1892	4,513	2,470	2,043
1893	4,969	2,455	2,514
1894	4,844	3,137	1,707
1895	4,989	2,791	2,198
1896	4,877	3,403	1,474
1897	5,152	2,892	2,260
1898	5,703	2,882	2,821
1899	5,935	3,796	2,139
1900	6,137	5,068 [137]	1,069
1901	6,605	7,894	-1,289
1902	5,705	3,502	2,203
1903	5,319	3,429	1,890
1904	5,322	2,717	2,605
1905	3,550 [138]	264	
Total			£57,246

Buxton the Main Areas of Residential Growth, 1882–1905

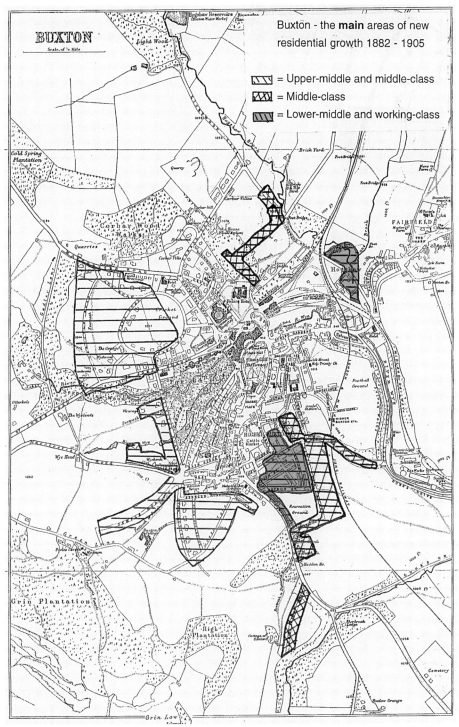

Buxton - the **main** areas of new residential growth 1882 - 1905

⬛ = Upper-middle and middle-class
⬛ = Middle-class
⬛ = Lower-middle and working-class

Chronological Summary of the Work of the Devonshire Hospital and Buxton Bath Charity, 1830–1904 [91]

Up to the mid 1860s the chair at the annual meeting was usually taken by a different aristocratic patron each year.

1830/31 Annual meeting held at the Great Hotel, Buxton on 12 September 1831, Chairman Viscount Strathallan. Balance sheet for the year 6 Sept 1830 to 12 Sept 1831 totalled £423 15s. 9d. Patients in the year 864 of whom: 724 were cured or much relieved, 52 relieved, 27 no better, 61 remain on books. An additional 443 patients received treatment but not pecuniary assistance.

1839/40 Annual meeting held at the Great Hotel 11 Sept 1840. Earl of Mount Edgcumbe in chair. Balance sheet for the year, 11 Sept 1839 to 7 Sept 1840 £1,203. Patients in the year, 1225 of whom: 924 'cured or much relieved', 128 'relieved', 65 'no better', 108 'remain on books'. An additional 749 patients received treatment but not pecuniary assistance. It was resolved that a donation of £10 would give life membership and power to send one patient annually. The charity is short of funds, £292 has been spent on a medical trustees room, a building for the use of patients, a dispensary so it was resolved that each hotel and lodging house keeper be requested to present the one-shilling subscription book and donation book to each visitor, a printed notice to that effect be hung up in each place. Two sermons had been preached which raised £83.

1850/51 Annual meeting held in the Great Hotel, 13 Sept 1850 . Rt. Hon. Henry Pierrepont in the chair. Balance sheet 10 Sept. 1849 to 13 Sept. 1850 £841. A total of 892 patients in the year of which: 694 'cured or much relieved', 96 'relieved', 16 'no better', 84 'on books'. No numbers given for those not receiving pecuniary assistance. Phillip Heacock was thanked for his benevolent exertions on behalf of the charity for the past 37 years. The rules now allowed that every contributor of one guinea may recommend a patient. Patients receive 5s. per week for subsistence.

1853/4 Annual Meeting held in the ballroom, 18 Sept 1854. President Lord Viscount Combermere, Sir Edward Bulwer Lytton Bart., MP in the chair. Balance sheet £989. Total patients for the year 1203 of which: 716 'cured or much relieved', 389 'somewhat relieved' 25 'no bette'r, 73 left irregularly without being discharged'. A further breakdown is given: 456 received full benefit and pecuniary assistance; 64 received medical advice, medicines and use of baths, 683 received medical advice and use of baths only. Note the use of 'somewhat relieved' rather than 'relieved' is a softening of the previous assessment measure. The trustees now include local worthies such as: Lord Bishop Spencer, Rev Hull Brown, Sydney Smithers (also treasurer),W. H. Robertson, Thos. Carstairs, W. P. Shipton (all three also hon medical officers). Mr James Wardley is secretary and paid £21pa. A sum of £57 8s. 6d. had been spent in advertising the object and rules of the charity at 100 railway stations. (as in earlier years)

The fortunes of the charity have increased markedly by this time. The question of accommodation was raised. The Duke of Devonshire had given land and £100, and the trustees estimated that £2,500 was needed to provide a hospital. The patients stay can now be extended to four weeks if needed. The subscribers list is now standing at approximately 500 with sixty life subscribers and four donations of between £100 and £200 had been made. The rules now allow for a one guinea subscriber to nominate a patient who would receive 5s. per week for 3 weeks plus treatment. A half guinea subscriber patient would receive 2s. 6d. per week and treatment for three weeks. A subscriber of less than half guinea but more than 2s. 6d. could nominate a patient who will receive treatment only.

1858/9 Annual Meeting, Field Marshal Lord Viscount Combermere GCB in the chair. Balance sheet £3,917. This is the first year of the establishment of the Devonshire Hospital. Total patients for the year 662 of which: 352 'cured or much relieved'; 256 'more or less relieved', 42 'no better'; 6 'discharged for breach of rules'; 4 'not being fit objects'; 2 'dead'. In addition 269 patients where treated out of the hospital as outpatients. The medical description has softened further from 'somewhat relieved' to 'more or less relieved'. The hospital has 120 beds.

1864. By this year the place of residence of patients was given. 985 patients were drawn from 240 places, e.g.

Alfreton 7	Barnsley 9	Bury 11	Bx & Burbage 16
Chesterfield 13	Derby 24	Glossop 6	Halifax 9
Huddersfield 19	Leeds 17	Leek 17	Liverpool 20
Macclesfield 31	Manchester 140	Nottingham 21	Newcastle u Lyne 10
Rochdale 26	Rotherham 13	Sheffield 71	Stockport 23
Todmorden 10			

Patients came from as far as York (2) Wellingborough (4) Bath (1) Holbeach (1) Maidenhead (1) but mostly were drawn from the midlands and north.

1866. This Annual report is W. H. Robertson's first as chairman, he succeeded after the death of E. W. Wilmot. Robertson wrote a preface in which he gave performance statistics from 1820 as follows:

1820–1838	14,906 patients of which: 1,206 'cured or much relieved'.
1838–1858	23,319 patients of which 16,575 'cured or much relieved', 5,859 'relieved in some degree', 885 'no better'.

1869. Annual report contains the first meteorological report from E. J. Sykes FMS the meteorologist. A meteorological station was made in the hospital grounds.

1878. The number of patients treated in the year was 1575 of which: 1459 'relieved' 55 'no better', 4 'no report', 22 'left of own request', 5 'drunkenness', 5 'died', 25 'left on books'. The medical description 'relieved' is now used in place of 'cured'.

In 1875 the trades and occupations of patients were listed for the first time and representative figures are given for 1878. In the report 120 different occupations are listed ranging from apparitor to carder to drayman to machinist to ropemaker to tinplate worker. Categories with ten or more are listed as follows:

Book keepers & Clerks 26 Bricklayers 10   Carders 10   Colliers & miners 72
Carters 19   Cutlers 14   Cotton operatives – male 44
Cotton Operatives – female 49   Domestic duties (chiefly married women) 403
Dressmakers 23   Engine drivers & stokers 15 Gardeners 30   Grooms & hostlers 16
Joiners & carpenters 38   Labourers 240   Machinists 26   Nurses 20
Painters 16   Seamstressers 24   Stonemasons 17   Weavers 22.
Also children under fourteen years 7

The largest category by far is 'Domestic duties (chiefly married women)'. This is the case right through the reports (in 1894 the figure was 739, in 1904 it was 755), the category being twenty five percent of the total. This suggests that particular female problems were treated, indeed, could have been something of a specialism. No specific work exists on this, though it is possible to identify some particular mention by the doctors. W. H. Robertson considered that the diseases which could be relieved by Buxton baths included:

> ... much of the deranged health incidental to middle-age in females – much of the uterine irregularity and disturbed condition incidental to females at various periods of life ...[92]

Dr Samuel Hyde included 'Diseases of Women' as a separate category of ailments for which the Buxton waters could be used indicating that:

> ... Irregular and painful menstruation, leucorrhoea, chronic ovaritis, neuralgia of the ovaries, ulcerations, and catarrh frequently derive much benefit from the Buxton bath ...[93]

However, by today's standards, it is likely that women were, more generally, under-represented in the hospital, at between thirty and thirty five percent of the total, given that three times the number of women suffer from rheumatoid arthritis than men.

1898. By 1898 the separate medical report section gave details and numbers of cases in each of several major categories:

Diseases of the locomotor system 2,356 cases includes:
chronic rheumatism, subacute rheumatism, lumbage, synovitis

Diseases of the Nervous system 322 cases includes:
Sciatica, Myelitis, Neurasthenia, Epilepsy, Vertigo

In addition smaller numbers of cases in other systems were included.

Diseases of the Circulatory system, 13 cases
Diseases of the Respiratory system, 17 cases
Diseases of the Alimentary system, 11 cases
Diseases of the Integumentary system 12 cases
Diseases of the Genito-Urinary system 10 cases
Diseases dependent upon blood states 18 cases
Diseases of Tropical Countries 1 case
Diseases involving more than one system 113 cases
Other Cases, Debility 44 cases
Surgical cases 19 cases includes: Sprained ankle, head wound, strangulated hernia (operation), Circular saw accident, Crushed foot (amputation), Blasting accident.

244

In the 1898 report accident wards and an operating room were being made, the cost to be found from subscriptions.

1904. The balance sheet to 31 December 1904 was £8,708. After the 1879/81 rebuild the hospital had 300 beds, 150 of which were allotted to the Cotton District Convalescent Fund for patients from the cotton manufacturing districts. The accident wards were funded separately from the main hospital. Patients in the year had been drawn from every county in England with small numbers also from Scotland, Ireland and Wales.

This annual report lists the number of patients 'cured' or relieved' in each decade from the opening of the hospital in 1859:

First decade	9,702	(1859/69)
Second decade	14,178	(1870/79)
Third decade	20,445	(1880/89)
Fourth decade	20,483	(1890/99)
1900	2,724	
1901	2,841	
1902	2,846	
1903	2,600	
1904	2,823	
Total	**78,642**	

CHAPTER FIVE, APPENDIX II

Principal Nineteenth-Century Buxton Doctors and their Main Publications on Buxton[94]

Those who were honorary medical advisers to the Buxton Bath Charity and Devonshire Hospital are marked thus *.

Armstrong, William [MRCS 1877], *Buxton, Its Waters, Baths and Accessory Methods of Treatment*, (with J. E. Harburn), Bristol. 1903 *The Baths and Methods of Use at Buxton*

Bell, Charles W., *A Brief Essay on the Use and Peculiarities of the Buxton waters* [MD Edin. 1833], 1856

*Bennet, Robert Ottiwell Gifford (1832–1902) [MRCS 1856; MD Edin. 1857], *Buxton and Its Medicinal Waters*, Manchester, 1892

Bennett, Charles J [MRCS 1864]

*Bradley, James Byron (1791–1871) [MD & BL Paris 1827; MRCP Lond. 1832]

What is the Proximate Cause of Gout and Rheumatism, and how the Buxton Waters Cure those Diseases?, 1867

*Braithwaite, John [MD Durham 1895]

Buckley, Charles W [MD London 1899]

*Buxton, Samuel[95] (1747–1826) [MD]

*Carstairs, Thomas (d. 1856) [MD Aberdeen 1850], *Bathing and the Buxton Waters*, London, 1847 & 1853

*Cumming, James (d. 1852) [MRCS & LSA 1828]

*Darwin, Reginald (1818–1892)[96] [MD]

*Dickson, Francis Kennedy[97] (1843–1907) [FRCP Edin. 1873; FRCS Edin. 1881]

*Drever, Thomas (1768–1849) (seasonal visitor)

*Flint, Peter (d. 1846)

Flint, George (d. 1862) [MRCS 1844; LSA 1830]

*Flint, William Henry (d. 1906) [MRCP Edin. 1883; LFPS Glas. 1883]

*Flint, Thomas Buxton [MRCS 1895; LRCP Lond. 1895]

Harburn, John English [LRCP&S Edin. 1896], *Buxton, Its Waters, Baths and Accessory Methods of Treatment*, (with W. Armstrong), Bristol. 1903

Hartley, John [LRCP&S Edin. 1895]

*Haslewood, Albert Octavius [MRCS 1864]

Hyde, Samuel (d. 1900) [MD St Andrews 1892; LRCP Edin. 1886; MRCS 1877], *Buxton: Its Baths and Climate*, Manchester, 1889. *The Therapeutic Value of Buxton waters*, 1895. *Notes from a Spa Practice*, 1895. *The Causes and Treatment of Rheumatism and Arthritis*, 1896. *The Treatment of Cardiac Affections by Baths, Climate and Exercises*, 1896

*Lorimer, George [MD Edin. & Paris 1872], *Health Resorts, Buxton*, London 1896. *A Guide to the Use of Buxton Waters*, Introduction and notes to W. H. Robertson's guide after his death

*Mayo, Paggen William (1763–1836) (Seasonal Visitor)

*Moore, Edward Duke[98] [LRCP Edin. 1859; LSA 1827; MRCS 1826]

*Moore, Milner M. [MD Durham 1880; LRCP 1864; MRCS 1863]

*Page, Thomas Jackson (d. 1844), *A Month at Buxton: or a Description of the Town and Neighbourhood, 1828 Brief Observations on the Buxton Waters*, Bakewell, 1830

*Pearson, John Armitage [FRCS 1856; MRCS 1826; LSA 1825], *Reports of Cases Treated at the Buxton Bath Charity and Devonshire Hospital between May 1st and October 31st 1860*, Liverpool, 1861

*Robertson, William Henry (1810–1897) [MD Edin. 1830; MRCP 1859; FRCP], *A Handbook to the Peak of Derbyshire and to the use of the Buxton Mineral Waters*, eleven editions 1854–1886. *Buxton and its waters*, London 1838. *A Guide to the Use of Buxton Waters*, at least twenty seven editions from 1840 to 1898

*Scudamore, Sir Charles (1779–1849) (seasonal visitor) [MD Glas. 1814; LCP 1814], *A Chemical and Medical Report of the Properties of the Mineral Waters of Buxton, Matlock, Cheltenham etc. London 1820. The Tepid Springs of Buxton*, London, 1833 and 1839.

*Shipton Arthur (1856–1937) [FRCS Edin. 1882; MRCS & LSA 1877]

*Shipton, Herbert (1865–1925) [LRCP Lond. 1888; MRCS 1888]

*Shipton, William Parker (1818–1895) [MRCS & LSA 1847]

Thompson, George H [LRCP Lond. 1888; MRCS 1888]

Thresh, John C [DSc Lond 1884; MD Vict. (Gold Medal) 1896], *Buxton as a Health Resort*, Buxton 1883

* Turner, Frederick [MRCS 1864; LSA 1865 Sheffield, TC Dublin & Lond.], Annual Health Reports as Medical Officer of Health

CHAPTER FIVE, APPENDIX III

A Comparison of the Priessnitz Water Cure and Contemporary Water Treatments at Buxton

Graefenberg – Vincenz Priessnitz

... Priessnitz the Water Doctor – I immediately started for Graefenberg and saw the clerk of the establishment and there was but one room, vacated that very morning in Priessnitz's own establishment. I immediately engaged it and found that I had been very fortunate in getting it as some Englishmen who came here six weeks ago are in a room with seven others. The room I have got is very good; well furnished but plain. I supped at the establishment the evening I arrived. I was introduced to a German gentleman who told me he had been affected just like myself and that he was perfectly cured in three months. He introduced me to Priessnitz. He is most benevolent looking. He looked very hard at me and said he would be with me at seven in the morning to see me going into my bath. This is his *pulse*. I am now going through the full treatment, baths of all kinds. The douche is a body of water as thick as my arm, falling from about twenty feet: it is something like paving stones falling on you but stirs up the circulation briskly. In Priessnitz's own establishment there is the advantage of a fine large bath and being close to the eating hall. There are a great many English here, who say they have derived the greatest benefit; there is also an Irish doctor who says he would not take £5,000 for the benefit he has received in six weeks. There are some here who think the living is not good; but I do not think so at all. The meat is not certainly so good as in England but I scarcely ever saw it better in Italy. The milk and butter are excellent. There are also good strawberries for breakfast. There are splendid walks and fountains through the mountains; the fountains are all named and there are finger posts pointing them out, so that by taking a glass of water at each, you get a long walk. The scenery all round is beautiful: the mountains not very high, but covered in wood to the top. The weather is very fine; but Priessnitz says the cure goes on better in cold weather. He has become exceedingly mild in his treatment latterly, so that the cure goes on slower, but, they say, more sure. At present I cannot give any opinion as to the system; but it would be hard to persuade anyone that the people you saw at dinner were all diseased in some way or other, did you not know it from the best authority. The English that have been here a long time are more enthusiastic about Priessnitz than even Captain Claridge. I have even heard it said that he is inspired: he certainly divines diseases in the most extraordinary way. He desires me to eat and work like a peasant: to be always in the open air but to avoid the sun. After breakfast I saw and chop wood and walk a great deal ... [99]

Buxton – The five rules of bathing.

First go into the bath about the middle of the day
Second – to go into the bath when the body is warm
Third – to go in with the feet first
Fourth – to remain in the water FIRST but a very short time
Fifth – to bathe on alternate days, or to miss every third day ... [100]

Buxton – Sir Charles Scudamore

... A gentleman, aged 50, originally of robust constitution, subject to acute gout since the age of 25, had suffered in an unusual degree from a continuation of painful symptoms during two months; for he had felt himself so much injured by the taking of Wilson's tincture, Reynolds' specific, and the wine of colchicum to a great extent, that he left this fit to its own course, and visited Buxton in his state of convalescence, being much affected in the upper and lower extremities, with frequent aching or shooting pains, lameness, debility, and so sensitive to changes of weather that there was a strong character of rheumatism in his disorder. This view of the complaint was confirmed by his suffering occasionally from lumbago.

He used four warm baths, beginning at 96°, and each time lessening a degree, and shortening his stay in the bath accordingly. He then had recourse to the natural bath, which he used with prudence and steadiness for six weeks; at first two days in succession, omitting the third; and then for three days, omitting the fourth; never remaining in the bath more than seven minutes. The pump was applied to the loins and to the weakened joints. Friction and shampooing were employed daily. I never witnessed a more striking example of the use of the Buxton bath. This gentleman was quite renovated in the active and comfortable use of his limbs, and gained equally in constitution strength and nervous energy. He drank the water at intervals, a pint daily, without any disagreement, and with much seeming benefit ...[101]

Buxton – Dr W. H. Robertson

... The use of the *douche*, or the forcible impulsion of the waters on different parts of the body by means of a double-actioned forcing-pump ... is more especially useful in indolent swellings of the joints, in cases where there is a sluggish condition of the vessels of a part; and an evident diminution of its sensibilities. It is of much service in old rheumatic cases, whether affecting the muscles of the back, or those of the extremities, and in cases where, as the consequence of sprains or other accidents, there is a debilitated condition of particular muscles ...[102]

Buxton – Dr John Armitage Pearson

... P. C., aetat 53, a Weighing Clerk. June 30th, 1860. Has rheumatism 5 months in knees and feet, arising from exposure to cold and wet as guard on the railway. Bowels open – tongue clean – no cough – sleeps well and appetite good. Ordered warm bath and the water. July 14th. Feels better – legs swell – continue baths and the water. July 20th. Discharged, *Very much improved* ...

... M. B., aetat 39, a Charwoman. August 18th 1860. Had Rheumatic Fever in January. Has now pain in all her joints – bowels costive – tongue white – pulse quick and feeble – slight cough – has palpitation sometimes when lying down. Ordered dose of physic – 3 warm baths. August 25th less pain – feels better – continue warm baths. September 1st. Bowels costive – physic – continue warm baths. September 8th. Discharged. *Much relieved.*[103]

Agents of the Devonshire Buxton Estate, 1848–1905 [90]

Agent	Service	Annual Salary at start and end of Service
Phillip Heacock (*c.* 1775–1851)	1805–1851	£560–705

Collections: Buxton, Hartington, Peak Forest, Edale. Also Tutbury.

Sydney Smithers (1795–1856)	1851–1856	£1,025–1,025

Collections: Buxton, Hartington, Peak Forest, Ashford, Highlow, Bonsal, Dore, Stoney Middleton, Tideswell, Wetton.

Edward Woollett Wilmot (1809–1864)	1856–1864	£1,125–1,125

Collections: Buxton, Tideswell, Hartington, Peak Forest, Wetton, Bonsall.

George Drewry (1816–1896)	1864–1896	£675–675 [91]

Collections: Buxton [inc. Building Estate from 1892], Tideswell, Hartington, Peak Forest, Wetton.

Frank Drewry (1853-retd. 1919)	1896–1905 (1919)	£600–750 [92]

Collections: Buxton [inc. Building Estate], Tideswell, Hartington, Peak Forest, Wetton.

Note: Direct comparisons are difficult to make because the responsibilities of the agents were different as indicated here and in the text.

Staff of the Devonshire Buxton Estate Office, 1848–1905 [93]

Staff Member	Service	Annual Salary at start and end of service [94]
Wm. Smith [Surveyor]	1851–1857	£100–120
Thos Bennett [Surveyor]	1855–1856	£80–80
John Dawn [Surveyor]	1857–1858	£75–80
Thos Everitt [Surveyor]	1857–1858	£75–80
Jas. Wardley [Chief Clerk]	1851–1889	£70–225
Samuel Turner [Sub-Agent]	1857–1876	£100–225
James Scott [Surveyor]	1860–1863	£90–105
Robert R. Duke [Surveyor/Archt]	1863–1905 [beyond]	£78–60 [95]
Chas F. Wardley [Clerk]	1872–1882	£26–90
J. D. Simpson [Surveyor]	1877–1901	£200–200
F. Drewry [Sub-Agent]	1877–1896	£220–300 [96]
John. W. Wardley [Cashier]	1883–1905 [beyond]	£100–220
J. H. Harrison [Clerk of Works]	1891–1905 [beyond]	£104–200
G. J. Hudson [Clerk]	1891–1905 [beyond]	£42–130
E. Brown [Clerk]	1894–1905	£18–76
W. Yeatman [Asst Clerk of Works]	1901–1905 [beyond]	£110–110
W. R. Bryden [Architect]	1903–1905 [beyond]	£100–100 [97]

Memorials in St John's Church to Sydney Smithers and Edward Woollett Wilmot [98]

'Erected by Public Subscription
To the Memory of
Sydney Smithers Esqre., J. P.
Agent to His Grace the Duke of Devonshire
for the Buxton Estate
From AD 1851 to 1856
In grateful recognition of his taste and judgement in
promoting the public interests under his charge; – more
especially in regard to the reconstruction and extension
of the Buxton Baths and Pleasure Grounds, and the provision
of a hospital for the patients of the Buxton Bath Charity
Obit July 8th 1856; Aetatis 61'

'Erected by Public Subscription
To the Memory of
Edward Woollett Wilmot, Esqre., J. P.
Agent to His Grace the Duke of Devonshire
for the Buxton Estate
From AD 1856 to 1864
In grateful recognition of his energy and judgement in
promoting the interests of the town and neighbourhood of
Buxton; – more especially with regard to the formation
and establishment of the Devonshire Hospital, and important
undertakings under the Health of Towns Acts.
Obit June 25th 1864; Aetatis 56'

The monuments are of similar style, that for Smithers is on the north wall, Wilmot's on the south. The tablets were described as being made of white marble surrounded by richly carved freestone from St Helens with inlaid enrichments and inscriptions in Egyptian green marble. They were designed free of charge by Henry Currey and made by Messrs James and Henry Pateson of Oxford Road, Manchester at a cost of 100 guineas. Both tablets were erected in December 1865. [99]

CHAPTER SIX, APPENDIX III

Duties of Architect – Buxton Estate [100]

1. To prepare plans and sections of all roads to be constructed, superintend the making of them keeping an account of the expenditure as the work proceeds certify for payments on account and for the final balance.
2. Negotiate the sales of building land make accurate plans of same stake out the land and see to the fences being correctly placed.
3. A plan or tracing of plots sold to be given to the purchaser without charge for same.
4. Before concluding negotiations for the sale of any plots of land the plan must be submitted to the Agent to be initialed by him if approved.
5. For ready reference draw and colour on a general plan or on an Ordnance map the plots of land as sold shewing the

building line or limit. The general surveys will be made and plotted by the surveyor, who has charge of all the estate plans and surveys, the architect to make copies of same for his own use.

6. To prepare and forward to Messrs Curry the Solicitors plans and the necessary instructions for the conveyance of land sold and see to the accuracy of the various covenants in the draft.

7. Examine and sign when approved all building plans and file copies of same with notes of any necessary particulars to be preserved and ultimately placed in the Estate Office.

8. To see that no additions are made to existing buildings and that no buildings or structures of any kind be erected on the land coloured light red or pink on which it is covenanted not to be built upon. Applications to make any such addition must be submitted by the Architect to the Agent for his opinion and decision.

9. All plans sections tracings measurements accounts letters &c. including all connected with or apertaining to the Architect's duties and work to be the property of the Agent who must have free access to them at all times he being the responsible head of all connected with the Buxton Estate.

Buxton July 10th 1899. Dear Sir, I am very much obliged to you for your very complete memo as to the duties of the Architect. – I hope it may be a very long time before I shall have any occasion again to refer to it – But it will be most useful to me. When I next see you I should like you to tell me what suggestions you once made to me about setting out some land for cottages in the Burbage Brickyard – I think it was only intended for gentlemen who had already built houses in the Park. Yours, F Drewry. [101]

Architecture by Henry Currey FRIBA (1820–1900) of 37 Norfolk Street, Strand, London E. C. in Buxton[85]

Building and Location	Date	Client
Hot and Natural Baths remodelling	1851–4	Devonshire Buxton Estate (DBE)
Devonshire Villas	1853	Messrs Sanders & Woolcott
Corbar Villa	1853	Mr Henry Shaw
The Market Hall	1857	The Market Hall Company.
Devonshire Hospital conversion	1859	Devonshire Hospital and Buxton Bath Charity Trustees
New Turkish Baths	1861	DBE
Christ Church, Burbage	1860	DBE
Dining Room to the Old hall Hotel	1860	DBE
Extensions to the Shakespeare Hotel	1860	DBE
New Parsonage, Park Road	1861	Buxton Anglican Churchwardens
Congregational Church	1861	Church Trustees
Wye House Asylum (original plan 1856)	1861	DBE
Hot Baths and Devonshire Colonnades	1863	DBE
Palace Hotel	1864–6	Palace Hotel Co.
Monuments to Sydney Smithers and E. W. Wilmot	1865	Free of charge for subscribers
Natural Baths re-roofing	1865–6	DBE
Hot Baths re-roofing	1868–9	DBE
Further modifications to both Baths	1869–70	DBE
Baths re-modelling	1875–7	DBE
Baths extensions	1886–8	DBE
Pump Room	1894	DBE

Attributed only further verification needed:

Building and Location	Date	Client
The Quadrant	1853–64	DBE
Nos. 1–3 Cavendish Villas, Broad Walk	1861	Mr C. F. Barnard
Nos. 4–6 Cavendish Villas, Broad Walk	1864	Mr Brian Bates
Cavendish House, Broad Walk	*c.*1866	
Derby House, Broad Walk	*c.*1866	
Dalton House, Broad Walk	*c.*1868	Mr John Milligan

Architecture by Robert Rippon Duke (1817–1909) 31 Spring Gardens, Buxton in Buxton[86]

Building and Location	Date	Client
Lodge to Poole's Cavern	1852	Devonshire Buxton Estate (DBE)
Thorncliffe Cottage, Hartington Street	1862	Mr J. C. Bates
Printing office, Eagle Street	1864	Mr J. C. Bates
New Dining and Refreshment Rooms at the Seven Stars Inn	1864	Mr James Smith
Three-light fountain, Quadrant	1868	Buxton Local Board
Extensions to Market Hall	1868	Market Hall Co.
Wesleyan Methodist Chapel, Fairfield	1868	Chapel Trustees
Six houses and seven cottages Bridge Street	1870	Himself
Park House, Manchester Road	1870–71	Himself
Trinity Church	1872	J. W. Taylor
Burlington Hotel	1874	DBE

Building and Location	Date	Client
The Knoll, Marlborough Road	1874	DBE
'Hamilton' and 'Arnside' Devonshire Road	1874	DBE
Argyle Villas, Broad Walk	c. 1875	E. C. Milligan
Charity Hot Baths, George Street and Natural Baths, The Square	1875–76	Devonshire Hospital and Buxton Bath Charity Trustees (DHBCC)
New Concert Hall and extensions including Skating Rink, Pavilion Gardens	1876	Buxton Improvements
Turners Memorial	1878	Subscriptions
Devonshire Hospital conversion	1879–82	DHBBC,
Alterations and extensions to Wesleyan Chapel, Market Place	1880	Chapel Trustees
Buxton Hydropathic Hotel, major conversion	1881	Buxton (House) Hydropathic Company Ltd. (Later Peak Hydropathic)
New Post Office, Cavendish Circus	1881	HM Postmaster
Renovation of St Peter's Church, Fairfield	1882	Churchwardens
Extensions to Royal Hotel	1882	Mr Thomas Barker
Building and Location	Date	Client
New Dining Room, Palace Hotel	1887*	Palace Hotel Co.
New west wing, Palace Hotel	1887*	Palace Hotel Co.
Devonshire Hospital new accident ward	1898	DHBBC
Attributed only further verification needed:		
Building and Location	Date	Client
Burbage House	1858	Mr R. Broome
Stanley Villas, Broad Walk	1867–8	
Lake Villas, Broad Walk	1866	
Cambridge Villas, Broad Walk	1867–8	
The Laurels, Marlborough Road	c. 1874	
The Balmoral, Marlborough Road	c. 1878	
Spring Bank, Marlborough Road	c. 1875	

* With W. R. Bryden

CHAPTER EIGHT, APPENDIX III

Architecture by William Radford Bryden FSA, FRIBA, MSA (b. 1851) 31 Spring Gardens and George Street Buxton in Buxton[87]

Building and Location	Date	Client
1884–1890		
Brooklands, Park Road	1885–6	Mr A. W. Slack
Union Club, Water Street	1886	Union Club Ltd
Ballroom and extensions Peak Hydro	1887	Peak Hydropathic Company Ltd
New west wing, Palace Hotel	1887*	The Palace Hotel Company
New Dining Room, Palace Hotel	1887*	The Palace Hotel Company
Alterations to roofs of Charity Hot Baths, George Street	1887	Devonshire Hospital and Buxton Bath Charity Trustees (DHBBC)
The Entertainment Stage (New theatre)	1889	Buxton Gardens Company
Wesleyan Chapel, Harpur Hill	c. 1889	Trustees
Southwood, St John's Rd	c. 1890	Miss Vernon Wentworth
House, Burlington Road	1890	Mr John Slack
Two detached houses, Park road	1890	Mr Abel Oram
New Ministers House, Hartington St Chapel	1890	Unitarian Trustees

Building and Location	Date	Client
1891–1900		
Pair of semi detached houses, Marlborough Mansions, Marlborough Road	1891	Mr W. P. Shipton
The Hawthorns, Burlington Road	1891–2	Mr David Sherratt
New Vicarage, Lismore Road	1893	Buxton Anglican Churchwardens
Three detached houses, Macclesfield Old Road	1894	Mr John Willoughby
Pair of semi detached houses, New Market Street	1895	Mr George Howe
Extensions to Fairfield Endowed Schools	1893–5	School Trustees
Shop conversion, Market Street	1895	Mr James Salt
Building and Location	Date	Client
Curator's House, The Serpentine	1896	Buxton Gardens Co.
Additions to Balmoral House, Marlborough Road	1896	Mrs James Beswick
Catholic Apostolic Church, Hardwick Square South	1896	Church Trustee
Elmwood and Elmbank, Burlington Road	1898	Mr William Wood
Lakenham and Inglethorpe, Burlington Road	1898	Mr William Wood
Wesleyan Methodist, Devonshire Road, Sunday Schools	1899	Wesleyan Trustees
Refreshment kiosk, Pavilion Gardens	1899	Buxton Gardens Company
1901–1905		
Extensions to St Peter's Church, Fairfield	1901	Churchwardens
Alterations to Northleigh, Devonshire road	1901	E. C. Milligan
New villa and alterations to Wiseman House, Marlborough Road	1901	Mr Rowland Swan
Buxton Hydropathic Laundry, Eagle street	1902–3	H. R. P. Lomas
Coachman's lodge, Branksome, Gadley Lane	1902	Mr Digby Johnson
Lightwood Road, three pairs of semi-detached houses	1903	Messrs Farrow & Brindley
Two sets of Four houses, Sylvan Cliff	1904	Mr F. Dalton
Two sets of Four houses, Sylvan Cliff	1904	Mr J. H. Holmes
Four three-storey houses, Sylvan Cliff	1904	Mr John M. Brown
Seventeen houses, Kents Bank Road	1904	Mr W. M. Bagshaw
Six three-storey houses, Green Lane	1904	Mr Mathew Bennett
Six houses, Holmfield (Germany), Burbage	1904	Mr George Holme
The Alison, Temple Road	1904	Mr W. H. Bradburne
Heathfield, Park Road	1905	Himself
Lightwood Road, one house	1905	Mr J. Brindley
Four houses at Can Holes, Burbage	1905	Mr J. Edge
Milnthorp Homes, Macclesfield Road	1904–05	Trustees for Mr J. Minlthorpe
1906–1910		
Two houses, Holmfield (Germany), Burbage	1906	Mr George Wardle
Four blocks of four houses houses for the continuation of Recreation road	1906	Mr W. M. Bagshaw
New Infants School, Queens Road, Fairfield	1907	Endowed School Board
Bungalow, Palace Road	1907	Mr Charles Binns
Cottage in Hogshaw	1907	Mr J. Needham
17 + 19 Lansdowne Road	1907	
Building and Location	Date	Client
Conversion old Post Office, Cavendish Circus into 5 shops	1908	
Lerryn, Temple Road	1908	Mr R. McDougal
Addition of billiard & smoke rooms, Balmoral House, Marlborough Road	1908	Mrs James Beswick
Williams Deacons Bank, Devonshire Colonnade	1909	Willaim Deacons Bank
Glass colonnading to the Hot Baths	1909	Buxton UDC
Additions to the Alison, College Road	1910	Mr W. H. Bradburne
St James Church, Harpur Hill	1910	Churchwardens
Parkfield, Carlisle Road	1910	Mr William Righton

Building and Location	Date	Client
Heatherton, Temple Road	1910	Mr H. Lancashire
Attributed only further verification needed:		
House, Park Road	1898	Misses Hannah and Mary Jane Barker
*With R. R. Duke		

Note: From 1908 Bryden was in partnership with Sidney Walton and the practice was known as Bryden & Walton.

CHAPTER EIGHT, APPENDIX IV

Architecture by George Edwin Garlick (c. 1863–c. 1932) 5 Terrace Road, Buxton in Buxton[88]

Building and Location	Date	Client
1888–1890		
Five houses, Hogshaw	1888	Mr E. T. Ash
Primitive Methodist Chapel, London Road	1889–90	Trustees
Alterations and additions to Peak Hydropathic, Terrace Road	1889–94	Peak Hydroparthic Company
Pair of semi-detached houses, Grange Road	1890	Mr W. Turner
Pair of terraced semi-detached houses, Leek Road (Green lane)	1890	Mr James Kirkland
Three shops and two houses, corner of London Road and Leek Road (Green Lane)	1890	Mr James Kirkland
Eagle parade, development of shops and accommodation, Market Place	1890	P. & F. Rowland, A. A. Hargreaves and others
1891–1895		
Detached Villa, (Moorcroft) Burlington Road	1891	Mr J. H. Lawson
Terrace of five houses and stables, Heath Street and New Market Street	1891	Mr Webster
Five cottages and stabling, Heath Street and New Market Street	1891	Mr Webster
The Towers, College Road	c. 1892	Mr Geo. Brocklehurst
Bungalow, Green lane	1892	Mr J. S. Blease
Pair of semi-detached houses, South Street	1892	Mr John Holmes
Terrace of five cottages, Hogshaw	1893	Dr R. O. G. Bennet
Terrace of four houses, London Road	1893	Mr J. Beswick
Terrace of three houses, Macclesfield Old Road	1893	The Misses Norton
Three Cottages, Market Street	1893	Mr A. Mycock
Pair semi-detached houses and shops South street	1893	Mr Geo. Brocklehurst
Estate of seventeen cottages and two pairs of semi-detached houses, Davenham Avenue and New Market Street	1894	C. T. & J. Hague
Terrace of three houses, Grange Road	1894	Mr J. H. Holmes
Detached house, (The Rowans), College Road	1894	Messrs Carter and Carruthers
Detached house, Green Lane	1894	Mr J. Worrall
Two terraces of three houses, Hardwick Square South	1894	Mr James Holme
Two villa residences, Spencer Road	1894	Mr I. Sutcliffe
Two villa residences, Spencer Road	1895	Mr Geo. Meachim
Primitive Methodist Manse, London Road	1895	Trustees
Pair of semi-detached houses, Grange Road	1895	Mr B. Thompson
Terrace of three houses, Hardwick Square East	1895	Mr H. O. Tebbe
Detached house, Macclesfield Road, Burbage	1895	Mr Sherbrook
Two Houses and stables on West Street	1895	Mr Geo. Ardern
Two cottages, Wye Street	1895	Mr F. J. Flint
Pair of semi-detached houses, West Street	1895	Mr T. Bentley

1896–1900

Building and Location	Date	Client
Detached house, Compton Road	1896	Mrs J. Worrall
Terrace of three cottages, Hogshaw	1896	Dr R. O. G. Bennet
Two groups of four cottages, Hogshaw	1896	Mr F. W. Booth
Terrace of seven cottages and store room, off Spring Gardens	1896	Mr W. T. Stott
Fruiterer's shop, West Street	1896	Mr James Stanway
House, Bridge Street	1897	Mr F. J. Flint
Pair semi-detached houses, Compton Road	1897	Mr G. J. Bagshaw
Pair of semi-detached houses, West Street/Road	1897	Mr R. B. Mortin
Detached house, Compton Road	1897	Mr G. J. Bagshaw
Two semi-detached cottages, Hogshaw	1897	Mr F. W. Booth
Five cottages, Victoria Avenue, off Holker Road	1897	Dr S. Hyde
Terrace of six houses, Victoria Avenue, off Holker Road	1897	Dr S. Hyde
Five terraces known as 'Beech Mount' 'Southcliffe', 'Woodlands', 'Rock Cliff', 'Green Mount' each of four houses and two terraces of three houses, Dale Road	1897–1900	Messrs Sugden & Hobson
Twenty cottages, Hogshaw	1897	Mr F. W. Booth
Twelve cottages, Hogshaw	1898	Mr F. W. Booth
Pair of semi-detached houses and shops, London Road	1898	Mr C. Jowett
Two houses, London Road	1898	Mr C. Jowett
Two terraces of four houses, Bennet Street	1898	Dr R. O. G. Bennet
Building and Location	Date	Client
Pair of semi-detached villas, Green lane	1898	Mr Edward White
Detached villa, Green Lane	1898	Mr Edward White
Detached House, Hogshaw	1899	Mr F. W. Booth
Two houses, Marlborough Road	1899	Mr B. Wardle
Two terraces each of four houses, Recreation Road	1899	Mr G. J. Bagshaw
Eight houses, Recreation Road	1899	Mr G. J. Bagshaw
Pair of semi-detached houses, Robertson Road	1899	Mr Geor. Brocklehurst
Four houses, Green Lane	1900	Mr E. White

1901–1910

Building and Location	Date	Client
Two houses, corner of Kents Bank and Recreation Roads	1901	Mr G. J. Bagshaw
Two terraced houses nos. 43 & 49 London Road	1901	Miss Wood
Five houses and stabling, New Market Street	1904	Mr George Howe
Three cottages, Green Lane	1905	Mrs Jane Webbe
Five houses, Macclesfield Old Road	1905	Mrs Jane Webbe
Flat roofed extension on Brunswick House, Hardwick Square East	1910	
Two houses, Park Road	nd	Mr & Mrs J. Whalley
Attributed only further verification needed:		
Brookfield House, Manchester Road	nd	
Longford Lodge, Moorlands and Strachur Park Road. (Some involvement with Barry Parker including the preparation of drawings)	1892	Mr Robert Parker

NB. George Garlick was joined by Charles Flint from 1896, the firm was known as Garlick & Flint

CHAPTER EIGHT, APPENDIX V

Architecture by William Holland (b. 1861) 9a Terrace Road and 12 Hardwick Street, Buxton in Buxton[89]

Building and Location	Date	Client
1893–1895		
Railway hotel stables, Bridge Street	1893	Chesterfield Brewing Company

Building and Location	Date	Client
Pair of semi-detached houses, Dale Road	1893	Mr J. B. Needham
Stables, Hardwick Cliff, Hardwick Square West	1893	Mr William Wood
Six houses and three cottages ('Doveside') Market street	1894	Mr James Nall Jnr.
Kinneswood, Palace Road	1894	Mr E. Hoy
Stables, Wye Street	1894	Mr T. W. Brittain
Oddfellows Hall and house, Market Street	1895	Duke of Devonshire Lodge of Oddfellows Buxton
Cottage, Market Street	1895	Mr James Nall Jnr.
Terrace of four houses Clifton Road	1895	Mr G. Gill
Two pairs semi-detached houses, Silverlands	1895	Mr A. Wild
Two houses and stabling, Grange Road	1895–96	Mrs Woolliscroft

1896–1901

Building and Location	Date	Client
Two villas, Park Road	1896	Mr T. Bakewell
A pair of semi-detached houses, Spencer Road	1896	Mr J. H. Holmes
Shops and stables, West Street	1896	Mr James Jones
Terrace of six houses, Recreation road	1897	Mr W. Webster
Three houses, off Silverlands Road	1897	Mr George Gregory
Pair of semi-detached houses, Robertson Road	1898	Mr J. H. Holmes
Detached house, Park Road	1898	Mrs M. Bromley
Holmlea, Corbar Road	1900	Mrs S. Pettitt
Additions to the Pendennis, Devonshire Rd	1901	Mrs M. Newton
Terraced house, London Road	1901	Mr H. Perks

CHAPTER EIGHT, APPENDIX VI

Architecture by Charles Heathcote FRIBA (1851–1938) 6 Princess Street, Mancheser and Wychwood, Buxton in Buxton[90]

Building and Location	Date	Client
Wychwood, St John's Road	1892	Himself
Southcroft, Carlisle Road	1896	Mr F. B. Benger
Alterations/Additions to the Peak Hydropathic	1896	The Buxton Hydropathic Co.
Conservatory, The Grange, Park Road	1896	Miss Alice Aldom
Detached House (Cheetham's Close)	1897	Miss E. Mothersill Park Road
Detached Staff House, Gadley Lane	1898	Mr Digby Johnson
Thornwood, Carlisle Road	1899	J. H. L. Seebohm

Architecture by Barry Parker FRIBA, MSA (1867–1947) and Raymond Unwin FRIBA (1863–1940) 6 & 7 The Quadrant, Buxton in Buxton

Building and Location	Date	Client
Longford Lodge, Moorlands and Strachur, Park Road§	1892	Mr Robert Parker
Pair semi-detached houses Faringford & Somersby, College Road*	1896–97	Mr R. Parker
Greenmoor, Carlisle Road	1898–99	Mrs Clara Bennett
Two pairs semi-detached houses, Cavanleck & Overlaw, Lightwood Ridge & Woodlea, Lightwood Road	c. 1900	
Additions and alterations to the Towers, Spencer and College Roads	1901	Mr Geo. Brocklehurst
Consulting and Waiting Rooms, No. 1 Broad Walk	1901–02	Dr W. Tweed
Additions to Longford Lodge, Park Road	1909	Mr B. Parker

*Barry Parker only

§Barry Parker in association with G. E. Garlick

Notes

Notes to Introduction

1. T. Hearne, *The Itinerary of John Leland the Antiquary*, vol. 7 (Oxford, 1769), p. 37.

2. J. Jones, *The Benefit of the auncient Bathes of Buckstones, which cureth most greevous sicknesses, never before published* (London, 1572).

3. T. Hobbes, *De Mirabilibus Pecci* (London, c.1666); Charles Cotton, *The Wonders of the Peake* (London, 1681).

4. See for example Sir J. Floyer, *An Enquiry into the Right Uses and Abuses of the Hot and Cold Temperate Baths in England* (London, 1697); T. Short MD, *The Natural, Experimental and Medical History of the Mineral Waters of Derbyshire, Lincolnshire and Yorkshire* (London, 1734).

5. A. Jewitt, *The History of Buxton and Visitors Guide et al.* (London and Buxton, 1811).

6. W. Turner, *Ancient Remains near Buxton – The Archæological Explorations of Micah Salt* (Buxton, 1899) is a good example.

7. C. R. Hart, *The North Derbyshire Archæological Survey* (Sheffield, 1984); P. Wroe, 'Roman roads in the Peak District', *Derbyshire Archæological Journal (DAJ)*, vol. CII (1982); Edward Tristram, 'Roman Buxton', *DAJ*, vol. xxxviii (1916); J. T. Leach, 'Notes on the supposed Roman Baths at Buxton', *Derbyshire Miscellany*, vol. 15, pt 4 (Autumn 1999).

8. A concise account is in M. Langham, 'Things written in the glasse windowes at Buxstons', *Derbyshire Miscellany*, vol. 15, pt 1 (Spring 1998).

9. I. Hall, *Georgian Buxton* (Matlock, 1984).

10. J. T. Leach, *The Book of Buxton* (Buckingham, 1987); T. Marchington has produced a broad sweep of the geography, population and physical growth of the town over 150 years from 1800. 'The development of Buxton and Matlock since 1800' MA thesis (1961); M. Langham and C. Wells, *A History of the Baths at Buxton* (Leek, 1997); A. F. Roberts, *Turnpike Roads Around Buxton* (Buxton, 1992); A. F. Roberts and J. T. Leach, *The Coal Mines of Buxton* (Cromford, 1985); Ros McCoola, *Theatre in the Hills* (Chapel-en-le-Frith, 1984).

11. D. Cannadine, *Lords & Landlords – The Aristocracy and the Towns, 1774–1967* (Leicester, 1980), p. 251; Addison handles the Victorian growth in two paragraphs regretting that, during this expansion, no architect to rank with Carr was employed. W Addison, *English Spas* (London, 1951), p. 90; Professor Hobsbawm, on the other hand, suggests that money was made out of Buxton. He observes '… the seventh Duke of Devonshire, left in a little temporary financial embarrassment of a million or so by an unusually free-spending Sixth Duke, was not obliged to sell even the more outlying of his numerous seats, but could fall back on the development of Barrow-in-Furness and Buxton Spa…' E. J. Hobsbawm, *Industry and Empire an Economic History of Britain Since 1750* (London, 1989).

12. Kathleen Denbigh, *A Hundred British Spas* (London, 1981), pp. v, 37.

13. Phyllis Hembry, *The English Spa 1560–1815: A Social History* (London, 1990), pp. 21–5, 216–27; Phyllis Hembry, edited and compiled by L. W. Cowie and Evelyn E. Cowie, *British Spas from 1815 to the Present – A Social History* (London, 1997), pp. 115–21, 179–82. The coverage superficial, and relies mainly upon older secondary sources.

14. Frederick Alderson, *The Inland Resorts and Spas of Britain* (Newton Abbot, 1973), pp. 17, 73.

15. See appendices 3.1 and 4.1 for detailed statistics.

16. M. Langham and C. Wells, *The Architect of Victorian Buxton* (Matlock, 1996; R Grundy Heape, *Buxton under the Dukes of Devonshire* (London, 1948). (His book is, unfortunately, not referenced.)

17. R. J. Morris (ed.), *Class, Power and Social Structure in British Nineteenth-century Towns* (Leicester, 1986), p. 8.

18. A. Briggs, *Victorian Cities* (Harmondsworth, 1968) is an excellent paradigm; D. Cannadine (ed.), *Patricians, Power and Politics in Nineteenth-century Towns* (Leicester, 1982), p. 6.

19. Such urban processes as described in R. J. Morris & R. Rodger (eds), *The Victorian City* (Harlow, 1993); D. Cannadine (ed.), *Patricians, Power and Politics in Nineteenth-century Towns* (Leicester, 1982); see also specific studies cited in chapter three.

20. J. Pearson, *Stags and Serpents* (London, 1983), p. 205.

21. Rev. F. Brodhurst, 'Sir William Cavendish – 1557', *Derbyshire Archaeological Journal*, xxix (1907), p. 90. Sir William Cavendish's pocket book carries an entry recording his marriage to Elizabeth Hardwycke, this being her family name. Her first husband was Robert Barlow (d. 1544) but she is best known as Bess of Hardwick; See genealogical chart at appendix Intro.1.

22. D. and S. Lysons, *Magna Britannia of Great Britain Vol 5. Derbyshire* (London, 1817) pp. xlviii–xlix, 147.

23. J. T. Leach, 'Buxton and the Cavendish families', *Derbyshire Archaeological Journal*, CVIII (1988), pp. 54–5.

24. M. J. Langham, 'Things written in the glasse windowes at Buxstons', *Derbyshire Miscellany*, vol. 15, pt 1 (Spring 1998).

25. Pearson, *op. cit.*, pp. 22, 30, 31, 33; Leach, *op. cit.* (1988), p. 55.

26. C. Cotton, *The Wonders of the Peake*, 4th edn (London, 1699), p. 24. The 'noble owner' was William, Earl of Devonshire.

27. R. Thornes and J. Leach, 'Buxton Hall', *Derbyshire Archaeological Journal*, vol. cxiv (1994).

28. M. J. Langham and C. Wells, *A History of the Baths at Buxton* (Leek, 1997), pp. 26–30.

29. Leach, *op. cit.*, (1988) p. 59.

30. *Ibid.*, p. 60.

31. Buxton Collections, Joseph Gould's Account for one year ending Ladyday 1802 T/4/5. Devonshire Collections, Chatsworth.

32. I. Hall, *Georgian Buxton* (Derbyshire Museum Service, 1984), gives a detailed account of the Fifth Duke's investment; T. Askey, 'The houses on Hall Bank in Buxton', *Buxton Archaeological and Natural History Society*, Bulletin no. 8 (Autumn 1989).

33. Buxton Collections, Joseph Gould's Account for one year ending Ladyday 1798 T/4/1. Devonshire Collections, Chatsworth.

34. Buxton Collections, Joseph Gould's Accounts 1800–1804, T/4/3–7 and Phillip Heacock's accounts 1805–7, T/4/8–10. Devonshire Collections, Chatsworth.

35. A Rental of His Grace the Duke of Devonshire's Estates at Buxton, Fairfield &c. for one year ending at Ladyday 1807 T/4/10. Devonshire Collections, Chatsworth.

36. A. Jewitt, *A History of Buxton* (London, 1811), pp. 51–65.

37. Letterbooks of P. Heacock A5/1512, 24 December 1824. Devonshire Collections, Chatsworth.

38. 'Several Particulars relating to the estates &c. in the Buxton Collection' T/4/12. Devonshire Collections, Chatsworth.

39. 'Indenture between the Sixth Duke of Devonshire and others and the Hon. Charles William, Viscount Milton', 1824. Terrier and papers accompanying map no. 4034 'Buxton Estate in 1922', Devonshire Collections, Chatsworth.

40. D. Cannadine, *Aspects of Aristocracy* (London, 1995), p. 170.

41. D. Cannadine, *op. cit.*, p. 171.

42. Buxton Tithe Award 1847: Map D2360/ 3/56a (P295), Award D2360/DL56b (P316), Derbyshire Record Office, Matlock.

43. Fairfield Tithe award Map D 2360/3/103a (P296) 1842. Schedule D2360 DL 1036 (P317), 24 August 1841. Derbyshire Record Office, Matlock.

44. 'Buxton Estate in 1922' Map 4034, Devonshire Collections, Chatsworth.

45. R. Bolton King, *Buxton College, 1675–1970* (Buxton, 1973), p. 20; The results of all these analyses are shown in the plan at appendix Intro.4.

46. *Buxton Advertiser*, 5 March, 9 April 1859.

47. Local Government Boards Provisional Orders Confirmation Act (no. 4) 1873, 36 and 37 Vict.

48. This summary is taken from J. T. Leach, 'Buxton and the Cavendish Families', *Derbyshire Archaeological Journal*, CVIII (1988), pp. 55–9.

49. He became the First Duke of Newcastle in 1665.

50. Plan no. 4897/347, 'Newcastle' Senior Atlas, Welbeck Woodhouse, quoted in J. Leach, *op cit*.

Notes to Chapter 1: Buxton 1811–1848

1. D. Cannadine, *Lords and Landlords - The Aristocracy and the Towns 1774–1967* (Leicester, 1980), pp. 251, 383.

2. Phyllis Hembry, *The English Spa 1560–1815, A Social History* (London, 1990), p. 227.

3. P. Heacock to John Heaton, 2 November 1813. Letterbook A5/1511. Devonshire Collections, Chatsworth.

4. A. Aspinall and E. A. Smith, *English Historical Documents 1783–1832* (London, 1959), pp. 533–4 (from the Fitzwilliam Mss).

5. P. Heacock to John Heaton, 30 July 1812. Letterbook A5/1511. Devonshire Collections, Chatsworth.

6. J. K. Walton, *The English Seaside Resort – A Social History 1715–1914* (Leicester, 1983), pp. 157–8.

7. 'Buxton Ballroom G. Bluett, Master, 1788', Buxton Museum, EY2000. Buxton Archaeological & Natural History Society (BANHS); O. Gomersal, 'Buxton Crescent Ballroom Subscription list', Occasional paper No. 6, *BANHS Bulletin*, Autumn 1988; see appendix 1.1.

8. In 1835 there were twelve titled subscribers out of a total of 30; in 1837 fourteen out of 22.

9. See appendix 1.2 .

10. Ernest Axon, *Historical Notes on Buxton and Its Inhabitants and Visitors*, Fourth Paper, November 1936. Axon identifies six writers of between 1772 and 1796 who comment upon the lack of trees and cultivation in Buxton; J. Lees-Milne, *The Bachelor Duke* (London, 1991), pp. 18–19. The auditor, James Abercromby, who superceded Heaton, encouraged the Duke to plant two million trees on his various estates between 1816 and 1817.

11. An analysis of this investment is given at appendix 3.3.

12. Heacock to Heaton, 3 May 1813; 11 October 1813. Letterbook A5/1511. Devonshire Collections, Chatsworth.

13. A. Jewitt, *The History of Buxton* (London, 1811), pp. 151–3, argues for a market on economic grounds; Heacock to Heaton, 8 September, 26 October, 2 November 1813, Letterbook A5/1511. Devonshire Collections, Chatsworth.

14. R. Simpson, *History & Antiquities of Derby* (Derby, 1826), p. 448; Maxwell Craven, *Bygone Derby* (Chichester, 1989), p. 53; A more detailed description of the Hot Baths is given in M. J. Langham & C. Wells, *A History of the Baths at Buxton* (Leek, 1997), pp. 45–6.

15. J. Denman MD, *Observations on Buxton Water* (London, 1801), pp. 49–50; Heacock to Heaton 26 December 1812. Letterbook A5/1511. Devonshire Collections, Chatsworth. Dr Drever was physician to HRH The Duke of York and Albany and to HRH Prince Leopold of Saxe-Coburg. He was also an honorary physician to the Buxton Bath Charity.

16. Sir C. Scudamore, MD, *A Chemical and Medical Report of the Properties of the Mineral Waters of Buxton, Matlock, Cheltenham* [*et al.*] London, 1820 and *The Analysis and Medical Account of the Tepid Springs of Buxton* (London, 1833, 1839); *DNB*, vol. xvii (London, 1909).

17. Architect to the Sixth Duke, he became Sir Jeffry Wyatville in 1827.

18. Sir C. Scudamore, MD, *op. cit.* (1820), p. 24; Accounts of Phillip Heacock, 1820–22 'T' Series, Devonshire Collections, Chatsworth.

19. Accounts of Phillip Heacock for 1829–32 'T' Series; Heacock to newspaper editors 3 June 1828. Letterbook

A5/1513. Devonshire Collections, Chatsworth.

20. J. K. Walton, *The English Seaside Resort – A Social History 1750–1914* (Leicester, 1983), pp. 19–22.

21. Heacock to J. Shaw, 10 March 1811, A5/1510; to J. White Jnr, 28 July 1811, A5/1510; to W. H. Chesck Esq., 14 March 1831, A5/1514. Devonshire Collections, Chatsworth. Parkgate was a small resort on the Wirral catering for local demand which had opened up in the late eighteenth century, J. K. Walton, *op. cit.*, p. 15.

22. Ros McCoola, *Theatre in the Hills* (Chapel-en-le-Frith, 1984), p. 29.

23. Helena Whitbread (ed.), *No Priest But Love – The Journals of Anne Lister from 1824–1826* (Otley, 1992), pp. 111–18.

24. A. B. Granville, *The Spas of England, 2. The Midlands & South* (London, 1841; Repr. Bath, 1971) pp. 27–8.

25. See M. J. Langham and C. Wells, *Buxton Waters – A History of Buxton the Spa* (Derby, 1986), p. 23, where seven Roman roads are identified; A. F. Roberts, *Turnpike Roads Around Buxton* (Buxton, 1992), pp. 174–5; A. Dodd and E. M. Dodd, *Peakland Roads and Trackways* (Ashbourne, 1980), pp. 130–45.

26. E. Rhodes, *Peak Scenery or the Derbyshire Tourist* (London, 1824), p. xxiii.

27. A. F. Roberts, *op. cit.*, p. 19–22.

28. Heacock to Mathew Frost, 29 December 1829 A5/1514, 29 January 1829 A5/1513, 4 March 1831, A5/1514. Devonshire Collections, Chatsworth.

29. For a useful record of coach and carrier services from 1811 to 1852 see A. F. Roberts, *op. cit.*, pp. 175–9.

30. J. Marshall, *The Cromford and High Peak Railway* (Halifax, 1996), p. 3.

31. Heacock to Brittlebank, 30 November 1824. Letterbook A5/1512 Devonshire Collections, Chatsworth.

32. J. Marshall, *op. cit.* (1996), p. 3.; Heacock to Jepson, 23 March 1831, Letterbook A5/1514. Devonshire Collections, Chatsworth.

33. J. Marshall, *op. cit.*, p. 14.

34. J. T. Leach, 'Grin Hill Buxton, A Major Limestone Quarry', *Derbyshire Archaeological Journal*, vol. 116 (1996), p. 114; J. Marshall, *op. cit.*, p. 17.

35. G. F. Chadwick, *The Works of Sir Joseph Paxton 1803–1865* (London, 1961), pp. 241–2. The Hon. George (afterwards Lord George) Cavendish, brother of Lord Burlington, the Seventh Duke.

36. *Buxton Herald & Gazette of Fashion*, Saturday 22 June 1844; Saturday 3 August 1844, 19 July and 25 October 1845, 27 June 1846.

37. Correspondence and Papers of Sir Joseph Paxton, P.422, 438, 442, 444, 484, 494, March 1846–February 1847. Devonshire Collections, Chatsworth; J. M. Stephenson, *The Peak Line* (Tisbury, nr Salisbury, 1982), pp. 9–11.

38. *Buxton Herald & Gazette of Fashion*, 8 June 1843.

39. 'Buxton Ballroom G. Bluett, Master, 1788', *op. cit.*,

40. Heacock to John Heaton, 30 March 1813. Letterbook A5/1511 Devonshire Collections, Chatsworth.

41. In 1844 the Duke wrote a 'Handbook of Chatsworth' in the form of a letter to his sister Harriet Cavendish which has been extracted and described in, The Duchess of Devonshire, *The House* (London, 1982).

42. D. Cannadine, *op. cit.*, pp. 169–70, offers an excellent

43. summary of the Bachelor Duke's extravagant lifestyle; J. Lees-Milne, *op. cit.*, p. 29.

Correspondence and Papers of Sir Joseph Paxton, P.254, 27 August 1844. Devonshire Collections, Chatsworth; J. Lees-Milne, *op. cit.*, p.163; D. Cannadine, *Aspects of Aristocracy* (Penguin edn, 1995), p. 170.

44. G. F. Chadwick, *op. cit.*, p. 241; Correspondence and Papers of Sir Joseph Paxton, P.229–241, 253, June to August 1844. Devonshire Collections, Chatsworth.

45. *Buxton Herald & Gazette of Fashion*, 4 September 1842; A verbatim account is given in R. Grundy Heape, *Buxton Under the Dukes of Devonshire* (London, 1948), pp. 70–2.

46. *Buxton Herald & Gazette of Fashion*, 4 October 1843.

47. Well dressing was an annual celebration, begun in 1840, which involved the decoration of the fountain with floral motifs to celebrate the provision of the water supply by the Duke of Devonshire. The custom, adapted by the Christian Church from pagan rites associated with the worship of springs, continues to this day.

48. *Buxton Herald & Gazette of Fashion*, 20 July and 4 September 1844, 26 June and 2 October 1847; Dr William Condell first accompanied the Duke on a tour to Constantinople in 1838 and retained the post of personal physician until the Duke's death in 1858. J. Lees-Milne, *op. cit.*, pp. 134, 213–15.

49. Correspondence and Papers of Sir Joseph Paxton, letter P24, 8 December 1835. Devonshire Collections, Chatsworth.

50. D. Fraser, *Urban Politics in Victorian England* (London, 1976), p. 31; E. Axon, *Historical Notes on Buxton, its inhabitants and Visitors*, paper XVII, November 1943; Buxton Vestry Book 1742–1818. See, for example, entries for 20 April 1813, 20 March 1815, 28 March 1816. Buxton Museum & Art Gallery.

51. Axon, *op. cit.* (1943).

52. 'Conditions of Sale by Auction of Freehold Property belonging to the township of Buxton' Mss. ML116, Langham Collection, Buxton.

53. A. R. Neeves 'A Pattern of Local Government Growth: Sheffield and its Building Regulations 1840–1914.' PhD thesis, University of Leicester, 1991, pp. 22, 125.

54. A. J. Ley, 'Building Control: its Development and Application 1840–1936.' MPhil, Open University, 1992, p. 62.

55. *Buxton Herald & Gazette of Fashion*, 16 June 1849.

56. 'Town Improvements', a lecture by E. W. Wilmot Esq., 2 December 1859, Buxton.

57. *Buxton Herald & Gazette of Fashion*, 20 August 1842.

58. Chapter five identifies, in some detail, the reasons for this.

59. Accounts of Phillip Heacock, 1818, 1828, 1834, 1842, 'T' Series, Devonshire Collections, Chatsworth.

60. *Buxton Herald & Gazette of Fashion*, 29 June 1844. See also 'The King of Saxony's Journey through England and Scotland in the year 1844' by Carl Gustav Carus (1789–1869), physician to the King of Saxony (1845, English translation 1846) in D. Rubinstein, *Victorian Homes* (Newton Abbot, 1974), pp. 19–20.

61. *Buxton Herald & Gazette of Fashion*, 8 June 1843; 29 June 1844.

62. G. F. Chadwick, *op. cit.*, pp. 54–5.

63. W. Adam, *Gem of the Peak* (London and Derby *et al.*).

64. Editions of 1845 and 1848, part IV, ch. 1.

65. Dr Shirley Foster, Department of English, University of Sheffield. 'Travel writing in the nineteenth century – the art of seeing' Paper given at Sheffield, 8 October 1997.

66. T. Rose, *The Counties of Chester, Derby & Nottingham,* with drawings by *T. Allom* (London, 1836), p. 66. Allom could have used a 'Claude Glass' to miniaturise landscape and produce model views in his highly picturesque engravings.

66. *Buxton Herald & Gazette of Fashion,* 1 October 1842.

Notes to Chapter 2: The Early Stages of Real Investment

1. A. J. P. Taylor, *From Napoleon to the Second International* (Harmondsworth, 2nd edn, 1995), p. 174.

2. D. Thompson, *England in the Nineteenth Century* (Harmondsworth, 7th edn, 1960), p. 96.

3. The *Buxton Herald & Gazette of Fashion* carried a list of visitors. Typical figures are from the 1847/48 seasons; S. Bagshaw *History, Gazetteer & Directory of Derbyshire* (1846); Census 1841 and 1851.

4. D. Orme, *The Buxton Guide and Excursive Companion* (Buxton, 1842), p. 10.

5. J. C. and H. B. Bates, *The Buxton Diamond* (Buxton, 1858), p. 3; W. H. Robertson, *A Handbook to the Peak of Derbyshire or Buxton in 1854* (London, 1854), p. 72; J. K. Walton, *The English Seaside Resort – A Social history 1715–1914* (Leicester, 1983), p. 133.

6. *Buxton Herald & Gazette of Fashion,* 16 June 1849.

7. *Ibid.*

8. A detailed account of the building of the Royal Hotel may be found in M. J. Langham and C. Wells, *The Architect of Victorian Buxton – A Biography of Robert Rippon Duke* (Matlock, 1996), pp. 25–32.

9. J. Leach, *Methodism in Buxton* (Buxton, 1985).

10. *Buxton Herald & Gazette of Fashion,* 16 June 1849.

11. W. H. Robertson, *Buxton Waters* (London, 1838), pp. 124–5: D. Orme, *The New Buxton Guide* (Buxton, 1823), p. 22; Chalybeate water (pronounced Kali-be-at) is iron bearing and was used principally for eye bathing and for cases of anaemia.

12. W. H. Robertson, *op. cit.,* p. 57.

13. 'Plan of Buxton Park – as laid out in building plots by Sir Joseph Paxton 1852'. Buxton Museum & Art Gallery, unlisted.

14. Development at Bournemouth, initiated by Sir George Tapps-Gervis and the Calverley estate at Tunbridge Wells by the architect Decimus Burton are smaller examples. W. Ashworth, *The Genesis of Modern British Town Planning* (London, 1965), pp. 42–5; W. H. Robertson *op. cit.,* p. 27. For examples of comparative growth of towns and cities see R. J. Morris, 'Urbanisation' in R. J. Morris and Richard Rodger (eds), *The Victorian City – 1820–1914* (London, 1993), ch. 2.

15. A full description of the new baths was given in the *Builder,* 20 August 1853.

16. G. F. Chadwick, *The Works of Sir Joseph Paxton 1803–1865* (London, 1961), pp. 156–7.

17. *Buxton Herald & Gazette of Fashion,* 11 September 1852.

18. *The Lancet,* 2 October 1852, p. 301.

19. R. N. Crook, 'Henry Currey and the Seventh Duke of Devonshire', RIBA, 1978, pp. 49, 78.

20. Note also that Edward Milner was a student of Paxton.

21. *Buxton Herald & Gazette of Fashion,* 20 July 1850.

22. W. L. Burn, *The Age of Equipoise* (London, 1964), p. 71.

23. *Official Descriptive, Illustrated Catalogue of the Great Exhibition 1851,* p. 769; J. M. Tomlinson, *Derbyshire Black Marble* (Matlock Bath, 1996), pp. 42, 61–2, 66. Derbyshire Black Marble was found at Ashford in the water and worked up to the end of the century. A variety of articles were produced by the spar workers using other stones local and imported to produce brightly coloured mosaics and patterns inlaid in the black stone. In 1860 there were six dealers and/or workers in marble and spar in Buxton.

24. *Buxton Herald & Gazette of Fashion,* 21 June 1851; P. Bailey, *Leisure and Class in Victorian England* (London, 1978), p. 81.

25. A. F. Roberts, *Turnpike Roads around Buxton* (Buxton, 1992), pp. 20, 171.

26. Accounts of Sydney Smithers One year to Ladyday & Michaelmas 1853, *passim.* Bound volume; ditto 1852, p. 39; Cashbook 1852 (labelled 1844), pp. 40–1. Devonshire Collections, Chatsworth.

27. In 1855 Edmund Buckley owned Lawson's Corner on Spring Gardens and new properties in the Quadrant.

28. 'Mortgage of freehold at Buxton and leaseholds at Holborn', Indenture dated 5.2.1853; Letter Henry Currey to Messrs Warry, Robins & Burges, Solicitors 9.10.1854. I am indebted to Louise Potter for allowing me to study deeds and papers relating to Devonshire Villas.

29. Open University Social Sciences Course Team (eds), *Understanding Society – Zoning In Cities* (London, 1970), pp. 367–8.

30. It is interesting to observe that this was also the case with the Devonshire development of Eastbourne in the early 1850s. R. N. Crook, *op. cit.,* p. 59.

31. J. K. Walton, *op. cit.,* p. 106.

32. White's *Directory of Derbyshire* (1857); *Buxton Herald & Gazette of Fashion,* 26 June 1856.

33. The Accounts of E. W. Wilmot One year to Ladyday & Michaelmas 1857 & 1858, *passim,* bound volume, Devonshire Collections, Chatsworth.

34. Recounted in Minutes of Local Board 'Committee appointed to make the necessary arrangements for laying of the foundation stone of the Town Hall' 15 June 1887. Buxton Museum (unlisted copy).

35. *Buxton Herald & Gazette of Fashion,* 19 June 1852.

36. Established by a deed of settlement 20.3.1851. Vestry minutes 26 and 31 October 1850, Buxton Vestry Book 1818, D4641/1/1 Derbyshire Record Office, Matlock. The chairman (Phillip Heacock) and twenty seven others signed the motion including: Brian Bates, Hotelier, Selim Bright, High Class Retailer, Samuel Turner, Builder and Church warden; Accounts of Sydney Smithers One year to Ladyday & Michaelmas 1851, Devonshire Collections, Chatsworth; The Company was re-constituted and incorporated with limited liability under the Companies Act 1862.

37. Act of Parliament William IV 3rd and 4th, chapter 90,

for lighting and watching of parishes in England and Wales.

38. *An Appeal to the Ratepayers of Buxton*, The Anti-Monopoly Society, Buxton, April 1851.
39. J. K. Walton, *op. cit.*, p. 136.
40. Vestry minutes 1852–59, Buxton Vestry Book 1818, D4641/1/1 Derbyshire Record Office, Matlock; *Buxton Herald & Gazette of Fashion*, 19 June 1852 and 21 June 1851; Accounts of Sydney Smithers One year to Ladyday & Michaelmas 1852, *passim*, bound volume, Devonshire Collections, Chatsworth.
41. W. H. Robertson, *op. cit.* (1854), p. 195; J. T. Leach, *The Book of Buxton* (Buckingham, 1987), p. 103; Accounts of Sydney Smithers One year to Ladyday & Michaelmas 1853, *passim*, bound volume, Devonshire Collections, Chatsworth.
42. Joyce C. Miles, 'The Rise of Suburban Exeter and the Naming of its Streets and Houses, *c.* 1801–1907' PhD, University of Leicester, 1990, p. 118; In the estate accounts for the half year to Michaelmas 1856 'sundry persons in higher and Lower Buxton' paid a total of £39 for a private water supply. Accounts of Edward Woollett Wilmot Half Year Ending 31 December 1856, bound volume, Devonshire Collections, Chatsworth.
43. 'Buxton Office 1856' entry 26 November 1856, Devonshire Collections, Chatsworth; *Buxton Advertiser*, 4 July 1856.
44. P. Bailey, *op. cit.*, p. 144; *Buxton Herald & Gazette of Fashion*, 2 July and 20 August 1853.
45. Handbill of Mechanics Institute dated 7 July 1856, Duke/MI/04, The Duke Papers, Buxton; M. J. Langham and C. Wells, *The Architect of Victorian Buxton – A Biography of Robert Rippon Duke* (Matlock, 1996), pp. 36–40; Viscount Combermere (1773–1865) had a distinguished military career. A Privy Councillor and Constable of the Tower of London, he was a regular visitor to Buxton and a President of the Buxton Bath Charity. R. Grundy Heape, *Buxton Under the Dukes of Devonshire* (London, 1948), pp. 62–3; *DNB*, vol. iv (1908); Lord John Manners became 7th Duke of Rutland in 1888. *DNB*, Second Supplement, vol. ii (1912).
46. See R. J. Morris and Richard Rodger (eds) *op. cit.* (1993), pp. 29–30, 34–5.
47. Violet Markham, *Paxton and the Bachelor Duke* (London, 1935), p. 115; Though agent in name at Chatsworth, Pax-

ton's increasing involvement in politics meant that his wife, Sarah, actually did the work. See Correspondence and Papers of Sir Joseph Paxton, for example P1026 Sarah to Joseph Paxton, 27 June 1853, Devonshire Collections, Chatsworth; *Buxton Herald and Gazette of Fashion*, 2 July 1853.
48. *Illustrated London News*, 26 August 1854; *The Builder*, 1852, p. 235, and 20 August 1853, pp. 535–7; W. H. Robertson, *op. cit.*
49. Lyon Playfair (1818–98) was a distinguished chemist. He was a member of the executive committee of the Great Exhibition and served on a number of Royal Commissions including Public Health (1844), Famine Commissioner to Ireland (1845), the Cattle Plague and the Re-Organisation of the Civil Service. His Parliamentary career spanned 1868 to 1892 and offices held included Postmaster-General and Vice-President of the Council. He became Baron Playfair of St Andrews in 1892. *DNB*, vol. xxii (1909); *Who Was Who*, 1897–1916.
50. Accounts of Sydney Smithers One year to Ladyday and Michaelmas 1852–55, *passim*, bound volumes, Devonshire Collections, Chatsworth.
51. *Buxton Herald and Gazette of Fashion*, 8 October 1853 and 7 October 1854.
52. W. L. Burn, *op. cit.* (1964).
53. B. W. Bentley advertisement, p. 1, *Buxton Advertiser*, 11 October 1856.
54. R. Grundy Heape, *op. cit.*, p. 77; Accounts of Sydney Smithers One year to Ladyday and Michaelmas 1855, bound volume, Devonshire Collections, Chatsworth.
55. Elizabeth Barton 'Edward Woollett Wilmot: The Duke of Devonshire's Agent in Buxton, 1856–64' *BANHS Bulletin*, no. 19, Spring 1995.
56. Accounts of Sydney Smithers One year to Ladyday and Michaelmas 1855. Bound volume, Devonshire Collections, Chatsworth.
57. Letter Wilmot to R. R. Duke, 15 November 1856, Duke/Archt/48, the Duke Papers, Buxton.
58. D. Cannadine, *Aspects of Aristocracy* (London, 1995), p. 171; *Lords and Landlords – The Aristocracy and the Towns 1774–1967* (Leicester, 1980), p. 233; W. L. Burn, *op. cit.*, p. 310.
59. *Buxton Advertiser*, 19 July 1856.

Notes to Chapter 3: Two Decades of Formative Growth

1. Appendix 3.1 gives the relevant statistics.
2. From 1860 to 1864 there were 54,000 houses built in Great Britain. This figure rose to 113,500 in 1875–79. D. Read, *The Age of Urban Democracy* (London, 1994), p. 52.
3. Robert Rippon Duke (1817–1909) came to Buxton in 1849 and, in a period of fifty years, was involved in practically every facet of the town's affairs, chiefly in the layout and architecture but also politically and socially. A detailed study of his life and work is in M. J. Langham and C. Wells, *The Architect of Victorian Buxton* (Matlock, 1996); See also chapter six.
4. See 'Report on the Sanitary Condition of the Labouring Population', Parliamentary Papers, 1842, vol. xxvi,

pp. 369–72, reprinted in C. Harvie, G. Martin, A. Scharf, *Industrialisation and Culture 1830–1914* (London 1970), pp. 137–41.
5. 'Town Improvements', a lecture by E. W. Wilmot Esq., 2 December 1859, Buxton, pp. 4, 7.
6. *Buxton Advertiser*, 29 January, 26 February, 5 March, 9 April, 18 June 1859; The boundaries are set out in the Introduction to this book. The inspector was called in by E. W. Wilmot to settle the boundary dispute with the neighbouring village of Fairfield which would lose some of its most valuable rateable property. Wilmot was adamant that the boundary must include all that land which would form urban Buxton if the estate was to continue to develop the town. Fairfield effectively lost out to Buxton

but the township supported its own Local Board and remained fiercely independent until, after prolonged resistance, it was incorporated with Buxton into one borough in 1917.

7. Buxton Local Board Minutes 17 October and 31 October, 1859, D 1323/1/1 pp. 23 and 26–7. Derbyshire Record Office, Matlock.

8. R Lambert 'Central and Local relations in Mid-Victorian England: The Local Government Act Office 1858–71' *Victorian Studies* (December, 1962), p. 128. Rawlinson, an eminent engineer, became Chief Inspector in 1861 and was ultimately knighted for his public service.

9. Buxton Local Board Minutes, 20 June, D 1323/1/1 p. 2. Derbyshire Record Office, Matlock. Josiah Taylor remained as Clerk, through the Urban District Council (formed 1894) to become the first Town Clerk of the Buxton Borough in 1917. His sixty years' service as a chief officer must be largely unparalleled in local government service.

10. R Lambert, *op. cit.*, p. 123; V. D. Lipman, *Local Government Areas 1834–1945* (Oxford 1949), p. 57.

11. R. Lambert, *op. cit.*, *passim*. Lambert's paper offers a very useful and detailed account of the work of the LGAO.

12. Buxton Local Board Minutes, 28 November 1859, D 1323/1/1 p. 32. Derbyshire Record Office, Matlock.

13. *Bye-Laws made by the Local Board of Buxton District*, Buxton, 1860, Buxton Museum LG2/51906; Buxton Local Board Minutes, 31 October, D 1323/1/1 pp. 26–7. Derbyshire Record Office, Matlock; *Buxton Advertiser*, 24 May 1862.

14. Borough of Buxton, *Abstract of Accounts for the year ended 31 March 1956*, pp. 124–5; Buxton Local Board Minutes, 17 January 1862. D1323/1/1. Derbyshire Record Office, Matlock.

15. D Read, *The Age of Urban Democracy* (London, 1994), p. 166. Professor Read quotes G. J. Goschen, President of the Local Government Board in 1871 'a chaos as regards authorities, a chaos as regards rates, and a worse chaos than all as regards areas' There were, for example, 27,069 different rating authorities and eighteen different types of rate. V. D. Lipman, *op. cit.*, p. 79.

16. *Buxton Advertiser*, 24 May 1862. But an amendment to the Local Government Act of 1861 had enabled ratepayers in Hartington Upper quarter to manage their own highways which the Buxton Local Board had been quick to implement. Buxton Local Board Minutes, August 1861, D1323/1/1.

17. *Buxton Advertiser*, 19 and 26 January, 2 February 1861. All the notable townsmen and tenants were there, many toasts were drunk and the evening was a 'most complete success'.

18. *Ibid.*, 10 May 1862.

19. G. P. Davis, 'Image and Reality in a Victorian Provincial City. A Working Class area of Bath 1830–1900' PhD Bath, 1981, p. 612.

20. W. L. Burn *The Age of Equipoise* (London, 1964), p. 167; Appendix 3.2 lists thirty influential townsmen in the early 1860s.

21. Buxton Local Board Minutes, 13 November, 11 December 1863, 8 January 1864, D1323/1/1, Derbyshire Record Office, Matlock.

22. 'Buxton Local Board Roll of Members from 1859' 352.365.9. Local Studies Library, Buxton.

23. See 'Correspondence and Papers of Sir Joseph Paxton', P1502, 25 February, P1526, 10 August, P1528, 13 August 1860, P1604, 15 March 1862. Devonshire Collections, Chatsworth.

24. J. K. Walton, *The English Seaside Resort – A Social History 1750–1914* (Leicester 1983), pp. 115–16.

25. *Buxton Advertiser*, 23 April 1864.

26. An account of the early history is in M. J. Langham and C. Wells, 'Notes of the Building of the Palace Hotel and Turner's Memorial' in *BANHS Bulletin*, no. 14, Occasional Paper 14, Autumn 1992.

27. The medical aspects are dealt with in chapter five.

28. See Walton, *op. cit.*, pp. 115–16.

29. Currey's original design for an unrealised Buxton Bath Charity Hospital were used for this asylum.

30. A more detailed account of development is in M. J. Langham and C. Wells, *The Architect of Victorian Buxton, op. cit.*, p. 61; N. Pevsner, *The Buildings of England – Derbyshire* (Harmondsworth, 1986), p. 117.

31. Buxton Local Board Minutes, 9 January 1863. *op. cit.*, D 1323/1/1 p. 285/6, Derbyshire Record Office, Matlock; See also M. J. Langham and C. Wells, *A History of the Baths at Buxton* (Leek, 1997), pp. 61–2.

32. See appendix 3.3.

33. See appendix 3.4.

34. See appendix 3.6.

35. Letterbooks of R. R. Duke, no. 1. August 1864–August 1866. Devonshire Collections, Chatsworth.

36. 'Fee Farm' and 'Chief Rents' are described in detail later in the chapter. The direct remittance of outright sales was, however, recommened in 1892 as described in chapter four.

37. Sheffield Town Council, for example, did not adopt the 1858 Act until 1864 and were slow to bring about improvements through local acts of parliament. A. R. Neeves, 'A Pattern of Local Government Growth: Sheffield and its Building Regulations 1840–1914', PhD, University of Leicester (1991), p. 257. However, Neeves points out (p. 206) that the willingness of smaller towns to adopt the Local government Act was not matched by their larger counterparts.

38. 'Buxton Local Board – Roll of Membership from 1859', Buxton Local Studies Library 352.365.9.

39. *Buxton Advertiser*, 14 June 1862.

40. Buxton Local Board Minutes, 2 May 1862, D1323/1/1, Derbyshire Record Office, Matlock.

41. The editor of the *Buxton Advertiser*, John Cumming Bates, founded the paper in 1852. He wielded a good deal of influence through his pen and was a prime mover in the formation of the Buxton Improvements Co. which developed the pavilion and gardens. M. Langham and C. Wells, 'J. C. Bates 1822–1899', in *Derbyshire Miscellany*, vol. 14, pt 4, Autumn 1996, pp. 104–12.

42. Account of G. Drewry 1868. *op. cit.*; Borough of Buxton, *Abstract of Accounts for the year ended 31 March 1956*, p. 132; M. J. Langham and C. Wells, *The Architect of Victorian Buxton, op. cit.*, pp. 64–5.

43. The Buxton Gas Act, 33 and 34 Vict. Session 1870.

44. Buxton Local Board Act, 36 and 37 Vict. 1873 (Ch. lvi).

45. Local Government Board's Provisional Orders Confirmation Act (No. 5) 36 and 37 Vict. 1873 (Ch. cxli).

46. A Series of papers relating to Lawson's Corner, ML64–174, Langham Papers, Buxton.

47. Buxton Local Board Minutes 9.10.79, D1323/1/8, Derbyshire Record Office, Matlock.

48. H. Fraser 'Municipal Socialism and Social Policy' in R. J. Morris and R. Rodger, *The Victorian City: 1820–1914* (Harlow, 1993), pp. 259–60.

49. A resume of Legislation on the subject of housing and sanitary affairs identifies six of the more important acts between 1860 and 1868. W. Ashworth, *The Genesis of Modern British Town Planning* (London, 1965), p. 62; In fact in addition to the Buxton Local Board Act of 1873 and its three associated Provisional Orders the town featured in only three other Provisional Orders up to 1881 viz. 1878 (Abingdon) 41 Vict. – Additional borrowing powers for gas undertaking; 1880 (Abingdon) 43 and 44 Vict. (Ch. xxxvi) – Provision for setting up of sinking funds and 1881 (Acton) 44 and 45 Vict. (Ch. clxii) – Provision for further borrowing for gas undertaking.

50. A useful explanation is provided by Heather A. Fuller, 'Landownership in Lindsey c. 1800–1866'. MA, Hull University (1974). Freehold estates may be held in fee simple, in fee tail or for life. In all three cases the tenant is considered to be the owner of the land but only fee simple estates can be passed on *ad infinitum* to an heir. An estate in fee simple has therefore come to resemble absolute ownership and represents the highest grade in the hierarchy of ownership structures. Estates held in fee tail can only be inherited by descendants of the original tenant, collateral relatives and ascendants being excluded. An estate held for life cannot be inherited.

51. I am indebted to Mr Martin Brooke-Taylor, solicitor, of Bennett, Brooke-Taylor and Wright, Buxton who, in three lunchtime meetings (3.12.96; 22.4.97 and 20.5.97) explained to me the finer legal points of these arrangements and their local application. The more modern legal term is 'Rent Charge'.

52. A. Offer, *Property and Politics 1870–1914* (Cambridge, 1981), pp. 115–18. Offer uses the map taken from the Liberal Urban land Enquiry of 1914 which identifies Chief Rents used in such towns as Bristol, Bath and Weston-Super-Mare in the West Country, Maryport and Sunderland in the North. Towns in Lancashire close to Buxton included Stockport, Stalybridge and Ashton. In nearby Bakewell the Duke of Rutland used leases for land sales.

53. *Ibid.* for Barrow; see D. Cannadine, *Lords and Landlords – The Aristocracy and the towns 1774–1967* (Leicester 1980), pp. 288–9 for Eastbourne where ninety year leases were offered with an option to purchase the freehold during the first ten years for thirty years (later twenty-five) annual lease charge; R. N. Crook, 'Henry Currey and the Seventh Duke of Devonshire' RIBA dissertation (1978), pp. 65–6.

54. A. Offer, *op. cit.*, p. 5 describes a Rent Charge as an example of 'incorporeal' tenure in that it is exercised *indirectly* as a charge or expectation in money, labour or kind.

55. 'Chief Rents at Buxton – Abstract of Form of Conveyance' Papers accompanying Map 4034, Devonshire Collections, Chatsworth.

56. Letterbooks of R. R. Duke, August 1866 to June 1871, unlisted – Buxton cupboard, Devonshire Collections, Chatsworth.

57. *Ibid.*, December 1876 to December 1882.

58. See W. Ashworth, *op. cit.*, pp. 24, 37–8 for other examples. R. J. Morris and R. Rodger, *op. cit.*, pp. 121–3, 129, 131–2; D. Cannadine, *op. cit.* (1980), ch. 6 *passim* on the Calthorpes at Edgbaston; R. Gurnham 'The Creation of Skegness as a Resort Town by the 9th Earl of Scarbrough' *Lincolnshire History and Archaeology*, vol. 7 (1972); Also J. Liddle on Southport in D. Cannadine (ed.), *Patricians, power and politics in nineteenth-century towns* (Leicester, 1982), p. 144.

59. Buxton Local Board Minutes 4 April 1862, 23 January and 6 February 1863 D1323/1/1. Derbyshire Record Office, Matlock. The first surveyor was also the Inspector of Nuisances and was part-time earning £20 p.a. as surveyor and, after he had asked for a rise, a further £10 p.a. as Inspector.

60. A useful summary may be found in A. J. Ley 'Building Control: Its development and application 1840–1936.' MPhil., Open University (1992), Appendix 8 (pp. 272–3).

61. Buxton Local Board Minutes 8 January 1864. D1323/1/1, Derbyshire Record Office, Matlock.

62. W. L. Burn, *op. cit.*, p. 219.

63. Buxton Local Board Minutes, *op. cit.*, 2 and 16 October 1863, Derbyshire Record Office, Matlock.

64. Chapter 6 deals with the role of the agents to the Devonshire Buxton Estate in some detail.

65. 7th Duke of Devonshire's Diaries, vol. 14, 30 October 1861; Vol 16, 1 April 1864, Devonshire Collections, Chatsworth.

66. *Ibid.*, vol. 16, 19 May 1864; 1 July 1864.

67. See appendices 3.6 and 3.7. George Drewry took this decision, see chapter six.

68. 'Buxton Land sales Book No. 2'. Plan nos 1–64 (1868–71) and tracings nos 66–139 (1872–87), Devonshire Collections, Chatsworth.

69. These valuations may be compared with private building land sold in Sylvan Park, Spring Gardens, Buxton in 1867 at 3s. 6d. per square yard. It is difficult to make meaningful comparisons with other towns since land values varied markedly. In the 1860s land for working class housing cost from 2s. 6d. to 5s. in Leeds but from £1 11s. to £3 2s. in Liverpool. J. Burnett, *A Social History of Housing 1815–1985*, 2nd edn (London, 1978), pp. 22–3; Commercial land in Deansgate, Manchester could be had for between £5 and £12 in 1862 but by 1871 had risen to £15 to £40 per square yard. W. Ashworth *op. cit.*, p. 100.

70. Plan of Buxton Park Building Land, 1877, in 'Fairfield Plans of Chief Rents' Bound Volume, Devonshire Collections, Chatsworth.

71. P. J. Aspinall 'Speculative Builders and the Development of Cleethorpes, 1850–1900', *Lincolnshire History and Archaeology*, vol. ii (1976), table 2.

72. C. G. Powell *An Economic History of the British Building Industry 1815–1979* (London, 1980), p. 52. Examples of middle-class houses in 1860s ranged from smallest of 1900 sq ft. at £500 to over 7600 sq ft. costing up to £2800. Typical cost per square foot was seven shillings.

73. Joyce C. Miles, *op. cit.*, pp. 42–3.

74. Professor Tarn refers to villas in Sheffield masquerading outwardly as detached houses but very often a pair with doors at either end rather than in the middle. J. N. Tarn,

Sheffield, in M. A Simpson and TH Lloyd, *Middle-Class Housing in Britain* (Newton Abbot, 1977), p. 180.

75. For example an 'Extract of Title for 10 and 12 Hartington Road' dated 7 July 1876 sets out the requirement upon Taylor and Simpson within the space of 12 calendar months to build two pairs of good substantial semi-detached dwelling houses with necessary offices and out-buildings and expend a sum of not less than £750 on each (pair); see also C. G. Powell, *op. cit.*, pp. 2–3.

76. The word 'slum' was in common usage by the 1840s. R Rodger, *Housing in Urban Britain 1780–1914* (Cambridge, 1989), p. 1.

77. G. P. Davis, *op. cit.*, p. 27 and *passim*; D. Cannadine 'Victorian Cities – How Different', in R. J. Morris and R. Rodger, *op. cit.*, p. 119.

78. 'Buxton Land sales Book, No. 1', A Series of 104 Plans of land sold between 1864 and 1867, Plan no. 58. Devonshire Collections, Chatsworth. Although the name sounds like one of the philanthropic housing societies (for example the Manchester Labourers Dwellings Co. or Leeds Industrial Dwellings Co. See J. Burnett, *op. cit.*, p. 175) it was, in fact, a joint stock company which boasted Henry Currie (*sic*) as its architect. *Buxton Advertiser*, 11 June 1864; Only seventeen cottages were actually built, Buxton O.S. 1897 and 1922.

79. W. H. Robertson's *Handbook of the Peak of Derbyshire* (1880), lists twenty-nine builders resident in the Buxton area of which about twelve were substantially involved in new house building. These included the better known names of James Brown (high class), Joseph Gladwin, Joseph Mortin and James Salt (pp. 282–83).

80. Subsequent chapters explore this related growth in the areas of water medicine, religion, commerce and building/architecture in more detail.

81. 'The Buxton Office 1856' *passim*, large folio; Accounts of E. W. Wilmot 1858–64 and G. Drewry 1864–71 *passim*, bound volumes, Devonshire Collections, Chatsworth.

82. 7th Duke's Diaries, vol. 20. Devonshire Collections, Chatsworth.

83. A more detailed history of the Pavilion Gardens is in M. J. Langham and C. Wells, *The Architect of Victorian Buxton, op. cit.*, chapter 4. For a Victorian gardenesque historical review see Hilary A. Taylor *et al.*, 'Pavilion Gardens Buxton – Survey Grounds development Plan', vol. 1, Parklands Consortium for High Peak Borough Council, 1996. Edward Milner was a student of Paxton and his connection with the Devonshire Estate architect, Henry Currey has been covered in chapter two. Milner was assisted at Buxton by his son Henry Ernest, see H. E. Milner, *The Art and Practice of Landscape Gardening* (London, 1890), pp. 95–7.

84. Account of Geo. Drewry one year to 30 June 1869. Devonshire Collections, Chatsworth.

85. D. Cannadine, *op. cit.* (1980), p. 282. In fact the Duke had to invest further in 1880 to try to increase the popularity of these amenities.

86. 7th Duke of Devonshire's Diaries, vol. 21, Devonshire Collections, Chatsworth.

87. S. Pollard, 'Barrow in Furness and the Seventh Duke of Devonshire' *Economic History Review*, 2nd series, vol. viii, no. 2 (1955), p. 213.

88. S. Pollard, *op. cit.*, p. 218, table 2. The summary of the Duke's commercial activity is based on this paper.

89. D. Cannadine, *op. cit.* (1980), pp. 268–9, 272–3, 283.

90. See chapter six.

91. R. Grundy Heape, *Buxton under the Dukes of Devonshire* (London, 1948), p. 107. He offers no evidence for the second assertion which is, in fact, borne out by the present research.

92. H. Leach, *The Duke of Devonshire – a Personal and Political Biography* (London, 1904), p. 25.

93. D. Cannadine, *op. cit.* (1980), pp. 231, 251, 382–3.

94. *Buxton Herald and Visitors Gazette*, 16 July 1902; D. Cannadine, *op. cit.* (1980), pp. 342, 345.

95. E. Bradbury (Strephon), *Pilgrimages in the Peak: Derbyshire Essays* (Buxton, 1879), p. 68.

96. Census 1861, Enumerator's returns; Census 53 & 54 Vic. c61, 1891 Tables of population; R. Lawton (ed.), *The Census and Social Structure* (London, 1978), p. 97.

97. Figures are for the Urban Sanitary District of Buxton and of Harrogate with Bilton.

98. Matlock Urban sanitary District with Matlock Bath and Scarthin Nick.

99. Ordnance Survey of Buxton, 1:2500, 1879; W. H. Robertson, *A Handbook of the Peak of Derbyshire* (Buxton, editions of 1861, 1875, 1880); Harrison Harrod and Co., *Directory of Derbyshire* (1860).

100. Figures for 4, 5 and 6 are taken from the *Buxton Advertiser* list of Visitors, 27 August 1859 and 30 August 1879 as typical of the growth in the season. The newspaper relied upon the accommodation provider to send in details of guests each week; thus these figure may understate the actual number of visitors in the weeks concerned, for example Robertson, *op. cit.* (1880), lists 390 apartment and boarding houses.

101. *Buxton Advertiser*, 1 January 1859.

102. W. H. Robertson, *A Handbook to the Peak of Derbyshire* (Buxton, 1861); Harrison Harrod and Co., *Directory of Derbyshire* (1860); *White's Directory of Derbyshire* (1857); M. Langham and C. Wells, *The Architect of Victorian Buxton* (Matlock 1996), pp. 297–304; Buxton census 1861.

103. Buxton Estate accounts of E. W. Wilmot 1859–64 and G. Drewry 1864–81 *passim*, Bound Ledgers, Devonshire Collections, Chatsworth. Note the relevant figures for urban Buxton have been extracted from these accounts which cover a wider area described as the 'Buxton Collection'.

104. Includes expenditure on waterworks (£508) including a new reservoir at Burbage, brickworks, including opening a new claybed (£1112) and new asylum (£2685 part).

105. Includes New asylum (£3137 balance), waterworks (£1193), Natural and Hot baths (£1523).

106. Includes waterworks (£1379) and £1355 paid to Joseph W. Lees for brick making. The increase from 1862 is largely due to modifications and additions to the baths generating greater income.

107. Marked reductions in all expenditure, re-assessment of rentals and increased income continuing from baths. The accounts audited and signed by the Duke personally.

108. Includes new billiard and dining room at the St Anne's Hotel and six new houses/shops in Spring Gardens (total £4708) also new tanks at the baths (£1626).

109. Includes balance on Spring Gardens property (£3888)

and Burlington Hotel (£1300 part).

110. Includes additions and repairs to baths (£2566).

111. Includes additions and repairs to baths (£5384).

112. Includes £4500 paid by the Devonshire Hospital for new stables in exchange for the Great Stables which were to be fully converted for hospital use.

113. Buxton Estate accounts of E. W. Wilmot 1859–64 and G. Drewry 1864–81, Bound Ledgers, Devonshire Collections, Chatsworth.

114. Includes both operating and maintenance costs except where separately indicated.

115. Includes new Turkish Baths part of building costs.

116. Completion of Turkish Baths installation.

117. Half year to 25 June.

118. Includes new roof to the Natural Baths spread over 1865/66 accounts.

119. Includes new roof at the Hot Baths and widening to colonnade spread over 1868/69 accounts.

120. Includes new tanks at the Hot Baths spread over 1870/71 accounts.

121. Includes additions and enlargements spread over 1876/7 accounts.

122. Borough of Buxton, *Abstract of Accounts year ending 31st March 1935*, pp. 172–3, 178–9 and *ibid.* (1956), pp. 124–5, 132–3.

123. Buxton Estate accounts of E. W. Wilmot 1859–64 and

124. Entries marked * are separately accounted for and were remitted direct to William Currey, the Devonshire Estate solicitor at 14 Great George Street, Westminster. They are *not* included as part of the annual accounts.

125. Undated additions to the Plan Book at footnote but datable to this period by their location and on the basis of estate business at the time.

126. Includes County Police for a lock-up and house (£500); Local Board for several plots of land (£4071), the cattle market (£746) and land in Ashwood Dale for a new Gas Works (£2133).

127. 'Counterpart Conveyances of Land on Chief Rents' and 'Schedule of the Fee Farm Rents', Papers accompanying Map 4034; 'Buxton Estate, Building Land Sold on Perpetual Chief Rent' A5/1785, Devonshire Collections, Chatsworth.

128. Includes only those years between 1859 and 1881 where there are ledger entries.

129. A preferential price for The Market Hall Co. in which the Devonshire Estate held shares.

130. Land at the Devonshire Hospital on token rent of 5s. p.a.

G. Drewry 1864–81, Bound Ledgers; Plan Book unnumbered 'Buxton Land Sales to 31st Dec. 1867', Devonshire Collections, Chatsworth.

Notes to Chapter 4: Buxton Comes of Age

1. See appendix 4.1.

2. The Urban District Council came into being in 1894.

3. *Buxton Advertiser*, 5 January 1895. E. C. Milligan's use of this familial term is significant. He is using the Seventh Dukes's own description of his predecessor in a familiar manner which shows the confidence of the UDC in its dealings with the Devonshire Estate. The Sixth Duke was a devoted and generous uncle to the Seventh Duke and his brother Lord George Cavendish. J. Lees-Milne, *The Bachelor Duke* (London, 1998), p. 53.

4. J. Leach, *The Book of Buxton* (Buckingham, 1987), p. 65; R. Grundy Heape, *Buxton under the Dukes of Devonshire* (London, 1948), pp. 73–4, 94.

5. The published LNWR timetable for July 1902 offered two journeys of 40 minutes or less and two of fifty minutes or less to Manchester in the morning. Three return trains were offered in the evening of fifty minutes or less. The slower services took, typically, one hour and five minutes.

6. *Buxton: Its History, Waters, Climate, Scenery etc.* Publicity booklet produced by C. J. Smilter of the Crescent Hotel as part of the town's publicity scheme, 1905, p. 6.

7. For a more detailed comparison of Buxton and Harrogate see chapter five.

8. For example, in the *Buxton Advertiser* of 23 January 1901 almost 40 per cent of the 535 listed visitors were staying at one of the four hydros.

9. *Buxton the Mountain Spa*, Official Handbook issued by the Bureau of Information, Buxton, 1912, pp. 37–8.

10. *The Times*, 22 June 1887; *Buxton Advertiser*, 8 June 1887.

11. *Buxton: Its History, Waters, Climate, Scenery etc., op. cit.* An edition of 1899 was sent to Queen Victoria. In 1905 Chas. Smilter took advantage of the visit of the King

and Queen to issue a revised edition.

12. See: Peak Dale Local History Group, *More than Just Dust* (Peak Dale, Buxton, 1989); J. T. Leach, 'Grin Hill Buxton, A Major Limestone Quarry', *Derbyshire Archaeological Journal*, vol. 116 (1996), p. 116–34; The contemporary local writer 'Strephon' rages against '… those utilitarian limestone quarrying men … despoiling … robbing the hills of their Alpine beauty …' E. Bradbury, *In the Derbyshire Highlands* (Buxton, 1881), pp. 176–8.

13. A. F. Roberts and J. T. Leach, *The Coal Mines of Buxton* (Cromford, 1985), pp. 69, 92.

14. Leonore Davidoff, 'Mastered for Life: Servant and Wife in Victorian and Edwardian England', *Journal of Social History*, 7 (1994), pp. 409–10.

15. The category 'servant' includes: 'general servants, potman, nurse/domestic servant, coachman, chambermaid, waitress, cook, housekeeper, governess, assists at home, laundress'.

16. D. Read, *The Age of Urban Democracy – England 1868–1914* (Harlow, 1994), pp. 27–9, 235–37; The description of social class, a key feature of Victorian society, is problematical in that historians use a range of different terms. For example, the class structure of Sheffield from the 1820s has been defined in terms of: 'middle-class employers', 'labour aristocrat', 'unskilled worker', Caroline Reid, 'Middle-class values and working-class culture in nineteenth-century Sheffield: the pursuit of respectability', in S. Pollard and C. Holmes, *Essays in the Economic and Social History of South Yorkshire* (Sheffield, 1976), pp. 275–7; The social structure offered through the census later in the century is much more detailed. See J. A. Banks, 'The Social Structure

of Nineteenth-Century England as seen through the Census', in R. Lawton (ed.), *op. cit.* (1978), pp. 179–223; A. L. Bowley, the leading Edwardian social statistician offers useful socio-economic measures – an annual income of £1000 to £5000 being seen as upper middle class, those earning between £300 and £999 as solid middle class: D. Read, *op. cit.* (1994), p. 391. In Buxton there was a growing 'petty bourgeoisie' or 'shopocracy' whose lifestyle, as demonstrated by type of house, employment of servants, religious following and activities in public life, would aspire to middle-class status. But there was also an influx of wealthy business people who built very substantial properties. Additionally, there was a class of artisan, single self-employed tradesmen and lodging house keepers who may be described as lower middle-class. To allow for social mobility and a degree of fluidity between social groups, it will be most meaningful to use, in this chapter, four broad class divisions of: upper middle, middle, lower middle and working class. These are reflected in types of houses and can be correlated with the occupation of the head of the household in the 1891 census. See also: D. Cannadine, *Class in Britain* (New Haven and London, 1998), pp. 9, 10, 20. M. A. Simpson, 'The West End of Glasgow, 1830–1914', in M. A. Simpson and T. H. Lloyd, *Middle-Class Housing in Britain* (Newton Abbot, 1977), p. 46; D. Read, *op. cit.* (1994), p. 391.

17. Correspondence S. M. Smith 'Duke/SMS/Fam 299–363' and R. R. Duke, 'Duke/RRD/Fam/ 39, 78, 85, 135,' The Duke Papers, Buxton. In 1905 there were at least three servant registry offices in Buxton.

18. Leonore Davidoff, *op. cit.* (1994), pp. 406–28. An interesting sociological and feminist perspective on the norms of control inherent in the master–servant relationship.

19. The 'self-selective' and partial nature of commercial directories is well recognised. R. Schola has assessed the value of some other sources including trade tokens, guild records and probate inventories finding these, inevitably, fragmentary and selective failing to match up to even the poorest of directories. R. Scola, 'Retailing in the Nineteenth-Century Town: Some Problems and Possibilities', in J. H. Johnson and C. G. Pooley (eds), *The Structure of Nineteenth-Century Cities* (Beckenham, 1983), p. 156. G. Shaw has analysed in detail the compilation and reliability of local directories concluding that, despite their limitations, trade directories remain the main source of information on the retail trade. G. Shaw, 'The Role of Retailing in the Urban Economy', *ibid.*, pp. 189–92 .

20. *Kelly's Directory of Derbyshire*, 1891 and 1904; *Bulmer's Directory of Derbyshire*, 1895.

21. J. M. Bentley and G. K. Fox, *Railways of the High Peak – Buxton to Ashbourne* (Stockport, 1997), pp. 7–8; J. Marshall, *The Cromford and High Peak Railway* (Halifax, 1996), p. 62.

22. D. Read, *op. cit.* (1994), p. 62; J Leach, *op. cit.* (1987), p. 94.

23. See S. B. Saul, 'House Building in England 1890–1914' *Economic History Review*, 2nd series, vol. 15, no. 1 (1962), pp. 120–1. In 1890 building was at a low ebb, recovering slowly to 1895, rising to a peak in 1898–99, then declining, to return to a peak in 1903. The extent to which Buxton matched this pattern will become clear as the chapter

proceeds.

24. J. C. Thresh, *Buxton as a Health Resort* (Buxton, 1883), pp. 36–8 in which he proposes modifications to the present system; J. Buckley, *Modern Buxton* (1886), p. 77 says the new installations were were paid for by a rate of £1 3s. 4d. in the pound. He quotes verbatim the technical paper read by Thresh at the banquet held on the opening of the new plant, pp. 69–72. See also 'Royal Commission on Labour, Dr John C. Thresh on Chelmsford and Maldon Rural Sanitary Districts', PP, vol. xxxv, part v (1893–94) pp. 84–5, in D. Rubinstein, *Victorian Homes* (Newton Abbot, 1974), pp. 230–3.

25. W. H. Grieves, 'Buxton Souvenir of the New Filter Beds', Buxton, 1904. The town was host to the Provincial Summer meeting of the Institute of Sanitary Engineers in 1902 where a paper on the sanitary works at Buxton was presented. Dr Thresh was the Chairman. *The Sanitary Record and Journal of Sanitary and Municipal Engineering*, 26 June (568–70), 3 July (15–18), 10 July (31–34), 24 July (89), 1902.

26. In a fulsome letter to E. C. Millican, chairman of the Local Board, Sir Robert Rawlinson expressed his great satisfaction with the new works and said that no town was more perfect in its sanitary arrangements: *The Builder*, 14 August 1886, p. 253; See for comparison articles in D. Rubinstein, *Victorian Homes* (Newton Abbot, 1974); S. Stevens Hellyer 'The Plumber and Sanitary Houses' pp. 82, 89–90; and H. J. Jennings, 'Our Homes and How to Beautify them', 1902, pp. 236, 239; M. J. Daunton gives an excellent resume of sanitary arrangements in England, see 'Public Place and Private Space in D. Fraser and A. Sutcliffe, *The Pursuit of Urban History* (London, 1983), pp. 228–33.

27. *Buxton Advertiser*, 29 December 1900; R. R. Duke, *An Autobiography 1817–1902* (Buxton, 1902), p. 17; Josiah Taylor, 'Statement of Evidence for Incorporation, 1912', Buxton Museum, LG6/51230.

28. W. H. Grieves, *op. cit.*, p. 1.

29. A. Hacker, *Buxton Thro' Other Glasses* (Derby, 1905), p. 51.

30. Buxton Local Board Streets Committee, Wednesday, 8 September 1880, D1323/2/3/7, Derbyshire Record Office, Matlock.

31. R. Rodger, *Housing in Urban Britain 1780–1914* (Cambridge, 1995), p. 4. The term 'jerry building' was in common use, see H. C. Burdett 'The Dwellings of the Middle Classes' Transactions of the Sanitary Institute of GB 1883–84 in D. Rubinstein *Victorian Homes* (Newton Abbot, 1974), pp. 237–41.

32. Although the Public Health Act of 1872 decreed all Local Boards to be urban sanitary authorities, Buxton Local Board did not use the term in its title; *Bye Laws made by the Local Board for the District of Buxton acting as the Urban Sanitary Authority with respect to new streets and buildings in the Urban Sanitary District of Buxton 1886*, Buxton Local Studies Library, 352.365.9. Subsequent byelaws dealt with: Nuisances (1886), Markets (1890), Omnibuses &c. (1891), Horses, Ponies, Mules and Asses (1890), Cemetary (1896), Sanitary Conveniences (1895), Pleasure Grounds (1898), Underground Bakehouses (1904), Luggage, Porters &c. (1904) see 'Statement of

Evidence for Incorporation, 1912' *op. cit.*, Buxton Museum, LG6/51230.

33. Local Government Board's Provisional Orders Confirmation (No. 4) Act 1886.

34. Buxton Local Board Act, 55&56 Vict (Ch. cxliv), 1892.

35. Local Government Board's Provisional Orders Confirmation Acts (no. 2) 1897 and (no. 2) 1901.

36. Buxton UDC Water Act 2 Edw. 7 (Ch. cxxv), 1902.

37. By 1904 in addition to the clerk there were: Treasurer, Medical Officer of Health, Surveyor and Water works Engineer, Gas Engineer and Manager, Librarian, Sanitary Inspector and of Markets and Hackney Carriages, Accountant, Collector, Electrical Engineer, Cemetery Superintendent.

38. See E. B. Klopfer, 'The Disease of Indifference – A Local Democratic Approach to Local Government Reform 1830–90', Oxford University DPhil, 1992, pp. 11, 326.

39. A. Offer, *Property and Politics 1870–1914* (Cambridge, 1981), p. 221; See appendix 4.2.

40. Of the members at the first meeting of the new Urban District Council in 1895 G. F. Barnard had been first elected in 1863, E. C. Milligan in 1873, J. E. Harrison in 1876 and J. Willoughby in 1878. See appendix 4.3.

41. Twenty architects submitted plans including the local architect W. R. Bryden. The town hall was paid for by a loan from the Local Government Board and £1900 from the insurance of the market hall fire of 1885. William Pollard, described as architect and surveyor, ran his own practice in King Street and, later, York Street Manchester. Buxton Local Board Minutes: 5, 28 March, 13, 15, 24 May, 5 June, 2 July, 20 August 1886; 7 May 1887. Derbyshire Record Office, Matlock, D1323/1/12.: *Slater's Directory of Manchester*, 1881 and 1891.

42. The Marquess of Hartington became the Eighth Duke of Devonshire in 1891; Nikolaus Pevsner described the building as '… rather poor, with a thin tower in the middle of the façade …' but this is to understate its undeniable grandeur for a town the size of Buxton. N. Pevsner, *Buildings of England – Derbyshire* (Harmondsworth, 1986), p. 113. A local historian and librarian has suggested that the plans were initially refused by the Local Government Board as being too ambitious for a place the size of Buxton and were only agreed on the basis that the three Buxton Fremasonry Lodges would be sited there. He does not, unfortunately, provide the evidence for this assertion. I. E. Burton, *The Duke of Connaught Lodge No. 246 of Mark Masons 100 – 1879–1979, A Short History*, August 1978, p. 13.

43. Plan dated 4.12.1889, Buxton Plans N–W, Folder 'T', Devonshire Collections, Chatsworth. The Local Board reached an agreement with the Estate which included other arrangements and it is clear that the authority was now negotiating from a firmer base. Buxton Local Board – Streets Committee, 8 November 1888, D1323/2/3/10, Derbyshire Record Office, Matlock.

44. See A. R. Neeves, 'A pattern of Local government Growth – Sheffield and its Building Regulations 1840–1914', PhD, University of Leicester (1991), p. 6; O. MacDonagh's five stages of local government development quoted by Neeves (pp. 9–13) can also be seen in Buxton's growth, they are: 1. Legislate to overcome basic social evils. The legislation was usually very compromised, thus … 2. Appointment of special officers to redraft and ensure that the act was carried into effect. 3. Calls for amendments in details leading to the equivalent demand for centralisation. 4. Recognition of the need for a slower process of tightening up loopholes, refining etc. 5. Application of legislation which gave executive officers discretion and their use of experts e.g. in medicine, engineering, to help smooth the path into law.

45. Buxton moved from a Local Board District to the more democratic constitution of the UDC based on the municipal pattern. K. B. Smellie, *A History of Local Government* (4th edn, London 1968), p. 39.

46. A. Offer, *Property and Politics 1870–1914* (Cambridge, 1981), p. 224.

47. Buxton was ahead of the boom in domestic investment by towns from the late 1890s, see A. Offer, *op. cit.*, p. 231.

48. He became Lord Avebury in 1900, *Concise DNB*, part II (Oxford, 1982), pp. 421–2.

49. A. Offer, *op. cit.*, p. 236.

50. George Cavendish was nephew to the Sixth Duke and brother of the seventh. He took the title Lord George Cavendish after his brother succeeded to the dukedom in 1858.

51. *McCalmont's Parliamentary Poll Book*, part i, p. 76.

52. A dinner was given by the chairman, Henry Cooke JP, in November 1877 attended by the notable townsmen who formed the Liberal registration Committee and by both George and Edward Cavendish. At this dinner Cooke declared himself to be a personal friend and fellow worker with Richard Cobden. *Buxton Advertiser*, 10 November 1877. The report of a political meeting in town in the *Buxton Advertiser*, 3 April 1880, is typical of many such meetings and shows the strength of support from the names of townsmen listed.

53. *High Peak News*, 31 January 1880.

54. John Frederick Cheetham was a wealthy businessman and an active Congregationalist from Stalybridge.

55. *Buxton Advertiser*, 17 April 1880. John Cumming Bates, the editor and a literary man, has used a contemporary quotation see, for example, W. D. Christie (ed.), *The Poetical Works of John Dryden* (London, 1881), p. 460.

56. The Third Reform Act consisted of two parts – a Franchise Bill (covering changes to the electorate) and a Re-distribution Bill (dealing with Parliamentary seats and constituencies). The House of Lords wished to see both of these bills enacted together and defied the Commons at the second reading of the Franchise Bill in 1884 which led to widespread popular unrest. Amongst many speeches given throughout the country by government and opposition, Lord Hartington spoke at a demonstration of some 30,000 people in Manchester in June 1884 where he put the reasonable Liberal case to bring about long needed changes in Parliamentary representation. He had, hovever, serious misgivings on the effect of any extension of electoral change in Ireland fearing this would increase the Nationalist vote in favour of agrarian revolution and affect the security of the loyal minority in the north. (His brother, Lord Frederick, had been assasinated in Phoenix Park, Dublin, in 1882 for which crime a Fenian gang were convicted). He was also in favour of government handling both franchise and redistribution bills together. During the months of

wrangling between the opposing factions within the cabinet he declared himself 'terribly sick of office' and offered to resign his cabinet position as war minister. The Franchise Act of 1884 gave the vote to all male householders and, indeed, greatly increased the Nationalist vote in Ireland. The Redistribution Act the following year divided the country, by and large, into single member constituencies with boundaries drawn for that purpose. See B. Holland, *The Life of Spencer Compton, Eighth Duke of Devonshire* (London, 1911), vol. i, pp. 392–404; *Cassell's History of England* (London, 1897), vol. viii, pp. 11–19; D. Cannadine, *The Decline and Fall of the British Aristocracy* (London, 1996), pp. 41–3; J. Pearson, *Stags and Serpents* (London, 1983), pp. 157–8, 167.

57. Cheetham may have suffered from a strong attack on his nonconformity. He was accused by his opponent of being a 'liberationist' and a leader of 'secularists at Stalybridge'. The vicar of Hope accused him of being an atheist but subsequently retracted the charge. *Buxton Advertiser*, 14 November 1885.

58. *Buxton Advertiser*, 5 December 1885. Members of the Sidebottom family were very active in local politics in Glossop with strong continuity of service as Councillor, Alderman and Mayor through the last quarter of the century. Glossop Mill owners also significantly influenced those of the working-class who were able to vote. J. Scott *et. al.*, *Glossop Dale, Manor and Borough* (Glossop, 1973), pp. 80–5; D. Read, *op. cit.* (1994), p. 154.

59. *Buxton Herald and Gazette of Fashion*, 18 March 1880. Significant Conservatives in town included: Medical Officer of Health, Dr Frederick Turner and Alfred Louis, businessman, who were both vice-chairmen of the local party. The chairman was Captain Darwin who served as chairman of the Local Board and as County Councillor. Others included hotel and lodging house keepers and tradespeople such as grocers and builders. The report in the newspaper includes at least six who were elected to the Local Board in the 1880s.

60. *Buxton Advertiser*, 26 June 1886. See also B. Holland, *op. cit.* (1911), vol. i, pp. 384–90.

61. William Sidebottom first stood for Derbyshire North in 1880 when he came fourth. In 1885 he fought a hard battle with Cheetham to take what had become the High Peak Division. He held the seat until 1900 advancing in his military career from Captain to Colonel through this time. His brother James (d. 1895) was Alderman for twenty-three years and Mayor eight times as well as a JP for Glossop, and Lancs and Derbyshire. *Buxton Advertiser*, 14 November and 5 December 1885; *McCalmont's Parliamentary Poll Book*, part ii, p. 56; *Manchester Guardian*, 5 February 1895; J. Scott *et. al.*, *op. cit.* (1973), p. 83.

62. *McCalmont's Parliamentary Poll Book*, p. 56; Partington kept the seat at the following three elections and became Junior Lord of Treasury; *Buxton Herald*, 26 September 1900. From 1885 Lord Edward Cavendish represented the Western Division of Derbyshire as a Liberal Unionist. At his death in May 1891 his son, Victor Cavendish (later Ninth Duke of Devonshire), was elected to succeed in the seat without contest.

63. *Buxton Advertiser*, Wednesday 24 July 1895.

64. *Buxton Advertiser*, Wednesday 7 July 1886.

65. V. D. Lipman, *Local Government Areas 1834–1945* (Oxford, 1949), pp. 81, 156.

66. B. Keith-Lucas, *English Local Government in the Nineteenth and Twentieth Centuries* (London, 1977), pp. 22–3.

67. The Derbyshire Red Book, Bemrose, Derby, 1890, 1893, 1896, 1899, 1902, 1907, 1919, 1911, 1915. In 1898 Capt Darwin RN served one term and in 1901 John Edward Schunk, gentleman of Wyelands did similarly.

68. The interests of the lime industry were strongly represented in Fairfield. When H. A. Hubbersty JP, lime merchant, became an alderman James Beswick described progressively as lime works manager then director, took the seat.

69. *Buxton Advertiser*, 13 February 1892, 2 March 1895, 19 February 1898.

70. B. Keith-Lucas, *op. cit.*, p. 23.

71. *Buxton Advertiser*, 19 March 1904.

72. E. B. Klopfer, *op. cit.*, pp. 330–1.

73. Appendix 4.3 identifies the local politicians in 1895 and 1904 with their occupation.

74. See D Read, *op. cit.* (1994), pp. 52, 247.

75. Sheffield experienced a real slump in building between 1891 and 1895. P. J. Aspinall, 'The Internal Structure of the House building Industry in Nineteenth Century Cities' in J. H. Johnson and C. G. Pooley (eds), *op. cit.* (1983), p. 102.

76. See appendices 4.5 and 4.6.

77. See appendix 4.8.

78. S. Pollard, *op. cit.* (1955), pp. 220–1; D. Cannadine, *op. cit.* (1995), p. 176.

79. W. L. Burn, *The Age of Equipoise* (London, 1964), p. 310; S. Pollard, *op. cit.*, p. 221.

80. D. Cannadine, *op. cit.* (1995), pp. 177–81.

81. F. A. Currey, eldest son of William and third generation head of the practice, was well aware of the difficulties of the Devonshire finances in the late 1880s and this, combined with the likelihood of a new regime under the Eighth Duke, may have urged the Curreys to initiate changes in accounting practice; Mr Charles Hamilton, who worked on the Duke's personal staff from 1894, observed that the estate accounts were kept in a very elaborate manner and detailed yearly variation reports were closely studied by the Duke. B. Holland, *op. cit.*, vol. ii, pp. 223–4. The direct remittance to Currey and Co. of receipts from ouright sales had been the practice between 1864 and 1878. See chapter 3 and appendix 3.6. also appendix 4.6.

82. In the description of the built environment which follows, the location of new roads can be seen from the plan at appendix 4.9. The description is a synthesis of data gathered largely from the following sources: Devonshire Buxton Estate Plans, Boxes 'B', 'F', 'H' and nos 1–303, Devonshire Collections, Chatsworth; Buxton Local Board Minutes Streets Committee 1872–1906, D1323/2/3/1–17, Derbyshire Record Office, Matlock; supplemented by fieldwork.

83. The opening up of Burlington Road was not without controversy. In 1876 when the first two houses were built the *Buxton Advertiser* described them as 'a blot on the landscape' (30.12.1876) but by 1890 was suggesting that the road would become one of the most popular in town (8.3.1890). The Local Board had some acrimonious ex-

changes over the delay and cost of building the necessary road bridges over the Wye river tributaries. Conflict arose between Devonshire Estate and Local Board interests. At one meeting the Chairman, E. C. Milligan, threatened to leave the chair, *Buxton Advertiser*, 8 and 15 March 1890.

84. The impact of these and other architects in Buxton is more fully described in chapter eight.

85. In nineteenth-century working-class housing architectural involvement was seen as an extra, what professor Tarn has described as '… the icing upon the building cake …' J. N. Tarn, *Working-Class Housing in 19th-Century Britain* (London 1971), p. 17.

86. *Bulmer's Directory of Derbyshire*, 1895, lists forty names under building trades, e.g. 'Builders, Contractors, Joiners, slaters, plasterers, painters,plumbers, gas fitters etc. in Buxton and its environs, pp. 117–206.

87. Most would be in the social statistician, Charles Booth's category of 'Regular Standard Earnings', some undoubtedly under 'High Class Labour' D. Read, *op. cit.* (1994), p. 238; The wage rates for craftsman in southern England ranged between 72 and 80 pence per ten hour day in the period, labourers from 46 to 55 pence per ten hour day. E. H. Phelps Brown and Sheila V. Hopkins, 'Seven Centuries of Building Wages', *Economica*, new series, vol. xxii, no. 87 (1955), pp. 195–206. Annual earnings in 1906: carpenters £98 p.a.; bricklayers £95 p.a. C. G. Powell, *An Economic History of the British Building Industry 1815–1979* (London, 1980), p. 76.

88. Recreation Road was renamed Heath Grove in 1910.

89. One acre of meadow at 'Crowestone' is shown on the 1847 Buxton Tithe Award, owned by the Buxton School Trustees. When the plans were considered by the Streets Committee on 28 August 1901 Mr Bagshaw retired for the duration. Later building took this terrace to thirty two houses and further contemporary building added two blocks of three at either end and a block of four opposite.

90. D. Cannadine, 'Residential Differentiation in Nineteenth-Century Towns: From Shapes on the Ground to Shapes in Society' in J. H. Johnson and C. G. Pooley (eds), *The Structure of Nineteenth-Century Cities* (Beckenham, 1983), pp. 238–40; also D. Cannadine, *op. cit.* (1998), p. 84.

91. Vera Brittain, *Testament of Youth* (London, 1978), pp. 53–6, 72.

92. According to his autobiography R. R. Duke laid out thirty-four roads during his forty years' service with the Estate. R. R. Duke, *An Autobiography 1817–1902* (Buxton, 1902), p. 17.

93. Two examples serve to make the point. The Estate offered strips of land in Hardwick Square in exchange for the public footpath from Spencer Rd to West Rd being made by the council. All three pieces of land concerned then to be given to the council as footpaths. Mr Drewry proposed that the making of Carlisle and Spencer Roads should be placed in the hands of their surveyor, R. R. Duke and that if Mr Hague (town surveyor) would consult with him an early start might be made. Buxton Local Board, Streets Committee, 3 October 1895, D1323/2/3/13, Derbyshire Record Office, Matlock. See also correspondence, R. R. Duke to J. Hague, 14 April and 3 August 1886, R. R. Duke to W. H. Grieves, 7 January 1897, R. R. Duke to R. Hulme (Chairman of Streets Committee), 10 May 1895. Letterbooks of R. R. Duke, Buxton Cupboard, Devonshire Collections, Chatsworth.

94. See Joyce C. Miles, *op. cit.*, pp. 295, 307, 342.

95. See appendix 4.8 and chapter five note 70.

96. *High Peak News*, 8 October 1881; *Buxton Advertiser*, 29 September 1883.

97. Buxton Local Board Act 1892, 55 and 56 Vict. (Ch. cxliv).

98. In 1894 the Chancellor of the Exchequer, Sir William Harcourt, proposed death duties of eight per cent on estates over one million pounds plus a graduated succession duty. The Duke of Devonshire's speech at Buxton came in the middle of the budget debate and may have contributed to the concessions subsequently won from the Chancellor. *Cassell's History of England* (1896), vol. viii, p. 564; The *Buxton Advertiser*, 13 June 1894, carried the Duke's speech verbatim.

99. The cost was just under £5,000. Buxton Estate Accounts of G. Drewry, 1892/93/94, Bound Ledgers, Devonshire Collections, Chatsworth.

100. J. K. Walton, *op. cit.* (1983), pp. 148–50; *Buxton Advertiser*, 26 December 1903.

101. Buxton Estate Accounts of F. Drewry, April 1905, Bound Ledgers, Devonshire Collections, Chatsworth. The total cost to the town over the sixty years was £145,560.

102. Buxton UDC Act 1904, 4 Edw. 7. (Ch. ccxxiv).

103. Its history has been carefully researched in Ros McCoola *Theatre in the Hills* (Chapel-en-le-Frith, 1984); see also C. Wells, *The Buxton Stage* (Disley, 1998).

104. From 1880 Buxton built a fine reputation for its lawn tennis tournament. It was run by the Buxton Gardens Company and included the Derbyshire Ladies and Gentlemen's singles and the All-England Ladies Doubles, a national championship which was staged at Buxton until 1954. R. Grundy Heape, *op. cit.*, pp. 112–15; M. Langham and C. Wells, *Buxton A Pictorial History* (Chichester, 1993), p. 132.

105. A history of the Devonshire Hospital and description of its central importance to the town's medical reputation is given in chapter five.

106. The *Buxton Advertiser* carried a detailed report of the visit in its 7 January 1905 issue.

107. A. Hacker, *Buxton Thro' Other Glasses* (Derby, 1905), pp. 13–14.

108. Census 53&54 Vict. c61, 1891 and 1911, 10 Edw. 7 and 1 Geo. 5 ch. 27, Tables of population; R. Lawton (ed.), *The Census and Social Structure* (London, 1978), p. 97.

109. Figures are for the Urban Sanitary District of Buxton.

110. Part of the civil parish of Buxton was added to the UDC in 1894.

111. Urban Sanitary District of Harrogate with Bilton.

112. By Local Govt. Order and Provisional Orders Confirmation Act 1900, the Municipal Borough was extended to include parts of the civil parishes of Bilton, Pannal and Starbeck.

113. Matlock Urban sanitary District with Matlock Bath and Scarthin Nick.

114. Ordnance Survey of Buxton, 1:2500, 1879; Map 4034 and accompanying papers, Devonshire Collections, Chatsworth.

115. Figures for 4, 5 and 6 are taken from the *Buxton Advertiser*

list of Visitors, 30 August 1879, 31 August 1889, 21 August 1895, 26 August 1905 as typical numbers in the high season. The newspaper relied upon the accommodation provider to send in details of guests each week, thus these figure may understate the actual number of visitors.

116. Borough of Buxton, *Abstract of Accounts year ending 31st March 1935*, pp. 166–79 and *ibid.* (1956), pp. 124–7, 132–7.

117. *Buxton Advertiser*, 5 January 1895; *Bulmer's Directory of Derbyshire*, 1895.

118. From 1894 Buxton was divided into four wards with three councillors elected to represent each ward.

119. W. H. Grieves, *Buxton, Souvenir of the New Sewage Filter Beds* (Buxton, 1904) p. 12; *Kelly's Directory of Derbyshire*, 1904; *Buxton Directory* (published by the *Buxton Advertiser*), 1906.

120. 'Counterpart Conveyances of Land on Chief Rents' and 'Schedule of the Fee Farm Rents', Papers accompanying Map 4034; 'Buxton Estate, Building Land Sold on Perpetual Chief Rent' A5/1785, Devonshire Collections, Chatsworth.

121. The higher figure here and in 1890 is for Eagle Parade, a newly developed terrace of substantial shops with accommodation above.

122. Detailed records cease after 1899. The later figures are extracted from the sources in note 1 above and verified against 'Buxton Estate Rentals 1905–1906', bound ledger, Devonshire Collections, Chatsworth.

123. 'Counterpart Conveyances of Land on Chief Rents' and 'Schedule of the Fee Farm Rents', Papers accompanying Map 4034; 'Buxton Estate, Building Land Sold on Perpetual Chief Rent' A5/1785, Devonshire Collections, Chatsworth.

124. 'Buxton Estate Rentals 1905–06' Bound Volume, Devonshire Collections, Chatsworth.

125. Buxton estate accounts of G. Drewry 1892–1895 and F. Drewry 1896–1906. Bound Ledgers, Devonshire Collections, Chatsworth.

126. Income consists of: Chief Rents for the current year *plus* a number of rents paid on account for the following year, small sales of land and interest, repayments for roads and sewer costs.

127. Payments consist of: Fixed charges, construction of roads and sewers, salaries and wages, management costs.

128. This is land and other premises sold by the estate which is entered in the Building Account in a memo in red ink. It is not to be found elsewhere in the accounts but it would have been forwarded, as capital, direct to Currey and Co at 14 Gt George St, Westminster, London. Revenue from earlier sales was handled in this manner (see chapter 3 and appendix 3.6).

129. The lower figures coincide with low expenditure on roads and sewers, thus reflect the road planning activity of the Devonshire Estate at this time.

130. Buxton Estate accounts of G. Drewry 1882–91, Bound Ledgers, Devonshire Collections, Chatsworth. Note the relevant figures for urban Buxton have been extracted from these accounts which cover a wider area described as the 'BuxtonCollection'.

131. Includes alterations to the Eagle Hotel and a new clock for the Devonshire Hospital.

132. Additions to baths, see baths accounts appendix 4.8.

133. Repairs to property much reduced in this year.

134. Buxton Estate accounts of G. Drewry 1882–1895 and F. Drewry 1896–1905, Bound Ledgers, Devonshire Collections, Chatsworth.

135. Includes new needle, vapour and massage baths, new waiting room, shops and water tower in the years 1887–88.

136. From 1892 the accounts are compiled for a calendar year, 1 January to 31 December.

137. Includes major work at the Hot Baths: new massage bath, hydraulic lift to upper floor and remodelling of the front of the baths in stone. Costed in the 1900–02 accounts.

138. The baths were sold to the Buxton UDC from 31 December 1904. This income represents the furniture, fixtures and fittings.

Notes to Chapter 5: Water Medicine

1. In 1905 Buxton had nine doctors who were Fellows of the Balneological and Climatological Society, Bath and Harrogate had sixteen each, Leamington and Malvern five each. Matlock had only one. *Journal of Balneology and Climatology*, vol. 9, pt 4, October 1905; See also *The Spas of Great Britain*, The Official Handbook of the British Spas Federation (1923 edn); T. D. Luke, *Spas and Health Resorts of the British Isles* (London, 1919).

2. M. J. Langham and C. Wells, *A History of the Baths at Buxton* (Leek, 1997), pp. 34–6, 43.

3. Phyllis Hembry, *The English Spa 1560–1815, A Social History* (London, 1990), pp. 163, 310–11; idem, *British Spas from 1815 to the Present, A Social History* (London, 1997), p. 4.

4. See chapter one; Dr Thomas Drever was an honorary physician to the Buxton Bath Charity and a seasonal visitor to Buxton. He was physician to the Duke of York and Albany and to Prince Leopold of Saxe-Coburg. Dr Jos. Denman lived at nearby Stoney Middleton and published *Observations on Buxton Water* in 1793, which ran to a second edition in 1801. In 1812 he bequeathed his estate at Stoney Middleton to his nephew Thomas who became the Lord Chief Justice in 1832 and Baron Denman of Dovedale. J. C. Cox, *Derbyshire*, 2nd edn (London, 1915), pp. 58–9.

5. A. B. Granville, *Spas of England and Principal Sea Bathing Places* (1841; repr. Bath, 1971), vols 1 and 2 *passim*.

6. Sir C. Scudamore, MD, *A Chemical and Medical Report of the Properties of the Mineral Waters of Buxton, Matlock, Cheltenham [et. al.]* (London, 1820), and *The Analysis and Medical Account of the Tepid Springs of Buxton* (London, 1833, 1839).

7. *Idem, The Tepid Springs of Buxton* (London, 1833), p. 25. Sir Charles Scudamore MD graduated at Glasgow in 1814 reading a thesis 'De Arthritide'. In 1820 he was appointed physician to Prince Leopold of Saxe-Gotha. He was knighted in Dublin in 1829 and also became an honorary member of Trinity College. Though a specialist in water medicine, he used a range of treatments including: bleeding, purgatives, colchicum, opium and

quinine and he published extensively on medical cases. *DNB*, vol. xvii (London, 1909).

8. Dr W. H. Robertson published *Buxton and its Waters* in 1838, when he also published on diet and regime and the nature and treatment of gout. He went on to write the very successful *Handbook to the Peak of Derbyshire* which ran to eleven known editions up to 1886, becoming *Robertson's Buxton Guide*, the standard work on Buxton and its baths. His sixpenny *Guide to the Buxton Mineral Waters* went to at least twenty seven editions and was still being published after his death in 1897. He also contributed a number of articles to *the Lancet*. See M. Langham and C. Wells, *Six Buxton Gentlemen* (Buxton, 1995), pp. 10–15; Annual Report of the Devonshire Hospital and Buxton Bath Charity, 1866. D4508/10/1 Derbyshire Record Office, Matlock.

9. Census 1841; *Buxton Herald*, 1 July 1848; *Bagshaw's Gazetteer and Directory of Derbyshire*, 1846.

10. B. Abel-Smith, *The Hospitals 1800–1948* (London, 1964), pp. 27, 31.

11. Dr Jones argued the case for a resident physician at Buxton and treatment for the poor, both to be paid for by levying a sliding scale of charges from a yeoman at three pence to a minister at one shilling, a duke at three pounds, ten shillings and an archbishop paying five pounds. The income to be split half to the physician and half for the poor. This he called the 'treasure of the bath' It is unlikely that Jones' proposal was adopted, in 1572 an act of parliament was passed for the punishment of vagabonds and for the relief of the poor and impotent which had a specific section dealing with Bath and Buckstone (Buxton). No diseased or impotent poor person, living on alms, was to visit the baths at these places unless they had a licence signed by two Justices of the Peace in their own locality. A petition to Queen Elizabeth in 1595 by the inhabitants of the village of Fairfield, adjacent to Buxton, setting out a case for a chapel and minister raised, inter alia, the question of the charitable upkeep of poor sick people who travelled to the baths at Buxton for treatment which suggests that, despite the act, this was still a problem. J. Jones, Dr, *The Benefit of the Auncient Bathes of Buckstones, which cureth most greevous sickness, never before published* (London, 1572), pp. 20–1; E. Axon, *Historical Notes on Buxton and its Inhabitants and Visitors*, paper no. 9, March–April 1940.

12. Copy of the Report of the Charity for the year 1785 reprinted in *Devonshire Hospital and Buxton Bath Charity Report 1866*, D4508/10/1, Derbyshire Record Office, Matlock; E. Axon, *Buxton Doctors Since 1700*, paper no. 8, December 1939.

13. A. Jewitt, *The History of Buxton* (London, 1811), pp. 65–6.

14. 'Buxton Bath Charity Annual Report 1822, printed in D. Orme, *The New Buxton Guide* (Macclesfield, 1823), pp. 19–22.

15. Some of the medical staff, Sir Joseph Paxton and trustee Bishop Spencer of Edge Moor were opposed to the plan. Henry Currey's redundant designs were used to build Wye House private asylum at Corbar overlooking the town. M. Langham and C. Wells, *The Architect of Victorian Buxton* (Matlock, 1996), pp. 141–3.

16. I am indebted to Mr M. Bryant, Senior Hydrotherapist

for sight of a plan of the ground-floor of the hospital c. 1878 just before conversion.

17. A detailed account of this conversion is in M. J. Langham and C. Wells, *The Architect of Victorian Buxton, op. cit.*, chs 7 and 8, pp. 141–89.

18. The architect's notebook gives a total of £26,049 which included £4,277 for the domed roof. Duke/DH/002, The Duke Papers, Buxton. The Buxton Bath Charity had a long association with the Cotton Districts Convalescent Fund which had its origins in the Lord Derby's Central (Executive) Relief Fund. This fund was set up in 1862 to alleviate suffering in the cotton famine brought about by the American Civil War (1861–65). In the winter of 1862/63 a hundred women under thirty years of age were selected by the relief committees of mill towns and came to Buxton for a change of air, rest and treatment. Funds remaining after the famine were made available for charitable provisions including Buxton and a convalescent home and children's sanatorium at Southport. See M. Langham and C. Wells, *op. cit.* (1996), pp. 146–7; *Devonshire Hospital and Buxton Bath Charity Report 1866*, D4508/10/1, Derbyshire Record Office, Matlock; Appendix 5.1 gives a summary of the work of the hospital taken from annual reports 1831 to 1904.

19. *Devonshire Hospital and Buxton Bath Charity Report 1898*, D4508/10/4, Derbyshire Record Office, Matlock. Dr F. K. Dickson, the owner and medical officer of the Wye House private Asylum (established in Buxton in 1859) was both hon. medical officer and consulting physician to the Devonshire Hospital, commencing his service in 1865.

20. Scudamore, 1833, *op. cit.*, pp. 25–33, cites his own case histories; J. A. Pearson, honorary physician to the charity, published details of 100 cases treated between May and October 1860. J. A. Pearson, *Reports of Cases Treated at the Buxton Bath Charity and Devonshire Hospital* (Liverpool, 1861). Other Buxton doctors simply used the hospital statistics, see for example, S. Hyde MD, *Buxton: Its baths and Climate* (London, 1898), pp. 32–4; W. H. Robertson, *A Guide to the Buxton Waters*, 15th edn (1867), pp. 51–3; J. C. Thresh, *Buxton as a Health Resort* (Buxton, 1883), pp. 72–3. Dr Thresh says '… it is impossible to say how many [visitors] go away cured or relieved; but the fact that the number increases … steadily year by year is one which requires no comment …' He goes on to set out cases and statistics drawn from the Devonshire Hospital. The doggerel of a patient, 'J. E. Todmorden', written in 1866 bears out the last point rather well. 'On my first visit to Devonshire Hospital, Buxton', Local Studies Library, Buxton, Devonshire Hospital box ,unlisted. From 1869 the hospital had its own weather station and an honorary meteorologist.

21. Accounts of Phillip Heacock, 1836–37, 'T' Series, Devonshire Collections, Chatsworth; A. B. Granville, *op. cit.* (1841), pp. 40, 42.

22. Medical rubbers in Buxton styled themselves as shampooers or galvanists. The term 'rubber' gave way to 'masseur' in about 1890, the adoption of the French terminology coincided with more sophisticated hydrotherapy treatments. R. Rolls, 'From balneology to physiotherapy: the development of physical treatment at Bath' in R. Rolls and Jean and J. Guy (eds), *A Pox on*

the Provinces: Proceedings of the 12th Congress of the British Society for the History of Medicine (Bath, 1990), p. 114.

23. See appendix 5.2 .

24. Buxton Herald, 23 July, 6 and 27 August 1842; Freebody's Directory of Derbyshire, 1852.

25. See appendix 1.2.

26. R. Price, 'Hydropathy in England 1840–70', Medical History, 25 (1981), pp. 269–80; D. Harley, 'A Sword in the Madman's Hand; Professional Opposition to Popular Consumption in the Waters Literature of Southern England and the Midlands, 1570–1870' in R. Porter (ed.), The Medical History of Waters and Spas, Medical History, Supplement no. 10, Wellcome Institute (London, 1990), p. 55; M. S. Legan, 'Hydropathy in America: A Nineteenth-century Panacea', Bulletin of the History of Medicine, vol. 45 (Baltimore, 1971), p. 271.

27. R. Metcalf, Life of Vincent Priessnitz: Founder of Hydropathy (Richmond Hill, Surrey, 1898); R. Price, op. cit., pp. 271–2; 'Priessnitzovy Lecebne Lazne a.s. Priessnitzi's Medicinal Spa', Internet http://info-jesenik.oz/en/historie/lazne.htm; Also http://www.info-jesenik.oz/en/.

28. R. Price, op. cit., pp. 270–3; R. T. Claridge, Hydropathy of the Cold Water Cure, 3rd edn (London, 1842); A Clergyman, A Few Pages on Hydropathy, or the Water Cure (London, 1843).

29. R. T. Claridge, op. cit., pp. 69–70, 125 et seq.

30. T. Smethurst, Hydrotherapia (London, 1843); J. Wilson, The Water Cure (London, 1843); A. Clergyman op. cit., The growth was rapid on the Continent and in England. Claridge (1842) lists forty six hydros in fifteen countries in Europe, Smethurst (1843) lists ninety eight in Europe including the four in England. A clergyman (1843) describes eleven establishments in England.

31. J. Culverwell, Hydropathy or the Cold Water Cure (London, 1842); A Medical Practitioner, Quacks and Quackery (London, 1844). The book is sub-titled A Remonstrance against the sanction given by the government, the press and the public to the quackeries of the day ... with remarks on homoeopathy, Hydropathy, Mesmerism, Mesmero -Phrenology. This Leeds medical practitioner equated homeopaths, hydropathists, mesmerists and mesmerophrenologists with bone-doctors, worm-doctors, wind and water doctors all as quacks but the latter four were lower in the scale. See also, Quackery, University of Toledo Libraries, Internet http://www.cl.utoledo.edu/canaday/quackery/quack3b.html; R. Porter, Health for sale: Quackery in England 1660–1850 (Manchester, 1989), pp. 52–5, 140–3, 188–9, 228–33.

32. Appendix 5.3 gives a verbatim account of a patient's experience under Priessnitz at Graefenberg and, for comparative purposes, contemporary accounts of treatment at Buxton; The contemporary Haydn's Dictionary of Dates, first published in 1842, offers a succinct description of hydropathy: '... a term applied to the treatment of diseases by cold water, practised by Hippocrates in the fourth century BC, by the Arabs in the tenth century AD, and revived by Dr Currie in 1797. A system was suggested in 1825 by Vincenz Priessnitz, of Graefenberg, in Austrian Silesia. The rational part of the doctrine was understood and maintained by Dr Sydenham, before 1689 ...' B. Vincent, Haydn's Dictionary of Dates, 15th

edn (London, 1876), p. 371; In a very full article Dr Alfred Martin places Priessnitz very much into historical context. A. Martin, 'Historical Sketch of Balneology', Medical Life, vol. 34, no. 5 (May 1927), pp. 257–301; See also H. B. Routh et al., 'Balneology, Mineral Water, and Spas in Historical perspective', Clinical Dermatology, 14, no. 6 (1996), pp. 551–4.

33. W. L. Burn, The Age of Equipoise (London, 1964), p. 209; The Lancet challenged, as an impertinent presumption, the assertion that the medical art was yet '... in its infant state ...' which had been made in the Morning Chronicle, vol. 1, 27 June 1846, p. 708.

34. R. Price, op. cit., p. 270.

35. R. Porter, op. cit. (1989), p. 231.

36. J. Culverwell, op. cit. (1842), pp. 44–5. Culverwell was a water practitioner himself with premises in the Strand and City, London where he prescribed a variety of shower baths, hot and cold medicated water and a douche bidet; The Lancet, 1842/43, vol. ii, pp. 271–2; The Lancet maintained this position, see 'Hydropathy and Hypochondriasis' 25 July 1863, pp. 101–3.

37. The Lancet, vol. i, 27 June 1846. The editorial refers to '... hydropathy – the water death, as we shall continue to call it ...'.

38. The Lancet, vol. ii, 1841–42, pp. 429–30. Dr James Wilson practised at Malvern from 1842.

39. A Medical Practitioner, Quacks and Quackery (London, 1844), pp. 55–6n.; Janet Browne, 'Spas and Sensibilities: Darwin at Malvern' in R. Porter (ed.), op. cit. (1990), p. 102, n. 3. Sir Francis Burdett underwent hydropathy for gout at Stansteadbury under Dr Edward Johnson; The Lancet, vol. i, 13 and 27 June 1846. Dr Ellis of Petersham was acquitted of the manslaughter of Richard Dresser but the case demonstrated the need for legal registration of medical practitioners; In 1852 The Lancet carried a letter from a correspondent in Leamington Prior recounting the death of a relation through hydropathy and suggesting that several other similar instances were known: The Lancet, vol. i, 24 January 1852.

40. The term hydropathic or hydro means a residential establishment, usually a hotel, where hydropathy was practised.

41. British and Foreign Medico-Chirurgical Review, vol. x, July–October 1852, pp. 121–8. A review of Hydropathy as Applied to Acute Diseases by T. B. Armitage (London, 1852).

42. Sir E. Bulwer Lytton Bart, Confessions of a Water Cure Patient, 3rd edn (London, 1847), p. 38.

43. See R. Porter, op. cit. (1989), p. 232; Janet Browne, op. cit., p. 102; Buxton Herald, 3 September 1842.

44. DNB, vol. xvii (London, 1909), pp. 1090–1.; Buxton Herald, 17 August 1843; R. Price, op. cit., p. 275; M. Stapleton, The Cambridge Guide to English Literature (London, 1983), pp. 111–12.

45. Buxton Herald, 3 September 1842, 8, 22 June, 17, 24, 31 August, 7, 14 September, 19 October 1843, 21 September 1844. The Buxton Herald reviewed: J. Wilson, The Water Cure; T. Smethurst, Hydrotherapia; and Sir C. Scudamore's account of his visit to Graefenberg.

46. Buxton Bath Charity Annual Report 1854. D4508/9/5. Derbyshire Record Office, Matlock; Notebook of RR

Duke, Duke/DH/02, The Duke Papers, Buxton. Bulwer-Lytton's family had ancient Derbyshire connections. But his connections with the Duke of Devonshire were contemporary. He joined with Charles Dickens in 1849 in an enterprise to support needy authors. His play 'Not so bad as we seem' was produced by Dickens at Devonshire House, London in the presence of the Queen and Consort, invited there by the Sixth Duke. *DNB*, vol. xvii (London, 1909; J. Lees-Milne, *The Bachelor Duke* (London, 1998), pp. 195–8.

47. *The Lancet*, 2 October 1852.

48. Analyses conducted included those by: Short (1734), Higgins (1782), Pearson (1784), Scudamore and Garden (1819), Playfair (1852), Muspratt (1860) and several more were conducted in the later part of the century. J. C. Thresh, *Buxton as a Health Resort* (Buxton, 1883), pp. 44–63; W. H Robertson, *A Handbook to the Peak of Derbyshire* (London, 1854), pp. 112–27.

49. W. H. Robertson, *op. cit.* (1854), pp. 125–43; T. Carstairs, *Bathing and the Buxton Waters* (London, 1847), pp. 15–16.

50. A detailed account is in M. Langham and C. Wells, *op. cit.* (1996) pp. 129–35.

51. Sir Charles Scudamore prescribed drugs, blistering and leeching as well as the water treatment. C. Scudamore, *op. cit.* (1839) pp. 52–63; Dr Page was a great believer in vapour baths. T. J. Page, *Brief Observations on the Buxton Waters*, 7th edn (Buxton, 1843), pp. 29–31; See appendix 5.2.

52. Miller's establishment was, however, described as a hydro in the commercial directories up to 1860. See the Derbyshire Directories of White, 1857, and Harrison and Harrod, 1860.

53. Matlock was developed by businessman turned hydropathist John Smedley (1803–74). At Malvern the two pioneering hydropathic doctors were James Manby Gully (1808–83) and James Wilson (d. 1867). Early resident doctors at Ilkley were Dr Rishchank from Silesia and Dr Macleod (d. 1875).

54. K. Rees, 'Medicine as a Commodity: Hydropathy in Matlock', *Bulletin of the Society for the Social History of Medicine*, no. 35 (June 1985), pp. 24–8; D. A. Barton, 'The Hydros of Matlock' unpublished paper, 6 May 1980. Matlock Local Studies Library, 942.51M; In 1866 there were nine hydros in Matlock. T Marchington, *op. cit.* (1960), p. 107.

55. Malvern, driven by Drs Gully and Wilson, had ten hydropathics by 1864. Ilkley, from the opening of Ben Rhydding in 1844 could boast six additional hydros and a similar number of hotels with hydropathic facilities. Phyllis Hembry, *op. cit.* (1997), pp. 173–5, 183–5.

56. The hydropathist, Richard Metcalf observed that Buxton and Harrogate were different from other resorts in terms of hydropathy for similar reasons. R. Metcalf, *The Rise and Progress of Hydropathy in England and Scotland*, 2nd edn (London, 1912), pp. 210–14. All three resorts had charity hospitals whose influence, in support of medical reputation, has already been discussed. The medical ethos in Buxton may best be seen through W. H. Robertson. For Bath see R. W. Falconer MD, *The Baths and Mineral Waters of Bath* (London, 1857), and on Harrogate, a particularly supportive paper, A. S. Myrtle MD, 'Hydrotherapeutics:

The Resources of Harrogate Specially Considered' *The British Medical Journal*, vol. I (April 1870), pp. 430–1. A German physician, Dr Mastalier, is described as operating a hydro at the house and pleasure grounds of Sydney Gardens, Bath, in 1843, but Bath did not develop at this time in to a hydropathic centre: A. Clergyman, *op. cit.*, pp. 11–12.

57. Robertson held firmly to this view throughout his life. In 1894 after a sixty-year career he stated that Buxton with its unique mineral water could not be considered as an ordinary health resort and that the Buxton Baths were quite distinct from the packs and medicated baths produced artificially in hydropathic establishments. In no sense could treatment at the Buxton mineral water baths be seen as identical to the peculiar system of hydropathy. G. Lorrimer MD, introduction to W. H. Robertson MD, *Guide to the Buxton Mineral Waters*, 27th edn (Buxton, *c.* 1898), pp. 15, 16.

58. J. M. Gully, *The Water Cure in Chronic Disease*, 2nd edn (London and Malvern, 1847).

59. *Ben Rydding: The Principles of Hydropathy and the Compressed air bath, together with a chapter on the improved Roman or Turkish bath. With illustrations by Theta*, by a graduate of the University of Edinburgh (London, 1859).

60. D. A. Barton, *op. cit.* (1980).

61. See, J. Culverwell, *op. cit.* (1842). A Medical Practitioner, *op. cit.* (1844), Sir Charles Scudamore, as already noted, operated an eclectic approach and would not have been alone in this.

62. *The Lancet*, 25 July 1863.

63. A. S Myrtle, *op. cit.* (1870); *Journal of Balneology and Climatology*, vol. 9, pt 2 (April 1905) Letter from the Buxton practitioner, Dr John Braithwaite; B. Abel-Smith, *op. cit.*, pp. 21–31.

64. '... Amongst the wants of the country are hydropathic institutions comprising every variety of bath, conducted by men of sound judgments and and acting upon sensible and scientific principles ...' *The Lancet*, Editorial, 25 July 1863.

65. J. Leach, 'The Revd James Shore of Bridgetown, Totnes' in *The Devon Historian*, no. 57 (October 1998), pp. 14–19; J. Buckley, *Modern Buxton* (Buxton, 1886), pp. 35–6; *Buxton, Its History etc.*; [C. Smilter] *Buxton* (guidebook, *c.* 1905.)

66. Harrogate was later than Buxton in hydro development. Attempts were made in the 1860s but it was 1878 before the Swan (later Harrogate) hydro was opened. This was followed by the Cairn in 1898 and the Harlow Manor: R. Metcalfe, *The Rise and Progress of Hydropathy in England and Scotland* (London, 1912), p. 213. Metcalfe gives Bath only a page of description and does not mention any hydros there, pp. 230–1.

67. See M. Langham and C. Wells, *op. cit.* (1996), ch. 6, for detailed description of the changes.

68. M. Langham and C. Wells, *op. cit.* (1997), pp. 64–5. The 'Sitz' bath from the Austrian sitting bath, was, paradoxically, part of the hydropathic system.

69. *Ibid.*, pp. 95–9 gives descriptions of almost fifty treatments available at Buxton, including some imported from Continental Europe e.g. Vichy Douche, Nauheim Bath, Fango Mud Packs.

70. The Buxton Estate accounts give 50,000 p.a. through the paying baths to which a further 25,000 may be added for the separate Charity Baths. This is based on 2,400 patients p.a. on a three-week stay taking, on average, ten baths. Accounts of George and Frank Drewry for Buxton Estate 1894–1905, bound volumes, Devonshire Collections, Chatsworth; *Devonshire Hospital Annual Report*, 1904. Comparisons are not straightforward due to differences in defining what was meant by a 'bath' but, as a broad indication, Bath in 1886 saw 86,223 bathers pass through the four city baths and Harrogate in 1904 gave 86,865 baths. G. P. Davis, 'Image and Reality in a Victorian Provincial City, A Working-Class area of Bath 1830–1900', PhD, Bath (1981), p. 51; R. Metcalfe, *The Rise and Progress of Hydropathy in England and Scotland*, 2nd edn (London, 1912), p. 219.

71. The considerable investment put into this has been seen in chapter four.

72. D. Read, *The Age of Urban Democracy* (Harlow, 1994), pp. 49–50.

73. Some of the difficulties experienced by medical people in this new profession are discussed in E. Klopfer, 'The Disease of Indifference – A Local democratic Approach to Local Government Reform 1830–90', Oxford University DPhil (1992), pp. 286–8.

74. *Medical Directory* (London, 1866, 1874, 1888).

75. Frederick Turner was the son of Samuel Turner, sub-agent to the Devonshire Buxton Estate and well respected townsman. Dr Turner qualified MRCS in 1864 and LSA in 1865. He retained his MOH position at Buxton and ran his own practice through the century and was still Medical Officer of Health in 1905 by which time he had been made a JP. He lived at Grafton House in the Quadrant for many years.

76. Comparative figures for England and Wales were: 1861 – 22.5; 1884 – 19.1; 1900 – 17.5 and for Bath; 1861 – 22; 1884 – 19.9; 1900 – 17.4. Buxton figures from: W. H. Robertson, *A Guide to the Buxton Waters*, 15th edn (Buxton, 1867), pp. 6–7; Buxton Medical Officer of Health Report, 1887, p. 5; R Grundy Heape, *Buxton Under the Dukes of Devonshire* (London, 1948), p. 144; Robertson/Lorimer, *A Guide to the Buxton Mineral Waters*, 27th edn (Buxton, 1898), p. 8. The figures for Bath and England and Wales are taken from G. P. Davis, *op. cit.* (1981), p. 410, who also gives a comparison with Cheltenham at 19, 17.8 and 15.5 per thousand for the same years. *Ibid.*, p. 412; See also D. Cannadine, *Lords and Landlords* (1980), p. 266 for other comparisons including Eastbourne (10.2 per 1000 in 1904) and Scarborough (14.8 per 1000 in 1904).

77. W. H. Robertson, *op. cit.* (1867), pp. 6–7; Idem, *Hand-book to Buxton and the Peak of Derbyshire* (1872), p. 49; (1875), p. 49; (1886), p. 34; J. C. Thresh, *op. cit.*, pp. 38–9; R. O. G. Bennet, *Buxton and Its Medicinal Waters* (Manchester, 1892), p. 11.

78. *The Sanitary Record and Journal of Sanitary and Municipal Engineering*, 10 July 1902, p. 32, Buxton Museum. LG6.

79. W. H. Robertson, *A Guide to the Use of the Buxton Waters* (Buxton, 1867), p. 25.

80. Idem, *A Hand-Book to the Peak of Derbyshire* (Buxton, 1875), p. 203.

81. *Ibid.*, pp. 209–10.

82. From 1898 the Devonshire Hospital annual report gave a detailed breakdown of numbers and cases. By far the largest number of cases were of diseases of the Locomotor system (2356 cases) which included rheumatic diseases. Diseases of the Nervous system followed (322 cases) including sciatica, myelitis and neurasthenia. Cases of diseases involving more than one system were the only other category where the annual case numbers went to three figures (113) and most of these involved rheumatism of one form or another. *Devonshire Hospital Annual Report, 1898*. D4508/10/4, Derbyshire Record Office, Matlock; Neurasthenia was a diagnosis much in vogue at the turn of the century. It was a term used to describe a broad range of conditions including general nervousness, the male equivalent of hysteria in women, minor depression and chronic fatigue. Edward Shorter offers a useful description of this condition as a psychosomatic illness. E. Shorter, *From Paralysis to Fatigue – A History of Psychosomatic Illness in the Modern Era* (New York, 1993), pp. 220–32.

83. S. Hyde, *Buxton: Its Baths and Climate* (Manchester, 1898), pp. 30–1, 52–4. Dr Hyde was very well respected as a water specialist and extensively published in the journals including *British Medical Journal, Lancet, Journal of British and Foreign Health Resorts*. See *Medical Directory 1900* (London, 1900); Examples are: 'The Natural Mineral Waters of Buxton: Their Indications and Modes of Application' *British Medical Journal*, vol. 2 (1894), December, p. 1302; 'Analysis of Two Hundred Cases of Sciatica', *Lancet*, vol. 1 (1896), May, p. 1281. He devised his own specialist treatment called 'The Thermal Cure'.

84. R. Rolls, 'From Balneology to Physiotherapy: the development of physical treatment at Bath' in R Rolls and Jean and J. Guy (eds), *A Pox on the Provinces: Proceedings of the 12th Congress of the British Society for the History of Medicine* (Bath 1990), pp. 111–18.

85. *Report of the Devonshire Hospital and Buxton Bath Charity, 1904*. Derbyshire Record Office, D4508/10/5.

86. S. Hyde, *op. cit.* (1898), pp. 43, 94–103; *Kelly's Directory of Derbyshire 1904*; Professional recognition for medical rubbers came through the Society of Trained Masseurs which was founded in 1894; by 1900 the membership had reached 250. The society then became the Incorporated Society of Trained Masseurs with professional and legal status. Examination entry into the profession included the theory of Galvanism and Faradism as well as the use of electric baths and radiant heat and light. Nicola R. Y. Clemence, 'Physiotherapy – A Hundred Years of Medical Rubbing?' *Norfolk and Norwich Institute for Medical Education Journal*, vol. 10 (Autumn 1993), pp. 31–6; E. M. Magill, *Notes on Galvanism and Faradism*, 2nd edn (London, 1919).

87. M. Worboys, 'Urban Advantage-Tuberculosis 1885–1925' Unpublished paper, Sheffield, 6 October 1997; C. J. Whitby, 'Notes on the Sanatorium Treatment of Pthisis and its Present Limitations', *Journal of Balneology and Climatology*, vol. 9, pt 1 (1905).

88. *Ibid.*, vol. 9, pt 4 (October 1905); vol. 10, pt 4, October 1906. In 1905 Buxton had twenty doctors in total.

89. *Ibid.*, vol. 10, pt 4, October 1906.

90. W. H. Robertson MD, *Guide to the Buxton Mineral Waters*, 27th edn (Buxton, c. 1898), p. 56.

91. Taken from the Annual reports [Devonshire Hospital and] Buxton Bath Charity, 1830–1904, D4508, Derbyshire Record Office, Matlock.
92. W. H. Robertson, *A Handbook to the Peak of Derbyshire and to the use of the Buxton Mineral Waters* (Buxton, 1875), p. 242.
93. S. Hyde, *Buxton: Its Baths and Climate* (Manchester, 1898), p. 33.
94. Main sources: Axon E. *Historical Notes on Buxton, Its Inhabitants and Visitors*, Paper 8, December 1939; Paper 14, March/April 1942; Jewitt, *The History of Buxton* (London, 1811); Annual reports [Devonshire Hospital and] Buxton Bath Charity, 1830–1904, D4508, Derbyshire Record Office, Matlock; *The Medical Directory 1845–1905* (London). A number of these doctors contributed to the professional journals such as, *The Lancet* and *British Medical Journal.*
95. He was an apothecary in 1769 and in 1779 was listed as the only medical man in Buxton. He acquired the degree of MD date unknown. *The Medical Regster for the Year 1779* (London).
96. Not listed in the *Medical Directory*. He was son of Sir Francis S. Darwin MD, of Breadsall Priory and grandson of Dr Erasmus Darwin. In 1846 he was described MD

in *Bagshaw's Directory of Derbyshire*, but he retired early from medical practice and became a JP. He lived at Fern House, London Road.
97. F. K. Dickson was the proprietor of the Wye House private lunatic asylum.
98. A doctor of note. He was formerly apothecary in ordinary to HM King William IV, Queen Adelaide and their household; HM King of Belgians; HM King of Hanover and the Duchess of Kent. He was also joint apothecary to Queen Victoria. He may have semi-retired to Buxton for he only served three years as an honorary medical officer of the Buxton Bath Charity, retiring in 1866 due to ill health.
99. A correspondent of the *Cork Southern Reporter*, reprinted in *Buxton Herald and Gazette of Fashion*, 19 October 1843.
100. T. J. Page, *Brief Observations on the Buxton Waters*, 7th edn (1843).
101. Sir C. Scudamore, *The Tepid Springs of Buxton* (London, 1833), pp. 27–8.
102. W. H. Robertson, *Buxton and Its Waters* (London, 1838), p. 97.
103. J. A. Pearson, *Reports of Cases treated at the Buxton Bath Charity* (Liverpool, 1861), pp. 21, 31.

Notes to Chapter 6: Agents of Change

1. See F. M. L. Thompson, *English Landed Society in the Nineteenth Century* (London, 1963), ch. VI; G. E. Mingay, *The Agrarian History of England and Wales*, vol. vi, 1750–1850 (Cambridge, 1989), pp. 591–617; D. Spring, *The English Landed Estate in the Nineteenth Century: Its Administration* (London, 1963). ch. IV.
2. R. G. Heape, *Buxton Under the Dukes of Devonshire* (London 1948), p. 56.
3. D. C. Moore, 'The Gentry', in G. E. Mingay (ed.), *The Victorian Countryside*, vol. 2 (London, 1981), pp. 383–98. The description in his chapter supports the notion of men like the Buxton agents being viewed as gentry; Burke's *History of the Commoners in Great Britain and Ireland* (vols I–IV, 1833–38) does not list any of the Buxton Agent families, though it will be seen in this chapter that their lifestyle was that of gentry. Frank Drewry made a brief entry in Kelly's *Handbook to the Titled, Landed and Official Classes* in 1924, after his retirement, and his son George, also a Devonshire estate land agent, had a substantial entry in the 1948 edition.
4. Appendix 6.1 shows the agents and staff at the Buxton Estate office 1848–1905.
5. *Transactions of the Surveyor's Institute*, *passim*. It is noticeable that, by 1919, all the agents to the Devonshire estates in Derbyshire and Yorkshire were members of the Land Agents Society. *Estates Gazette*, 15 November 1919.
6. Caleb Garth to his daughter's suitor, Fred Vincy, in George Eliot, *Middlemarch* (Penguin edn, 1994), p. 561.
7. Heacock to John Heaton 30 March 1813. P. Heacock's letterbooks A5/155, Devonshire Collections, Chatsworth.
8. E. W and G. R. ''Tis Sixty Years Since', reprinted from the *Buxton Advertiser*, 24 March 1906, p. 10; R. G. Heape, *op. cit.* (1948), pp. 55–6.

9. See E. Richards '… some agents behaved with as much patrician style as their masters …' in *The Land Agent*, in G. E. Mingay (ed.), *The Victorian Countryside* (London 1981), p. 440. As noted in chapter one, he made an early assessment and adjustment (upwards) of rentals in Buxton.
10. P. Lead, *Agents of Revolution* (Keele, 1989). John Gilbert (1724–95) the land agent and Thomas Gilbert (1720–98) a lawyer were, *inter alia*, prime movers in the construction of the Bridgewater canal: p. 14, 33.
11. G. E. Mingay, *op. cit.* (1989), p. 595. Blaikie actually took a cut in salary in 1822 , from £650 to £550 to help Thomas Coke of Norfolk, the First Earl, out of difficulties in the agricultural depression after the Napoleonic Wars.
12. F. M. L. Thompson, *op. cit.* (1963), p. 156.
13. He was a contributor to the great agricultural survey of Derbyshire published 1811. J. Farey, *General View of the Agriculture and Minerals of Derbyshire* (1811; repr. Peak District Historical Mines Society, 1989), p. xx.
14. Letterbook of Phillip Heacock A5/1512, Devonshire Collections, Chatsworth.
15. G. E. Mingay, *op. cit.* (1989), p. 592; E. Richards, 'The Land Agent', in G. E. Mingay, *op. cit.* (1981), p. 439. He suggests that many proprietors handed over to their agents almost all the responsibility for running their properties to the point where the agent became the 'alter ego' of the landlord.
16. Accounts of Phillip Heacock, 1812, 1831, 1832, 1834, 1835, 1839. Devonshire Collections, Chatsworth; Poll Book for the Northern Division of Derbyshire 1837; R. G. Heape, *op. cit* (1948), asserts that he was a Tory but does not say where he obtained this information, p. 56.
17. The Fifth Duke's wife, Georgiana, did not trust Heaton and called him the 'corkscrew ' also 'knave of spades'

see The Earl of Bessborough, *Georgiana, Extracts from the Correspondence* . . (London, 1955), pp. 66–73 *et seq.*; J. Lees-Milne, *The Bachelor Duke* (London, 1998), p. 18.

18. A. B. Granville, *Spas of England*, vol. 2 (1841), p. 49.

19. *Buxton Herald*, 21 June 1851.

20. M. J. Langham and C. Wells, *op. cit.* (1996), p. 33; Alexander Beresford-Hope (1820–87), politician, author and architect. He was a prominent member of the Cambridge Camden Society (founded 1839) which formed the aesthetic side of the Oxford Movement. He inherited Lord Beresford's English Estates in 1854. He founded the *Saturday Review* in 1855 and was president of the Institute of Architects 1865–67. *Concise DNB to 1930* (Oxford, 1948); L. E. Elliot-Binns, *Religion in the Victorian Era* (London, 1936), p. 230.

21. Letter Thomas Carstairs (Dr) to Duke of Devonshire, 10 February 1851; (Revd) Hull Brown to Duke of Devonshire, 12 February 1851. Buxton Museum, 66.3.66.4.66.5.

22. *Buxton Herald*, 21 June 1851; Letter Thos Warren to the Duke of Devonshire, 16 August 1848. Buxton Museum, 66.1.

23. D. Spring, *op. cit.* (1963), pp. 99–100.

24. Simon F. Ivery to the Duke of Devonshire, 17 February 1851. Buxton Museum, 66.6. His uncle was Sir Oswald Mosley Bt of Rolleston Hall, Staffs.

25. Devonshire Estate Accounts Books, Folio, *passim*. Devonshire Collections, Chatsworth; The Stavely estate was sold in 1829 to pay debts. J. Lees-Milne, *op. cit.* (1998) p. 91.

26. Smithers was responsible, from 1851, for ten main collections: *Ashford* including: Great Longston, Little Longston, Monsal Dale, Wardlow, Holme, Bakewell, Sheldon, Upper Haddon, Brushfield, and Blackwell. *Highlow* inc: Eyam, Eyam Woodlands, Hathersage, Hathersage Outseats, Offerton and Shatton. *Bonsal. Dore. Stoney Middleton* inc:Eyam and of the Cottage, Chief and Pasture rents at Stoney Middleton, Eyam, Eyam Woodlands, Foolow and Abney. *Hartington* inc: Flagg, Chelmorton, the Peak Tithes and the Rectory of Youlgreave, Meadow Place, One Ash and Callinglow Granges. *Peak Forest* inc: Forestry, Chapel-en-le-Frith, Fernilee, Barmor, Rushup Edge and Edale. *Tideswell* inc: Wormhill, Great Hucklow and Wheston. *Wetton* inc: Alstonfield, Castern, Throwley and Cowlow in County of Stafford. *Buxton* inc: Fairfield, Fernilee, Wormhill and part of Hartington Upper Quarter. Devonshire Estate Accounts, Folio, Devonshire Collections, Chatsworth.

27. Caird wrote: '. . . The selection of a properly qualified agent or steward is, on every large estate, a matter of the utmost importance. Honesty and uprightness are indispensable, capacity and personal activity, with an inquiring and unprejudiced mind, sound judgment, and decision of character, are all necessary. An agent should be capable of choosing a class of tenantry who would aid him in the improvement of his employer's estates; he should be able to consult with and advise them in the management of their farms, pointing out resources which they may have overlooked; he should study the proper subdivision of farms and fences; the best arrangement of farm buildings and the most economical mode of constructing them; he should be

competent to decide on the fields that need drainage, so that while necessary improvements are not neglected, the money of his employer may not be needlessly expended. The presence of such an agent is visible at once in the general air of comfort, activity, and progress which animates all classes connected with the estate which he superintends …', J. Caird, *English Agriculture in 1850–51* (London, 1852), p. 493: D. G. F. MacDonald, *Hints on Farming and Estate Management* (London, 1865), pp. 188–90.

28. The Cavendish motto, *Cavendo tutus* – Secure by caution, is seen at work through this chapter in the selection of successive agents.

29. Elizabeth Barton, 'Edward Woollett Wilmot: The Duke of Devonshire's Agent in Buxton, 1856–64', *BANHS Bulletin*, no. 19 (Spring 1995), p. 10; N Pevsner, *The Buildings of England, Cheshire* (Harmondsworth, 1971), pp. 125–6.

30. *Buxton Advertiser*, 2 July 1864, 9 July 1864 quoting the *Congleton, Sandbach and Crewe Advertiser*.

31. The son of a baronet, he married Emma, daughter of Sir Francis Sacheverell Darwin of Breadsall Priory and Sydnope Hall, near Darley Dale. Her grandfather was Dr Erasmus Darwin, philosopher, physician and scientist of Breadsall Priory (d. 1802) who was also the grandfather of Charles Robert Darwin, the eminent naturalist but by a different wife. The Thoroton Society of Nottinghamshire, 'In Emma's Footsteps', Paper prepared for an excursion on Saturday 23 September 1995; J. C. Cox, *Derbyshire*, 2nd edn (London, 1915), pp. 57–8.

32. Wilmot's policy was to convince the inhabitants of the need to work together to achieve common goals to benefit the whole town. In this he echoed Samuel Smiles' 'mutual understanding of common interests' A. Briggs, *Victorian People* (London, 1990), p. 141. Smiles published *Self-Help* in 1859.

33. K. C. Edwards *The Park Estate, Nottingham*, in M. A. Simpson and T. H. Lloyd, *Middle-Class Housing in Britain* (Newton Abbot, 1977), pp. 156, 159.

34. E. W. Wilmot was responsible for six collections: Buxton, Tideswell, Hartington, Peak Forest, Wetton, Bonsall. These formed a geographically compact portfolio. Devonshire Buxton Accounts, folio, 1856/57; R. G. Heape, *op. cit.* (1948), p. 78.

35. 'Buxton Office 1856', Folio. Devonshire Collections, Chatsworth. The suede covered large folio runs from 13 September 1856 to 25 March 1889.

36. D. Spring, *op. cit.* (1963), pp. 119–20; J. O. Parker, *The Oxley Papers* (Colchester, 1964), pp. 110–11; Wilmot was a JP.

37. 'Estate Register Buxton Office 1857', Folio. Devonshire Collections, Chatsworth.

38. Contemporary Directories and the 1861 census give his address as Wye Head but this designates the area rather than the specific residence. I am indebted to Mrs Elizabeth Barton for revisiting her research notes to verify this, 1.6.1999.

39. Elizabeth Barton, *op. cit.* (1995), pp. 17–18.

40. Devonshire Buxton Accounts 1856 to 1864, Folio, Devonshire Collections Chatsworth.

41. *Buxton Advertiser*, 2, 9, 16 July 1864; See appendix 6.2.

42. D. Cannadine, *Lords and Landlords, The Aristocracy and*

the Towns 1774–1967 (Leicester, 1980), pp. 262–4.

43. F. M. L. Thompson, *op. cit.* (1963), p. 157; D. Spring, *op. cit.* (1963), p. 102. Formal training was not known until the opening of the Royal Agricultural College at Cirencester in 1845. By 1882 most of the students trained there became land agents. There was no separate land agents' society until 1902 and no formal examinations until 1920s. Some of the elite of the profession joined the exclusive Surveyors' Club, formed in 1834. In 1886 it was claimed that a great majority of the leading agents of the day were members of the Surveyors Institution. George Drewry was not one of them. E, Richards, *op. cit.* (1981), pp. 444–5; J. V. Beckett, *The Aristocracy in England 1660–1914* (Oxford, 1986), p. 144.

44. D. Spring, *op. cit.* (1963), p. 13. The Seventh Duke of Devonshire had sought the Duke of Bedford's advice in 1858, reckoning him to be a first rate man of business. *Ibid.*, p. 51.

45. Sir Anthony Buller, formerly a judge in Bengal, died 1866, he was the son of John Buller of Morval in Cornwall. *Burke's Landed Gentry*, vol. 1 (1846).

46. Lord Chesham, second Baron, acceded in 1863 and was a cousin of the Seventh Duke of Devonshire. His father (raised to the peerage in 1858) was Charles Compton Cavendish, 4th son of George Cavendish, the First Earl of Burlington (2nd creation). V. Gibbs, *The Complete Peerage* (London, 1913).

47. Drewry won many prizes and made substantial money from sales. A sale of thirty animals at Holker in 1878 realised just under £20,000 and the Duke gave him a gift of £1,000. *Buxton Advertiser*, 18 April 1896.

48. When George Drewry first came to Holker the Seventh Duke was still the Earl of Burlington. He served the Duke for forty-six years right through the time of the Devonshire investments at Barrow, living close by and, clearly, providing unwavering support. *Buxton Advertiser*, 18 November 1876, quoting the *Agricultural Gazette*.

49. For example, the Duke visited Holker to inspect his shorthorn cattle immediately after the first ship launching at Barrow in 1873. D. Spring, 'The English Landed Estate in the Age of Coal and Iron: 1830–1880', *Journal of Economic History*, vol. xi (1951), p. 11.

50. J. O. Parker, *op. cit.* (1964), pp. 88–133.

51. *Buxton Advertiser*, 18 April 1896.

52. Jas Wardley was variously described as Land Agent's assistant or sub-agent, but he was, essentially, an administrator.

53. Folder dated 3.12.1872 a series of eleven drawings. An Inner folder dated 8.4.1874, No. 1A. A series of six drawings. Devonshire Collections, Chatsworth.

54. A short biography is given in M. Langham and C. Wells, *Six Buxton Gentlemen* (Buxton, 1995), pp. 3–9.

55. As Marian Sharples has pointed out, tact was a very important asset in maintaining good landowner–tenant relationships which could so easily be destroyed by arrogant land agents. Marion Sharples, 'The Fawkes family and their Estates in Wharfedale, 1818–1936' *Leeds Thoresby Society*, 2nd series (1997); E. W. and G. R., *op. cit.* (1906), p. 8; M. Langham and C. Wells, *op. cit.* (1995), p. 5.

56. Clerk of Works Notebook (Samuel Turner) 1866. L/113/6. Devonshire Collections, Chatsworth.

57. Letter R. R. Duke to Sarah M. Smith, 4 October 1876. Duke/RRD/Fam/36. Duke Papers, Buxton.

58. A full account of his life is in M. J. Langham and C. Wells, *The Architect of Victorian Buxton, A Biography of Robert Rippon Duke* (Matlock, 1996); See also chapter eight.

59. D. Cannadine, *op. cit.* (1980), pp. 118, 262–3.

60. Letterbooks of R. R. Duke, no. 6, September 1892 to April 1895, Devonshire Collections, Chatsworth.

61. Letterbooks of R. R. Duke, no. 5, May 1888 to September 1892, Devonshire Collections, Chatsworth.

62. *Ibid.*, no. 2, August 1866 to June 1871.

63. See letters, 29 November 1865, 14 March and 16 May 1866, 8 April 1867. *Ibid.*, no. 1, August 1864 to August 1866 and 2 August 1866 to June 1871.

64. *Ibid.*, no. 2, August 1866 to June 1871. Mr Moore was at the office of Currey and Co. Gt George Street, W1. At this time William Currey was the head of the legal practice which handled the Devonshire finances. From 1886 his son Francis Alfred took over.

65. *Ibid.*, no. 1, August 1864 to August 1866.

66. *Ibid.*, no. 2, August 1866 to June 1871.

67. Heather Fuller's discussion of arrangements between absentee owner and resident agent is relevant to the Buxton situation of absentee agent and resident surveyor. Heather A. Fuller, 'Land Ownership in Lindsey with particular reference to the Role of the Large Landowner as an Agent of Agricultural Improvement and Landscape Change'. MA thesis, University of Hull (1974), p. 149.

68. Letterbooks of R. R. Duke, no. 3, December 1876 to July 1883; See also appendix 3.7.

69. *Buxton Advertiser*, 10 November 1877, in the same edition an article from the *Harrogate Herald* suggested that the Northern resort was vying to become as good as Buxton and trying to extend its season in similar manner to Buxton.

70. Accounts of George Drewry, 1877. Bound Volume, Devonshire Collections, Chatsworth. Noticeably F. Drewry was paid £5 p.a. less than the Chief Clerk J. Wardley.

71. John. D. Simpson had taken drawing lessons from Robert R. Duke.

72. Letterbook F. Drewry, July 1878 to January 1886, contains 400 letters across the range of estate business. He was sent correspondence to deal with by his father. Devonshire Collections, Chatsworth.

73. Letterbooks of R. R. Duke, no. 3, December 1876 to July 1883. Devonshire Collections, Chatsworth.

74. Devonshire Hospital Minute Book, 31 March 1877. Unlisted. Devonshire Royal Hospital archive, now at the County Record Office, Matlock.

75. Census 1891.

76. *Kelly's Directory of Derbyshire* (1881); Accounts of George Drewry, 1892, Folio. Devonshire Collections, Chatsworth.

77. Buxton Local Board, Streets Committee D1323/2/3/12, February 1892 to May 1895. Derbyshire Record Office, Matlock.

78. Duke/Dev/04. The Duke Papers, Buxton.

79. *Buxton Advertiser*, 11 April 1896.

80. The Drewry family provided the Devonshire estate with three generations of agent for, at the time of Frank's

retirement in 1919 his son, George Hayward, was appointed to the Woodlands, Peak Forest and Highlow estates. He was a member of the Surveyors Institution and lived at Hargate Hall near Wormhill. *Estates Gazette*, 15 November 1919; *Transactions of Surveyors Institution* (1919–20); *Kelly's Handbook to Titled, Landed and Official Classes* (1948).

81. D. Cannadine, *Decline and Fall of the British Aristocracy* (London, 1996), pp. 89, 124; D. Spring, *op. cit.* (1951), pp. 3–24.

82. *Buxton Calling*, 1925, Buxton Bureau of Information, p. 102.

83. In 1896 the Royal Commission on the Land in Wales and Monmouthshire set down a form of proper training for land agents. D. Spring, *op. cit.* (1963), pp. 100–1; and the Land Agent's Society was formed in 1902, see note 43; See appendix 6.3.

84. E. Richards, *op. cit.* (1981), p. 444. Cost of management in the 1880s was variable. On a large well managed estate the cost could be as low as 4 per cent. Richards does not say how the figure is derived. The Buxton figures are based on total costs of office and salaries as a percentage of turnover for sample years 1852, 1862, 1870, 1880, 1890. The figures must be viewed with caution, however because of differing agent portfolios and the difficulty in separating out accounts; Devonshire Buxton Accounts, Bound Volumes, *passim*. Devonshire Collections, Chatsworth.

85. F. M. L Thompson, *op. cit.* (1963), p. 151.

86. In addition to the studies already cited J. T. Ward has carried out several studies with a northern focus including: 'The Earls Fitzwilliam and the Wentworth Woodhouse Estate in the Nineteenth Century', *Yorkshire Bulletin of Economic and Social Research*, XII, I (1960); and 'West Riding Landowners and Mining in the Nineteenth Century' *ibid.*, XV, I (1963).

87. J. Bateman, *The Great Landowners of Great Britain and Ireland* (1876; repr. Leicester, 1971), p. 505.

88. R. R. Duke, privately printed pamphlet, 31 May 1906. Duke/DH/011, Duke Papers, Buxton.

89. Caleb Garth, land agent, speaking to his wife in George Eliot, *Middlemarch* (1872; Penguin edn, 1994), p. 403.

90. Taken from Buxton Estate Accounts 1851–1905 *passim*. Devonshire Collections, Chatsworth.

91. Includes £75 p.a. expenses. G. Drewry was also agent for three other major estates during this time.

92. £750 in 1905. He retired in 1919.

93. Taken from Buxton Estate Accounts 1851–1905, *passim*, Devonshire Collections, Chatsworth.

94. Or 1905 where [beyond] is used.

95. Part-time post. Retired 1901 but paid to 1908 as Consulting Architect.

96. Resident Agent from 1892, Agent from 1896.

97. Part-time post.

98. Taken from a hand-written record made by Robert Rippon Duke. Duke/Archt 30 and 31, Duke Papers, Buxton .

99. *Buxton Advertiser*, 23 December 1865.

100. Transcription of hand-written description 1899, by Robert Rippon Duke, Architect to the Estate. Duke/Dev/02, Duke Papers, Buxton.

101. Duke/Dev/03. Duke Papers, Buxton.

Notes to Chapter 7: Religious Belief – The Mortar Between the Stone

1. L. E. Elliot-Binns, *Religion in the Victorian Era* (London, 1936), p. 420.

2. The term 'denomination' is used here to describe a stage of development between a 'sect' and a church' See H. Davies, *Worship and Theology in England*, Vol. iv (Cambridge, 1996 edn), p. 148.

3. D. Read, *The Age of Urban Democracy* (London, 1994), p. 69; Between 1869 and 1885 in the Diocese of Manchester £730,000 was spent on building over 100 new churches. In 1873 the cost of churches was £5–£10 per sitting for the majority, though the cost, for some, could be higher at £10–£12. C. G. Powell, *An Economic History of the British Building Industry 1815–1979* (London, 1980), p. 58; Elliot-Binns points out that no period since the Reformation can compare with the amount of church building in the Victorian era: *op. cit.* (1964), pp. 353–5.

4. D. Bebbington, *Victorian Nonconformity* (Bangor, 1992), p. 24.

5. H. McLeod, *Class and Religion in the Late Victorian City* (London, 1974), p. 24.

6. Caroline Reid offers a definition of 'respectability' as essentially a social expression of a behavioural conditioning which permeated inner attitudes, outer appearance and general social conduct. She offers a detailed case-study of class and lifestyle differences in Sheffield, including the distinction between the 'rough' and the 'respectable', Caroline Reid, 'Middle-class values and working-class culture in Nineteenth century Sheffield' in S. Pollard and C. Holmes, *Essays in the Economic and Social History of South Yorkshire* (Sheffield, 1976), pp. 275–91.

7. O Chadwick, *The Victorian Church*, pt II (London, 1970), p. 268.

8. H. McLeod, *op. cit.* (1974), pp. 139–40, 219.

9. Beatrice Webb, 'My Apprenticeship', in C. Harvie *et al.*, *Industrialisation and Culture 1830–1914* (London, 1970), pp. 146–7; O. Chadwick, *op. cit.*, pp. 263–9.

10. H. McLeod, *Religion and the Working Class in Nineteenth Century Britain* (London, 1984), p. 26; G. K. Horridge, *The Salvation Army Origins and Early Days: 1865–1900* (Godalming, 1993), p. 228.

11. O. Chadwick, *op. cit.*, p. 267; H. McLeod, *op. cit.* (1974), p. 155.

12. D. Fraser, 'Politics and the Victorian City' in *Urban History Yearbook* (1979), pp. 32–45.

13. D. Thomson, *England in the Nineteenth Century* (Harmondsworth, 1960 edn), p. 107.

14. The other four are described later. They were: the Wesley Methodist Chapel in Higher Buxton, the Independent Chapel in Spring Gardens, the Presbyterian Chapel on the Market Place and the Primitive Methodists who met in a room in Higher Buxton. D. Orme, *The Buxton Guide* (Buxton, 1842), p. 10; J. Leach, *Methodism in Buxton* (Buxton, 1985), p. 12; The chapel on the Market Place had a stone above the door inscribed 'Presbyterian

Chapel 1725' though the chapel trust had always been for Protestant Dissenters, not for Presbyterians or Unitarians. E. Axon, *Historical Notes on Buxton Its Inhabitants and Visitors*, paper XXII (1947), *passim*; The term Unitarian was not commonly used in the North West; it will be seen later that the term was not applied to the new Hartington Street Chapel until the middle of the last century.

15. Cicely Williams, *The Parish Church of St John the Baptist, Buxton* (1988).
16. The incumbents styled themselves 'Perpetual Curates' until the 1868 Act of Parliament allowed use of the title 'Vicar'. The residence built in 1861, in Buxton Park, for Rev. Edward Weighall was known as the 'New Parsonage'; The 1878 OS map indicated that the church could seat 1,000.
17. Cicely M. Williams, *op. cit.* (1988).
18. James Medland Taylor (1834–1909) and his brother, Henry Taylor (b. 1837) were architects for many churches in the Manchester area, producing unusual, inventive, 'quirky' designs. St James was certainly unusual, in random coursed stone with a hexagonal crossing tower and spire adjacent to an apsidal chancel. N. Pevsner, *op. cit.*, *Derbyshire*, p. 116; *South Lancashire*, p. 43 and *passim*.
19. The chasuble, alb, stole, maniple and amice were worn. J. J. Stark, *St Anne's Church, Buxton* (*c.* 1967), p. 2; H. Davies *op. cit.* (1996), vol. iv, pp. 127–8.
20. J. J. Stark, *op. cit.* (*c.* 1967). The 1878 OS map describes the church as St John the Baptist.
21. J. J. Stark, *op. cit.*, p. 2; O. Chadwick, *op. cit.* (1970), p. 323.
22. 'Musings of Memory by an Old Buxtonian', reprinted from the *Buxton Herald*, 25 June 1902.
23. Letter to J. W. Taylor, 5 May 1904. D247 B/G8, Derbyshire Record Office, Matlock.
24. E. W. and G. R. ''Tis Sixty years Since – A Few Recollections of Buxton' p. 22, reprinted from the *Buxton Advertiser*, 24 March 1906.
25. English Church Union founded in 1859 to support the Anglo-Catholic ritual had the following objects:
    1. To Defend and maintain unimpaired the doctrine and discipline of the Church of England
    2. To afford counsel, protection and assistance to all persons, lay and clerical, suffering under unjust aggression of hindrance in spiritual matters
    3. In general, so to promote the interests of religion as to be, by God's help, a lasting witness for the advancement of His glory and the good of His Church. L. E. Elliot-Binns, *op. cit.* (1964), p. 235. At the anniversary of the Buxton Branch in 1896 the Dean of Chichester gave an address and the Provost of Cumbrae preached at the high celebration of the Eucharist in St James' Church. *Buxton Advertiser*, 15 August 1896.
26. *Buxton Advertiser*, 6 June 1896; 'Musings of Memory by an Old Buxtonian' *op. cit.* (1902), pp. 11–12.
27. The family of Miss Mirilees owned an engineering business in Stockport.
28. St John's Church Buxton, Handwritten Report by Rev. C. C. Nation, D1751A/P1 41. Derbyshire Record Office, Matlock.
29. Cicely Williams, *op. cit.*; Correspondence of C. Heathcote 1895–6, D1752A/P1 30–35, Derbyshire Record Office, Matlock.
30. Estimates by W. R. Bryden, 1896, D1752A/P141–2; Letters W. R. Bryden to Rev. C. C. Nation, February 1896 to January 1897, D1752A/P1 47–59. Derbyshire Record Office, Matlock; *Buxton Advertiser*, 9 May 1896.
31. Report from Sir A. Blomfield, 9 April 1895, D1751A/P1 49. Derbyshire Record Office, Matlock; St John's had been built on oak piles to secure the footings in wet foundation soil.
32. Correspondence from Sir Arthur Blomfield's firm spans 1896–1909. D1751A/P1 41–120, Derbyshire Record Office, Matlock.
33. *Buxton Advertiser*, 11 March 1893.
34. Register of Services, St Mary's Church 1897–1905, D1754/4/1. Derbyshire Record Office, Matlock.
35. From 1884 Buxton had left Lichfield to join the new diocese of Southwell. The diocese of Derby was not created until 1927.
36. Professionals such as Dr W. H. Robertson and Dr F. Turner MOH, substantial hoteliers such as J. H. Lawson and P. Le Gros and G. F. Barnard, Wines and Spirits Merchant. In the period of this study there were sixty-nine elected members of the Local Authority, of these one third were active in the Anglican Church. The term 'active' means more than just a worshipper, thus, for example, a member, or trustee or sidesman.
37. L. E. Elliot-Binns, *op. cit.* (1964), ch. 12.
38. J. W. Taylor, *Trinity Episcopal Chapel* (Buxton, 1888), p. 8.
39. J. W. Taylor, *op. cit.* (1888), p. 7; J. W. Taylor, *These Fifty Years 1873–1923* (Buxton, 1923).
40. J. W. Taylor, *op. cit.* (1888), pp. 10–11.
41. D. Newsome, 'Newman and the Oxford Movement' in A. Symondson (ed.), *The Victorian Crisis of Faith* (London, 1970), p. 73; J. W. Taylor *op. cit.* (1888), p. 20; It is noticeable that the high Anglican, Dr W. H. Robertson did not mention Trinity Chapel in his well-known guidebooks, see W. H. Robertson, *Buxton and the Peak of Derbyshire* (Buxton, 1872, 1875), pp. 148–9; (1886), pp. 127–9.
42. H. McLeod, *op. cit.* (1974), p. 172.
43. M. Langham and C. Wells, *Six Buxton Gentlemen* (Buxton, 1995), p. 43.
44. D. A. Prendergast, *Catholicity in Buxton* (Liverpool, 1935), p. 5.
45. Samuel Grimshawe III (1811–83) graduated BA 1830, 1833 from Brazenose College Oxford. He took his MA in the same year as Edward Manning and was influenced by him and by John Henry Newman as the Oxford Movement was being formed. Grimshawe converted to the Roman Church in 1851, the same year as Manning. G. Hancock, *Goyt Valley and its People* (1996), pp. 20–3; *Concise DNB, Origins – 1930* (Oxford, 1948); *Buxton Advertiser*, 20 July 1861.
46. J. J. Scholes was a 'pupil clerk' of the RC architect Joseph Ireland in which capacity he supervised the building of Ireland's Classical Revival RC church at Hassop near Bakewell. N. Pevsner, *op. cit.*, *Derbyshire* (Harmondsworth, 1986), pp. 116, 238; St Anne's RC and the Congregational churches were the last major contracts

of R. R. Duke before his building firm encountered financial difficulties and he moved into surveying and architecture. M. Langham and C. Wells, *The Architect of Victorian Buxton* (Matlock), pp. 52–7.

47. Pope Pius IX had declared the doctrine of the immaculate conception as dogma in 1854. Opposition in Europe by the Dominicans and others of the Medieval Church to the declaration had led to an increasing conflict with the Holy See over the succeeding six or seven years. Manning's defence of the sacerdotal and royal office of the papacy from what he termed the animosity against the pure and inflexible laws of Christianity and hatred of authority, order and rule both sacred and civil, was a clear indication of his stance on Papal Infallibility which he successfully advocated in England. L. E. Elliot-Binns, *op. cit.* (1964), pp. 128–30; *Buxton Advertiser*, 20 July 1861 reported his sermon in full.

48. O. Chadwick, *op. cit.* (1970), pt II, p. 241.

49. D. A. Prendergast, *op. cit.*, p. 17.

50. Manning has been described as an ecclesiastical statesman, diplomatist and great preacher. He did much to overcome the resistance by the 'old' Catholic families to the newer converts and to raise the standards of the priesthood. He advocated temporal power and Papal Infallibility and was himself autocratic and ultramontane as Archbishop. By his patriotism, involvement in moral and philanthropic enterprises and his vigorous and witty preaching he achieved a degree of popularity with ordinary people not matched by other ecclesiastical dignitaries. H. Davies, *op. cit.* (1996), vol. iv, p. 342; O. Chadwick, *op. cit.*, pt II, pp. 251–4; Elliot-Binns, *op. cit.* (1964), pp. 128–30.

51. Letter R. R. Duke to Rev. J. Power, 27 November 1882, Letterbooks of R. R. Duke, Buxton Cupboard, Devonshire Collections, Chatsworth; D. A. Prendergast, *op. cit.*, pp. 7–9; The Presentation convent (a teaching order) remains today, though somewhat depleted from a high in 1935 of ten nuns, two novices and a postulant.

52. John Wesley preached in Buxton in 1783 at the age of eighty, later that year he preached at Fairfield Anglican church. The movement in Buxton was then small. E. Axon, *op. cit.* (1947). Growth was slow in the early part of the nineteenth century: J. Leach, *op. cit.* (1985), p. 6; Professor Briggs notes that the Nonconformists were far more important than their numbers in influencing in the city. His observation of Methodists being passive is not borne out in Buxton, however. A. Briggs, *Victorian Cities* (Harmondsworth, 1971), pp. 68–9.

53. D. W. Woodhead, *Buxton Wesley Chapel* (Buxton, 1949), p. 23. The earlier chapel had existed since 1797.

54. The so-called Fly Sheet controversy involved the publication in 1849 of pamphlets accusing prominent Wesleyan leaders of despotism and appealing for a more liberal form of government. G. K. Horridge, *op. cit.* (1993), p. 4; O. Chadwick, *op. cit.* (1970), pt I, ch. 6. See also H. D. Rack, 'Wesleyan Methodism 1849–1902', in R. Davies, A. R. George, G. Rupp, *A History of the Methodist Church in Great Britain* (London, 1983), vol. 3, pp. 120–2.

55. Rev. Robert Newton (1780–1854), preached at London, Liverpool, Manchester, Leeds and Stockport. He was president of the Wesleyan conference 1824, 1832, 1840, 1848; Jabez Bunting (1779–1858) served at headquarters, London 1833, was president of the theological institute 1835, and organised the connection and its severance from the Anglican church; John Hannah (the Elder) (1792–1867) delegate to United States of Wesleyan conference 1824, 1856. President of conference 1842, 1851. Tutor at the Wesleyan Theological Institution, Didsbury, Lancs, 1843–67; Jonathan Crowther (1794–1856) General Superintendent of the Wesleyan Missions in India, 1837–43. Tutor at the Didsbury Institution 1849, examiner at Wesley College, Sheffield. *Concise DNB, Origins – 1930* (Oxford, 1948).

56. The church would accommodate a congregation of 350 and the schoolroom 100 pupils. James Wilson (1816–1900), a Methodist, designed Kingswood Methodist School, Lansdown (1851), Cheltenham College in 1841–43 (many later additions) and Westminster Methodist College, Horseferry Road in 1849–51 (chapel 1872) also a number of churches in Bath and North Somerset. R. Dixon, S. Muthesius, *Victorian Architecture* (London, 1978), pp. 231, 270; N. Pevsner, *Buildings of England – North Somerset and Bristol* (Harmondsworth, 1958), *passim*. He reputedly designed the Wesleyan Church at Chapeltown, Sheffield.

57. Minute Book Wesleyan Circuit Buxton, D3568/2/1, Derbyshire Record Office, Matlock; D. W. Woodhead, *op. cit.* (1949), p. 26.

58. *Ibid.*, pp. 28–9, describes the additions in some detail.

59. *Ibid.*, p. 31; *Buxton Advertiser*, 24 May 1873.

60. The sixteen trustees for this chapel included a number of solid citizens: Millican, draper; Raynor, grocer; Vernon, butcher; White, butcher; Lomas, baker; T. Webster, lodging-house keeper; E. Webster, spa maker.

61. D. W. Woodhead, *op. cit.* (1949), p. 31; Sir Robert Perks (1849–1934), a railway lawyer and businessman, was Liberal MP for Louth division from 1892 to 1910. An active Methodist, he was the originator of an influential nonconformist parliamentary committee and worked successfully for Methodist Union which was achieved in 1932. *Concise DNB 1901–1970* (Oxford, 1982).

62. Minute Book Wesleyan Circuit Buxton, D3568/2/1, Derbyshire Record Office, Matlock; D. W. Woodhead *op. cit.*, p. 32.

63. J. Leach, *op. cit.* (1985), p. 9.

64. The schism which gave rise to the formation of Primitive Methodists had its origins on a hill called Mow Cop on the Staffordshire–Cheshire border in 1807. Here several thousand people gathered for a full day of praying, preaching and hymn singing. The Wesleyan Conference, preoccupied with issues of leadership and discipline, determined that such 'camp meetings' were not desirable and expelled the leader, Hugh Bourne, from the movement. Thus alienated Bourne, a carpenter, and William Clowes, a potter joined with the 'Magic Methodists' of Delamere Forest in Cheshire, one of several groups existing at this time on the margins of official Methodism. They subsequently formed the Primitive Methodist movement in 1812. Appealing strongly to the working class with an evangelical, bible and repentance based doctrine, the movement grew to 200,000 members by the end of the century. It is reputed that Hugh Bourne visited

Buxton in 1820, in which year missionaries from Macclesfield, fifteen miles away, also visited. Due to the town's remoteness, it was difficult to sustain a regular visiting preacher and it proved equally difficult to find accommodation for services. H. McLeod, *op. cit.* (1984), p. 26; E. Axon, *op. cit.*, paper XXII (1947); J. Leach, *op. cit.* (1985), p. 12–13.

65. E. Axon, *op. cit.*, paper XXII (1947); *Buxton Herald*, 23 July 1842.

66. *Buxton Herald*, 21 May 1890.

67. Records of the Congregational Church Buxton incip. Ad 1854. D3657/1/1, Derbyshire Record Office, Matlock.

68. D. Bebbington, *Victorian Nonconformity* (Bangor, 1992), p. 15.

69. *Buxton Herald*, 21 May 1890.

70. F. A. Holmes JP (1870–1947), amateur archaeologist and natural historian, was a close friend of Dr J. W. Jackson, archaeologist, of Manchester University. He fought a long and successful campaign to preserve access to Dovedale in Derbyshire, now managed by the National Trust. P. Browning 'Dovedale and its Unsleeping Sentinel' *National Trust Magazine* (Spring 1981); R. Procter, 'Notes and Records' *Bulletin of the Buxton Archaeological and Natural History Society*, 16 (Autumn 1993).

71. E. Axon, *op. cit.*, XXII; J. Leach *op. cit.* (1985), p. 14; At least thirteen stones remain including one inscribed with the architect (G. E. Garlick), contractor (A. Wild) and minister (Rev. I. J. Hardy). Fieldwork 13.10.99.

72. Its founder William Booth had become a minister of the Methodist New Connexion in 1854 evangelising in London, Brighouse and Gateshead. He resigned in 1862 because the movement would not allow him and his wife, Catherine, to return to evangelistic work. The Booths decided to work with the destitute and drunk setting up a mission in the East End of London in 1865. From these revivalist beginnings the movement developed into a highly organised army of about 100,000 evangelistic soldiers by the end of the century, taking the name 'Salvation Army' in 1879. This achievement in only thirty-five years was due to the intense zeal and leadership of its founder, but also to his absolute autocracy. G. K. Horridge, *op. cit.* (1993), pp. 14–15; H. Davies, *op. cit.*, vol. iv, pp. 166–7; L. E. Elliot-Binns, *op. cit.* (1964), pp. 425–6. On Booth's leadership style Horridge says: '... Above all the Booth family were unquestionably in charge and orders had to be obeyed to the letter. This was maintained throughout the rank structure. Always the senior officer's word was true unless that officer were anti-Booth or was otherwise discredited in the eyes of the Booths ... A mass of detailed paperwork and reports [had] to be regularly attended to ...', p. 88.

73. G. K. Horridge, *op. cit.* (1993), p. 44, table.

74. Census 1891; *Bulmers Directory of Derbyshire, 1895*, p. 127; *Buxton Herald and Gazette of Fsshion*, 5 May, 3 November, 15 December 1886.

75. *Buxton Herald*, 16 July 1902; *Buxton Advertiser*, 7 January 1905 lists no services. In 1906 the premises on Torr Street were described as Salvation Army offices. *Buxton Directory, 1906*.

76. The origins of Independent Congregationalism in Buxton may be traced to the visit of two prominent

Congregationalists in 1802, James Alexander Haldane and Thomas Wilson. Both were evangelical enthusiasts, Haldane preached in the Assembly Room in Buxton and in villages around. Wilson passed through Buxton on visits to his wife's father, Arthur Clegg, in Manchester. Wilson and Haldane met in Buxton in 1804 and from this time regular services were held in private houses and, from 1810, in an Independent chapel in Spring Gardens. The land for the chapel was purchased by Wilson's father-in-law, Arthur Clegg and of the eleven trustees only one was resident in Buxton. Early preachers included four of the leading Congregational ministers in the north, Haldane, himself, returned in 1814 and Wilson provided ministers from Hoxton Academy of which he was the long-time treasurer. The cause was active until about 1827, certainly in that year as many as 131 inhabitants were prepared to sign a petition for the minister to be allowed to officiate in the Presbyterian Chapel on Hall Bank, but after this time the Spring Gardens chapel opened only intermittently, usually in the season, until the 1840s. James Alexander Haldane (1768–1851) Religious writer, first Congregational minister in Scotland 1799, founded Society for Propagating the Gospel at Home 1797, Baptist 1808; Thomas Wilson (1764–1843), a Nonconformist benefactor and son of a ribbon and gauze manufacturer, engaged extensively in building and repairing chapels for Congregationalists. *Concise DNB, Origins to 1930* (Oxford, 1948). He had close Derbyshire links, being brother-in-law to Thomas Bateman senior (1760–1847), father of William and grandfather of Thomas the pioneer archaeologists. B. M. Marsden, *The Barrow Knight* (Eldwick, 1988), pp. 6, 7, 44. The ministers were: Revs. Samuel Bradley of Manchester, James Boden and James Mather both of Sheffield, and Benjamin Boothroyd of Pontefract, later of Huddersfield. 'Records of the Congregational Church Buxton. A.D. 1854'. D3657/1/1, Derbyshire Record Office, Matlock.

77. Manuscript history of the church written by Rev T. G. Potter in 'Records of the Congregational Church Buxton incip. A.D. 1854'. D3657/1/1, Derbyshire Record Office, Matlock.

78. Rev T. G. Potter is unable to contain a degree of smugness as he recounts how he thought the Duke would have instructed Sir Joseph to '... take the thing in hand and write to ... [Wilmot] ...' Manuscript history of the church written by Rev T. G. Potter in 'Records of the Congregational Church Buxton incip. A.D. 1854'. D3657/1/1, Derbyshire Record Office, Matlock; 'Buxton Office 1856' Entry dated 27 January 1857, Devonshire Collections, Chatsworth.

79. Rev. Dr Raffles (1788–1863) was reaching the end of a long life in the ministry which had included fifty one years as minister of Newington Chapel and its successor, Great George Street, Liverpool. He was one of the chief founders and organisers of the Lancashire Independent College at Whalley Range, Manchester. *Concise DNB, Origins – 1930* (Oxford, 1948); *Buxton Advertiser*, 13 July 1861.

80. C. Binfield, *So Down to Prayers – Studies in English Nonconformity 1780–1820* (London, 1977), p. 28. Shaw was assured of widespread support. Subscriptions making up the total cost of £2,785 had come from Congregationalists

in London (£133), Manchester (£488) and more than sixteen other towns including, Blackburn, Bradford, Sheffield, Stockport, Liverpool, Ashton and Lancaster (£712). Buxton contributed £912 which included Shaw's contribution of £500 plus a further £202. The radical MP for Sheffield and joint founder of the Lancashire Independent College, George Hadfield, gave £100. The Duke of Devonshire's contribution was a modest £20 and E. W. Wilmot, the agent, noticeably gave only £1. Building Fund, Statement of Accounts 13 August 1865, Records of the Congregational Church, Buxton, D3657/1/1 and Accounts Book, 1858–1864, D3657/12/1. Derbyshire Record Office, Matlock.

81. C. Binfield, op. cit. (1977), p. 79–80; For biographical note on Edward Baines see J. Briggs and I. Sellers (eds), *Victorian Nonconformity* (London, 1971), p. 177; C. Porteous, *Pill Boxes and Bandages, A documentary biography of the first two generations of Robinsons of Chesterfield 1839–1916* (Chesterfield, 1961), pp. 150, 174–5; Bebbington, op. cit. (1992), pp. 30–1, mentions Sir Titus Salt, alpaca manufacturer of Saltaire, a noted Congregationalist, in similar terms.

82. Henry Shaw's death was sudden and occurred at the close of Morning Service. Congregational Church, Hardwick Mount, Buxton, *Manual 1911*.

83. As members, women had voting rights in the church but their influence in management and on committees (other than in the Sunday School or in specifically female concerns) was limited. For example, it would be unlikely for a woman to serve on a church building committee but membership of a lesser committee such as one dealing with the interior fabric might be found.

84. Congregational Church, Hardwick Mount, Buxton, *Manual 1911*, pp. 22–6; The Congregational Church Buxton, *The Church's Story – Triple Jubilee 1810–1960*; Buxton Local Board Committee Minutes, 1878–80, 4 October 1878, D1323/1/8, Derbyshire Record Office, Matlock; Land Sales Book, tracings 66–139, 1872–1887, plan no. 118, Devonshire Collections, Chatsworth; see also chapter eight.

85. J. W. Taylor, op. cit. (1888), p. 16 (his italics); O. Chadwick, op. cit. (1970), p. 255; *Buxton Advertiser*, 13 July 1861.

86. Taylor served one term on the Local Board, but was probably temperamentally unfitted for such representational work. Henry Shaw jnr. was co-opted to fill a vacancy caused by the retirement of J. C. Bates but remained in this 'local shopocracy' for only one year, it was, clearly, not for him either. J. W. Taylor was founder chairman of the Buxton Protestant Electoral Association, formed in 1899 to encourage people to take a protestant rather than political stance in voting for the Parliamentary candidate, whether liberal or conservative, who gave the fullest assent to protestant principles. By the turn of the century this association could count on 250 voters in the High Peak Division and Rev. Robert Rew, the Congregational minister was an active member. Association minutes 1899–1901 D247 B/G1 and papers G2(2), G19 and 20, G24. Derbyshire Record Office, Matlock.

87. Ernest Axon FSA (1868–1947), whose work informs this book, was for fifty years a librarian, completing his career as deputy city librarian of Manchester. He was a prolific writer, presenting papers to the Lancashire and Cheshire Antiquarian and the Unitarian Historical Societies amongst others. He presented a series of twenty-two important papers to the Buxton Archaeological and Natural History Society between 1934 and 1947. These 'Historical Notes on Buxton and its Inhabitants and Visitors' were published in full in the *Buxton Advertiser. Lancashire and Cheshire Antiquarian Society Bulletin*, LIX (1947), pp. 237–40. Axon, a firm Unitarian, is at pains to argue that Dr Clegg was not orthodox in the sense of being a Trinitarian Calvinist. He describes him as semi-Arian and influenced by Arminianism and thus carefully argues that the genesis of the Buxton chapel itself was not strictly orthodox. The division between orthodox and unorthodox belief stems from the Trinitarian controversy at a meeting in Salter's Hall Presbyterian Church in 1719. The Unitarians led the way in developing a distinct philosophy combining Biblical religion with a reduction of the supernatural to the natural, the mysterious to the rational and the depreciation of faith in favour of the good works of charity; what Professor Davies has described as 'rationalistic moralism' H. Davies, op. cit., vol. iii (1996), pp. 3, 76. The Semi-Arians, subsequently Biblical Unitarians, were radical, intellectual theologians who sought to revise the Book of Common Prayer to support the dignity of worship, rather than practise free prayer: *Ibid.*, vol. iii, pp. 76–80. The Arminian influence would allow Clegg to lay emphasis on the voluntary aspects of personality, the forming of habits and emulating Christ by increasing conformity between the heart and way of life: *Ibid.*, vol, III, p. 195. He argues that, whilst the church may not of been Unitarian from the beginning, each minister has been in the right line of Unitarian ancestry. E. Axon, 'Buxton Chapel (Hartington Road [Unitarian] Church 1725–1925', *Transactions of the Unitarian Historical Society* (1926), p. 4.

88. E. Axon, op. cit. (1926), pp. 5–6.

89. The trust deed of 1729 refers to an assembly of Protestant Dissenters, making no mention of Presbyterians or Unitarians and this was not altered by the revision of the trust deed required for the new chapel in Hartington Street in 1875. Of the first trustees only five out of a total of twenty-eight were Buxton people and this has been the pattern throughout the life of this church in Buxton. The first 150 years of its history were chequered. From its beginning the chapel received a grant from the Presbyterian Fund and was able to accumulate a small endowment but this grant was withdrawn and re-awarded at times coinciding with the closure of the chapel or its restricted seasonal opening. The chapel and manse at the top of Hall Bank were constantly in need of repair. Between 1783 and 1823 the minister George Buxton let the manse which became the Kings Head Inn and delivered a regular income to the chapel. By 1825 it was admitted that there were no persons of Unitarian sentiment in Buxton and attempts by the Congregationalists to obtain possession of the chapel may have induced the trustees to do more than simply make it available to the few worshippers. 'Extracts from Declaration of Trust, 9 February 1876' by courtesy of Bennett Brooke-Taylor and Wright, Solicitors, 4 The Quadrant Buxton. Until the middle of this century the new chapel was always referred to as 'The Hartington Street Chapel'.

90. Meeting of trustees 15 September 1869, Minute Book, 1855–1907, D1332J/U1, Derbyshire Record Office, Matlock.

91. 'Buxton Chapel' Appeal for funds, D1323J/U11, Derbyshire Record Office, Matlock.

92. R. K. Webb notes that Manchester College was a principal source of Unitarian Ministers for much of the nineteenth century. R. K. Webb 'The Faith of Nineteenth Century Unitarians: A Curious Incident' in R. J. Helmstadter and B. Lightman (Eds) *Victorian Faith in Crisis* (London, 1990), p. 130; At least five new Unitarian churches were built in the environs of Manchester in the 1870s. N. Pevsner, *Buildings of England, South Lancashire* (London, 1989); *ibid., Cheshire* (1971).

93. N. Pevsner, *op. cit., South Lancashire* (1989), and *Cheshire* (1971), attributes the following to Thos Worthington: Altrincham (1872), Hyde (1878) , Salford (1874), Gorton (1869/70), Monton (1875).

94. Correspondence with Department for Culture, Media and Sport, 9 September 1999; *Buxton Advertiser*, 22 May 1875.

95. *Buxton Advertiser*, 22 May 1875. Charles Beard (1827–88) was minister at Hyde Chapel, Gee Cross and at Renshaw Street Chapel, Liverpool. An academic, he was a lecturer and vice-president of University College, Liverpool and published religious writings. He was the son of John Relly Beard (1800–76) minister at Salford and indefatigable Unitarian publicist. *Concise DNB, Origins – 1930* (Oxford, 1948); R. K. Webb, *op. cit.* (1990), p. 137.

96. He reverted to Anglicanism in which he was first ordained. E. Axon, *op. cit.* (1926), pp. 22–3.

97. *Buxton Advertiser*, 22 May 1875 The local press saw the main aim of this church as meeting the needs of visitors and observed that a further body of Christians as yet unprovided for were the members of the Scotch kirk who visit in increasing numbers every year.

98. The Lancashire and Cheshire Provincial Assembly and the East Cheshire Christian Union. E. Axon *op. cit.,* paper XXII (1947).

99. H. McLeod, *op. cit.* (1974), p. 250.

100. *Buxton Advertiser*, 22 July 1896; How relevant to Buxton was the sermon preached, in the same year, by the Rev Brooke Herford, then Minister at Rosslyn Hill, on the opening of a new chapel in West Hampstead: '... As he washed the feet of his disciples, so they might build baths and wash-houses; as he healed the sick, so they might best follow him by supporting the hospitals ...' *Hampstead and Highgate Express*, 18 January 1896, quoted in H. McLeod, *op. cit.* (1974), p. 250, n. 162.

101. R. K. Jones, citing J. F. Molloy says there were in 1892 forty seven congregations in England numbering 6,000 communicants. 'The Catholic Apostolic Church: A Study in Diffused Commitment' in M. Hill (ed.), *A Sociological Yearbook of Religion in Britain*, 5 (London, 1972), pp. 146, n. 17. At the end of the century in London the Catholic Apostolic membership, at 3,232, was only two per cent of the figure for Church of England. O. Chadwick, *op. cit.* (1970), p. 235.

102. *Buxton Advertiser*, 18 March 1899. This was, at one time, a popular description; the main London church in Gordon Square, built 1854, was known as the Irvingite church. Edward Irving went to London, from his native Scotland, in 1822 to be minister of the Caledonian chapel in Hatton Garden. His charismatic preaching drew large congregations such that in 1827 a new church in Regent Square was built. His belief that the church, through time, had neglected the second coming of Christ which was imminent, drew him to Henry Drummond, the Member of Parliament for West Surrey. Between 1826 and 1830 Drummond held annual conferences at his country house, Albury, Surrey which were attended by clergy and laity of different denominations. From these conferences was born the Catholic Apostolic movement. G. L. Standring, *Albury and the Catholic Apostolic Church* (Albury, 1985), pp. 13–14, 52–4; H. Davies, *op. cit.* (1996), vol. iv, pp. 153–4, 162; M. Hennell, *Sons of the Prophets – Evangelical Leaders of the Victorian Church* (London 1979), pp. 9–12; C. G. Flegg, 'The Catholic Apostolic Church: Its History, Ecclesiology, Liturgy and Eschatology', Open University PhD thesis (1990), p. 36.

103. As the movement grew churches other than the founding Apostle's Chapel at Albury Park in Surrey were referred to as 'Particular Churches': C. G. Flegg, *op. cit.* (1990), p. 129; G. L. Standring, *op. cit.* (1985), pp. 37–8, 68–9; H. Davies, *op. cit.* (1996), vol. iv, p. 156.

104. J. B. Cardale (1802–77), founder member with Drummond was a wealthy solicitor who retired at the age of thirty to devoted himself to the movement after receiving a call from God to be an apostle. He devised the Liturgy from the Greek, Roman and Anglican churches which was adopted in 1842. G. L. Standring, *op. cit.* (1985), pp. 23–4; K. W. Stevenson, *op. cit.* (1979), pp. 23, 24.

105. The last Angel, Karl Schrey of the church in Siegen, Westphalia, died in 1960 aged ninety. G. L. Standring, *op. cit.* (1985), p. 15. In Great Britain the last Priest was Dr D. L. Davson of Paddington Church who died in 1971. K. W. Stevenson, *op. cit.* (1979), p. 27.

106. Irving was discharged as a minister in the Church of Scotland by his presbytery in Annan for his unorthodox doctrine of the incarnation. Ironically, on returning from Annan to the movement he had helped to form in London he found himself sidelined and was not appointed as an Apostle. L. E. Elliot-Binns, *op. cit.* (1964), p. 57. H. Davies, *op. cit.* (1996), vol. iv, pp. 154, 156.

107. The book of regulations of 1878 set out the duties of ministers and members and church discipline. The highly regarded, liturgy was issued as a definitive eighth edition in 1880. G. L. Standring, *op. cit.* (1985), pp. 22, 57–8; K. W. Stevenson, 'The Catholic Apostolic Church – Its History and its Eucharist', *Studia Liturgica*, vol. 13, no. 1 (1979) offers a very good description of the development of the liturgy.

108. Personal correspondence P. C. Whitfield, secretary to the trustees, Catholic Apostolic Trust Property, 2 The Cloisters, Gordon Square, London WC1H 0AG, 5 July 1999; *Sutton's History of and Guide to Buxton* (1882); *Bulmer's Directory of Derbyshire, 1895* records that the chapel cost £100 in 1885. The chapel is not recorded on the 1878 OS map, nor on local plans of 1885 (C. F. Wardley) and 1887 (J. Buckley).

109. C. G. Flegg, *op. cit.* (1990), p. 1; The Macmillan sixteen volume *Encyclopedia of Religion* (1987 edn) does not

contain a reference, though the church is mentioned in an entry for Edward Irving; A brief description is, however, contained in F. L. Cross and E. A. Livingstone (eds), *The Oxford Dictionary of the Christian Church*, 3rd edn (Oxford, 1997), p. 306.

110. The Manchester Church was rebuilt, to seat 300, in 1867. A very good description of the liturgy and vestments worn by the clergy is given in: *The Free Lance*, vol. ii (7 September 1867), pp. 76–7.

111. *Buxton Advertiser*, 19 August 1896.

112. *Buxton Herald and Gazette of Fashion*, 17 November 1886, 5 January 1887 *et seq.*

113. There was argument over whether it constituted a public building, whether it would interfere with the property, Delrow Terrace, just below in Darwin Street, and problems over the building line. It was approved on the casting vote of the chairman. *Buxton Advertiser*, 9 May 1896; Buxton Local Board Streets Committee Minutes, D1323/2/3/113, May 1895 to April 1898, Derbyshire Record Office, Matlock.

114. Fourfold consisting of Apostle, Prophet, Evangelist and Pastor.

115. Verbatim report in *Buxton Advertiser*, 19 August 1896; G. L. Standring, *op. cit.* (1985), p. 87.

116. The *Buxton Advertiser* described the church as of 'Early English Gothic' design to accommodate 100 persons in the body of the building and made the point that the chancel would occupy a considerable portion of the building in order to suit the requirements of the services, '… which are very elaborate …', 6 June 1896; The stained-glass symbols included vines and leaves also a chalice and host; R. K. Jones offers a good description of the way in which the architecture of the movement was ordered and set out for liturgical worship in *op. cit.* (1972), p. 145.

117. Reflecting the practice of 'tithing' introduced in 1836 and the use of three bags for the different offerings. G. L. Standring, *op. cit.* (1985), p. 87; fieldwork 29.6.1999, I am obliged to Mr Phil Brennan, minister of the Church of God in Buxton, for allowing me access to the church and its remaining artifacts.

118. *Buxton Advertiser*, 18 March 1899. Noticeably after the service officials and ministers took lunch at the Peak Hydro but the choir and members of the congregation were entertained to tea in the evening at Fleetwood's restaurant in Spring gardens. At this time there were nine London churches and just over fifty in the rest of England. R. K. Jones *op. cit.*, pp. 154–7.

119. *Buxton Advertiser*, 7 January 1905. After the opening of the new church local guide books listed the church services, see *Guide to Buxton and the Peak District*, Ward Lock edn (Buxton 1896, 1902–3). It was felt that teaching and instruction should not be part of the framework of liturgical worship, hence the separate weekday services. G. L. Standring, *op. cit.* (1985), pp. 36, 78.

120. C. G. Flegg, *op. cit.* (1990), pp. 455–8; G. L. Standring describes this belief as 'other-worldliness'. Mrs Cecil F. Alexander who wrote 'All things Bright and Beautiful' was an active promoter of the Oxford Movement but her verse 'The rich man in his castle/the poor man at his gate/God made them, high or lowly/ and ordered their estate', exemplifies this belief. *Hymns Ancient and Modern*, 1st edn, no. 573; R. K. Jones *op. cit.*, p. 141.

121. The annual *Buxton Guide* included the church up to 1946. In 1947 it was let to the Plymouth Brethren. R. K. Jones, *op. cit.* (1972), p. 154.

122. H. Davies, *op. cit.* (1996), vol. iv, p. 162; Dr Elliot-Binns has suggested that the movement '… played very little part in the development of Victorian religion in England, being of too high-flown a nature to commend itself to English people and having to face the greater attractions on the one hand of the revived church life of the Oxford movement, and of Spiritualism on the other …' *op. cit.* (1936; 3rd imp. 1964), pp. 57–8. It, nevertheless, met the spiritual needs of some including those at the resort of Buxton.

123. For completeness it should be noted that at the end of the century there were meetings of Gospel movements and the Society of Friends in the Town Hall and a YMCA in Spring Gardens.

124. C. Binfield, *op. cit.* (1977), p. 28; The Catholic Apostolics were, of course, anxious to emphasise their non-sectarianism '… they were one indeed with their brethren in every division of Christendom …' Chief minister at the laying of the foundation stone, *Buxton Advertiser*, 19 August 1896; See also G. L. Standing, *op. cit* (1985), p. 72–3.

125. It may be observed that Freemasonry provided a source of ritual if not belief, through the four lodges active in the town during the period. These were Phoenix Lodge of St Anne 1235 (1868) and Chapter (1872); Buxton Lodge 1688 (1877); Duke of Connaught Lodge of Mark Master Masons 246 (1879).) This was by no means an alternative to church membership; many masons were active in the church and several Anglican incumbents were masons. Freemasonry was as much a part of the social fabric as religion and, indeed, provided a quasi-religious ritual as part of its ceremony. Activities, other than closed rituals, were reported in the press. A good, if later, example is given in the programme for the dedication of a new Masonic temple in the Old Court House in Buxton. A litany was incorporated in the proceedings which included: dedication, opening prayer, anthem, invocation prayers, gospel and psalm readings, hymns, the use of incense and a benediction. Freemasonry might rank alongside any of the denominations described in this chapter, no less than forty-two percent of the local authority members were freemasons. Of lesser importance were the Oddfellows and Foresters but a detailed examination of the influence of these organisations must await separate study. S. Taylor, *History of Freemasonry in Buxton and Longnor* (Buxton, 1906), *passim*; 'Dedication Programme' Ancient, Free and Accepted Masons of England, Provincial Grand Lodge of Derbyshire, 1957.

126. [Sir H. H. Bashford], *Augustus Carp by Himself – Being the Autobiography of a Really Good Man* (1924; Woodbridge edn, 1985), p. 129.

Notes to Chapter 8: Shape and Style: The Influence of Architects

1. N. Pevsner *et al.*, *The Buildings of England, passim.*
2. C. Stewart, *The Stones of Manchester* (London, 1956), p. 16.
3. Doreen Yarwood, *A Chronology of Western Architecture* (London, 1987); Helena Barrett and J. Phillips, *Suburban Style – The British Home 1840–1960* (London, 1987), pp. 54–5, 86–7, 90–9; R. Dixon and S. Muthesius, *Victorian Architecture* (London, 1985), pp. 17–28. The Royal Institute of British Architects (RIBA) received its Royal Charter in 1837, the Architectural Association was founded in 1847 and numerous provincial societies were set up. Also influential was the Society of Architects, a rival to the RIBA in the 1890s, Barry Parker was a member. CorrespondenceM. K. Miller to RIBA in G. F. Armitage biographical file, RIBA London; R. Dixon and S. Muthesius, *op. cit.*, 2nd edn (1985), pp. 11–12; W. L. Burn, *The Age of Equipoise* (London, 1964), p. 213; Jenkins suggests that Victoria's reign saw the rise of architecture from the category of trade to that of an academically disciplined profession. F. Jenkins, 'The Victorian Architectural Profession', in P. Ferriday (ed.), *Victorian Architecture* (London, 1963), p. 47.
4. Doreen Yarwood, *op. cit.* (1987); R. Dixon and S. Muthesius, *op. cit.* (1985), pp. 25–6.
5. J. Betjeman, in P. Ferriday, *op. cit.* (1963), p. 15.
6. Exemplified, perhaps, by the competition for the Houses of Parliament in 1835, producing ninety-six entries of which only six were not in the Gothic style. Charles Barry, who won with help from A. W. N. Pugin, produced a building with much Gothic detail but the building is not Gothic in the principles of its design. Barry was a Neo-Classicist and would have preferred to have built the Houses of Parliament in the Italianate style. R. Dixon and S. Muthesius, *op. cit.* (1985), pp. 155–8. N. Pevsner, *Some Architectural Writers of the Nineteenth Century* (Oxford, 1972), pp. 301–2.
7. J. Ruskin, 'Lectures on Architecture and Painting' in D. Rubinstein, *Victorian Homes* (Newton Abbot, 1974), pp. 56–8.
8. N. Pevsner, in P. Ferriday, *op. cit.*, p. 31.
9. W. H. Robertson in 'Robert R. Duke, Surveyor etc, Buxton, Testimonials' p. 16. Duke/Archt/55, The Duke papers, Buxton.
10. Henry Currey (1820–1900) was brother to William (1819–86) who took on the post of solicitor to the Duke of Devonshire at the death of their father, Benjamin, in 1846. Henry Currey was articled to Decimus Burton (1800–81) and in the office of William Cubitt (1791–1863). R. N. Crook, 'Henry Currey and the Seventh Duke of Devonshire' (RIBA: London, 1978), pp. 3–4; A. Felstead *et al.*, *Directory of British Architects 1834–1900* (RIBA: London, 1993).
11. R. N. Crook, *op. cit.* (1978), p. 13; For example: Nos 1–3 Cavendish Terrace (1861), built for local the wine and spirit merchant G. F. Barnard, Cavendish House (*c.* 1866), Derby House (*c.* 1866), Dalton House built for John Milligan, the draper, in 1868. Dept of Environment Report SK0573SE with correspondence by Mrs J. Whibberley, owner, 12.7.1997; Devonshire Buxton Accounts 1860, Devonshire Collections, Chatsworth.
12. Wye House Asylum built from the original designs for a new Charity hospital in Sylvan Park. (See chapter five).
13. They were later named 'Grosvenor Terrace', OS Map, 1878, and 'Villas', J. C. Bates, *Views in Buxton and Neighbourhood* (Buxton, *c.* 1866).
14. See M. Langham and C. Wells, *A History of the Baths at Buxton* (Leek, 1997), pp. 61–9.
15. 'Memorandum and Articles of Association, Buxton Palace Hotel Co.', 1868. Duke/Pal/07. The Duke of Devonshire was a major investor; others included Edward Tootal, James Bancroft, director of the LNW Railway and J. W. Lees, Cotton Spinner of Oldham; local investors included Robert Broome, quarry owner of Burbage, John Milligan the draper and J. C. Bates of the *Buxton Advertiser*; Appendix 8.1 lists Currey's known work in Buxton.
16. R. Crook, *op. cit.* (1978) offers a useful biography.
17. J. Gloag, *Victorian Taste* (Newton Abbot, 1979), ch. IV.
18. A position which has been fully described in chapter six.
19. His handwritten library catalogue runs to sixteen pages and includes: *Picturesque Designs in Architecture*, Rickman's *Gothic Architecture*, *Cottage Homes of England*, *Gothic Ornament* and *Principles of Christian Architecture* by Pugin. Duke/RRD/Fam/120, The Duke Papers, Buxton.
20. George Myers, known as Pugin's Builder, moved from Hull to set up business in London. Patricia Spencer-Silver, *Pugin's Builder – The Life and Work of George Myers* (Hull, 1993), *passim*; Argyle Villas probably built for E. C. Milligan, draper and local politician. *Buxton Guide and Directory* (1876); Plan 4.10.1871 Buxton Plans and Buxton Estate Accounts 1874–75, Devonshire Collections, Chatsworth.
21. He later designed a hydraulic passenger lift in the house which ran off the town mains water. His letter to the chairman of the Local Board in 1886 ran: '... I write to ask when I may have water to work my lift. It is very exasperating after so large an expenditure to wait so many months ... I assure you that last week I was put to serious inconvenience and this week have been put to even more Inconvenience ... I should not like to think that I am boycotted but it looks very much like it. It may be fun for the Board or officials but it is no trifling matter here ...' R. R. Duke to E. C. Milligan, 9 February, to J. Hague 15 and 26 January 1886, Letterbooks of R. R. Duke, Devonshire Collections, Chatsworth.
22. C. Stewart, *op. cit.* (1956), p. 37; R. Dixon and S. Muthesius, *op. cit.* (1985), pp. 127–8.
23. His fee for the two was £114 and for the Knoll £58, which represents about 4.5 per cent of the total cost. Devonshire Buxton Accounts 1873–74 and 1875. Devonshire Collections, Chatsworth.
24. All three had worked together in The Princes Park, Liverpool in 1843: see chapter two.
25. A detailed account of the building of the large octagonal concert hall is in M. Langham and C. Wells, *The Architect of Victorian Buxton* (Matlock, 1996), ch. 4.
26. *The Engineer*, 27 January 1882.
27. N. Pevsner, in P. Ferriday, *op. cit.* (1963), p. 28.
28. *The Art Journal* (1851), p. 126; Patricia Spencer-Silver, *op.*

cit. (1993), pp. 154–5.

29. R. Dixon and S. Muthesius, *op. cit.* (1985), pp. 107–8.

30. Correspondence (13.12.99) with Dr Peter Smith, formerly Planning Architect in charge of the Alexandra Palace Development team to whom I am grateful for copies of articles in: *Illustrated London News* (1850); 'Bibliography New Series' No. 60, Architectural Association Library; *Victoria and Albert Museum Catalogue* item 135 'Sydney Smirke and Alfred Stevens model of the Proposed Reading Room of the British Museum *c.* 1853'; P. Smith, 'The Roof of the Great Hall at Alexandra Palace 1863–1986'. Dr Smith suspects that there was an (undeclared) aim to exceed the diameter of the dome of St Peter's, Rome (138 ft) in a number of these projects. R. R. Duke had copies of the exhibition catalogue of 1862 in his library. Duke/RRD/Fam/120, The Duke Papers, Buxton.

31. R. R. Duke, 'Devonshire Hospital', privately printed pamphlet, 1 October 1902. Duke/DH/010, *ibid.*

32. Appendix 8.2 lists R. R. Duke's work in Buxton.

33. I. E. Burton, 'Education in Buxton Yesterday and Today' undated mss, Buxton Library, 373.4251; William Pollard (b. 1853) was articled to Robert Boyle of Manchester (1868–74) and set up a practice in King Street Manchester. He became LRIBA in 1911. RIBA Library record 13.1.00.

34. *Who's Who in Architecture* (London, 1914); A. Felstead *et. al.*, *op. cit.* (1993); C. Wells and M. Langham, 'William Radford Bryden FRIBA' Occasional Paper no. 28; BANHS Bulletin no. 28 (Autumn 1999). E. M. Barry was Professor of Architecture at King's College London, 1873–80.

35. See M. Langham and C. Wells, *op. cit.* (1996), pp. 192–4.

36. The Buxton Improvements Company was renamed 'The Buxton Gardens Company' in 1888.

37. The Misses Barker kept apartments at 11 St John's Road. Plan No. 49, 24 August 1898, 'Fairfield Plans of Chief Rents; Plan of Buxton Cricket Ground, 16 May 1927, Buxton Plans N–W Folder P, Devonshire Collections, Chatsworth.

38. The other, for local hotelier J. H. Lawson, was designed by G. E. Garlick (1891).

39. William Wood had stores on High Street and Spring Gardens; Appendix 8.3 lists Bryden's work in Buxton.

40. Letter R. R. Duke to W. R. Bryden, 18 January 1886, Letterbooks of R. R. Duke, Devonshire Collections, Chatsworth; Wm Holland to R. R. Duke, 17 March 1905 re. references. Duke/Archt/18, The Duke Papers, Buxton.

41. *Buxton Herald*, 4 June, 23 September 1896.

42. I am indebted to Mrs Mary Burton (née Garlick) of Bishops Lane, Burbage for information about her family 13.6.1997; Appendix 8.4 lists Garlick's work in Buxton.

43. Appendix 8.5 lists Holland's work in Buxton.

44. Plans 39 (December 1892) and 47 (28 July 1896), Plans of Fairfield Chief Rents; Building Plans BP/F/47, Devonshire Collections, Chatsworth; Frederick, William Booth was a Fairfield builder and this is an interesting example of private enterprise providing working-class housing. J. N. Tarn, *Five-percent Philanthropy – An Account of housing in Urban Areas between 1840 and 1914* (Cambridge, 1973).

45. Data gathered principally from: Buxton Building Plans, Boxes B, F and H, Devonshire Collection, Chatsworth and Minutes of the Buxton Local Board/UDC 'Streets' Committee, Derbyshire Record Office, Matlock.

46. *Building News*, 16 April 1897.

47. He won the RIBA Medal of Merit in 1867/68 and became ARIBA in 1871, FRIBA in 1884. *Manchester Guardian*, 29 January 1938; W. Burnett Tracey, *Manchester and Salford at the Close of the Nineteenth Century* (1899), Manchester Public Library; A. S. Gray, *Edwardian Architecture* (London, 1985), p. 208; A. Felstead *et al.*, *op. cit.* (1993), p. 429.

48. Interestingly he bought the land from Robert Parker, father of Barry Parker. 'Fairfield Plans of Chief Rents, Plan no. 36; Buxton Accounts half year to 31 December 1891. Devonshire Collections, Chatsworth.

49. Plan of Wychwood approved 14 May 1892. BP/F/36/3, Devonshire Collections, Chatsworth; Letter from Mary Heathcote at Wychwood to Sarah Smith dated 6 January 1894 referring to a children's party. Duke/SMS/Gen/351, The Duke Papers, Buxton .

50. The Peak Hydropathic had a very chequered history and most architects in town worked on its many extensions at some time or another.

51. F. Baden Benger was manager of F. B. Benger and Co. Ltd, Manufacturing Chemists of Mary Street, Strangeways, Manchester. *Kelly's Directory of Manchester* (1891). The firm later became well known as 'Benger's Foods' producing processed foods for infants and invalids. *Slater's Manchester Directories* (1905, 1911).

52. In 1891 Schill Modera and Co, Shippers, Herman Schill was a partner: *ibid.*

53. Appendix 8.6 lists his known work in Buxton.

54. Huon Matear (1856–1945) was articled to James Francis Doyle (1840/41–1913) and was in partnership with him from 1882 to 1887. He won the competition for the Courts of Justice and the Police and Fire Stations at York in 1889. His design (with F. W. Simon) for the Liverpool Cotton Exchange in Old Hall Street (1905–6) has been described as having few Edwardian parallels outside London. Only the cast-iron side elevation remains. Interestingly he designed a pavilion for the caterers Spiers and Pond at the Liverpool Exhibition (1886) and that of Paris (1888). Spiers and Pond were to open a luxurious hotel in Buxton by architect Thomas Garner in 1901. A. S. Gray, *op. cit.* (1985), p. 258; A Felstead *et al.*, *op. cit* (1993), p. 607; N. Pevsner, *op. cit.*, *South Lancashire* (1989), pp. 148, 162.

55. *The Builder*, 2 December 1899, p. 512; Plan BP122/N/1–2, BP/F/40/1, BP/122N/3–4, and Fairfield Plans of Chief Rents, no. 40, Devonshire Collections, Chatsworth.

56. Letters R. R. Duke to Mr [B.] Parker, 17 and 28 August 1896, Letterbooks of R. R. Duke; Plan dated 8 October 1896 gives Barry Parker's address as 'Moorlands' Buxton. BP/H27/15. Devonshire Collections, Chatsworth.

57. Letter Bennett Brooke-Taylor and Wright, Solicitors, Buxton to Mrs S. Cooper, Longford Lodge, 2 April 1996.

58. Mervyn Miller credits them to Barry Parker. M. K. Miller 'To Speak of Planning is to Speak of Unwin – The Contribution of Sir Raymond Unwin (1863–1940) to the Evolution of British Town Planning' PhD thesis, University of Birmingham (1981), pp. 75–6. Only Longford Lodge remains today and this closely matches a plan

drawn by G. E. Garlick. His plans for the other two were in a similar style, but none of these plans were approved by the Devonshire Estate. A plan by Parker and Unwin for additions to Longford Lodge dated 30 June 1909 does, however, match Garlick's earlier plan. Buxton Plans BP/F35–2, 4, 6, 8, 12, 13 dated 1892 and 16 dated 1909. Devonshire Collections, Chatsworth.

59. Bank Hall Lodge was designed by Eden Nesfield, 1873. N. Pevsner, *op. cit.*, *Derbyshire* (1986), p.125.

60. C. Binfield, *So Down To Prayers – Studies in English Nonconformity 1780–1920* (London, 1977), pp.174–85, offers a fluent description of Armitage's work and his contribution to *art nouveau* and the Domestic Revival; Head and Pike, *Cheshire at the Opening of the Twentieth Century* (1904), Manchester Public Library.

61. In 1891 Frederick Smallman had six vegetarian dining rooms in central Manchester including two on Piccadilly. In 1900 he had nine. He also owned several properties in Higher Buxton. *Kelly's Directory of Manchester* (1891); *Slater's Manchester and Salford 1900, 1905*; Register of Electors, High Peak, 1901. Derbyshire Record Office, Matlock.

62. 'William Larner Sugden' Obituary in the *Leek Times*, 22–29 June 1901. Larner Sugden and his father William (1820/21–1892) were prolific architects in Leek. A list of their works is in G. A. Lovenbury 'The House of Sugden' Mss 1975, copy by courtesy of Mr O. Gomersal, Buxton. Wm Sugden and Son came second in a competition for extensions to a Buxton Hydropathic in 1888. R. Harper, *Victorian Architectural Competitions* (London, 1983), p. 28. A usefully brief description of the early life of Barry Parker and Raymond Unwin is in M. Miller, *Letchworth – The First Garden City* (Chichester, 1989), pp. 43–5.

63. *The Builder*, 4 December 1897; *The Building News*, 27 July 1900.

64. Note on Plan no. 10 BP/64/N, Devonshire Collections, Chatsworth. Parker and Unwin suffered similar stringencies over the gates for Farringford and Somersby.

65. N. Pevsner, *op. cit.*, *Derbyshire* (1986), p.116; M. Miller, *op. cit.* (1989), p.45; Horace Townsend wrote '… the 'new architect' nowadays designs the interior furniture, hangings and so forth, unlike his predecessor …' Horace Townsend 'Notes on Country and Suburban House Design by C. F. Voysey' *The Studio* April 1899, quoted in D. Rubinstein, *op. cit.* (1974), pp. 62–4.

66. *Buxton Directory* (1906, 1908); M. Miller, *op. cit.* (1981), illustration L1 gives their address on the Letchworth plan of 1906 as Buxton and Baldock Herts.

67. *The Building News*, 23 June 1893, 19 July, 26 July 1895; *The Builder*, 14 December 1901; These were published in a private pamphlet at Buxton in 1895 and its reception provided the stimulus for a book of lectures and illustrations, B. Parker and R. Unwin *The Art of Building a Home* (London, 1901). The preface by Parker gave the address Quadrant, Buxton.

68. N. Pevsner, *op. cit.*, *Derbyshire* (1986), p.116n.

69. The 'Alison' was built for W. H. Bradburne, of Avenham, College Road, and designed as two houses one larger than the other, Bradburne's intention was to let the smaller of the two; Henry Lancashire of J. H. Lancashire and Co. Stockbrokers, 46 Pall Mall near King Street,

Manchester moved from 'One Ash' in Spencer Road to his newly built 'Heatherton'. *Slater's Manchester Directories*, 1911 and 1912. The house was later bought by Thomas Neilson Brown of the Manchester Departmental Store, Aflick and Brown. It was renamed Hartington House in 1953, becoming part of the Buxton College, and is now apartments known as Temple Court. Plans BP 47/1–4 R [Alison], BP 47/1–4 [Heatherton] Devonshire Collections, Chatsworth; Bolton King, *Buxton College 1675–1970* (Buxton, 1973), p. 71; Plans BP 32/1–4 and correspondence [Lerryn], Devonshire Collections, Chatsworth. Robert McDougal moved from 'Kingscroft', Green Lane to Temple Road. His father, Arthur McDougal lived at 'Lyndhurst' The Park, Buxton and was a founder of the City Flour Mills in Manchester named after him. Robert, his son, became head of the firm McDougal's Flour. He was a Radical Liberal who stood for parliament unsuccessfully three times in the High Peak Division. A noted philanthropist, he was knighted for his benevolent works which included the purchase, for the National Trust, of 100 acres in Dove Dale. *Transactions of the Manchester Literary and Philosophical Society*, vol. lvii (1912/13), pp. xxx, xxxi; vol. lxxxiii (1938/39), pp. v, vi.

70. R. H. Brooks had his business at 7 Dale street, Manchester. I am indebted to Mr Gerald Fitzgerald for information on Mr Brooks and the house deeds. (12.2.00); The practice of John Bowden was at 14 Ridgefield, Manchester and he was active between 1868 and 1899 as a surveyor and architect though his death in 1905 suggests that a (younger?) partner did the design; A. Felstead, *op. cit.* (1993); RIBA library correspondence 10.04.2000.

71. The choice of the house name 'Brantwood' is interesting, did the Misses Taylor have a particular interest in John Ruskin, or his house on Coniston Water perhaps?; Plans BP/22/1–4 [Filleigh], BP30/1–4 [Brantwood] Devonshire Collections, Chatsworth.

72. Charles Swain had an office at 12 Exchange Street Manchester, but he moved to Buxton in the early 1920s. The Misses Sarah and Mary Jane Taylor came from Sherwood Rise Nottingham to Buxton. James H Vickery, a Congregationalist, had his iron, tinplate, wire and metal merchants business at 21 Bradshaw street, Shudehill, Manchester.

73. John Henry Orme was a local solicitor.

74. Correspondence survives from at least twenty four different addresses. Duke/SMS/Gen/ 340–405, The Duke Papers, Buxton.

75. Could the house be named after the Charlotte Brontë novel *Villette* (published 1853), perhaps? The connection with Belgium is tenuous, but the novel may have been a favourite of Miss Gibbs.

76. Flockton and Gibbs, who were responsible for the Mappin Art Gallery (1886–88) became Flockton, Gibbs and Flockton in 1895 and in 1902 Edward Mitchell Gibbs became the senior partner. RIBA Biography File, C. B. Flockton (1867–1945).

77. W. Burnett Tracey, *Manchester and Salford at the Close of the Nineteenth Century* (Manchester, 1899); J. Potter Briscoe, *Contemporary Biographies – Derbyshire*, 1901.

78. W. Burnett Tracey, *op. cit.* (1899).

79. *Slater's Manchester and Salford*, 1905 and 1911.

80. Thomas Garner (1839–1906) was a pupil of the Gothic

Revivalist architect Sir George Gilbert Scott (1811–78) and in partnership with George Frederick Bodley (1827–1907) from 1869 to 1898. I. Wodehouse, *British Architects 1840–1976* (Detroit, 1978); J. M. Richards, *Who's Who in Architecture from 1400 to Present Day* (London, 1977).

81. R. Dixon and S. Muthesius, *op. cit.* (1985), pp. 51–2.

82. It had a short commercial life, after use as a discharge centre for Canadian troops in the First War it never re-opened as an hotel.

83. *Architectural Review*, October 1976, quoted in Ros McCoola, *Theatre in the Hills* (Chapel-en-le-Frith, 1984), p. 51n. Of the 400 or so theatres built between 1880 and 1912 Matcham was responsible for at least 150 of them, they included: Grand Theatre Blackpool (1894), Grand Opera House, Belfast (1895), Leeds Empire (1898), London Hippodrome (1899–1900) and Coliseum Theatre (1904). '… The choice of Matcham was an inspired one …' C. Wells, *The Buxton Stage* (Disley, 1998), pp. 33–5; R. Dixon and S. Muthesius, *op. cit.* (1985), p. 262.

84. *Buxton the Mountain Spa*, Official Handbook issued by the Bureau of Information, Buxton 1912.

85. A wide range of sources have been used to compile this record including Buxton Building Plans and Devonshire Buxton Accounts in the Devonshire Collection, Chatsworth and the minutes of the Buxton Local Board/UDC 'Streets' Committee in the Derbyshire Record Office, Matlock. The work is ongoing.

86. A wide range of sources have been used to compile this record including Buxton Building Plans in the Devonshire Collection, Chatsworth, the minutes of the Buxton

Local Board/UDC 'Streets' Committee in the Derbyshire Record Office, Matlock and the 'Duke Papers' at Buxton. The work is ongoing.

87. The chief sources for this compilation are the Buxton Building Plans in the Devonshire Collection, Chatsworth and the minutes of the Buxton Local Board/UDC 'Streets' Committee in the Derbyshire Record Office, Matlock. Where possible these have been verified by field-work. For the sake of completeness in architectural style, known commissions up to 1910 are included. Research is ongoing.

88. The chief sources for this compilation are the Buxton Building Plans in the Devonshire Collection, Chatsworth and the minutes of the Buxton Local Board/UDC 'Streets' Committee in the Derbyshire Record Office, Matlock. Where possible these have been verified by field-work. For the sake of completeness in architectural style, known commissions up to 1910 are included. Research is ongoing.

89. The chief sources for this compilation are the Buxton Building Plans in the Devonshire Collection, Chatsworth and the minutes of the Buxton Local Board/UDC 'Streets' Committee in the Derbyshire Record Office, Matlock. Where possible these have been verified by field-work. Work is ongoing.

90. A wide range of sources have been used to compile this record including Buxton Building Plans in the Devonshire Collection, Chatsworth, the minutes of the Buxton Local Board/UDC 'Streets' Committee in the Derbyshire Record Office, Matlock and architectural periodicals (see text). The work is ongoing.

Notes to Chapter 9: Buxton: an Estate-resort … Poised for Constant Re-invention …

1. Phyllis Hembry, *op. cit.* (1997), *passim*; J. Smedley, *Practical Hydropathy*, 8th edn (1866); Mrs Smedley, *Manual of Practical Hydropathy for Ladies and Children*, 4th edn (c. 1866).

2. Phyllis Hembry, *op. cit.* (1997), pp. 85–6.

3. Eastbourne: D. Cannadine *op. cit.* (1980), *passim*; Barrow: S. Pollard, *op. cit.* (1955). There were other estates developed by the Seventh Duke not so prominent as these three; at Chiswick see F. M. L. Thompson, *The Rise of Suburbia* (Leicester, 1982), p. 109; Keighley see M. Langham and C. Wells, *op. cit.* (1996), p. 104; Carlisle see D. Cannadine, *op. cit.* (1980), p. 382.

4. *Ibid.*, pp. 234–6.

5. R. Rodger, *Housing in Urban Britain 1780–1940* (Cambridge 1989), pp. 38–43.

6. R. Grundy Heape, *op. cit.* (1948), p. 56.

7. W. G. Baxter, *Scenes and Incidents in Buxton* (Manchester, c. 1885); Edward Bradbury, *Pilgrimages in the Peak* (1879); *In the Derbyshire Highlands 1881*; *All About Derbyshire* (Buxton and London, 1884).

8. J. A. Pearson, *op. cit.* (1861); Annual Report [Devonshire Hospital and] Buxton Bath Charity 1876–1886, D4508/10/2, Derbyshire Record Office, Matlock.

9. The use of the adjective 'exponential' is apposite. Local Board borrowing 1886 to 1893 was £46,916; from 1894 to 1901 it was £84,381 and from 1902 to 1904, £268,796. Borough of Buxton, *Abstract of Accounts year ending 31*

March 1935 and *1956 op. cit.*,

10. Percy H. Currey (b. 1864) should not be confused with Percivall Currey FRIBA son of Henry Currey. P. H. Currey was responsible for a number of interesting Derbyshire churches usually with his partner Charles Clayton Thompson FRIBA. They included: St John Evangelist Nottingham Road Ilkeston, 1894, St Bartholomew, Nightingale Road, Osmaston Derby, 1927, and St Stephen Sinfin Lane Mickleover, 1935 and the outstanding Kelham Hall New Chapel, near Newark. Also All Saints Totley, 1924, in the Diocese of Sheffield, formerly Derby. N. Pevsner, *Derbyshire* (1986), *Yorkshire: The West Riding* (1959); *Who's Who in Architecture* (1914); *The Architect's Journal*, 14 January 1931.

11. N. Pevsner, Derbyshire, *op. cit.* (1986), p. 117.

12. M. Langham, *Buxton Community School – Origins and Early History* (Buxton, 1997), pp. 25, 31.

13. M. Langham and C. Wells, *op. cit.* (1996), p. 263.

14. Buxton Plans, Boxes BP, *passim*, The Devonshire Collections, Chatsworth.

15. Buxton and Fairfield incorporation, scrapbook of contemporary notices and newspaper cuttings, ML120, The Langham Collection, Buxton.

16. Housing and Town Planning Committee 1918–1945, D1323/2/18/1. Derbyshire Record Office, Matlock .

17. Raymond Unwin, for twelve years in architectural practice in Buxton, was a major contributor to the Town

and Country Planning Act of 1919.

18. Housing and Town Planning Committee 1918–1945, D1323/2/18/1. Derbyshire Record Office, Matlock.

19. Vera Brittain, *op. cit.* (1978 edn), pp. 164–204.

20. Sale catalogues, Brown and Nesbitt Papers, D247. Derbyshire Record Office, Matlock.

21. Buxton – Official Handbook, Bureau of Information, 1914 and 1921.

22. T. D. Luke, *op. cit.* (1919), pp. 8–12.

23. See M. Langham and C. Wells, *op. cit.* (1997), pp. 95–9 for definitions of treatments.

24. British Spas Federation Official Handbook, *The Spas of Great Britain* (1930) is an example.

25. Corbar Hall, designed as Corbar Villa by Henry Currey 1853 for the Congregationalist Henry Shaw.

26. Devonshire Royal Hospital Appeal for Funds Booklet, 1937. ML 140 The Langham Collection, Buxton.

27. Ros McCoola, *op. cit.* (1984), pp. 73–85; Buxton Borough Official Guide, 1937.

28. C. Wells, *op. cit.* (1998), pp. 94–5.

29. S. Hyde, *op. cit.* (1898), p. 6.

Bibliography

Primary Sources

Devonshire Collections, Chatsworth

Accounts, Buxton Collections, 'T' Series
Joseph Gould 1798–1804
Phillip Heacock 1805–42
Several Particulars relating to the estates 1824
Accounts, Bound volumes (Buxton cupboard)
Sydney Smithers 1851–56
Cashbook 1852 (labelled 1844)
Edward Woollett Wilmot 1856–64
George Drewry 1865–95
Francis Drewry 1896–1908
Buxton Estate Rentals 1905–6
Estate Books and Registers
'The Buxton Office 1856' Large Folio (Buxton Cupboard)
'Estate Register Buxton Office 1857', Folio. (Buxton Cupboard)
Clerk of Works Notebook (Samuel Turner) 1866. L/113/6.
Letterbooks and Correspondence
P. Heacock letterbooks, A5/1510–A5/1514.
Correspondence and Papers of Sir Joseph Paxton, P24–P1604
Letterbooks of R. R. Duke a series of seven: 1864–99 (Buxton Cupboard)

Diaries of 7th Duke of Devonshire, vols 14; 16; 20; 21
Letterbook F. Drewry, July 1878–January 1886
Maps and Plans
'Buxton Estate in 1922' Map 4034 with Terrier and accompanying conveyancing papers. Based on OS 1:2500 1878 survey, revised 1897, reprinted 1902–3
OS 1878 survey of Buxton 10.56 ft to one statute mile (41.66 ft.:1 inch)
OS 1898 Buxton 1:2500
Buxton Plans, Boxes 'B', 'F', 'H' and seven boxes containing nos 1–303
Buxton Land sales Book, no. 1. Plan nos 1–104 (1864–67) (shelved with Buxton Plans)
Buxton Land sales Book, no. 2. Plan nos 1–64 (1868–71) and tracings nos. 66–139 (1872–87) (shelved with Buxton Plans)
Plan of Buxton Park Building Land 1877 in 'Fairfield Plans of Chief Rents' Bound volume (shelved with Buxton Plans)
Folder dated 3.12.1872 a series of 11 drawings. An inner folder dated 8.4.1874, no. 1A. A series of 6 drawings (shelved with Buxton Plans)

Derbyshire Record Office, Matlock

Buxton Tithe Award 1847: Map D2360/3/56a (P295), Award D2360/DL56b (P316)
Fairfield Tithe award Map D 2360/3/103a (P296) 1842. Schedule D2360 DL 1036 (P317) 24th August 1841.
Buxton Vestry Book 1818, D4641/1/1
Buxton Local Board main and Streets Committee Minutes 1859–94; Regsters of Mortgages 1862–95; Registers of Title Deeds 1859–95 (D1323)
Buxton UDC main and Streets Committee Minutes 1895–1908; Regsters of Mortgages 1895–1908; Registers of Title Deeds 1895–1908 (D1323)
Buxton UDC, Housing and Town Planning Committee Minutes 1918–45, D1323/2/18/1
Devonshire Hospital & Buxton Bath Charity Reports 1831, 1836, 1840, 1850, 1854, 1859–75, 1876–86, 1887–93, 1894–1900, 1901–1904 (D4508)
Devonshire Hospital Minute Book, 1877. Unlisted Devonshire Royal Hospital archive. (Now at the County Records Office, Matlock)
St Mary's Church Buxton, Register of Services (D1754)
St John the Baptist Church, Buxton, correspondence, papers, estimates, reports (D1751)
St Anne's Church, Buxton, records (D1753)
St James Church, Buxton, correspondence, papers, estimates, reports (D1752)

Wesleyan Methodist Circuit Buxton, Minute Book, accounts, Sunday School (D3568)
Primitive Methodist Circuit, Buxton, minutes (D3568)
Wesleyan Methodist, Devonshire Park, Buxton, minutes, accounts, other papers (D3568)
Unitarian Chapel (Hartington Road) Buxton, minutes and other papers (D1332)
Congregational Church, Buxton, records, building fund, accounts, trust deed (D3657)
Buxton Protestant Electoral Federation, minutes and various records (D247)
Register of Electors, High Peak, 1895, 1899, 1901, 1903, 1905
Brown & Nesbitt Papers, Sales Catalogues, D247
Buxton Museum & Art Gallery
'Buxton Ballroom G. Bluett, Master, 1788', Buxton Museum; EY2000. Buxton Archaeological & Natural History Society (BANHS)
Buxton Vestry Book 1742–1818
'Plan of Buxton Park – as laid out in building plots by Sir Joseph Paxton 1852'; Unlisted.
Bye-Laws made by the Local Board of Buxton District, Buxton 1860, LG2/51906.
Josiah Taylor, Buxton UDC, 'Statement of Evidence for Incorporation 1912' LG6/51230
Letters: Dr Thomas Carstairs, Revd Hull Brown, Thos Warren,

Simon F. Ivery all to the Duke of Devonshire; 66.1, 66.3, 66.4, 66.5, 66.6.

Order regarding chimney firing;LG4/51262

Buxton Local Studies Library

'Buxton Local Board Roll of Members from 1859', 1902–3, 1906–7, 352–365.9; 1890–91, 1899–1900, 1901–2, 1903–4, 1905–96, 352.042

Buxton UDC, *Bye Laws made by the Local Board for the District of Buxton acting as the Urban Sanitary Authority with respect to new streets and buildings in the Urban Sanitary District of Buxton 1886*; 352.365.9.

'J. E. Todmorden', 'On my first visit to Devonshire Hospital, Buxton'; Devonshire Hospital box, unlisted.

'Dedication Programme' Ancient, Free and Accepted Masons of England, Provincial Grand Lodge of Derbyshire, 1957

The Langham Collection, a series of historical papers relating to Buxton, 14 St James Terrace, Buxton

'Conditions of Sale by Auction of Freehold Property belonging to the township of Buxton' Mss. ML116

Documents relating to 'Lawson's Corner' Buxton 1871–76. ML 64–107A

Buxton and Fairfield Incorporation, scrapbook of contemporary notices and newspaper cuttings, ML120

Devonshire Royal Hospital Appeal for Funds Booklet, 1937, ML140

The Duke Papers, An archive of papers relating to the R. R. Duke and A. W. Smith families, 14 St James Terrace, Buxton

Buxton Mechanics Institute papers Duke/MI/01–06

R. R. Duke, Architectural Business Duke/Archt/01–56

Devonshire Hospital Papers Duke/DH/01–38

Devonshire Buxton Estate Business Duke/Dev/01–05

Family Correspondence of R. R. Duke, Duke/RRD/Fam/01–160

Family Correspondence of S. M. Smith, Duke/SMS/Fam/01–385

General correspondence of S. M. Smith, Duke/SMS/Gen/01–485

Buxton Improvements/Gardens Company, Duke/Impco/01–11

Palace Hotel, Duke/Pal/01–20

Buxton Local Board, Duke/Locbd/01–04

Documents in private hands

'Mortgage of freehold at Buxton and leaseholds at Holborn', Indenture dated 5.2.1853; Letter Henry Currey to Messrs Warry, Robins & Burges, Solicitors 9.10.1854. Mrs Louise Potter, Buxton.

'Declaration of Trust 9 February 1876' Buxton Unitarian Church Bennett Brooke-Taylor & Wright, Solicitors, 4 The Quadrant Buxton

Parliamentary Acts and Orders

Census 1841, 1851, 1861, 1871, 1881, 1891

The Buxton Gas Act, 33 & 34 Vict. Session1870

Buxton Local Board Act, 36 & 37 Vict. 1873

Local Government Boards Provisional Orders Confirmation Act (no. 4) 1873, 36 & 37 Vict.

Local Government Board's Provisional Orders Confirmation Act (no. 5) 36 & 37 Vict. 1873

Local Government Boards Provisional Orders 1878 (Abingdon) 41 Vict.

Local Government Boards Provisional Orders1880 (Abingdon)

43 & 44Vict.

Local Government Boards Provisional Orders1881 (Acton) 44 & 45 Vict.

Local Government Board's Provisional Orders Confirmation (no. 4) Act 1886

Buxton Local Board Act, 55&56 Vict. 1892.

Local Government Board's Provisional Orders Confirmation Acts (no 2) 1897 and (no. 2.) 1901.

Buxton UDC Water Act, 1902 2 Edw 7.

Buxton UDC Act 1904, 4 Edw. 7.

Newspapers and Periodicals

The Architect's Journal

The Art Journal

Journal of Balneology and Climatology

The British Architect

British Medical Journal

British and Foreign Medico-Chirurgical Review

The Builder

Building News

Buxton Advertiser and List of Visitors

Buxton Herald & Gazette of Fashion

The Engineer

Estates Gazette

The Free Lance (published by John Heywood, Manchester)

The Graphic

High Peak News

Illustrated London News

The Lancet

Leek Times

Manchester Guardian

Manchester – Transactions of the Literary & Philospohical Society

Notes & Queries

The Sanitary Record and Journal of Sanitary and Municipal Engineering

Transactions of the Surveyor's Institute

The Times

Directories and Registers

S. Bagshaw, *History, Gazetteer & Directory of Derbyshire*, 1846

Bulmer's Directory of Derbyshire, 1895

Burke's History of the Commoners in Great Britain & Ireland, 1833–38

Burke's Landed Gentry 1846

Buxton Guide & Directory, 1876

The Buxton Directory, 1906, 1908, 1912

The Derbyshire Red Book, Bemrose, Derby, 1890, 1893, 1896, 1899, 1902, 1907, 1919, 1911, 1915.

Freebody's Directory of the Towns of Derbyshire, 1852

V. Gibbs, *The Complete Peerage* (London, 1913)

Harrison & Harrod & Co., *Directory of Derbyshire* 1860

J. G. Harrod & Co., *Postal & Commercial Directory of Derby-shire*, 1870

Kelly's Directory of Derbyshire, 1881, 1891 and 1904, 1916

Kelly's Handbook to the Titled, Landed and Official Classes, 1924 & 1948

Kelly's Directory of Manchester, 1891

McCalmont's Parliamentary Poll Book, Parts I and II

The Medical Directory, 1845–1905, London

The Medical Regster for the Year 1779, London

Pigot & Co's Commercial Directory for Derbyshire, 1835

Poll Book for the Northern Division of Derbyshire, 1837

Slater's Directory of Manchester/Salford 1881, 1891, 1900, 1905, 1911, 1912

White's *Directory of Derbyshire*, 1857

Who's Who in Architecture, London,1914

Who Was Who 1897–1916

Maps and Surveys

1876 Buxton, High Peak News Office n.t.s.

Buxton 1887, n.t.s. J. Buckley (original by R. R. Duke) Buxton.

Street Map of Buxton, 1882, The Herald Office, Buxton

Buxton *c.* 1904, 11/2 inch–1/4 mile A. C. Black London

OS Buxton 1898 1:2500 (1897 revision)

OS Buxton 1922 1:2500

Buxton 1923, 11/2 inch–1/4 mile, Ward Lock & Co. Ltd, London

Buxton, 1923. 6 miles to 1 inch, John Bartholomew

Contemporary Printed Material

W. Adam, *Gem of the Peak* (London and Derby editions of 1845 and 1848)

W. Adam, *Buxton, Chatsworth, Bakewell, Haddon Hall & Castleton* (Derby, *c.* 1858)

The Anti-Monopoly Society, *An Appeal to the Ratepayers of Buxton* (Buxton, April 1851)

W. Armstrong and J. E Harburn, *Buxton, Its Waters, Baths and Accessory Methods of Treatment* (Bristol, 1903)

J. Bateman, *The Great Landowners of Great Britain and Ireland* (1876; repr. Leicester, 1971); also 4th edn (London, 1883)

J. C. and H. B. Bates, *The Buxton Diamond* (Buxton, 1858)

J. C. Bates, *Views in Buxton and Neighbourhood* (Buxton *c.* 1866)

W. G. Baxter *Scenes and Incidences in Buxton*, 2nd edn (Manchester, *c.* 1886)

Borough of Buxton, *Abstract of Accounts for the year ended 31 March 1935*; and edn of 1956

R. O. G. Bennet, *Buxton and Its Medicinal Waters* (Manchester, 1892)

E. Bradbury (Strephon), *Pilgrimages in the Peak: Derbyshire Essays* (Buxton, 1879)

E. Bradbury, *In the Derbyshire Highlands* (Buxton, 1881

E. Bradbury, *All About Derbyshire* (Buxton and London, 1884)

J. Buckley, *Modern Buxton* (Buxton, 1886)

Sir E. Bulwer-Lytton Bart, *Confessions of a Water Cure Patient*, 3rd edn (London, 1847)

W. Burnett Tracey, *Manchester and Salford at the Close of the Nineteenth Century* (Manchester, 1899)

Buxton and Derbyshire and *Views of Buxton*, published by F. Wright, Spring Gardens (Buxton, *c.* 1900)

Buxton Bureau of Information, Official Handbooks for 1912; 1914; 1921; 1925; 1927; 1928; 1935; 1937; 1938; 1939; 1940; 1946 1948;

J Caird, *English Agriculture in 1850–51* (London, 1852)

T. Carstairs, *Bathing and the Buxton Waters* (London, 1847, 1853)

Charles Cotton *The Wonders of the Peake* (1681; 4th edn London, 1699)

R. T. Claridge, *Hydropathy or the Cold Water Cure*, 3rd edn (London, 1842)

A Clergyman, *A Few Pages on Hydropathy, or the Water Cure* (London, 1843)

Congregational Church, Hardwick Mount, Buxton, *Manual 1911*

J. Culverwell, *Hydropathy or the Cold Water Cure* (London, 1842)

J. Denman (MD) *Observations on Buxton Water* (London, 1793, 1801)

R. R. Duke, *An Autobiography 1817–1902* (Buxton, 1902)

R. W. Falconer MD., *The Baths and Mineral Waters of Bath* (London, 1857)

J. Farey, *General View of the Agriculture and Minerals of Derbyshire* (1811; repr. Peak District Historical Mines Society, 1989)

Sir J. Floyer, *An Enquiry into the Right Uses and Abuses of the Hot and Cold Temperate Baths in England* (London, 1697)

Graduate of the University of Edinburgh, *Ben Rydding: The Principles of Hydropathy and the Compressed air bath, together with a chapter on the improved Roman or Turkish bath. With illustrations by Theta*, by a graduate of the University of Edinburgh (London, 1859)

A. B. Granville, *Spas of England and Principal Sea Bathing Places* (1841; repr. Bath, 1971), vols 1 and 2

Great Exhibition 1851 – Official Descriptive, Illustrated Catalogue

W. H. Grieves, 'Buxton Souvenir of the New Filter Beds' (Buxton, 1904)

J. M. Gully, *The water Cure in Chronic Disease*, 2nd edn (London and Malvern, 1847).

Head and Pike, *Cheshire at the Opening of the Twentieth Century* (1904)

S. Hyde MD, 'The Natural Mineral Waters of Buxton: their indications and modes of application' *British Medical Journal*, vol. II (December 1894)

S. Hyde MD, 'Analysis of two hundred cases of Sciatica' *The Lancet*, vol. 1 (May 1896)

S. Hyde MD, *Buxton: Its Baths and Climate* (London, 1898)

A. Jewitt, *The History of Buxton and Visitors Guide* (London and Buxton, 1811)

A. Hacker, *Buxton Thro' Other Glasses* (Derby, 1905)

T. Hearne, *The Itinerary of John Leland the Antiquary* Oxford 1769

T. Hobbes, *De Mirabilibus Pecci__* (London, *c.* 1636)

J. Jones, *The Benefit of the auncient Bathes of Buckstones, which cureth most greevous sicknesses, never before published* (London, 1572)

G. Lorimer, *Health Resorts, Buxton* (London, 1896)

D. G. F. MacDonald, *Hints on Farming and Estate Management* (London, 1865)

E. M. Magill, *Notes on Galvanism and Faradism*, 2nd edn (London, 1919)

A Medical Practitioner, *Quacks and Quackery* (London, 1844)

H. E. Milner, *The Art and Practice of Landscape Gardening* (London, 1890)

A. S. Myrtle MD, 'Hydrotherapeutics: The Resources of Harrogate Specially Considered', *The British Medical Journal*, vol. 1 (1870)

D. Orme, *The New Buxton Guide* (Macclesfield, 1823)

D. Orme, *The Buxton Guide and Excursive Companion* (Buxton, 1842)

J. A. Pearson, *Reports of Cases Treated at the Buxton Bath Charity and Devonshire Hospital* (Liverpool, 1861)

T. J. Page, *Brief Observations on the Buxton Waters*, 7th edn (Buxton, 1843)

B. Parker and R. Unwin, *The Art of Building a Home* (London, 1901)

J. Potter Briscoe, *Contemporary Biographies Derbyshire* (1901)

E. Rhodes, *Peak Scenery or the Derbyshire Tourist* (London, 1824)

W. H. Robertson, *Buxton Waters* (London, 1838)

W. H. Robertson, *A Handbook to the Peak of Derbyshire or Buxton in 1854* (London, 1854; and editions of 1861, 1862, 1866, 1868, 1872, 1875, 1880, 1886)

W. H. Robertson, *A Guide to the use of the Buxton Mineral Waters* (Buxton, 1867, 1869 and c. 1898)

W. H. Robertson, 'The medical value of the nitrogenous tepid waters of Buxton', *The Lancet*, 27 July 1872

T. Rose, *The Counties of Chester, Derby and Nottingham*, with drawings by T. Allom (London, 1836)

J. Ruskin, 'Lectures on Architecture and Painting' in D. Rubinstein, *Victorian Homes* (Newton Abbot, 1974), pp. 56–8.

Sir C. Scudamore, MD, *A Chemical and Medical Report of the Properties of the Mineral Waters of Buxton, Matlock, Cheltenham [et al.]* (London, 1820)

Sir C. Scudamore, MD, *The Analysis and Medical Account of the Tepid Springs of Buxton* (London, 1833, 1839)

T. Short, MD, *The Natural, Experimental and Medical History of the Mineral Waters of Derbyshire, Lincolnshire and Yorkshire* (London, 1734)

J. Smedley, *Practical Hydropathy*, 8th edn (1866)

Caroline Anne Smedley, *Manual of Practical Hydropathy for Ladies and Children*, 4th edn (c. 1866)

T. Smethurst, *Hydrotherapia* (London, 1843)

[C. J. Smilter], *Buxton: Its History, Waters, Climate, Scenery etc.* (Buxton, 1899, 1905)

Sutton's History of and Guide to Buxton (1882)

J. W. Taylor, *Trinity Episcopal Chapel* (Buxton, 1888)

J. W. Taylor *These Fifty Years 1873–1923* (Buxton, 1923)

H. Townsend, 'Notes on Country and Suburban House Design by C. F. Voysey', *The Studio* (April 1899), quoted in D. Rubinstein, *Victorian Homes* (Newton Abbot, 1974)

J. C. Thresh, *Buxton as a Health Resort* (Buxton 1883)

W. Turner *Ancient Remains near Buxton – The Archæological Explorations of Micah Salt* (Buxton, 1899)

Ward Lock, *Guide to Buxton and the Peak District* (Buxton, 1884, 1896, 1902–3).

Beatrice Webb, 'My Apprenticeship', 1884, in C. Harvie *et al.*, *Industrialisation and Culture 1830–1914* (London, 1970)

C. J. Whitby, 'Notes on the Sanatorium Treatment of Pthisis and its Present Limitations', *Journal of Balneology and Climatology*, vol. 9, pt 1 (1905)

E. W. Wilmot Esq., 'Town Improvements', a lecture given 2 December 1859 (Buxton, 1859)

J. Wilson, *The Water Cure* (London, 1843)

Unpublished Manuscripts and Papers

D. A. Barton, 'The hydros of Matlock' 6 May 1980. Matlock Local Studies Library, 942.51M

I. E. Burton, 'Education in Buxton Yesterday and Today' n.d., Buxton Library, 373.4251

R. N. Crook, 'Henry Currey and the Seventh Duke of Devonshire'. RIBA 1978

G P Davis, 'Image and reality in a Victorian provincial city. a working-class area of Bath 1830–1900', PhD thesis Bath, 1981

C. G. Flegg, 'The Catholic Apostolic Church: its history, ecclesiology, liturgy and eschatology', PhD thesis, Oxford University, 1990

Dr Shirley Foster, 'Travel writing in the 19th century – the art of seeing', paper given at University of Sheffield, 8 October 1997

Heather A. Fuller, 'Land ownership in Lindsey c. 1800–66, with particular reference to the role of the large landowner as an agent of agricultural improvement and landscape change', MA thesis, University of Hull, 1974

E. B. Klopfer, 'The disease of indifference – a local democratic approach to local government reform 1830–90', Oxford University DPhil, 1992

M. Langham and C. Wells, *Six Buxton Gentlemen*, privately printed and distributed (Buxton, 1995)

A. J. Ley, 'Building control: its development and application 1840–1936', Oxford University MPhil, 1992

T. Marchington, 'The development of Buxton and Matlock since 1800', MA thesis, Cambridge University, 1961

Joyce C. Miles, 'The rise of suburban Exeter and the naming of its streets and houses, c. 1801–1907', PhD thesis, University of Leicester, 1990

M. K. Miller, 'To speak of planning is to speak of Unwin – the contribution of Sir Raymond Unwin (1863–1940) to the evolution of British town planning', PhD thesis, University of Birmingham, 1981

A. R. Neeves, 'A pattern of local government growth: Sheffield and its building regulations 1840–1914', PhD thesis, University of Leicester, 1991

Hilary A. Taylor *et al.*, 'Pavilion Gardens Buxton – Survey Grounds Development Plan', vol. 1, Parklands Consortium for High Peak Borough Council, 1996

Thoroton Society of Nottinghamshire, 'In Emma's footsteps', paper to accompany an excursion Saturday, 23 September, 1995. Nottingham

M. Worboys, 'Urban advantage – tuberculosis 1885–1925', paper given at University of Sheffield, 6 October 1997

Correspondence and interviews

P. C. Whitfield, secretary to the trustees, Catholic Apostolic Trust Property, 2 The Cloisters, Gordon Square, London WC1H 0AG, 5 July 1999

Department for Culture, Media and Sport, 9 September 1999, listing and description of Hartington Road Chapel

Dr Peter Smith, formerly Planning Architect in charge of the Alexandra Palace Development team, 13 December 1999, information on dome constructions

Mrs Mary Barton (née Garlick) of Burbage, Buxton for information about her family 13 June 1997

RIBA Library, Portland Place London, Biography files and correspondence 13 January and 10 April 2000

R. Price, The Wellcome Institute for the History of Medicine, sources on hydropathy, 11 November 1997.

Mrs J. Whibberley, of Dalton House, Broad Walk, correspondence July 1997 and Department of Environment Report SK0573SE

Published books

B. Abel-Smith, *The Hospitals 1800–1948* (London, 1964)

W Addison, *English Spas* (London, 1951)

F. Alderson, *The Inland Resorts and Spas of Britain* (Newton Abbott 1973)

W. Ashworth, *The Genesis of Modern British Town Planning* (London, 1965)

A. Aspinall and E. A. Smith, *English Historical Documents 1783–1832* (London, 1959)

P. J. Aspinall, 'The Internal Structure of the House building Industry in Nineteenth-Century Cities' in J. H. Johnson and C. G. Pooley (eds), *The Structure of Nineteenth-Century Cities* (Beckenham, 1983)

P. Bailey, *Leisure and Class in Victorian England* (London, 1978)

J. A. Banks, 'The Social Structure of Nineteenth-Century England as seen through the Census', in R. Lawton (ed.), *The Census and Social Structure* (London, 1978)

Helena Barrett and J. Phillips, *Suburban Style – The British Home 1840–1960* (London, 1987)

[Sir H. H. Bashford], *Augustus Carp by Himself – Being the Autobiography of a Really Good Man* (1924; Woodbridge, 1985)

D. Bebbington, *Victorian Nonconformity* (Bangor, 1992)

J. V. Beckett, *The Aristocracy in England 1660–1914* (Oxford, 1986)

J. M. Bentley and G. K. Fox, *Railways of the High Peak – Buxton to Ashbourne* (Stockport, 1997)

Bessborough, The Earl of, *Georgiana, Extracts from the Correspondence ...* (London, 1955)

C. Binfield, *So Down to Prayers – Studies in English Nonconformity 1780–1820* (London, 1977)

H. Blackburn, *Randolph Caldecott: A personal memoire of his early art career* (London, 1886)

R. Bolton King, *Buxton College 1675–1970* (Buxton 1973)

A. Bower, *The Water Cure* (Derby, 1985)

A. Briggs, *Victorian Cities* (Harmondsworth, 1968).

A. Briggs, *Victorian People* (London, 1990)

J. Briggs and I. Sellers (eds), *Victorian Nonconformity* (London, 1971)

Vera Brittain, *Testament of Youth* (London, 1978)

British Spas Federation, *The Spas of Great Britain*, Official Handbook, editions of 1923 and 1930

H. C. Burdett, 'The Dwellings of the Middle Classes', *Transactions of the Sanitary Institute of GB 1883–84*, in D. Rubinstein *Victorian Homes* (Newton Abbot, 1974)

W. L. Burn, *The Age of Equipoise* (London, 1964)

J. Burnett, *A Social History of Housing 1815–1985* 2nd edn (London, 1978)

D. Cannadine, *Lords and Landlords – The Aristocracy and the Towns 1774–1967* (Leicester, 1980)

D. Cannadine (ed.), *Patricians, power and politics in nineteenth-century towns* (Leicester, 1982)

D. Cannadine, 'Residential Differentiation in Nineteenth-Century Towns: From Shapes on the Ground to Shapes in Society', in J. H. Johnson and C. G. Pooley (eds), *The Structure of Nineteenth Century Cities* (Beckenham, 1983)

D. Cannadine, 'Victorian Cities – How Different' in R. J. Morris and R. Rodger, *The Victorian City* (Harlow, 1993)

D. Cannadine, *Aspects of Aristocracy* (London, 1995)

D. Cannadine, *The Decline and Fall of the British Aristocracy* (London, 1996)

D. Cannadine, *Class in Britain* (New Haven and London, 1998)

Cassell's History of England vol. viii (London, 1897)

G. F. Chadwick, *The Works of Sir Joseph Paxton 1803–1865* (London, 1961)

O Chadwick, *The Victorian Church*, pt II (London, 1970)

W. D. Christie (ed.), *The Poetical Works of John Dryden* (London, 1881)

J. C. Cox, *Derbyshire*, 2nd edn (London, 1915)

Congregational Church Buxton, *The Church's Story – Triple Jubilee 1810–1960*.

M. Craven, *Bygone Derby* (Chichester, 1989)

F. L. Cross and E. A. Livingstone (eds), *The Oxford Dictionary of the Christian Church*, 3rd edn (Oxford, 1997)

M. J. Daunton, 'Public Place and Private Space' in D. Fraser and A. Sutcliffe, *The Pursuit of Urban History* (London, 1983)

H. Davies, *Worship and Theology in England*, vols III and IV (Cambridge 1996)

Kathleen Denbigh, *A Hundred British Spas* (London, 1981)

R. Dixon and S. Muthesius, *Victorian Architecture* (London, 1978)

The Duchess of Devonshire, *The House* (London, 1982)

Dictionary of National Biography, 1908/9 and second supplement 1912; Concise Version to 1930 (Oxford 1948 edn); 1901–1970 (Oxford, 1982)

A. Dodd and E. M. Dodd, *Peak land Roads and Trackways* (Ashbourne, 1980)

K. C. Edwards, 'The Park Estate, Nottingham', in M. A. Simpson and T. H. Lloyd, *Middle-Class Housing in Britain*

(Newton Abbot, 1977)

George Eliot, *Middlemarch* (1872; Penguin edn, 1994)

L. E. Elliot-Binns, *Religion in the Victorian Era* (London, 1936; 3rd imp. 1964)

A. Felstead *et al.*, *Directory of British Architects 1834–1900* (RIBA, London, 1993)

Amanda Foreman, *Georgiana Duchess of Devonshire* (London, 1998)

D. Fraser, *Urban Politics in Victorian England* (London, 1976)

D. Fraser, 'Politics and the Victorian City' in *Urban History Yearbook* (1979)

H. Fraser, 'Municipal Socialism and Social Policy' in R. J. Morris and R. Rodger, *The Victorian City, 1820–1914* (Harlow, 1993)

J. Gloag, *Victorian Taste* (Newton Abbot, 1979)

A. S. Gray, *Edwardian Architecture* (London, 1985)

R Grundy Heape, *Buxton under the Dukes of Devonshire* (London, 1948)

G. Hancock, *Goyt Valley and its People* (Chesterfield, 1996)

I. Hall, *Georgian Buxton* (Matlock, 1984)

R. Harper, *Victorian Architectural Competitions* (London, 1983)

C. R. Hart, *The North Derbyshire Archæological Survey* (Sheffield, 1984)

C. Harvie, G. Martin and A. Scharf, *Industrialisation and Culture 1830–1914* (London, 1970)

Phyllis Hembry, *The English Spa 1560–1815: A Social History* (London, 1990)

Phyllis Hembry, edited and compiled by L. W. Cowie and Evelyn E. Cowie, *British Spas from 1815 to the Present – A Social History* (London, 1997)

M. Hennell, *Sons of the Prophets – Evangelical Leaders of the Victorian Church* (London, 1979)

E. J. Hobsbawm, *Industry and Empire an Economic History of Britain since 1750* (London, 1989)

B. Holland, *The Life of Spencer Compton, Eighth Duke of Devonshire*, 2 vols (London, 1911)

G. K. Horridge, *The Salvation Army Origins and Early Days: 1865–1900* (Godalming, 1993)

Hymns Ancient and Modern (London, *c.* 1900)

F. Jenkins, 'The Victorian Architectural Profession', in P. Ferriday (ed.), *Victorian Architecture* (London, 1963), p. 47

R. K. Jones, 'The Catholic Apostolic Church: A Study in Diffused Commitment' in M. Hlill (ed.), *A Sociological Yearbook of Religion in Britain*, 5 (London, 1972)

B. Keith-Lucas, *English Local Government in the Nineteenth and Twentieth Centuries* (London, 1977)

M. Langham and C. Wells, *Buxton Waters – A History of Buxton the Spa* (Derby, 1986)

M. Langham and C. Wells, *Buxton: A Pictorial History* (Chichester, 1993)

M. Langham and C. Wells, *The Architect of Victorian Buxton – A Biography of Robert Rippon Duke* (Matlock, 1996)

M. Langham and C. Wells, *A History of the Baths at Buxton* (Leek, 1997)

M. Langham, *Buxton Community School – Origins and Early History* (Buxton, 1997)

R. Lawton (ed.), *The Census and Social Structure* (London, 1978)

H. Leach *The Duke of Devonshire – A Personal and Political Biography* (London, 1904)

J. T. Leach, *Methodism in Buxton* (Buxton, 1985)

J. T. Leach, *The Book of Buxton* (Buckingham, 1987)

P. Lead, *Agents of Revolution* (Keele, 1989)

J. Lees-Milne, *The Bachelor Duke* (London, 1991)

V. D. Lipman, *Local Government Areas 1834–1945* (Oxford 1949)

T. H. Lloyd, *Middle-Class Housing in Britain* (Newton Abbot, 1977)

T. D. Luke, *Spas and Health Resorts of the British Isles* (London, 1919)

D. and S. Lysons, *Magna Britannia of Great Britain, vol. 5, Derbyshire* (London, 1817)

Macmillan, *Encyclopedia of Religion* (1987 edn)

H. McLeod, *Class and Religion in the Late Victorian City* (London, 1974)

H. McLeod, *Religion and the Working Class in Nineteenth Century Britain* (London, 1984)

Ros McCoola, *Theatre in the Hills* (Chapel-en-le-Frith, 1984)

Violet Markham, *Paxton and the Bachelor Duke* (London, 1935)

B. M. Marsden, *The Barrow Knight* (Eldwick, 1988)

J. Marshall, *The Cromford and High Peak Railway* (Halifax 1996)

R. Metcalf, *Life of Vincent Priessnitz: Founder of Hydropathy* (Richmond Hill, Surrey, 1898)

R. Metcalf, *The Rise and Progress of Hydropathy in England and Scotland*, 2nd edn (London, 1912)

M. Miller, *Letchworth – The First Garden City* (Chichester, 1989)

G. E. Mingay, *The Agrarian History of England and Wales*, vol. VI, 1750–1850 (Cambridge, 1989)

D. C. Moore, 'The Gentry', in G. E. Mingay (ed.), *The Victorian Countryside*, vol. 2 (London, 1981)

R. J. Morris (ed.), *Class, power and social structure in British nineteenth-century towns* (Leicester 1986)

R. J. Morris and R. Rodger (eds), *The Victorian City* (Harlow, 1993)

D. Newsome, 'Newman and the Oxford Movement' in A. Symondson (ed.), *The Victorian Crisis of Faith* (London, 1970)

A. Offer, *Property and Politics 1870–1914* (Cambridge, 1981)

Open University Social Sciences Course Team (eds), *Understanding Society, Readings in the Social Sciences* (London, 1970)

J. O. Parker, *The Oxley Papers* (Colchester, 1964)

Peak Dale Local History Group, *More than Just Dust* (Peak Dale, Buxton, 1989)

J. Pearson, *Stags and Serpents* (London, 1983)

N. Pevsner, *Some Architectural Writers of the Nineteenth Century* (Oxford, 1972)

N. Pevsner, *Buildings of England – Derbyshire* (1986); *Cheshire* (1971); *North Somerset and Bristol* (1958); *South Lancashire* (1989); *North Lancashire* (1969); *Staffordshire* (1975); *Yorkshire: York and The East Riding* (1972); *Yorkshire: The North Riding* (1978); *Yorkshire: The West Riding* (1959)

C. Porteous, *Pill Boxes and Bandages, A documentary biography of the first two generations of Robinsons of Chesterfield 1839–1916* (Chesterfield, 1961)

R. Porter, *Health for sale: Quackery in England 1660–1850* (Manchester 1989)

R. Porter, *The Greatest Benefit to Mankind – A Medical History of Humanity from Antiquity to the Present* (London, 1999 edn)

C. G. Powell, *An Economic History of the British Building Industry 1815–1979* (London, 1980)

296

D. A. Prendergast, *Catholicity in Buxton* (Liverpool, 1935)

H. D. Rack, 'Wesleyan Methodism 1849–1902', in R. Davies, A. R. George and G. Rupp, *A History of the Methodist Church in Great Britain*, vol. 3 (London, 1983)

Caroline Reid, 'Middle-class values and working-class culture in nineteenth-century Sheffield: the pursuit of respectability', in S. Pollard and C. Holmes, *Essays in the Economic and Social History of South Yorkshire* (Sheffield, 1976)

D. Read, *The Age of Urban Democracy* (London, 1994)

E. Richards, 'The Land Agent', in G. E. Mingay (ed.), *The Victorian Countryside*, vol. 2 (London, 1981)

J. M. Richards, *Who's Who in Architecture from 1400 to Present Day* (London, 1977)

J. Richardson, *The Local Historian's Encyclopedia* (New Barnet, 1993 edn)

A. F. Roberts and J. T. Leach, *The Coal Mines of Buxton* (Cromford, 1985)

A. F. Roberts, *Turnpike Roads Around Buxton* (Buxton, 1992)

R Rodger, *Housing in Urban Britain 1780–1914* (Cambridge, 1989)

D. Rubinstein, *Victorian Homes* (Newton Abbot, 1974)

R. Scola, 'Retailing in the nineteenth-century town: some problems and possibilities', in J. H. Johnson and C. G. Pooley (eds), *The Structure of Nineteenth-Century Cities* (Beckenham, 1983)

J. Scott *et al.*, *Glossop Dale, Manor and Borough* (Glossop, 1973)

G. Shaw, 'The role of retailing in the urban economy' in J. H. Johnson and C. G. Pooley (eds), *The Structure of Nineteenth-Century Cities* (Beckenham, 1983)

E. Shorter, *From Paralysis to Fatigue – A History of Psychosomatic Illness in the Modern Era* (New York, 1993)

M. A . Simpson, 'The West End of Glasgow 1830–1914' in M. A. Simpson and T. H. Lloyd, *Middle-Class Housing in Britain* (Newton Abbot, 1977)

R. Simpson, *History and Antiquities of Derby* (Derby, 1826)

K. B. Smellie, *A History of Local Government*, 4th edn (London, 1968)

Patricia Spencer-Silver, *Pugin's Builder – The Life and Work of George Myers* (Hull, 1993)

D. Spring, *The English Landed Estate in the Nineteenth Century: Its Administration* (London, 1963)

G. L. Standring, *Albury and the Catholic Apostolic Church* (Albury, 1985)

M. Stapleton, *The Cambridge Guide to English Literature* (London, 1983)

J. J. Stark, *St Anne's Church, Buxton.* (*c.* 1967)

J. M. Stephenson, *The Peak Line* (Tisbury nr Salisbury, 1982)

C. Stewart, *The Stones of Manchester* (London, 1956)

J. N. Tarn, *Working-Class Housing in 19th-Century Britain* (London, 1971)

J. N. Tarn, *The Peak District National Park – Its Architecture* (Bakewell, 1971).

J. N. Tarn, *Five per cent Philanthropy – An Account of housing in Urban Areas between 1840 and 1914* (Cambridge, 1973)

J. N. Tarn, 'Sheffield', in M. A Simpson and T. H. Lloyd, *Middle-Class housing in Britain* (Newton Abbot, 1977)

A. J. P. Taylor, *From Napoleon to the Second International*, 2nd edn (Harmondsworth, 1995)

S. Taylor, *History of Freemasonry in Buxton and Longnor* (Buxton, 1906)

D. Thompson, *England in the Nineteenth Century*, 7th edn (Harmondsworth, 1960)

F. M. L Thompson, *English Landed Society in the Nineteenth Century* (London, 1963)

F. M. L Thompson, *The Rise of Suburbia* (Leicester, 1982)

J. M. Tomlinson, *Derbyshire Black Marble* (Matlock Bath), 1996

J. K. Walton, *The English Seaside Resort – A Social History 1715–1914* (Leicester, 1983)

B. Vincent, *Haydn's Dictionary of Dates*, 15th edn (London, 1876)

R. K. Webb, 'The Faith of Nineteenth-Century Unitarians: A Curious Incident' in R. J. Helmstadter and B. Lightman (eds), *Victorian Faith in Crisis* (London, 1990)

C. Wells, *The Buxton Stage* (Disley, 1998)

Helena Whitbread (ed.), *No Priest But Love – The Journals of Anne Lister from 1824 to 1826* (Otley, 1992)

Cicely Williams, *The Parish Church of St John the Baptist, Buxton* (1988

I. Wodehouse, *British Architects 1840–1976* (Detroit, 1978)

D. W. Woodhead, *Buxton Wesley Chapel* (Buxton, 1949)

Doreen Yarwood, *A Chronology of Western Architecture* (London, 1987)

Published papers

T. Askey, 'The houses on Hall Bank in Buxton', *Buxton Archaeological and Natural History Society*, Bulletin, no. 8 (Autumn 1989)

P. J. Aspinall, 'Speculative builders and the development of Cleethorpes, 1850–1900', *Lincolnshire History and Archaeology*, vol. II (1976)

E. Axon, *Historical Notes on Buxton and Its Inhabitants and Visitors*, Papers: Fourth, November 1936; Seventh, November 1938; Eighth, December 1939; Ninth, March–April 1940; XI, November 1940; [XIV] (un-numbered) March 1942; XVII, November 1943; XIX, November [1944]; XXI, June–August 1946; XXII, March–May 1947, *Buxton Advertiser*

E. Axon, 'Buxton Chapel (Hartington Road [Unitarian] Church 1725–1925', *Transactions of the Unitarian Historical Society* (1926)

[Ernest Axon] – Obituary (AJH), *Lancashire and Cheshire Antiquarian Society Bulletin*, LIX (1947)

Elizabeth Barton 'Edward Woollett Wilmot: the Duke of Devonshire's agent in Buxton, 1856–64', *Bulletin of the Buxton Archaeological and Natural History Society*, no. 19 (Spring 1995)

F. Brodhurst (Rev.), 'Sir William Cavendish – 1557', *Derbyshire Archaeological Journal*, XXIX (1907)

Janet Browne, 'Spas and sensibilities: Darwin at Malvern' in R. Porter (ed.), *The Medical History of Waters and Spas*, *Medical History*, Supplement no. 10, Wellcome Institute, London (1990)

P. Browning 'Dovedale and its unsleeping sentinel', *National Trust Magazine* (Spring 1981)

I. E. Burton, *The Duke of Connaught Lodge, no. 246 of Mark Masons 100: 1879–1979, A Short History* (August 1978)

Nicola R. Y. Clemence, 'Physiotherapy – a hundred years of medical rubbing?', *Norfolk and Norwich Institute for Medical Education Journal*, vol. 10 (Autumn 1993)

Leonore Davidoff, 'Mastered for life: servant and wife in Victorian and Edwardian England', *Journal of Social History*, 7 (1994)

O. Gomersal, 'Buxton Crescent Ballroom subscription list', Occasional paper, no. 6., *Buxton Archaeological and Natural History Society*, Bulletin, no. 6 (Autumn 1988)

R. Gurnham 'The creation of Skegness as a resort town by the 9th Earl of Scarbrough', *Lincolnshire History and Archaeology*, vol. 7 (1972)

D. Harley, 'A Sword in the Madman's Hand; professional opposition to popular consumption in the Waters literature of Southern England and the Midlands, 1570–1870', in R. Porter (ed.), *The Medical History of Waters and Spas*, *Medical History*, Supplement no. 10, Wellcome Institute, London (1990)

R Lambert 'Central and local relations in mid-Victorian England: the Local Government Act Office 1858–71', *Victorian Studies* (December 1962)

M. Langham and C. Wells, 'Notes of the building of the Palace Hotel and Turner's Memorial', *Buxton Archaeological and Natural History Society*, Bulletin no. 14, Occasional Paper 14 (Autumn 1992)

M. Langham and C. Wells, 'J. C. Bates 1822–1899', *Derbyshire Miscellany*, vol. 14, pt 4 (Autumn 1996)

M. Langham, 'Things written in the glasse windowes at Buxstons', *Derbyshire Miscellany*, vol. 15, pt I (Spring 1998)

J. T. Leach, 'Buxton and the Cavendish families', *Derbyshire Archaeological Journal* CVIII (1988)

J. T. Leach, 'Grin Hill, Buxton, A major limestone quarry', *Derbyshire Archaeological Journal*, vol. 116 (1996)

J. T. Leach, 'The Revd James Shore of Bridgetown, Totnes', in *The Devon Historian*, no. 57 (October 1998)

J. T. Leach, 'Notes on the supposed Roman Baths at Buxton', *Derbyshire Miscellany*, vol. 15, pt 4 (Autumn 1999)

M. S. Legan, 'Hydropathy in America: a nineteenth-century panacea', *Bulletin of the History of Medicine*, vol. 45 (Baltimore, 1971)

A. Martin, 'Historical sketch of Balneology', *Medical Life*, vol. 34, no. 5 (May 1927)

E. H. Phelps Brown and Sheila V. Hopkins, 'Seven centuries of building wages', *Economica*, new series, vol. XXII, no. 87 (1955)

S. Pollard, 'Barrow in Furness and the Seventh Duke of Devonshire', *Economic History Review*, 2nd series, vol. VIII, no. 2 (1955)

'Priessnitzovy Lecebne Lazne a.s. Priessnitzi's Medicinal Spa', Internet http://info-jesenik.oz/en/historie/lazne.htm; also http://www.info-jesenik.oz/en/

R. Price, 'Hydropathy in England 1840–70', *Medical History*, vol. 25 (1981)

R. Procter, 'Notes and records', *Buxton Archaeological and Natural History Society*, Bulletin, no. 16 (Autumn 1993)

K. Rees, 'Medicine as a commodity: hydropathy in Matlock', *Bulletin of the Society for the Social History of Medicine*, no. 35 (June 1985)

R. Rolls, 'From balneology to physiotherapy: the development of physical treatment at Bath' R. Rolls and Jean and J. Guy (eds), *A Pox on the Provinces: Proceedings of the 12th Congress of the British Society for the History of Medicine* (Bath, 1990)

H. B. Routh *et al.*, 'Balneology, mineral water, and spas in historical perspective', *Clinical Dermatology*, 14, no. 6 (1996)

S. B. Saul, 'House building in England, 1890–1914', *Economic History Review*, 2nd series, vol. 15, no. 1 (1962)

Marion Sharples, 'The Fawkes family and their estates in Wharfedale, 1818–1936', *Leeds Thoresby Society*, 2nd series (1997)

D. Spring, 'The English landed estate in the age of coal and iron: 1830–1880', *Journal of Economic History* vol. XI (1951)

K. W. Stevenson, 'The Catholic Apostolic Church – its history and its Eucharist', *Studia Liturgica*, vol. 13, no. 1 (1979)

R. Thornes and J. Leach, 'Buxton Hall', *Derbyshire Archaeological Journal*, vol. CXIV (1994)

Toledo, University of:, *Quackery*, Libraries, Internet http://www.cl.utoledo.edu/canaday/ quackery/quack3b.html

E. Tristram 'Roman Buxton', *Derbyshire Archaeological Journal*, vol. XXXVIII (1916)

J. T. Ward 'The Earls Fitzwilliam and the Wentworth Woodhouse estate in the nineteenth century', *Yorkshire Bulletin of Economic and Social Research*, XII, I (1960)

J. T. Ward 'West Riding landowners and mining in the nineteenth century', *Yorkshire Bulletin of Economic and Social Research*, XV, I (1963)

C. Wells and M. Langham, 'William Radford Bryden FRIBA' Occasional Paper, no. 28., *Buxton Archaeological and Natural History Society*, Bulletin, no. 28 (Autumn 1999)

P. Wroe, 'Roman roads in the Peak District', *Derbyshire Archaeological Journal*, vol. CII (1982)

Index

C

302